Nellie Bly's World

VOLUME I

1887-1888

Nellie Bly's World

Volume 1: 1887-1888

From articles originally published in The New York World

Transcribed and Edited by David Blixt

Cover by Robert Kauzlaric

ISBN-13: 978-1944540890

Published by Sordelet Ink
www.sordeletink.com

Nellie Bly's World

Volume I
1887-1888

The Complete Reporting of
Elizabeth Cochrane

Introduction by David Blixt

Books by Nellie Bly

Ten Days in a Mad-House

Six Months In Mexico

Nellie Bly's Book: Around the World in 72 Days

the Lost Novels

the Mystery of Central Park

Eva the Adventuress

New York by Night

Alta Lynn, m.d.

Wayne's Faithful Sweetheart

Little Luckie

Dolly the Coquette

In Love With a Stranger

the Love of Three Girls

Little Penny, Child of the Streets

Pretty Merribelle

Twins & Rivals

David Blixt's Bly Novels

What Girls Are Good For
Charity Girl
Clever Girl

FOR BROOKE KROEGER

THE FIRST AND FINAL AUTHORITY
ON ALL THINGS BLY

CONTENTS

Nellie Bly's "World"

Introduction by David Blixt

Who Is Nellie Bly?

I was somewhat nervous about my visit to Mrs. Grant. I only knew of her as the wife of the famous general; the successful hostess for eight years in the White House; the woman who had, in making a tour of the world, been received as a queen in every civilized land. Would any one wonder then at my apprehension, when women of so meaner light so often try to parry all attempts to approach? But I was wrong.

"My son tells me," Mrs. Grant said, with a pleasant laugh, after greetings had been exchanged and she had drawn me by the hand to the chair and seated herself on a lounge most cordially near, "that Nellie Bly is a little scamp,"—

"Oh, no, no," I broke in, but holding her finger up playfully, she continued:

"That, not being content with exposing the Blackwell's Island Insane Asylum—yes, and benefitting it wonderfully—and exposing Phelps, the great Albany lobbyist, she needs must got to Central Park and allow herself to be 'mashed,' and then tell all about it in the World, so that now none of the men dare wink at a girl while out driving, lest she be Nellie Bly."

"Why, that's a shame," I replied, and we both laughed, I fear not altogether in pity of the men.

—excerpt from "Our First Ladies,"
New York World, Nov. 28, 1888

"When a charming young lady comes into your office and smilingly announces that she wants to ask you a few questions regarding the possibility of improving New York's moral tone, don't stop to parley. Just say: 'Excuse me, Nellie Bly,' and shin down the fire-escape."

—*Puck Magazine*, Nov. 7, 1888.

Nellie Bly kept nudging my arm.

First it was hearing her praised by Stockard Channing's First Lady on *The West Wing,* my favorite TV show. Then a reference to her reporting in a story about *One Flew Over The Cuckoo's Nest.* Finally, reading an article in *The Atlantic* on silent films starring daredevil women, most of whom were based on, you guessed it, Nellie Bly.

Thick as I am, even I can get a message. Hint firmly received, in April of 2016 I started researching Bly, with an eye to writing a novel about the "plucky girl reporter."

I had no idea she was about to change my life.

First I wrote the novel, which took nearly two years. I had intended that book to be a one-off, but that wasn't good enough for Bly, whose life was far too interesting to let it go at one book.

Nudge.

Then, researching the next novel, I discovered *eleven full-length novels by Bly herself* that had been lost for 125 years. Another year of my life transcribing and editing those, preparing them for publication.

Nudge.

Thanks to the research for my own novels, I had already collected a few dozen Bly articles. When I started seeing the links between her lost novels and her reporting, I set about collecting more, thinking to include them with the novels so readers could enjoy the sources of her inspiration.

That was when I realized no one had ever collected all her reporting.

Nudge.

Born in 1864, Elizabeth Jane Cochrane—better known today by her *nom-de-plume*—had an astonishing career as a reporter, spanning thirty-seven years. In that time she entirely redefined the role of women in newspapers, helped to invent undercover reporting, and was instrumental in starting (and later rejecting) "stunt" journalism. She showed that a woman reporter need not be confined to the "women's pages" of a newspaper, but rather deserved headlines all her own. She was the inspiration for countless women to enter the field. She was also the basis for the comic book character Lois Lane.

The real Lois Lane, however, never needed a Superman.

Today she is best remembered for the stunts, beginning with her ten days undercover as a "bogus lunatic" to expose the inhumane conditions at the Blackwell's Island Insane Asylum, and culminating with her race around the globe to beat the fictional record set by Jules Verne's *Around The World In 80 Days*.

But while those two stunts will forever be the headlines to her legacy, they were just a drop in the ocean of her work as a journalist.

It is important to remember this: Nellie Bly was a reporter. While she certainly rode the tide of sensationalist journalism to fame, the vast majority of her reporting work was done, not in disguise, but in her own person. Self-trained, she was a remarkably skilled interviewer, eliciting from prominent figures a candor not usually seen. She also had a natural instinct for what makes a good story.

Most of all, she had a unique point of view. She told stories about the inconvenient people in Victorian New York society: the poor, the sick, the downtrodden. She was interested in orphans and women—*especially* women. Bly was forever telling stories of prominent or remarkable women. She was also relentless in ferreting out schemes meant to swindle poor women of their hard-earned pay. Having been cheated of her inheritance after her father's death, having had to earn a living before accidentally discovering her calling as a reporter, she never lost the twin tools that made Nellie Bly such an outstanding journalist: her empathy, and her outrage.

Bly's reporting divides neatly into four periods: her time at the *Pittsburg Dispatch* (1885-1887), her first explosive stint at Joseph Pulitzer's *New York World* (1887-1890), her return to the *World* (1893-1896), and her last hurrah in William Randolph Hearst's *New York Evening Journal* (1914-1922).

Setting out to collect and publish all of her articles, I started by compiling a list. I came up with an astonishing 488 distinct pieces of journalism. An incredible body of work that has hardly been scratched by any collection.

Gathering them, however, proved a challenge.

Online sites had selected articles from her time at *The New York World*, either transcribed or scans of the originals. But they hardly comprised a comprehensive collection, numbering maybe two dozen in all. There are volumes purporting to be the "complete works of Nellie Bly" but those turned out to be compilations of her three non-fiction books: *Ten Days In A Mad-House, Six Months In Mexico*, and *Around The World In 72 Days*, with her one known novel, *The Mystery Of Central Park*, thrown in. Far from "complete."

Even volumes that *did* include her short-form reporting (the vast majority of her work) were woefully inadequate, containing less than twenty of her *World* articles, leaving over a hundred untouched. Moreover, no volume contained anything from either her early years at the *Dispatch* or her twilight years at the *New York Evening-Journal*, her longest run and most prolific time.

So I settled in. I was incredibly fortunate to have made early contact with Bly biographer Brooke Kroeger (whose book *Nellie Bly: Daredevil, Reporter, Feminist* remains the single best biography of Bly). Through her I obtained several articles I was missing, and she directed my attention to the places where I might find the others. By contacting libraries, sorting through newspaper collections (especially at the Fulton's History website) I managed to gather the articles for this volume.

My ultimate goal is that all of Bly's writing be made available, so that a reader may begin with her early work among the workshop girls in Pittsburgh to her salad days as the scourge of New York scoundrels, through her never-before-seen novels, back into her reporting, and finally, after she was widowed and had lost her fortune, her work reporting on World War I and its aftermath.

However, due to the pandemic of 2020 closing libraries across the country, I was unable to access the *Dispatch* and *Evening Journal* records as quickly as I would have liked. Hence starting this series with her reporting for the *New York World*.

As stated above, Bly's career at the *World* splits very neatly into two sections: 1887-1890, and 1893-1896 (with a very brief stint in 1895 where she works for the *Chicago Times-Herald*). However, as I compiled the articles from the first set of years, I encountered an unexpected problem—I had too much material!

Thus I have broken down *Nellie Bly's World* into four volumes. This first volume covers the years 1887-1888, starting with her cannon-blast debut on Blackwell's Island. From there she exposes a so-called Mesmerist, tricks the self-proclaimed "King of the Lobby" in Albany, and outs a serial procurer of girls in Central Park. She goes after frauds in all walks of life, be they mediums and spiritualists, matrimonial agencies, or sweatshops that promise to train women for work only to fleece them of their cash. She also visits the poor and the fallen.

She undertakes lighthearted stories as well, from lessons in ballet dancing and fencing to a job as a chorus girl. But Bly is quite serious when she spends three weeks posing the question, "Should Women Propose?"

Most interesting, at least to me, are her interviews, from the female members of Buffalo Bill Cody's "Wild West Show" to the wives of the candidates for president, from New York's executioner to Belva Lockwood, running for the Oval Office. Her longest piece of 1888 is a series of interviews with all the living First Ladies, where she gleans never-before-revealed stories of their lives in the White House.

In short, 1887-1888 encapsulates Bly's entire career, alternating between death-defying stunts and heartfelt interviews, leavened with some frivolity and deepened with some misery.

❧

It is important, when reading these articles, to remember what Nellie Bly's world was like. Electricity was relatively new, and magnetism was all the rage. Bicycles were new, replacing roller-skates as the latest fad. Bustles were on the way out. The American Civil War was only a generation past, and photographic cameras were on the cusp of being made commercially affordable to the general public, but were still too expensive to print in newspapers. Horses, trains, and streetcars were the three standard forms of transportation.

1887 and 1888 were exciting years. They saw the first appearance of Sherlock Holmes in *A Study In Scarlet*, published in *Beeton's Christmas Annual*. They saw Bloody Sunday in Ireland. They saw four spies hanged in the Haymarket Affair. They saw the Great Blizzard of 1888 shut down the American East Coast and kill 400 people. They saw Susan B. Anthony organize the first international Congress For Women's Rights. They saw London in the grip of Jack The Ripper. They saw the filming of the very first motion picture. They saw Vincent Van Gogh cut off his own ear. And they saw a plucky young journalist named Nellie Bly emerge from an insane asylum to tackle fraudsters and charlatans of all walks of life.

A caveat: these articles are products of their time. While certainly enlightened for her era, Bly engages in all the ethnic, cultural, and racial stereotypes of Victorian New York. She pens descriptions and employs dialects for certain subjects that are clearly offensive to any modern reader. There are many off-hand references to "colored" people. Please read with care for yourself.

INCIDENTS IN THE LIFE OF THE BRILLIANT NELLIE BLY—SHE WRITES ONLY FOR THE GREAT **SUNDAY WORLD.** READ HER **NEXT SUNDAY.**

Unlike my work editing Bly's "Lost Novels," I have done very little to these articles. As I hope these volumes to be of use to scholars as well as the general public, I have confined myself to fixing obvious errors, such as not closing quotations, or a headline editor spelling her name *Nelly*. Sometimes names within the stories are misspelled, and if I could not verify the name myself, I chose the most frequently-used version from within the story.

This means I have left in place several of the grammatical peculiarities of the time that I excised from the "Lost Novels." One in particular is the style of not capitalizing a word after an exclamation mark. Not a constant rule, it was used when Bly wished to emphasize a sound or word, very much in line with Shakespeare's ecphonetic 'O', then continue with the same thought. Another is not capitalizing the words "street" or "avenue" when giving an address, or the use of "practice" as a noun and "practise" as a verb.

I have retained most period spellings, such as "to-day" "centre" or "indorse," because they occur so frequently and therefore become recognizable as a style. Whereas the rarely-used "wilful" and "skilful" I have corrected to "willful" and "skillful" purely for ease of reading.

I have also kept all of the original paragraph breaks—or lack thereof. Space in a newspaper being at a premium, Bly (or her editor) often mashes together what should be several separate paragraphs into one.

The *World* was a pioneer when it came to using art to sell a story. Photographs were too hard to reproduce, so Pulitzer's team created a process wherein etchings could be rapidly created for reproduction. With this in mind, I have included the original artwork by Walt McDougall, who illustrated much of Bly's work during this period.

One last formatting note: the habit at the time was to put the name of your own paper in small caps and italicize other papers. Hence when Bly references her own paper, it is printed THE WORLD, but if she is referring to a rival paper, it is printed the *Sun*. It is perhaps the least petty part of the New York newspaper wars of the late 19th Century.

Most of the articles can be understood from the context. Occasionally, such as with her interview with Belva Lockwood, Bly assumes a knowledge on the part of her reader that we no longer share. In such cases I have added a foreword to the article in question, giving the necessary information. Sometimes, however, the reporting surrounding one of these articles is important. When this is the case, I have added a note directing readers where to find a more complete set of articles, if available.

All of these articles were transcribed by yours truly, therefore any faults or infelicities are mine alone. If anyone is interested in checking my work against an original article, I'll be happy to provide that article. Visit *www.davidblixt.com* and drop me an email.

I owe several people a world of thanks, most especially my family for undertaking this lengthy journey with me. Thanks to Rob Kauzlaric for his gorgeous covers and his endless insights. Thanks as ever to my parents for their enthusiasm and support. Stephanie at the New York State Library. And deepest gratitude to both Brooke Kroeger and Matthew Goodman, whose own books about Bly remain the gold standard.

She's nudging me again to say that's enough from me. I'll just ask you to keep this in mind: Bly turned twenty-four years old during the span of this collection, though the *World* pretended she was much younger.

These articles were written by a woman in her middle twenties doing what was considered a "man's job," and doing it splendidly. While she pioneered the art of a female reporter putting herself in danger for a story, there is a reason we remember her name when so many of her imitators are forgotten. This is because Elizabeth Cochrane was far more than a mere "stunt girl."

She was Nellie Bly.

— David Blixt
Chicago, 2021

Nellie Bly's World

Volume I

BEHIND ASYLUM BARS

SUNDAY, OCTOBER 9, 1887

THE MYSTERY OF THE UNKNOWN INSANE GIRL

REMARKABLE STORY OF THE SUCCESSFUL IMPERSONATION OF INSANITY

HOW NELLIE BROWN DECEIVED JUDGES, REPORTERS AND MEDICAL EXPERTS

SHE TELLS HER STORY OF HOW SHE PASSED AT BELLEVUE HOSPITAL

Studying the Role of Insanity Before Her Mirror and Practising It at the Temporary Home for Women—Arrested and Brought Before Judge Duffy—He Declares She is Some Mother's Darling and Resembles His Sister—Committed to the Care of the Physicians for the Insane at Bellevue—Experts Declare Her Demented—Harsh Treatment of the Insane at Bellevue—"Charity Patients Should Not Complain"—Vivid Pictures of Hospital Life—How Our Esteemed Contemporaries Have Followed a False Trail—Some Needed Light Afforded Them—Chapters of Absorbing Interest in the Experience of a Feminine "Amateur Casual."

I.

ON the 22d of September I was asked by THE WORLD if I could have myself committed to one of the Asylums for the Insane in New York, with a view to writing a plain and unvarnished narrative of the treatment of the patients therein and the methods of management, &c. Did I think I had the courage to go through such an ordeal as the mission would demand? Could I assume the characteristics of insanity to such a degree that I could pass the doctors, live for a week among the insane without the authorities there finding out that I was only a "chiel amang 'em takin' notes?" I said I believed I could. I had some faith in my own ability as an actress and thought I could assume insanity long enough to accomplish any mission intrusted to me. Could I pass a week in the insane ward at Blackwell's Island? I said I could and I would. And I did. My instructions were simply to go on with my work as soon as I felt that I was ready. I was to chronicle faithfully the experiences I underwent, and when once within the walls of the asylum to find out and describe its inside workings, which are always so effectually hidden by white-capped nurses, as well as by bolts and bars, from the knowledge of the public. "We do not ask you to go there for the purpose of making sensational revelations. Write up things as you find them, good or bad; give praise or blame as you think best, and the truth all the time. But I am afraid of that chronic smile of yours," said the editor. "I will smile no more," I said, and I went away to execute my delicate and, as I found out, difficult mission.

THE PRELIMINARIES.

All the preliminary preparations for my ordeal were left to be planned by myself. Only one thing was decided upon, namely, that I should pass under the pseudonym of Nellie Brown, the initials of which would agree with my own name and my linen, so that there would be no difficulty in keeping track of my movements and assisting me out of any difficulties or dangers I might get into. There were ways of getting into the insane ward, but I did not know them. I might adopt one of two courses. Either I could feign insanity at the house of friends, and get myself committed on the decision of two competent physicians, or I could go to my goal by way of the police courts. On reflection I thought it wiser not to inflict myself upon my friends or to get any good-natured doctors to assist me in my purpose. Besides, to get to Blackwell's Island my friends would have had to feign poverty, and, unfortunately for the end I had in view, my acquaintance with the struggling poor, except my own self, was only very superficial. So I determined upon the plan which led me to the successful accomplishment of my mission and to which the bulk of the following narrative will be devoted. I succeeded in getting committed to the insane ward at Blackwell's Island, where I spent ten days and nights and had an experience which I shall never forget. I took upon myself to enact the part of a poor, unfortunate crazy girl, and felt it my duty not to shirk any of the disagreeable results that should follow. I became one of the city's insane wards for that length of time, experienced much, and saw and heard more of the treatment accorded to this helpless class of our population, and when I had seen and heard enough, my release was promptly secured. I left the insane ward with pleasure and regret—pleasure that I was once more able to enjoy the free breath of heaven; regret that I could not have brought with me some of the unfortunate women who lived and suffered with me, and who, I am convinced are just as sane as I was and am now myself. But here let me say one thing: From the moment I entered the insane ward on the island I made no attempt to keep up the assumed role of insanity. I talked and acted just as I do in ordinary life. Yet strange to say, the more sanely I talked and acted, the crazier I was thought to be by all except one physician, whose kindness and gentle ways I shall not soon forget.

PREPARING FOR THE ORDEAL.

But to return to my work and my mission. After receiving my instructions I returned to my boarding-house, and when evening came I began to practice the role in which I was to make my debut on the morrow. What a difficult task, I thought, to appear before a crowd of people and convince them that I was insane. I had never been near insane persons before in my life and had not the faintest idea of what their actions were like. And then to be examined by a number of learned physicians who make insanity a specialty and who daily come in contact with insane people! How could I hope to pass these doctors and convince them that I was crazy? I feared that they could not be deceived. I began to think my task a hopeless one. But it had to be done. So I flew to the mirror and examined my face. I remembered all I had read of the doings of crazy people, how first of all they must have staring eyes, and so I opened mine as wide as possible and stared unblinkingly at my own reflection. I assure you the sight was not reassuring, even to myself, especially in the dead of night. I tried to turn the gas up higher in hopes that it would raise my courage. I succeeded only partially, but I consoled myself with the thought that in a few nights more I would not be there, but locked up in a cell with a lot of lunatics. The weather was not cold; but nevertheless when I thought of what was to come, wintery chills ran races up and down my back in very mockery of the perspiration which was slowly but surely taking the curl out of my bangs. Between times, practicing before the mirror and picturing my future as a lunatic, I

NELLIE PRACTICES INSANITY AT HOME.

read snatches of improbable and impossible ghost stories, so that when the dawn came to chase away the night I felt that I was in a fit mood for my mission, yet hungry enough to feel keenly that I wanted my breakfast. Slowly and sadly I took my morning bath and quietly bade farewell to a few of the most precious articles known to modern civilization. Tenderly I put my tooth-brush aside, and, when taking a final rub of the soap, I murmured, "It may be for days, and it may be—for longer." Then I donned the old clothing I had selected for the occasion. I was in the mood to look at everything through very serious glasses. It's just as well to take a last "fond look," I mused, for who could tell but that the strain of playing crazy and being shut up with a crowd of mad people might turn my own brain and I would never get back. But not once did I think of shirking my mission. Calmly, outwardly at least, I went out to my crazy business. I walked down Second avenue. It had been arranged that I should enter one of the many temporary homes or shelters for females, and that once in I should do the best I could to get forwarded on my journey to Blackwell's Island. The place selected was the Temporary Home for Females, 84 Second avenue.

IN THE TEMPORARY HOME

II.

I was left to begin my career as Nellie Brown, the insane girl. As I walked down the avenue I tried to assume the look which maidens wear in pictures entitled "Dreaming." I passed through the little paved yard to the entrance of the Home. I pulled the bell, which sounded loud enough for a church chime, and nervously awaited the opening of the door to the home which I intended should ere long cast me forth and out upon the charity of the police. The door was thrown back with a vengeance, and a short, yellow-haired girl of some thirteen summers stood before me.

"Is the matron in?" I asked, faintly.

"Yes, she's in; she's busy. Go to the back parlor," answered the girl in a loud voice, without one change in her peculiarly matured face.

I followed these not overkind or polite instructions and found myself in a dark, uncomfortable back-parlor. There I awaited the arrival of my hostess. I had been seated some twenty minutes at the least, when a slender woman, clad in a plain dark dress entered and, stopping before me, ejaculated inquiringly, "Well?"

"Are you the matron?" I asked.

"No," she replied, "the matron is sick; I am her assistant. What do you want?"

"I want to stay here for a few days, if you can accommodate me."

AT THE TEMPORARY HOME FOR WOMEN.

"Well, I have no single rooms; we are so crowded, but if you will occupy a room with another girl, I shall do that much for you."

"I shall be glad of that," I answered. "How much do you charge?" I had brought only about 70 cents along with me, knowing full well that the sooner my funds were exhausted the sooner I should be put out, and to be put out was what I was working for.

"We charge thirty cents a night," was her reply to my question, and with that I paid her for one night's lodging, and she left me on the plea of having something else to look after. Left to amuse myself as best I could, I took a survey of my surroundings. By the time I had become familiar with my quarters a bell, which rivaled the door-bell in its loudness, began clanging in the basement, and simultaneously women went trooping down-stairs from all parts of the house. I imagined, from the obvious signs, that dinner was served, but as no one had said anything to me I made no effort to follow in the hungry train. Yet I did wish that some one would invite me down and I was glad when the assistant matron came up and asked me if I did not want something to eat. I replied that I did, and then I asked her what her name was. Mrs. Stanard, she said, and I immediately wrote it down in a notebook I had taken with me for the purpose of making memoranda, and in which I had written several pages of utter nonsense for inquisitive scientists. Thus equipped I awaited developments. But my dinner—well, I followed Mrs. Stanard down the uncarpeted stairs into the basement, where a large number of women were eating. She found room for me at a table with three other women. The short-haired slavey who had opened the door now put in an appearance as waiter. Placing her arms akimbo and staring me out of countenance she said:

NELLIE'S FIRST MEAL AT THE HOME.

"Boiled mutton, boiled beef, beans, potatoes, coffee or tea?"

"Beef, potatoes, coffee and bread," I responded.

"Bread goes in," she explained,

as she made her way to the kitchen, which was in the rear. It was not very long before she returned with what I had ordered on a large, badly battered tray, which she banged down before me. I began my simple meal. It was not very enticing, so while making a feint of eating I watched the others. After dinner I went upstairs and resumed my former place in the back parlor. I was quite cold and uncomfortable, and had fully made up my mind that I could not endure that sort of business long, so the sooner I assumed my insane points the sooner I would be released from enforced idleness. Ah, that was indeed the longest day I had ever lived. I listlessly watched the women in the front parlor, where all sat except myself. One did nothing but read and scratch her head and occasionally call out mildly, "Georgie," without lifting her eyes from her book. "Georgie" was her over-frisky boy, who had more noise in him than any child I ever saw before. He did everything that was rude and unmannerly, I thought, and the mother never said a word unless she heard some one else yell at him. Another woman always kept going to sleep and waking herself up with her own snoring. I really felt wickedly thankful it was only herself she awakened. The majority of the women sat there doing nothing, but there were a few who made lace and knitted unceasingly. The enormous doorbell seemed to be going all the time, and so did the short-haired girl. The latter was, besides, one of those girls who sing all the time snatches of all the songs and hymns that have been composed for the last fifty years. There is such a thing as martyrdom in these days. The ringing of the bell brought more people who wanted shelter for the night. Excepting one woman, who was from the country on a day's shopping expedition, they were working women, some of them with children. As it drew toward evening Mrs. Stanard came to me and said:

SHE BEGINS TO SHOW SIGNS.

"What is wrong with you? Have you some sorrow or trouble?"

"No," I said, almost stunned at the suggestion. "Why?"

"Oh, because," she said, womanlike, "I can see it in your face. It tells the story of a great trouble."

"Yes, everything is so sad," I said, in a haphazard way, which I had intended to reflect my craziness.

"But you must not allow that to worry you. We all have our troubles, but we get over them in good time. What kind of work are you trying to get?"

"I do not know; it's all so sad," I replied.

"Would you like to be a nurse for children and wear a nice white cap and apron?" she asked.

I put my handkerchief up to my face to hide a smile, and replied in a muffled tone, "I never worked; I don't know how."

"But you must learn," she urged; "all these women here work."

"Do they?" I said, in a low, thrilling whisper. "Why, they look horrible to me; just like crazy women. I am so afraid of them."

"They don't look very nice," she answered, assentingly, "but they are good, honest working women. We do not keep crazy people here."

I again used my handkerchief to hide a smile, as I thought that before morning she would at least think she had one crazy person among her flock.

"They all look crazy," I asserted again, "and I am afraid of them. There are so many crazy people about, and one can never tell what they will do. Then there are so many murders committed, and the police never catch the murderers," and I finished with a sob that would have broken up an audience of blasé critics. She gave a sudden and convulsive start, and I knew my first stroke had gone home. It was amusing to see what a remarkably short time it took her to get up from her chair and to whisper hurriedly: "I'll come back to talk with you after a while." I knew she would not come back, and she did not. When the supper-bell rang I went along with the others to the basement and partook of the evening meal, which was similar to dinner, except that there was a smaller bill of fare and more people, the women who are employed outside during the day having returned. After the evening meal we all adjourned to the parlors, where all sat, or stood, as there were not chairs enough to go round. I watched two women, who seemed of all the crowd to be the most sociable, and I selected them as the ones to work out my salvation, or, more properly speaking, my condemnation and conviction. Excusing myself and saying that I felt lonely, I asked if I might join their company. They graciously consented, so with my hat and gloves on, which no one had asked me to lay aside, I sat down and listened to the rather wearisome conversation, in which I took no part, merely keeping up my sad look, saying "Yes," or "No," or "I can't say," to their observations. Several times I told them I thought everybody in the house looked crazy, but they were slow to catch on to my very original remark. One said her name was Mrs. King and that she was a Southern woman. Then she said that I had a Southern accent. She asked me bluntly if I did not really come from the South. I said "Yes." The other woman got to talking about the Boston boats and asked me if I knew at what time they left. For a moment I forgot my role of assumed insanity, and told her the correct hour of departure. She then asked me what work I was going to do or if I had ever done any. I replied that I thought it very sad that there were so many working people in the world. She said in reply that she had been unfortunate and had come to New York, where she had worked at correcting proofs on a medical dictionary for some time, but that her health had given way under the task and that she was now going to Boston again. When the maid came to tell us to go to bed I remarked that I was afraid, and again ventured the assertion that all the women in the house seemed to be crazy. The nurse insisted on my going to bed. I asked if I could not sit on the stairs, but she said decisively:

"No; for every one in the house would think you were crazy." Finally I allowed them to take me to a room.

A KIND SOUL DISCOVERED.

Here I must introduce a new personage by name into my narrative. It is the woman who had been a proof-reader and was about to return to Boston. She was a Mrs. Caine, who was as courageous as she was good-hearted. She came into my room and sat and talked with me a long time, taking down my hair with gentle ways. She tried to persuade me to undress and go to bed, but I stubbornly refused to do so. During this time a number of the inmates of the house had gathered around us. They expressed themselves in various ways. "Poor loon!" they said. "Why, she's crazy enough!" "I am afraid to stay with such a crazy being in house." "She will murder us all before morning." One woman was for sending for a policeman to take me away at once. They were all in a terrible and real state of fright. No one wanted to be responsible for me, and the woman who was to occupy the room with me declared that she would not stay with that "crazy woman" for all the money of the Vanderbilts. It was then that Mrs. Caine said she would stay with me. I told her I would like to have her do so. So she was left with me. She didn't undress, but lay down on the bed, watchful of my movements. She tried to induce me to lie down, but I was afraid to do this. I knew that if I once gave way I should fall asleep and dream as pleasantly and peacefully as a child. I should, to use a slang expression, be liable to give myself dead away. I had made up my mind to stay awake all night. So I insisted on sitting on the side of the bed and staring blankly at vacancy. My poor companion was put into a wretched state of unhappiness. Every few moments she would rise up to look at me. She told me that my eyes shone terribly brightly and then began to question me, asking me where I had lived, how long I had been in New York, what I had been doing, and many things besides. To all her questionings I had but one response—I told her that I had forgotten everything, that ever since my headache had come on I could not remember.

Poor soul! How cruelly I tortured her, and what a kind heart she had! But how I tortured all of them! One of them dreamed of me–as a nightmare. After I had been in the room an hour or so I was myself startled by hearing a woman screaming in the next room. I began to imagine that I was really in an insane asylum. Mrs. Caine woke up, looked around, frightened, and listened. She then went out and into the next room, and I heard her asking another woman some questions. When she came back she told me that the woman had had a hideous nightmare. She had been dreaming of me. She had seen me, she said, rushing at her with a knife in my hand, with the intention of killing her. In trying to escape me she had fortunately been able to scream, and so to awaken herself and scare off her nightmare. Then Mrs. Caine got into bed again, considerably agitated, but very sleepy. I was weary, too, but I had braced myself up to the work, and was determined to keep awake all night so as to carry on my work of impersonation to a successful end in the morning. I heard midnight. I had yet six hours to wait for daylight. The time passed with excruciating slowness. Minutes appeared hours. The noises in the house and on the avenue ceased. I kept thinking about the sad events of my life. I began at the beginning and, after living over again fifteen or twenty years of my existence, found I had only spanned over a space of five minutes. Failing to find anything more to think about of the past I turned by thoughts bravely to the future, wondering, first, what the next day would bring forth, then making plans for the carrying out of my project. I wondered if I should be able to pass over the river to the goal of my strange ambition to become eventually an inmate of the halls inhabited by my mentally wrecked sisters. And then, once in, what would be my experience? And after? How to get out. Bah! I said, they will get me out.

I looked out towards the window and hailed with joy the slight shimmer of dawn. The light grew strong and gray, but the silence strikingly still. My companion slept. I had still an hour or two to pass over. Fortunately I found some employment for my mental activity. Robert Bruce in his captivity had won confidence in the future and passed his time as pleasantly as possible under the circumstances by watching the celebrated spider building his web. I had less noble vermin to interest me. Yet I believe I made some valuable discoveries in natural history. I was about dropping off to sleep in spite of myself, when I was suddenly startled to wakefulness. I thought I heard something crawl and fall down upon the counterpane with an almost inaudible thud. I had the opportunity of studying these interesting animals very thoroughly. They had evidently come for breakfast, and were not a little disappointed to find that their principal *plat* was not there. They scampered up and down the pillow, came together, seemed to hold interesting converse, and acted in every way as if they were puzzled by the absence of an appetizing breakfast. After one consultation of some length they finally disappeared, seeking victims otherwhere, and leaving me to pass the long minutes by giving my attention to cockroaches, whose size and agility were something of a surprise to me.

SYMPATHY IN TROUBLE.

My room companion had been sound asleep for a long time, but she now woke up, and expressed surprise at seeing me still awake and apparently as lively as a cricket. She was as sympathetic as ever. She came to me and took my hands and tried her best to console me, and asked me if I did not want to go home. She kept me upstairs until nearly everybody was out of the house, and then took me down to the basement for coffee and a bun. After that, partaken in silence, I went back to my room, where I sat down, moping. Mrs. Caine grew more and more anxious. "What is to be done?" she kept exclaiming. "Where are your friends?" "No," I answered, "I have no friends, but I have some trunks. Where are they? I want them." The good woman tried to pacify me, saying that they would be found in good time. She believed that I was insane. Yet I forgive her. It is only after one is in trouble that one realizes how little sympathy and kindness there are in the world. The women in the Home who were not afraid of me had wanted to have some amusement at my expense, and so they had bothered me with questions and remarks that had I been insane would have been cruel and inhumane. Only this one woman among the crowd, pretty and delicate Mrs. Caine, displayed true womanly feeling. She compelled the others to cease teasing me and took the bed of the woman who refused to sleep near me. She protested against the suggestion to leave me alone and to have me locked up for the night so that I could harm no one. She insisted on remaining with me in order to administer aid should I need it. She smoothed my hair and bathed my brow and talked as soothingly to me as a mother would do to an ailing child. By every means she tried to have me go to bed and rest, and when it drew toward morning she got up and wrapped a blanket around me for fear I might get cold; then she kissed me on the brow and whispered, compassionately: "Poor child, poor child!" How much I admired that little woman's courage and kindness. How I longed to reassure her and whisper that I was not insane, and how I hoped that, if any poor girl should ever be so unfortunate as to be what I was pretending to be, she might meet with one who possessed the same spirit of human kindness possessed by Mrs. Ruth Caine.

THE ADVENT OF THE POLICE

III.

But to return to my story. I kept up my rôle until the assistant matron, Mrs. Stanard, came in. She tried to persuade me to be calm. I began to see clearly that she wanted to get me out of the house at all hazards, quietly if possible. This I did not want. I refused to move, but kept up ever the refrain of my lost trunks. Finally some one suggested that an officer be sent for. After awhile Mrs. Stanard put on her bonnet and went out. Then I knew that I was making an advance toward the home of the insane. Soon she returned, bringing with her two policemen—big, strong men—who entered the room rather unceremoniously, evidently expecting to meet with a person violently crazy. The name of one of them was Tom Bockert. When they entered I pretended not to see them. "I want you to take her quietly," said Mrs. Stanard. "If she don't come along quietly," responded one of the men, "I will drag her through the streets." I still took no notice of them, but certainly wished to avoid raising a scandal outside. Fortunately Mrs. Caine came to my rescue. She told the officers about my outcries for my lost trunks, and together they made up a plan to get me to go along with them quietly by telling me they would go with me to look for my lost effects. They asked me if I would go. I said I was afraid to go alone. Mrs. Stanard then said she would accompany me, and she arranged that the two policemen should follow us at a respectful distance. She tied on my veil for me, and we left the house by the basement and started across town, the two officers following at some distance behind. We walked along very quietly and finally came to the station-house, which the good woman assured me was the express office and that there we should certainly find my missing effects. I went inside with fear and trembling, for good reason.

BEFORE CAPT. MCCULLAGH.

I remembered the police station well because only ten days before I had been there and had seen Capt. McCullagh, from whom I had asked for information in a case which I had written as a reporter. If he were in, would be not recognize me? And then all would be lost so far as getting to the island was concerned. I pulled my sailor hat as low down over my face as I possibly could, and prepared for the ordeal. Sure enough there was sturdy Capt. McCullagh standing near the desk. "Are you Nellie Brown?" he asked. I said I supposed I was. "Where do you come from?" he asked. I told him I did not know, and then Mrs. Stanard gave him a lot of informa-

IN THE HANDS OF THE POLICE.

tion about me—told him how strangely I had acted at her home; how I had not slept a wink all night, and that in her opinion I was a poor unfortunate who had been driven crazy by inhuman treatment. There was some discussion between Mrs. Standard and the two officers, and Tom Bockert was told to take us down to the court in a car.

"Come along," Bockert said, "I will find your trunk for you." We all went together, Mrs. Stanard, Tom Bockert and his companion and myself. I said it was very kind of them to go with me, and I should not soon forget them. As we walked along I kept up my refrain about my trucks, injecting occasionally some remark about the dirty condition of the streets and the curious character of the people we met on the way. "I don't think I have ever seen such people before," I said. "Who are they?" I asked, and my companions looked upon me with expressions of pity, evidently believing I was a foreigner, an emigrant or something of the sort. They told me that the people around me were working people. I remarked once more that I thought there were too many working people in the world for the amount of work to be done, at which remark Policeman P. T. Bockert eyed me closely, evidently thinking that my mind was gone for good. We passed several other policemen, who generally asked my sturdy guardians what was the matter with me. By this time quite a number of ragged children were following us too, and they passed remarks about me that were to me original as well as amusing.

"What's she up for?" "Say, kop, where did ye get her?" "Where did yer pull 'er?" "She's a daisy!"

Poor Mrs. Stanard was more frightened than I was. The whole situation grew interesting, but I still had fears for my fate before the judge.

SEARCHING FOR LOST TRUNKS.

At last we came to a low building, and Tom Bockert kindly volunteered the information: "Here's the express office. We shall soon find those trunks of yours."

I said that a great many people seemed to have lost their trunks. "Yes," he said, "nearly all these people are looking for trunks."

I said, "They all seem to be foreigners, too." "Yes," said Tom, "they are all foreigners, just landed. They have all lost their trunks, and it takes most of our time to help find them for them."

We entered the court-room. It was the Essex Market Police courtroom. At last the question of my sanity or insanity was to be decided. Judge Duffy sat behind the high desk, wearing a look which seemed to indicate that he was dealing out the milk of human kindness by wholesale. I rather feared I would not get the fate I sought because of the kindness I saw on every line of his face, and it was with rather a sinking heart that I followed Mrs. Stanard as she answered the summons to go up to the desk where Tom Bockert had just given an account of the affair. "Come here," said an officer. "What is your name?"

"Nellie Brown," I replied, with a little accent, "I have lost my trunks, and would like if you could find them." "When did you come to New York?" he asked. "I did not come to New York," I replied (while I added mentally, "because I have been here for some time.") "But you are in New York now," said the man. "No," I said, looking as incredulous as I thought a crazy person could, "I did not come to New York." "That girl is from the West," he said, in a tone that made me tremble. "She has a Western accent." Some one else who had been listening to the brief dialogue here asserted that he had lived South and that my accent was Southern, while another officer was positive it was Eastern. I felt much relieved when the first spokesman turned to the Judge and said, "Judge, here is a peculiar case of a young woman who doesn't know who she is or where she came from. You had better attend to it at once."

I commenced to shake with more than the cold, and I looked around at the strange crowd about me, composed of poorly dressed men and women with stories printed on their faces of hard lives, abuse and poverty. Some were consulting eagerly with friends, while others sat still with a look of utter hopelessness. Everywhere was a sprinkling of well-dressed, well-fed officers watching the scene passively and almost indifferently. It was only an old story with them. One more unfortunate added to a long list which had long since ceased to be of any interest or concern to them.

BEFORE JUDGE DUFFY.

"Come here, girl, and lift your veil," called out Judge Duffy in tones which surprised me by a harshness when I did not think from the kindly face he possessed.

"Who are you speaking to?" I inquired, in my stateliest manner.

"Come here, my dear, and lift your veil. You know the Queen of England, if she were here, would have to lift her veil," he said very kindly.

"That is much better," I replied. "I am not the Queen of England, but I'll lift my veil."

As I did so the little judge looked at me, and then, in a very kind and gentle tone, he said:

"My dear child, what is wrong?"

"Nothing is wrong except that I have lost my trunks, and this man," indicating Policeman Bockert, "promised to bring me where they could be found."

"What do you know about this child?" asked the Judge, sternly, of Mrs. Stanard, who stood, pale and trembling, by my side.

NELLIE BEFORE JUDGE DUFFY.

"I know nothing of her except that she came to the home yesterday and asked to remain overnight."

"The home! What do you mean by the home?" asked Judge Duffy, quickly.

"It is a temporary home kept for working-women at No. 84 Second Avenue."

"What is your position there?"

"I am assistant matron."

"Well, tell us all you know of the case."

"When I was going into the home yesterday I noticed her coming down the avenue. She was all alone. I had just got into the house when the bell rang and she came in. When I talked with her she wanted to know if she could stay all night, and I said she could. After awhile she said all the people in the house looked crazy, and she was afraid of them. Then she would not go to bed, but sat up all the night."

"Had she any money?"

"Yes," I replied, answering for her, "I paid her for everything, and the eating was the worst I ever tried."

There was a general smile at this, and some murmurs of "She's not so crazy on the food question."

"Poor child," said Judge Duffy, "she is well dressed, and a lady. Her English is perfect, and I would stake everything on her being a good girl. I am positive she is somebody's darling."

At this announcement everybody laughed, and I put my handkerchief over my face and endeavored to choke the laughter that threatened to spoil my plans, in despite of my resolutions.

"I mean she is some woman's darling," hastily amended the Judge. "I am sure some one is searching for her. Poor girl, I will be good to her, for she looks like my sister, who is dead."

There was a hush for a moment after this announcement, and the officers glanced at me more kindly, while I silently blessed the kind-hearted Judge, and hoped that any poor creatures who might be afflicted as I pretended to be should have as kindly a man to deal with as Judge Duffy.

"I wish the reporters were here," he said at last. "They would be able to find out something about her."

I got very much frightened at this, for if there is any one who can ferret out a mystery it is a reporter. I felt that I would rather face a mass of expert doctors, policemen, and detectives than two bright specimens of my craft, so I said:

"I don't see why all this is needed to help me find my trunks. These men are impudent and I do not want to be stared at. I will go away. I don't want to stay here."

So saying, I pulled down my veil and secretly hoped the reporters would be detained elsewhere until I was sent to the asylum.

"I don't know what to do with the poor child," said the worried Judge. "She must be taken care of."

"Send her to the Island," suggested one of the officers.

"Oh, don't!" said Mrs. Stanard in evident alarm. "Don't! She is a lady and it would kill her to be put on the Island."

For once I felt like shaking the good woman. To think the Island was just the place I wanted to reach and here she was trying to keep me from going there! It was very kind of her, but rather provoking under the circumstances.

"There has been some foul work here," said the Judge. "I believe this child has been drugged and brought to this city. Make out the papers and we will send her to Bellevue for examination. Probably in a few days the effect of the drug will pass off and she will be able to tell us a story that will be startling. If the reporters would only come!"

I dreaded them, so I said something about not wishing to stay there any longer to be gazed at. Judge Duffy then told Policeman Bockert to take me to the back office. After we were seated there Judge Duffy came in and asked me if my home was in Cuba.

"Yes," I replied with a smile. "How did you know?"

"Oh, I knew it, my dear. Now, tell me where was it. In what part of Cuba?"

"On the hacienda," I replied.

"Ah," said the Judge, "on a farm. Do you remember Havana?"

"Si, señor," I answered; "it is near home. How did you know?"

"Oh, I knew all about it. Now, won't you tell me the name of your home?" he asked persuasively.

"That's what I forget," I answered sadly. "I have a headache all the time, and it makes me forget things. I don't want them to trouble me. Everybody is asking me questions, and it makes my head worse," and in truth it did.

"Well, no one shall trouble you any more. Sit down here and rest awhile," and the genial Judge left me alone with Mrs. Stanard.

A REPORTER INTERVIEWS HER.

Just then an officer came in with a reporter. I was so frightened, and thought I would be recognized as a journalist, so I turned my head away and said, "I don't want to see any reporters; I will not see any; the Judge said I was not to be troubled."

"Well, there is no insanity in that," said the man who had brought the reporter, and together they left the room. Once again I had a fit of fear. Had I gone too far in not wanting to see a reporter, and was my sanity detected? If I had given the impression that I was sane, I was determined to undo it, so I jumped up and ran back and forward through the office, Mrs. Stanard clinging terrified to my arm.

"I won't stay here; I want my trunks! Why do they bother me with so many people?" and thus I kept on until the ambulance surgeon came in, accompanied by the Judge.

THE AMBULANCE APPEARS.

"Here is a poor girl who has been drugged," explained the Judge. "She looks like my sister, and any one can see she is a good girl. I am interested in the child, and I would do as much for her as if she were my own. I want you to be kind to her," he said to the ambulance surgeon. Then turning to Mrs. Stanard, he asked her if she could not keep me for a few days until my case was inquired into. Fortunately, she said she could not, because all the women at the home were afraid of me, and would leave if I were kept there. I was very much afraid she would keep me if the pay was assured her, and so I said something about the bad cooking and that I did not intend to go back to the home. Then came the examination. The doctor looked clever and I had not one hope of deceiving him, but I determined to keep up the farce. "Put out your tongue," he ordered, briskly. I gave an inward chuckle at the thought. "Put out your tongue when I tell you," he said. "I don't want to," I answered truthfully enough. "You must. You are sick, and I am a doctor." "I am not sick and never was. I only want my trunks." But I put out my tongue, which he looked at in a sagacious manner. Then he felt my pulse and listened to the beating of my heart. I had not the least idea how the heart of an insane person beat, so I held my breath all the while he listened, until when he quit I had to give a gasp to regain it. Then he tried the effect of the light on the pupils of my eyes. Holding his hand within a half inch of my face, he told me to look at it, then jerking it hastily away he would examine my eyes. I was puzzled to know what insanity was like in the eye, so I thought the best thing under the circumstances was to stare. This I did. I held my eyes riveted unblinkingly upon his hand, and when he removed it I exerted all my strength to still keep my eyes from blinking. "What drugs have you been taking?" he then asked me. "Drugs!" I repeated wonderingly. "I do not know what drugs are." "The pupils of her eyes have been enlarged ever since she came to the home. They have not changed once," explained Mrs. Stanard. I wondered how she knew whether they had or not, but I kept quiet. "I believe she has been using belladonna," said the doctor, and for the first time I was thankful that I was a little near-sighted, which of course answers for the enlargement of the pupils. I thought I might as well be truthful when I could without injuring my case, so I told him I was near-sighted, that I was not in the least ill, had never been sick, and that no one had a right to detain me when I wanted to find my trunks. I wanted to go home. He wrote a lot of things in a long, slender book, and then said he was going to take me home. The Judge told him to take me and to be kind to me, and to tell the people at the hospital to be kind to me, and to do all they could for me. If we only had more such men as Judge Duffy, the poor unfortunates would not find life all darkness.

IN THE AMBULANCE WAGON.

I began to have more confidence in my own ability now, since one Judge, one doctor and a mass of people had pronounced me insane, and I put on my veil quite gladly when I was told that I was to be taken in a carriage and that afterward I could go home. "I am so glad to go with you," I said, and I meant it. I was very glad indeed. Once more, guarded by Policeman Bockert, I walked through the little crowded court-room. I felt quite proud of myself as I went out a side door into an alleyway, where the ambulance was waiting. Near the closed and barred gates was a small office occupied by several men and large books. We all went in there, and when they began to ask me questions the doctor interposed and said he had all the papers and that it was useless to ask me anything further, because I was unable to answer questions. This was a great relief to me, for my nerves were already feeling the strain. A rough-looking man wanted to put me into the ambulance, but I refused his aid so decidedly that the doctor and policeman told him to desist, and they performed that gallant office themselves. I did not enter the ambulance without protest. I made the remark that I had never seen a carriage of that make before, and that I did not want to ride in it, but after awhile I let them persuade me, as I had right along intended to do. I shall never forget that ride. After I was put in flat on the yellow blanket the doctor got in and sat near the door. The large gates were swung open and the curious crowd which had collected swayed back to make way for the ambulance as it backed out. How they tried to get a glimpse at the supposed crazy girl! The doctor saw that I did not like the people gazing at me and considerately put down the curtains, after asking my wishes in regard to it. Still that did not keep the people away. The children raced after us, yelling all sorts of slang expressions and trying to get a peep under the curtains. It was quite an interesting drive, but I must say that it was an excruciatingly rough one. I held on, only there was not much to hold on to, and the driver drove as if he feared some one would catch up with us.

IN BELLEVUE HOSPITAL

IV.

At last Bellevue was reached, the third station on my way to the Island. I had passed through successfully the ordeals at the home and at Essex Market Police Court, and now felt confident that I should not fail. The ambulance stopped with a sudden jerk and the doctor jumped out. "How many have you?" I heard some one inquire. "Only one, for the pavilion," was the reply. A rough-looking man came forward, and catching hold of me attempted to drag me out as if I had the strength of an elephant and would resist. The doctor, seeing my look of disgust, ordered him to leave me alone, saying that he would take charge of me himself. He then lifted me carefully out and I walked with the grace of a queen past the crowd that had gathered curious to see the new unfortunate. Together with the doctor I entered a small dark office, where there were several men. The one behind the desk opened a book and began on the long string of questions which had been asked me so often. I refused to answer, and the doctor told him it was not necessary to trouble me further, as he had all the papers made out, and I was too insane to be able to tell anything that would be of consequence. I felt relieved that it was so easy here, as, though still undaunted, I had begun to feel faint for want of food. The order was then given to take me to the insane pavilion, and a muscular man came forward and caught me so tightly by the arm that a pain ran clear through me. It made me angry, and for a moment I forgot my rôle as I turned to him and said: "How dare you touch me?" At this he loosened his hold somewhat, and I shook him off with more strength than I thought I possessed. "I will go with no one but this man," I said, pointing to the ambulance-surgeon. "The judge said that he was to take care of me, and I will go with no one else." At this the surgeon said that he would take me, and so we went arm in arm, following the man who had at first been so rough with me. We passed through the well-cared-for grounds and finally reached the insane ward. A white-capped nurse was there to receive me. "This young girl is to wait here for the boat," said the surgeon, and then he started to leave me. I begged him not to go or to take me with him, but he said he wanted to get his dinner first, and that I should wait there for him. When I insisted on accompanying him he claimed that he had to assist at an amputation, and it would not look well for me to be present. It was evident that he believed he was dealing with an insane person. Just then the most horrible insane cries came from a yard in the rear. With all my bravery I felt a chill at the prospect of being shut up with a fellow-creature who was really insane. The doctor evidently noticed my nervousness, for he said to the attendant: "What a noise the carpenters make." Turning to me he offered me explanation to the effect that new buildings were being erected, and that the noise came from some of the workmen engaged upon it. I told him I did not want to stay there without him, and to pacify me he promised soon to return. He left me and I found myself at last an occupant of an insane asylum.

SOME INTERIOR ARRANGEMENTS.

I stood at the door and contemplated the scene before me. The long, uncarpeted hall was scrubbed to that peculiar whiteness seen only in public institutions. In the rear of the hall were large iron doors fastened by a padlock. Several stiff-looking benches and a number of willow chairs were the only articles of furniture. On either side of the hall were doors leading into what I supposed and what proved to be bedrooms. Near the entrance door, on the right-hand side, was a small sitting-room for the nurses, and opposite it was a room where dinner was dished out. A nurse in a black dress, white cap and apron and armed with a bunch of keys had charge of the hall. I soon learned her name, Miss Ball. An old Irishwoman was maid of all work. I heard her called Mary, and I am glad to know that there is such a good-hearted woman in that place. I experienced only kindness and the utmost consideration from her. There were only three patients, as they are called. I made the fourth. I thought I might as well begin work at once, for I still expected that the very first doctor might declare me sane and send me out again into the wide, wide world. So I went down to the rear of the room and introduced myself to one of the women and asked her all about herself. Her name, she said, was Miss Anne Neville, and she had been sick from overwork. She had been working as a chambermaid, and when her health gave way she was sent to some Sisters' Home to be treated. Her nephew, who was a waiter, was out of work, and, being unable to pay her expenses at the Home, had had her transferred to Bellevue.

"Is there anything wrong with you mentally as well?" I asked her.

"No," she said. "The doctors have been asking me many curious questions and confusing me as much as possible, but I have nothing wrong with my brain."

"Do you know that only insane people are sent to this pavilion?" I asked.

"Yes, I know; but I am unable to do anything. The doctors refuse to listen to me, and it is useless to say anything to the nurses."

AMONG THE INSANE PATIENTS.

Satisfied from various reasons that Miss Neville was as sane as I was myself, I transferred my attentions to one of the other patients. I found her in need of medical aid and quite silly mentally, although I have seen many women in the lower walks of life, whose sanity was never questioned, who were not any brighter.

The third patient, Mrs. Fox, would not say much. She was very quiet, and after telling me that her case was hopeless refused to talk. I began now to feel surer of my position, and I determined that no doctor should convince me that I was sane so long as I had the hope of accomplishing my mission. A small, fair-complexioned nurse arrived, and, after putting on her cap, told Miss Ball to go to dinner. The new nurse, Miss Scott by name, came to me and said, rudely:

"Take off your hat."

"I shall not take off my hat," I answered. "I am waiting for the boat and I shall not remove it."

"Well, you are not going on any boat. You might as well know it now as later. You are in an asylum for the insane."

Although fully aware of that fact, her unvarnished words gave me a shock. "I did not want to come here; I am not sick or insane, and I will not stay," I said.

"It will be a long time before you get out if you don't do as you are told," answered Miss Scott. "You might as well take off your hat, or I shall use force, and if I am not able to do it, I have but to touch a bell and I shall get assistance. Will you take it off?"

"No, I will not. I am cold, and I want my hat on, and you can't make me take it off."

"I shall give you a few more minutes, and if you don't take it off then I shall use force, and I warn you it will not be very gentle."

"If you take my hat off I shall take your cap off; so now."

Miss Scott was called to the door then, and as I feared that an exhibition of temper might show too much sanity I took off my hat and gloves and was sitting quietly looking into space when she returned. I was hungry, and was quite pleased to see Mary make preparations for dinner. The preparations were simple. She merely pulled a straight bench up along the side of a bare table and ordered the patients to gather 'round the feast. Then she brought out a small tin plate on which was a piece of boiled meat and a potato. It could not have been colder had it been cooked the week before, and it had no chance to make acquaintance with salt or pepper. I would not go up to the table, so Mary came to where I sat in a corner and while handing out the tin plate asked:

AN INSANITY EXPERT AT WORK.

"Have ye any pennies about ye, dearie?"

"What?" I said in my surprise.

"Have ye any pennies, dearie, that ye could give me. They'll take them all from ye any way, dearie, so I might as well have them."

I understood it fully now, but I had no intention of feeing Mary so early in the game, fearing it would have an influence on her treatment of me, so I said I had lost my purse, which was quite true. But though I did not give Mary any money, she was none the less kind to me. When I objected to the tin plate in which she had brought my food she fetched a china one for me, and when I found it impossible to eat the food she presented she gave me a glass of milk and a soda cracker.

ONLY A CHARITY WARD.

All the windows in the hall were open and the cold air began to tell on my Southern blood. It grew so cold indeed as to be almost unbearable, and I complained of it to Miss Scott and Miss Ball. But they answered curtly that as I was in a charity place I could not expect much else. All the other women were suffering from the cold, and the nurses themselves had to wear heavy garments to keep themselves warm. I asked if I could go to bed. They said "No!" At last Miss Scott got an old gray shawl and shaking some of the moths out of it told me to put it on. "It's rather a bad looking shawl," I said. "Well, some people would get along better if they were not so proud," said Miss Scott. "People on charity should not expect anything and should not complain." So I put the moth-eaten shawl with all its musty smell around me, and sat down on a wicker chair, wondering what would come next, whether I should freeze to death or survive. My nose was very cold, so I covered up my head and was in a half doze when the shawl was suddenly jerked from my face and a strange man and Miss Scott stood before me. The man proved to be a doctor, and his first

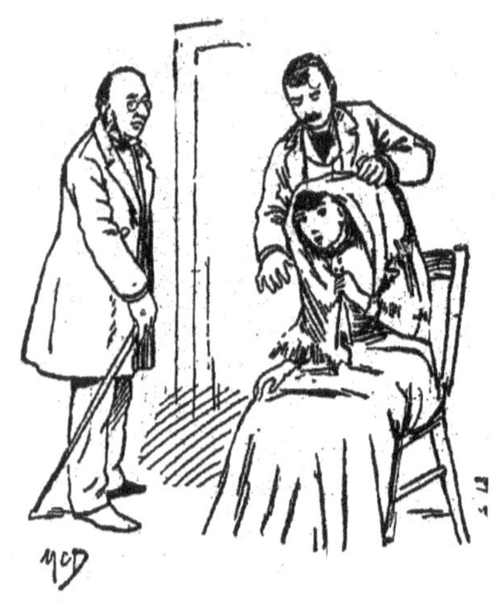
POSITIVELY DEMENTED.

greetings were, "I've seen that face before." "Then you know me?" I asked with a great show of eagerness that I did not feel. "I think I do. Where did you come from?" "From home." "Where is home?" "Don't you know? Cuba." He then sat down beside me, felt my pulse, and examined my tongue, and at last said: "Tell Miss Scott all about yourself." "No, I will not. I will not talk with women." "What do you do in New York?" "Nothing." "Can you work?" "No, Señor." "Tell me, are you a woman of the town?" "I do not understand you," I replied, heartily disgusted with him.

"I mean have you allowed the men to provide for you and keep you?"

I felt like slapping him in the face, but I had to maintain my composure, so I simply said: "I do not know what you are talking about. I always lived at home."

POSITIVELY DEMENTED.

After many more questions, fully as useless and senseless, he left me and began to talk with the nurse. "Positively demented," he said. "I consider it a hopeless case. She needs to be put where some one will take care of her."

And so I passed my second medical expert.

After this, I began to have a smaller regard for the ability of doctors than I ever had before, and a greater one for myself. I felt sure now that no doctor could tell whether people were insane or not, so long as the case was not violent.

Later in the afternoon a boy and a woman came. The woman sat down on a bench, while the boy went in and talked with Miss Scott. In a short time he came out, and, just nodding good-by to the woman, who was his mother, went away. She did not look insane, but as she was German I could not learn her story. Her name, however, was Mrs. Louise Schanz. She seemed quite lost, but when the nurses put her at some sewing she did her work well and quickly. At 3 in the afternoon all the patients were given a gruel broth, and at 5 a cup of tea and a piece of bread. I was favored, for when they saw that it was impossible for me to eat the bread or drink the stuff honored by the name of tea they gave me a cup of milk and a cracker, the same as I had had at noon. Just as the gas was being lighted another patient was added. She was a young girl, twenty-five years old. She told me that she had just gotten up from a sick bed. Her appearance confirmed her story. She looked like one who had had a severe attack of fever. "I am now suffering from nervous debility," she said, "and my friends have sent me here to be treated for it." I did not tell her where she was and she seemed quite satisfied. At 6.15 Miss Ball said that she wanted to go away, and so we would all have to go to bed. Then each of us—we now numbered six—were assigned a room and told to undress. I did so, and was given a short cotton-flannel gown to wear during the night. Then she took every particle of the clothing I had worn during the day, and making it up in a bundle labeled it "Brown" and took it away. The iron-barred window was locked, and Miss Ball, after giving me an extra blanket, which, she said, was a favor rarely granted, went out and left me alone. The bed was not a comfortable one. It was so hard, indeed, that I could not make a dent in it, and the pillow was stuffed with straw. Under the sheet was an oilcloth spread. As the night grew colder I tried to warm that oilcloth. I kept on trying, but when morning dawned and it was still as cold as when I went to bed, and had reduced me, too, to the temperature of an iceberg, I gave it up as an impossible task.

ANOTHER REPORTER TURNS UP.

I had hoped to get some rest on this my first night in an insane asylum. But I was doomed to disappointment. When the night nurses came in they were curious to see me and to find out what I was like. No sooner had they left than I heard some one at my door inquiring for Nellie Brown, and I began to tremble, fearing always that my sanity would be discovered. By listening to the conversation I found it was a reporter in search of me, and I heard him ask for my clothing so that he might examine it. I listened quite anxiously to the talk about me, and was relieved to learn that I was considered hopelessly insane. That was encouraging. After the reporter left I heard new arrivals, and I learned that a doctor was there and intended to see me. For what purpose I knew not, and I imagined all sorts of horrible things, such as examinations and the rest of it, and when they got to my room I was shaking with more than fear. "Nellie Brown, here is the doctor; he wishes to speak with you," said the nurse. If that's all he wanted I thought I could endure it. I removed the blanket which I had put over my head in my sudden fright and looked up. The sight was reassuring.

A HANDSOME DOCTOR.

He was a handsome young man. He had the air and address of a gentleman. The air he wore was somewhat deceptive. He came forward, seated himself on the side of my bed, and put his arm soothingly around my shoulders. It was a terrible task to play insane before this young man, and only a girl can sympathize with me in my position.

"How do you feel to-night, Nellie?" he asked, easily.

"Oh, I feel all right."

"But you are sick, you know," he said.

"Oh, am I?" I replied, and I turned my head on the pillow and smiled.

"When did you leave Cuba, Nellie?"

"Oh, you know my home?" I asked.

"Yes, very well. Don't you remember me? I remember you."

"Do you?" and I mentally said I should not forget him. He was accompanied by a friend who never ventured a remark, but stood staring at me as I lay in bed. After a great many questions, to which I answered truthfully, he left me. Then came other troubles. All night long the nurses read one to the other aloud, and I know that the other patients, as well as myself, were unable to sleep. Every half-hour or hour they would walk heavily down the halls, their boot-heels resounding like the march of a private of dragoons, and take a look at every patient. Of course this helped to keep us awake. Then, as it came toward morning, they began to beat eggs for breakfast, and the sound made me realize how horribly hungry I was. Occasional yells and cries came from the male department, and that did not aid in making the night pass more cheerfully. Then the ambulance-gong, as it brought in more unfortunates, sounded as a knell to life and liberty. Thus I passed my first night as an insane girl at Bellevue.

THE GOAL IN SIGHT

V.

At 6 o'clock on Sunday morning, Sept. 25, the nurses pulled the covering from my bed. "Come, it's time for you to get out of bed," they said, and opened the window and let in the cold breeze. My clothing was then returned to me. After dressing I was shown to a washstand, where all the other patients were trying to rid their faces of all traces of sleep. At 7 o'clock we were given some horrible mess, which Mary told us was chicken broth. The cold, from which we had suffered enough the day previous, was bitter, and when I complained to the nurse she said it was one of the rules of the institution not to turn the heat on until October, and so we would have to endure it, as the steam-pipes had not even been put in order. The night nurses then, arming themselves with scissors, began to play manicure on the patients. They cut my nails to the quick, as they did those of several of the other patients. Shortly after this a handsome young doctor made his appearance and I was conducted into the sitting-room. "Who are you?" he asked. "Nellie Moreno," I replied. "Then why did you give the name of Brown?" he asked. "What is wrong with you?" "Nothing. I did not want to come here, but they brought me. I want to go away. Won't you let me out?"

WHO IS THIS MAN?

"If I take you out will you stay with me? Won't you run away from me when you get on the street?"

"I can't promise that I will not," I answered, with a smile and a sigh, for he was handsome.

He asked me many other questions. Did I ever see faces on the wall? Did I ever hear voices around? I answered him to the best of my ability. "Do you ever hear voices at night?" he asked. "Yes, there is so much talking I cannot sleep." "I thought so," he said to himself. Then turning to me, he asked: "What do these voices say?" "Well, I do not listen to them always. But sometimes, very often, they talk about Nellie Brown and then on other subjects that do not interest me half so much," I answered truthfully. "That will do," he said to Miss Scott, who was just on the outside. "Can I go away?" I asked. "Yes," he said, with a satisfied laugh, "we'll soon send you away." "It is so very cold here, I want to go out," I said. "That's true," he said to Miss Scott. "The cold is almost unbearable in here, and you will have some cases of pneumonia if you are not careful."

TESTS FOR INSANITY.

With this I was led away and another patient was taken in. I sat right outside the door and waited to hear how he would test the sanity of the other patients. With little variation the examination was exactly the same as mine. All the patients were asked if they saw faces on the wall, heard voices, and what they said. I might also add each patient denied any such peculiar freaks of sight and hearing. At 10 o'clock we were given a cup of unsalted beef tea; at noon a bit of cold meat and a potato, at 3 o'clock a cup of oatmeal gruel and at 5.30 a cup of tea and a slice of unbuttered bread. We were all cold and hungry. After the physician left we were given shawls and told to walk up and down the halls in order to get warm. During the day the pavilion was visited by a number of people who were curious to see the crazy girl from Cuba. I kept my head covered, on the plea of being cold, for fear some of the reporters would recognize me. Some of the visitors were apparently in search of a missing girl, for I was made take down the shawl repeatedly, and after they looked at me they would say, "I don't know her," "or "she is not the one," for which I was secretly thankful. Warden O'Rourke visited me and tried his arts on an examination. Then he brought some well-dressed women and some gentlemen at different times to have a glance at the mysterious Nellie Brown.

PRAISE OF THE REPORTERS.

The reporters were the most troublesome. Such a number of them! And they were all so bright and clever that I was terribly frightened lest they should see that I was sane. They were very kind and nice to me, and very gentle in all their questionings. My late visitor the night previous came to the window while some reporters were interviewing me in the sitting-room and told the nurse to allow them to see me as they would be of assistance in finding some clue as to my identity.

In the afternoon Dr. Field came and examined me. He asked me only a few questions, and one that had no bearing on such a case. The chief question was of my home and friends, and if I had any lovers or had ever been married. The other patients were asked the same questions. As the doctor was about to leave the pavilion Miss Tillie Mayard discovered that she was in an insane ward. She went to Dr. Field and asked him why she had been sent there. "Have you just found out you are in an insane asylum?" asked the doctor. "Yes, my friends said they were sending me to a convalescent ward to be treated for nervous debility, from which I am suffering since my illness. I want to get out of this place immediately." "Well, you won't get out in a hurry," he said, with a quick laugh. "If you know anything at all," she responded, "you should be able to tell that I am perfectly sane. Why don't you test me?" "We know all we want to on that score," said the Doctor, and he left the poor girl condemned to an insane asylum, probably for life, without giving her one feeble chance to prove her sanity.

Sunday night was but a repetition of Saturday. All night long we were kept awake by the talk of the nurses and their heavy walking through the uncarpeted halls. On Monday morning we were told that we should be taken away at 1.30. The nurses questioned me unceasingly about my home, and all seemed to have an idea that I had a lover who had cast me forth on the world and wrecked my brain. The morning brought many reporters. How untiring they are in their efforts to get something new. Miss Scott refused to allow

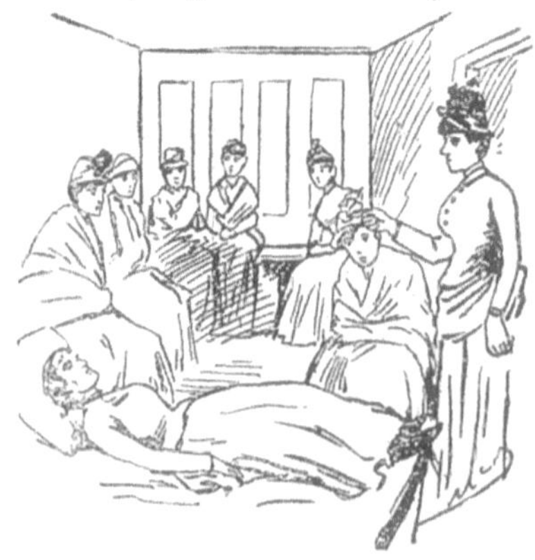

ON BOARD THE ISLAND BOAT.

me to be seen, however, and for this I was thankful. Had they been given free access to me, I should probably not have been a mystery long, for many of them knew me by sight. Warden O'Rourke came for a final visit and had a short conversation with me. He wrote his name in my note-book, saying to the nurse that I would forget all about it in an hour. I smiled and thought I wasn't sure of that. Other people called to see me, but none knew me or could give any information about me.

LEAVING BELLEVUE.

Noon came. I grew nervous as the time approached to leave for the Island. I dreaded every new arrival, fearful that my secret would be discovered at the last moment. Then I was given a shawl and my hat and gloves. I could hardly put them on, my nerves were so unstrung. At last the attendant arrived, and I bade good-by to Mary as I slipped "a few pennies" into her hand. "God bless you," she said; "I shall pray for you. Cheer up, dearie. You are young, and will get over this." I told her I hoped so, and then I said good-by to Miss Scott in Spanish. The rough-looking attendant twisted his arms around mine, and half led, half dragged me to an ambulance. A crowd of the students had assembled, and they watched us curiously. I put the shawl over my face and sank thankfully into the wagon. Miss Neville, Miss Mayard, Mrs. Fox, and Mrs. Schanz were all put in after me, one at a time. A man got in with us; the doors were locked, and we were driven out of the gates in great style on toward the insane asylum and victory! The patients made no move to escape. The odor of the male attendant's breath was enough to make one's head swim.

When we reached the wharf such a mob of people crowded around the wagon that the police were called to put them away, so that we could reach the boat. I was the last of the procession. I was escorted down the plank, the fresh breeze blowing the attendant's whisky breath into my face until I staggered. I was taken into a dirty cabin, where I found my companions seated on a narrow bench. The small windows were closed, and, with the smell of the filthy room, the air was stifling. At one end of the cabin was a small bunk in such a condition that I had to hold my nose when I went near it. A sick girl was put on it. An old woman, with an enormous bonnet and a dirty basket filled with chunks of bread and bits of scrap meat, completed our company. The door was guarded by two female attendants. One was clad in a dress made of bed-ticking and the other was dressed with some attempt at style. They were coarse, massive women, and expectorated tobacco juice about on the floor in a manner more skillful than charming. One of these fearful creatures seemed to have much faith in the power of the glance on insane people, for when any one of us would move or go to look out of the high window she would say, "Sit down," and would lower her brows and glare in a way that was simply terrifying. While guarding the door they talked with some men on the outside. They discussed the number of patients and then their own affairs in a manner neither edifying nor refined.

The boat stopped and the old woman and the sick girl were taken off. The rest of us were told to sit still. At the next stop my companions were taken off, one at a time. I was last, and it seemed to require a man and a woman to lead me up the plank to reach the shore. An ambulance was standing there, and in it were the four other patients.

"What is this place?" I asked of the man, who had his fingers sunk into the flesh of my arm.

"Blackwell's Island, an insane place, where you'll never get out of."

With this I was shoved into the ambulance, the spring-board was put up, an officer and a mail-carrier jumped on behind, and I was swiftly driven to the Insane Asylum on Blackwell's Island. Of my ten days' experience there I have yet to tell.

NELLIE BLY

Inside the Madhouse

Sunday, October 16, 1887

NELLIE BLY'S EXPERIENCE IN THE BLACKWELL'S ISLAND ASYLUM

Continuation of the Story of Ten Days With Lunatics

How the City's Unfortunate Wards are Fed and Treated

The Terrors of Cold Baths and Cruel, Unsympathetic Nurses

Attendants Who Harass and Abuse Patients and Laugh at Their Miseries

---

Doctors who Flirt with Pretty Nurses—A Queer Medical Examination that Did Not Examine—Inmates of Hall No. 6—At the Piano—Taking Away Her Clothes—A Long Wait in the Cold for Supper—No Knives Nor Forks—Food Unsalted and Unfit—Half Drowned in an Icy Bath—Soap Only Once a Week—Put to Bed in Damp Clothing—Noises at Night—The Horror of Fire in a Locked and Barred Room—Hair Combed with a Public Comb—Nurses Who Vex and Annoy Patients—Holding Them Under Water Until Half Downed—Punishing Unfortunates Who Appeal for Protection—Attendants Curse Nellie—Set Free at Last.

AS THE wagon was rapidly driven through the beautiful lawns up to the asylum my feelings of satisfaction at having attained the object of my work were greatly dampened by the look of distress on the faces of my companions. Poor women, they had no hopes of a speedy delivery! On the wagon sped, and I, as well as my comrades, gave a despairing farewell glance at freedom as we came in sight of the long stone buildings. We passed one low building, and the stench was so horrible that I was compelled to hold my breath, and I mentally decided that it was the kitchen. I afterward found I was correct in my surmise, and smiled at the signboard at the end of the walk: "Visitors are not allowed on this road." I don't think the sign would be necessary if they once tried the road, especially on a warm day.

The wagon stopped, and the nurse and officer in charge told us to get out. The nurse added: "Thank God! they came quietly." We obeyed orders to go ahead up a flight of narrow stone steps, which had evidently been built for the accommodation of people who climb stairs three at a time. I wondered if my companions knew where we were, so I said to Miss Tillie Mayard: "Where are we?" "At the Blackwell's Island Lunatic Asylum," she answered sadly. "Are you crazy?" I asked. "No," she replied, "but as we have been sent here we will have to be quiet until we find some means of escape. They will be few, though, if all the doctors, as Dr. Field, refuse to listen to me or give me a chance to prove my sanity." We were ushered into a narrow vestibule and the door was locked behind us.

In spite of the knowledge of my sanity and the assurance that I would be released in a few days, my heart gave a sharp twinge. Pronounced insane by four expert doctors and shut up behind the unmerciful bolts and bars of a madhouse! Not to be confined alone, but to be a companion, day and night, of senseless, chattering lunatics; to sleep with them, to eat with them, to be considered one of them, was an uncomfortable position. Timidly we followed the nurse up the long uncarpeted hall to a room filled by so-called crazy women. We were told to sit down, and some of the patients kindly made room for us. They looked at us curiously and one came up to me and asked: "Who sent you here?" "The doctors," I answered. "What for?" she persisted. "Well, they say I am insane," I admitted. "Insane!" she repeated incredulously. "It cannot be seen in your face."

This woman was too clever, I concluded, and was glad to answer the roughly given orders to follow the nurse to see the doctor. This nurse, Miss Grupe, by the way, had a nice German face, and if I had not detected certain hard lines about the mouth I might have expected, as did my companions, to receive but kindness from her. She left us in a small waiting-room at the end of the hall, and left us alone while she went into a small office opening into the sitting or receiving-room. "I like to go down in the wagon," she said to the invisible party on the inside. "It helps to break up the day." He answered her that the open air improved her looks, and she again appeared before us all smiles and simpers.

THE INSANE ASYLUM.

"Come here, Tillie Mayard," she said. Miss Mayard obeyed, and, though I could not see into the office, I could hear her gently but firmly pleading her case. All her remarks were as rational as any I ever heard, and I thought no good physician could help but be impressed with her story. She told of her recent illness, that she was suffering from nervous debility. She begged that they try all their tests for insanity, if they had any, and give her justice. Poor girl, how my heart ached for her! I determined then and there that I would try by every means to make my mission of benefit to my suffering sisters; that I would show how they are committed without ample trial. Without one word of sympathy or encouragement she was brought back to where we sat.

Mrs. Louise Schanz was taken into the presence of Dr. Kinier, the medical man. "Your name?" he asked, loudly. She answered in German, saying she did not speak English nor could she understand it. However, when he said Mrs. Louise Schanz, she said "Yah, yah." Then he tried other questions, and when he found she could not understand one word of English, he said to Miss Grupe: "You are German; speak to her for me." Miss Grupe proved to be one of those people who are ashamed of their nationality and she refused, saying she could understand but few words of her mother tongue. "You know you speak German. Ask this woman what her husband does," and they both laughed as if they were enjoying a joke. "I can't speak but a few words," she protested, but at last she managed to ascertain the occupation of Mr. Schanz. "Now, what was the use of lying to me?" asked the doctor, with a laugh which dispelled the rudeness. "I can't speak any more," she said, and she did not.

Thus was Mrs. Louise Schanz consigned to the asylum without a chance of making herself understood. Can such carelessness be excused, I wonder, when it is so easy to get an interpreter? If the confinement was but for a few days one might question the necessity. But here was a woman taken without her own consent from the free world to an asylum and there given no chance to prove her sanity. Confined most probably for

THE FRONT HALLWAY.

life behind asylum bars, without even being told in her language the why and wherefore. Compare this with a criminal, who is given every chance to prove his innocence. Who would not rather be a murderer and take the chance for life than be declared insane, without hope of escape? Mrs. Schanz begged in German to know where she was, and pleaded for liberty. Her voice broken by sobs, she was led unheard out to us.

Mrs. Fox was then put through this weak, trifling examination and brought from the office, convicted. Miss Annie Neville took her turn, and I was again left to the last. I had by this time determined to act as I do when free, except that I would refuse to tell who I was or where my home was.

THEY EXAMINE HER AGAIN.

BUT THE DOCTOR PAID MORE ATTENTION TO THE NURSE THAN TO HIS PATIENT.

"Nellie Brown, the doctor wants you," said Miss Grupe. I went in and was told to sit down opposite Dr. Kinier at the desk. "What is your name?" he asked, without looking up. "Nellie Brown," I replied easily. "Where is your home?" writing what I had said down in a large book. "In Cuba." "Oh!" he ejaculated, with sudden understanding—then, addressing the nurse: "Did you see anything in the papers about her?" "Yes," she replied, "I saw a long account of this girl in the *Sun* on Sunday." Then the doctor said: "Keep her here until I go to the office and see the notice again." He left us and I was relieved of my hat and shawl. On his return he said he had been unable to find the paper, but he related the story of my debut, as he had read it, to the nurse. "What's the color of her eyes?" Miss Grupe looked, and answered "gray," although everybody had always said my eyes were brown or hazel. "What's your age?" he asked; and as I answered, "Nineteen last May," he turned to the nurse, and said, "When do you get your next pass?" This I ascertained was a leave of absence or "a day off." "Next Saturday," she said, with a laugh. "You will go to town?" and they both laughed as she answered in the affirmative, and he said:

"Measure her." I was stood under a measure, and it was brought down tightly on my head. "What is it?" asked the doctor. "Now you know

I can't tell," she said. "Yes, you can; go ahead. What height?" "I don't know; there are some figures there, but I can't tell." "Yes, you can. Now look and tell me." "I can't; do it yourself," and they laughed again as the doctor left his place at the desk and came forward to see for himself. "Five feet five inches; don't you see?" he said, taking her hand and touching the figures. By her voice I knew she did not understand yet, but that was no concern of mine, as the doctor seemed to find a pleasure in aiding her. Then I was put on the scales, and she worked around until she got them to balance. "How much?" asked the doctor, having resumed his position at the desk. "I don't know. You will have to see for yourself," she replied, calling him by his Christian name, which I have forgotten. He turned and also addressing her by her baptismal name, he said: "You are getting too fresh!" and they both laughed. I then told the weight—112 pounds—to the nurse, and she in turn told the doctor. "What time are you going to supper?" he asked, and she told him. He gave the nurse more attention than he did me, and asked her six questions to every one of me. Then he wrote my fate in the book before him. I said, "I am not sick and I do not want to stay here. No one has a right to shut me up in this manner." He took no notice of my remarks, and having completed his writings, as well as his talk with the nurse for the moment, he said that would do, and with my companions, I went back to the sitting-room.

THE RECEPTION-ROOM.

"You play the piano?" they asked. "Oh, yes; ever since I was a child," I replied. Then they insisted that I should play, and they seated me on a wooden chair before an old-fashioned square. I struck a few notes, and the untuned response sent a grinding chill through me. "How horrible," I exclaimed, turning to a nurse, Miss McCarten, who stood at my side. "I never touched a piano as much out of tune." "It's a pity of you," she said spitefully, "we'll have to get one made to order for you." I began to play the variations of "Home Sweet Home." The talking ceased and every patient sat silent, while my cold fingers moved slowly and stiffly over the keyboard. I finished in an aimless fashion and refused all requests to play more. Not seeing an available place to sit, I still occupied the chair in the front of the piano while I "sized up" my surroundings.

It was a long, bare room, with bare yellow benches encircling it. These benches, which were perfectly straight, and just as uncomfortable, would hold five people, although in almost every instance six were crowded on them. Barred windows, built about five feet from the floor, faced the two double doors which led into the hall. The bare white walls were somewhat relieved by three lithographs, one of Fritz Emmet and the others of negro minstrels. In the centre of the room was a large table covered with a white bed-spread and around it sat the nurses. Everything was spotlessly clean and I thought what good workers the nurses must be to keep such order. In a few days after how I laughed at my own stupidity to think the nurses would work. When they found I would not play any more, Miss McCarten came up to me saying roughly: "Get away from here," and closed the piano with a bang.

"Brown, come here," was the next order I got from a rough, red-faced woman at the table.

"What have you on?" "My clothing," I replied. She lifted my dress and skirts and wrote down one pair shoes, one pair stockings, one cloth dress, one straw sailor hat, and so on.

AT SUPPER.

RANCID BUTTER, WEAK TEA AND FIVE PRUNES HER UNINVITING PORTION.

This examination over, we heard some one yell, "Go out into the hall." One of the patients kindly explained that this was an invitation to supper. We late comers tried to keep together, so we entered the hall and stood at the door where all the women had crowded. How we shivered as we stood there! The windows were open and the draught went whizzing through the hall. The patients looked blue with cold, and the minutes stretched into a quarter of an hour. At last one of the nurses went forward and unlocked a door, through which we all crowded to a landing of the stairway. Here again came a long halt directly before an open window. "How very imprudent for the attendants to keep these thinly clad women standing here in the cold," said Miss Neville. I looked at the poor crazy captives shivering, and added emphatically, "It's horribly brutal." While they stood there I thought I would not relish supper that night. They looked so lost and hopeless. Some were chattering foolish nonsense to invisible persons, others were laughing or crying aimlessly, and one old gray-haired woman was nudging me, and, with winks and sage noddings of the head and pitiful uplifting of the eyes and hands, was assuring me that I must not mind the poor creatures as they were all mad. "Stop at the heater," was then ordered, "and get in line, two by two." "Mary, get a companion." "How many times must I tell you to keep in line?" "Stand still," and, as the orders were issued, a shove and a push were administered, and often a slap on the ears. After this third and final halt we were marched into a long, narrow dining-room, where a rush was made for the table.

The table reached the length of the room and was uncovered and uninviting. Long benches without backs were put for the patients to sit on, and over these they had to crawl in order to face the table. Placed close together all along the table were large dressing-bowls filled with a pinkish-looking stuff which the patients called tea. By each bowl was laid a piece of bread, cut thick and buttered. A small saucer containing five prunes accompanied the bread. One fat woman made a rush, and jerking up several saucers from those around her emptied their contents into her own saucer. Then while holding to her own bowl she lifted up another and drained its contents at one gulp. This she did to a second bowl in shorter time than it takes to tell it. Indeed, I was so amused at her successful grabbings that when I looked at my own share the woman opposite, without so much as by your leave, grabbed my bread and left me without any.

Another patient seeing this kindly offered me hers, but I declined with thanks and turned to the nurse and asked for more. As she flung a thick piece down on the table she made some remark about the fact that if I forgot where my home was I had not forgotten how to eat. I tried the bread, but the butter was so horrible that one could not eat it. A blue-eyed German girl on the opposite side of the table told me I could have bread unbuttered if I wished, and that very few were able to eat the butter. I turned my attention to the prunes and found that very few of them would be sufficient. A patient near asked me to give them to her. I did so. My bowl of tea was all that was left. I tasted and one taste was enough. It had no sugar and it tasted as if it had been made in copper. It was as weak as water. This was also transferred to a hungrier patient in spite of the protest of Miss Neville. "You must force the food down," she said, "else you will be sick, and who know but with these surroundings you may go crazy. To have a good brain the stomach must be cared for." "It is impossible for me to eat that stuff," I replied, and despite all her urging I ate nothing that night.

It did not require much time for the patients to consume all that was eatable on the table, and then we got our orders to form in line in the hall. When this was done the doors before us were unlocked and we were ordered to proceed back to the sitting-room. Many of the patients crowded near us, and I was again urged to play, both by them and by the nurses. To please the patients I promised to play and Miss Tillie Mayard was to sing. The first thing she asked me to play was "Rock-a-bye Baby," and I did so. She sang it beautifully.

IN THE BATH.

SCRUBBED WITH SOFT SOAP AND PUT TO BED IN A WET GOWN.

A few more songs and we were told to go with Miss Grupe. We were taken into a cold, wet bathroom, and I was ordered to undress. Did I protest? Well, I never grew so earnest in my life as when I tried to beg off. They said if I did not they would use force and that it would not be very gentle. At this I noticed one of the craziest women in the ward standing by the filled bathtub with a large discolored rag in her hands. She was chattering away to herself and chuckling in a manner which seemed to me fiendish. I knew now what was to be done with me. I shivered. They began to undress me and one by one they pulled off my clothes. At last everything was gone excepting one garment. "I will not remove it," I said vehemently, but they took it off. I gave one glance at the group of patients gathered at the door watching the scene, and I jumped into the bathtub with more energy than grace.

The water was ice-cold, and I again began to protest. How useless it all was. I begged, at least, that the patients be made to go away, but was ordered to shut up. The crazy woman began to scrub me. I can find no other word that will express it but scrubbing. From a small tin pan she took some soft soap and rubbed it all over me, even all over my face and my pretty hair. I was at last past seeing or speaking, although I had begged that my hair be left untouched. Rub, rub, rub went the old woman, chattering to herself. My teeth chattered and my limbs were goose-fleshed and blue with cold. Suddenly I got, one after the other, three buckets of water over my head—ice-cold water, too—into my eyes, my ears, my nose and my mouth. I think I experienced some of the sensations of a drowning person as they dragged me, gasping, shivering and quaking, from the tub. For once I did look insane, as they put me, dripping wet, into a short canton flannel slip, labeled across the extreme end in large black letters, "Lunatic Asylum, B. I., H. 6." The letters meant Blackwell's Island, Hall 6.

By this time Miss Mayard had been undressed, and, much as I hated my recent bath, I would have taken another if by it I could have saved her the experience. Imagine plunging that sick girl into a cold bath when it made me, who have never been ill, shake as if with ague. I heard her explain to Miss Grupe that her head was still sore from her illness. Her hair was short and had mostly come out, and she asked that the crazy woman be made to rub more gently, but Miss Grupe said: "There isn't much fear of hurting you. Shut up, or you'll get it worse." Miss Mayard did shut up, and that was my last look at her for the night.

I was hurried into a room where there were six beds, and had been put into bed when some one came along and jerked me out again, saying: "Nellie Brown has to be put in a room alone to-night, for I suppose she's noisy." I was taken to room 28 and left to try and make an impression on the bed. It was an impossible task. The bed had been made high in the centre and sloping on either side. At the first touch my head flooded the pillow with water, and my wet slip transferred some of its dampness to the sheet. When Miss Grupe came in I asked if I could not have a night-gown. "We have not such things in this institution," she said. "I do not like to sleep without," I replied. "Well, I don't care about that," she said. "You are in a public institution now, and you can't expect to get anything. This is charity, and you should be thankful for what you get." "But the city pays to keep these places up," I urged, "and pays people to be kind to the unfortunates brought here." "Well, you don't need to expect any kindness here, for you won't get it," she said, and she went out and closed the door.

A sheet and an oilcloth were under me and a sheet and black wool blanket above. I never felt anything so annoying as that wool blanket as I tried to keep it around my shoulders to stop the chills from getting underneath. When I pulled it up I left my feet bare and when I pulled it down my shoulders were exposed. There was absolutely nothing in the room but the bed and myself. As the door had been locked I imagined I should be left alone for the night, but I heard the sound of the heavy tread of two women down the hall. They stopped at every door, unlocked it and in a few moments I could hear them relock it. This they did without the least attempt at quietness down the whole length of the opposite side of the hall and up to my room. Here they paused. The key was inserted in the lock and turned. I watched those about to enter. In they came, dressed in brown and white striped dresses, fastened by brass buttons, large white aprons, a heavy green cord about the waist, from which dangled a bunch of large keys, and small white caps on their heads. Being dressed as were the attendants of the day, I knew they were nurses. The first one carried a lantern, and she flashed its light into my face while she said to her assistant: "This is Nellie

HER BEDROOM.

Brown." Looking at her, I asked: "Who are you?" "The night nurse, my dear," she replied, and wishing that I would sleep well she went out and locked the door after her. Several times during the night they came into my room, and even had I been able to sleep, the unlocking of the heavy door, their loud talking and heavy tread would have awakened me.

THE HORROR OF FIRE.

ESCAPE PRACTICALLY IMPOSSIBLE IN CASE THE BUILDING SHOULD BURN.

I could not sleep, so I lay in bed picturing to myself the horrors in case a fire should break out in the asylum. Every door is locked separately and the windows are heavily barred, so that escape is impossible. In the one building alone there are, I think Dr. Ingram told me, some 300 women. They are locked, one to ten to a room. It is impossible to get out unless these doors are unlocked. A fire is not improbable, but one of the most likely occurrences. Should the building burn, the jailers or nurses would never think of releasing their crazy patients. This I can prove to you later when I come to tell of their cruel treatment of the poor things intrusted to their care. As I say, in case of fire, not a dozen women could escape. All would be left to roast to death. Even if the nurses were kind, which they are not, it would require more presence of mind than women of their class possess to risk the flames and their own lives while they unlocked the hundred doors for the insane prisoners. Unless there is a change there will some day be a tale of horror never equaled.

In this connection is an amusing incident which happened just previous to my release. I was talking with Dr. Ingram about many things, and at last told him what I thought would be the result of a fire. "The nurses are expected to open the doors," he said. "But you know positively that they would not wait to do that," I said, "and these women would burn to death." He sat silent, unable to contradict my assertion. "Why don't you have it changed?" I asked. "What can I do?" he replied. "I offer suggestions until my brain is tired, but what good does it do? What would you do?" he asked, turning to me, the proclaimed insane girl. "Well, I should insist on them having locks put in, as I have seen in some places, that by turning a crank at the end of the hall you can lock or unlock every door on the one side. Then there would be some chance of escape. Now, every door being locked separately, there is absolutely none." Dr. Ingram turned to me with an anxious look on his kind face as he asked slowly: "Nellie Brown, what institution have you been an inmate of before you came here?" "None. I never was confined in any institution, except boarding-school, in my life." "Where then did you see the locks you have described?" I had seen them in the new Western Penitentiary at Pittsburg, Pa., but I did not dare say so. I merely answered: "Oh, I have seen them in a place I was in—I mean as a visitor." "There is only one place I know of where they have those locks," he said, sadly, "and that is at Sing Sing. The inference is conclusive." I laughed very heartily over the implied accusation, and tried to assure him that I had never, up to date, been an inmate of Sing Sing or even ever visited it.

Just as the morning began to dawn I went to sleep. It did not seem many moments until I was rudely awakened and told to get up, the window being opened and the clothing pulled off me. My hair was still wet and I had pains all through me, as if I had the rheumatism. Some clothing was flung on the floor and I was told to put it on. I asked for my own, but was told to take what I got and keep quiet by the apparently head nurse, Miss Grady. I looked at it. One underskirt made of coarse dark cotton goods and a cheap white calico dress with a black spot in it. I tied the strings of the skirt around me and put on the little dress. It was made, as are all those worn by the patients, into a straight tight waist sewed on to a straight skirt. As I buttoned the waist I noticed the underskirt was about six inches longer than the upper, and for a moment I sat down on the bed and laughed at my own appearance. No woman ever longed for a mirror more than I did at that moment.

I saw the other patients hurrying past in the hall, so I decided not to lose anything that might be going on. We numbered forty-five patients in Hall 6, and were sent to the bathroom, where there were two coarse towels. I watched crazy patients who had the most dangerous eruptions all over their faces dry on the towels and then saw women with clean skins turn to use them. I went to the bathtub and washed my face at the running faucet and my underskirt did duty for a towel.

THE FIRST MORNING.

COMBED WITH A PUBLIC COMB, THE BREAKFAST AND THE UNIFORM.

Before I had completed my ablutions a bench was brought into the bathroom. Miss Grupe and Miss McCarten came in with combs in their hands. We were told to sit down on the bench, and the hair of forty-five women was combed with one patient, two nurses, and six combs. As I saw some of the sore heads combed I thought this was another dose I had not bargained for. Miss Tillie Mayard had her own comb, but it was taken from her by Miss Grady. Oh, that combing! I never realized before what the expression "I'll give you a combing" meant, but I knew then. My hair, all matted and wet from the night previous, was pulled and jerked, and, after expostulating to no avail, I set my teeth and endured the pain. They refused to give me my hairpins, and my hair was arranged in one plait and tied with a red cotton rag. My curly bangs refused to stay back.

After this we went to the sitting-room and I looked for my companions. At first I looked vainly, unable to distinguish them from the other patients, but after awhile I recognized Miss Mayard by her short hair. "How did you sleep after your cold bath?" "I almost froze, and then the noise kept me awake. It's dreadful! My nerves were so unstrung before I came here, and I fear I shall not be able to stand the strain." I did the best I could to cheer her. I asked that we be given additional clothing, at least as much as custom says women shall wear, but they told me to shut up; that we had as much as they intended to give us.

We were compelled to get up at 6 o'clock, and at 7.15 we were told to collect in the hall, where the experience of waiting, as on the evening previous, was repeated. When we got into the dining-room at last we found a bowl of cold tea, a slice of buttered bread and a saucer of oatmeal, with molasses on it, for each patient. I was hungry, but the food would not down. I asked for unbuttered bread and was given it. I cannot tell you of anything which is the same dirty, black color. It was hard, and in places nothing more than dried dough. I found a spider in my slice, so I did not eat it. I tried the oatmeal and molasses, but it was wretched, and so I endeavored, but without much show of success, to choke down the tea.

After we were back to the sitting-room a number of women were ordered to make the beds, and some of the patients were put to scrubbing and others given different duties which covered all the work in the hall. It is not the attendants who keep the institution so nice for the poor patients, as I had always thought, but the patients, who do it all themselves—even to cleaning the nurses' bedrooms and caring for their clothing.

About 9.30 the new patients, of which I was one, were told to go out to see the doctor. I was taken in and my lungs and my heart were examined by the flirty young doctor who was the first to see us the day we entered. The one who made out the report, if I mistake not, was the Assistant Superintendent, Ingram. A few questions and I was allowed to return to the sitting-room.

AN INSANE HALL.

I came in and saw Miss Grady with my note-book and long lead pencil, bought just for the occasion. "I want my book and pencil,"

I said quite truthfully. "It helps me remember things." I was very anxious to get it to make notes in and was disappointed when she said: "You can't have it, so shut up." Some days after I asked Dr. Ingram if I could have it, and he promised to consider the matter. When I again referred to it, he said that Miss Grady said I only brought a book there; that I had no pencil. I was provoked and insisted that I had, whereupon I was advised to fight against the imaginations of my brain.

After the housework was completed by the patients, and as the day was fine, but cold, we were told to go out in the hall and get on shawls and hats for a walk. Poor patients! How eager they were for a breath of air; how eager for a slight release from their prison. They went swiftly into the hall and there was a skirmish for hats. Such hats!

THE VIOLENT PATIENTS.

UNSPEAKABLE SCENES IN THE YARD—THE EVIL OF ENFORCED IDLENESS.

We had not gone many paces when I saw, proceeding from every walk, long lines of women guarded by nurses. How many there were! Every way I looked I could see them in the queer dresses, comical straw hats and shawls, marching slowly around. I eagerly watched the passing lines and a thrill of horror crept over me at the sight. Vacant eyes and meaningless faces, and their tongues uttered meaningless nonsense. One crowd passed and I noted, by nose as well as eyes, that they were fearfully dirty. "Who are they?" I asked of a patient near me. "They are considered the most violent on the island," she replied. "They are from the Lodge, the first building with the high steps." Some were yelling, some were cursing, others were singing or praying or preaching, as the fancy struck them, and they made up the most miserable collection of humanity I had ever seen. As the din of their passing faded in the distance there came another sight I can never forget:

A long cable rope fastened to wide leather belts, and these belts locked around the waists of fifty-two women. At the end of the rope was a heavy iron cart, and in it two women—one nursing a sore foot, another screaming at some nurse, saying: "You beat me and I shall not forget it. You want to kill me," and then she would sob and cry. The women "on the rope," as the patients call it, were each busy on their individual freaks. Some were yelling all the while. One who had blue eyes saw me look at her, and she turned as far as she could, talking and smiling, with that terrible, horrifying look of absolute insanity stamped on her. The doctors might safely judge on her case. The horror of that sight to one who had never been near an insane person before was something unspeakable. "God help them," breathed Miss Neville. "It is so dreadful I cannot look." On they passed, but for their places to be filled by more. Can you imagine the sight? According to one of the physicians there are 1,600 insane women on Blackwell's Island.

I was annoyed a great deal by nurses who had heard my romantic story calling to those in charge of us to ask which one I was. I was pointed out repeatedly.

It was not long until the dinner hour arrived, and I was so hungry that I felt I could eat anything. The same old story of standing for a half and three-quarters of an hour in the hall was repeated before we got down to our dinners. The bowls in which we had had our tea were now filled with soup, and on a plate was one cold boiled potato and a chunk of beef, which on investigation, proved to be slightly spoiled. There were no knives or forks, and the patients looked fairly savage as they took the tough beef in their fingers and pulled in opposition to their teeth. Those toothless or with poor teeth could not eat it. One tablespoon was given for the soup, and a piece of bread was the final entrée. Butter is never allowed at dinner nor coffee or tea. Miss Mayard could not eat, and I saw many of the sick ones turn away in disgust. I was getting very weak from the want of food and tried to eat a slice of bread. After the first few bites hunger asserted itself, and I was able to eat all but the crusts of the one slice.

Supt. Dent went through the sitting-room, giving an occasional "How do you do?" "How are you to-day?" here and there among the patients. His voice was as cold as the hall, and the patients made no movement to tell him of their sufferings. I asked some of them to tell how they were suffering from the cold and insufficiency of clothing, but they replied that the nurse would beat them if they told.

I was never so tired as I grew sitting on those benches. Several of the patients would sit on one foot or sideways to make a change, but they were always reproved and told to sit up straight. If they talked they were scolded and told to shut up; if they wanted to walk around in order to take the stiffness out of them, they were told to sit down and be still. What, excepting torture, would produce insanity quicker than this treatment? Here is a class of women sent to be cured? I would like the expert physicians who are condemning me for my action, which has proven their ability, to take a perfectly sane and healthy woman, shut her up and make her sit from 6 A.M. until 8 P.M. on straight-back benches, do not allow her to talk or move during these hours, give her no reading and let her know nothing of the world or its doings, give her bad food and harsh treatment, and see how long it will take to make her insane. Two months would make her a mental and physical wreck.

BAD FOOD AND WORSE HELP.

WHEN ONE FALLS ILL THE NATURAL THING IS TO SIMPLY DIE.

I have described my first day in the asylum, and as my other nine were exactly the same in the general run of things it would be tiresome to tell about each. In giving this story I expect to be contradicted by many who are exposed. I merely tell in common words, without exaggeration, of my life in a mad-house for ten days. The eating was one of the most horrible things. Excepting the first two days after I entered the asylum, there was no salt for the food. The hungry and even famishing women made an attempt to eat the horrible messes. Mustard and vinegar were put on meat and in soup to give it a taste, but it only helped to make it worse. Even that was all consumed after two days, and the patients had to try to choke down fresh fish, just boiled in water, without salt, pepper or butter; mutton, beef and potatoes without the faintest seasoning. The most insane refused to swallow the food and were threatened with punishment. In our short walks we passed the kitchen where food was prepared for the nurses and doctors. There we got glimpses of melons and grapes and all kinds of fruits, beautiful white bread and nice meats, and the hungry feeling would be increased tenfold. I spoke to some of the physicians, but it had no effect, and when I was taken away the food was yet unsalted.

My heart ached to see the sick patients grow sicker over the table. I saw Miss Tillie Mayard so suddenly overcome at a bite that she had to rush from the dining-room and then got a scolding for doing so. When the patients complained of the food they were told to shut up; that they would not have as good if they were at home, and that it was too good for charity patients.

A German girl, Louise—I have forgotten her last name—did not eat for several days and at last one morning she was missing. From the conversation of the nurses I found she was suffering from a high fever. Poor thing! She told me she unceasingly prayed for death. I watched the nurses make a patient carry such food as the well ones were refusing up to Louise's room. Think of that stuff for a fever patient! Of course, she refused it. Then I saw a nurse, Miss McCarten, go to test her temperature, and she returned with a report of it being some 150 degrees. I smiled at the report, and Miss Grupe, seeing it, asked me how high my temperature had ever run. I refused to answer. Miss Grady then decided to try her ability. She returned with the report of 99 degrees.

Miss Tillie Mayard suffered more than any of us from the cold, and yet she tried to follow my advice to be cheerful and try to keep up for a short time. Supt. Dent brought in a man to see me. He felt my pulse and my head and examined my tongue. I told them how cold it was, and assured them that I did not need medical aid, but that Miss Mayard did and they should transfer their attentions to her. They did not answer me, and I was pleased to see Miss Mayard leave her place and come forward to them. She spoke to the doctors and told them she was ill, but they paid no attention to her. The nurses came and dragged her back to the bench, and after the doctors left they said, "After awhile, when you see that the doctors will not notice you, you will quit running up to them." Before the doctors left me I heard one say—I cannot give it in his exact words—that my pulse and eyes were not that of an insane girl, but Supt. Dent assured him that in cases such as mine such tests failed. After watching me for awhile he said my face was the brightest he had ever seen for a lunatic. The nurses had on heavy undergarments and coats, but they refused to give us shawls.

Nearly all night long I listened to a woman cry about the cold and beg for God to let her die. Another one yelled "Murder!" at frequent intervals and "Police!" at others until my flesh felt creepy.

The second morning, after we had begun our endless "set" for the day, two of the nurses, assisted by some patients, brought the woman in who had begged the night previous for God to take her home. I was not surprised at her prayer. She appeared easily seventy years old and she was blind. Although the halls were freezing cold that old woman had no more clothing on than the rest of us, which I have described. When she was brought into the sitting-room and placed on the hard bench, she cried: "Oh, what are you doing with me? I am cold, so cold. Why can't I stay in bed or have a shawl?" and then she would get up and endeavor to feel her way to leave the room. Sometimes the attendants would jerk her back to the bench, and again they would let her walk and heartlessly laugh when she bumped against the table or the edge of the benches. At one time she said the heavy shoes which charity provides hurt her feet and she took them off. The nurses made two patients put them on her again, and when she did it several times and fought against having them on, I counted seven people at her at once trying to put the shoes on. The old woman then tried to lie down on the bench, but they pulled her up again. It sounded so pitiful to hear her cry: "Oh, give me a pillow and pull the covers over me, I am so cold."

At this I saw Miss Grupe sit down on her and run her cold hands over the old woman's face and down inside the neck of her dress. At the old woman's cries she laughed savagely, as did the other nurses, and repeated her cruel action. That day the old woman was carried away to another ward.

MADE MAD BY SURROUNDINGS.

THE TRAGIC CASE OF MISS TILLIE MAYARD—VERY NEAR TO DETECTION.

Miss Tillie Mayard suffered greatly from cold. One morning she sat on the bench next to me and was livid with the cold. Her limbs shook and her teeth chattered. I spoke to the three attendants who sat with coats on at the table in the centre of the floor. "It is cruel to lock people up and then freeze them," I said. They replied she had on as much as any of the rest, and she would get no more. Just then Miss Mayard took a fit and every patient looked frightened. Miss Neville caught her in her arms and held her, although the nurses roughly said: "Let her fall on the floor and it will teach her a lesson." Miss Neville told them what she thought of their actions, and then I got orders to make my appearance in the office.

Just as I reached there Supt. Dent came to the door and I told him how we were suffering from the cold, and of Miss Mayard's condition. Doubtless I spoke incoherently, for I told of the state of the food, the treatment of the nurses and their refusal to give more clothing, the condition of Miss Mayard, and the nurses telling us, because the asylum was a public institution, we could not expect even kindness. Assuring him that I needed no medical aid, I told him to go to Miss Mayard. He did so. From Miss Neville and other patients I learned what transpired. Miss Mayard was still in the fit, and he caught her roughly between the eye-brows or thereabouts, and pinched until her face was crimson from the rush of blood to the head, and her senses returned. All day afterwards she suffered from terrible headache, and from that on she grew worse.

Insane? Yes, insane; and as I watched the insanity slowly creep over the mind that had appeared to be all right I secretly cursed the doctors, the nurses and all public institutions. Some one may say that she was insane at some time previous to her consignment to the asylum. Then if she were, was this the proper place to send a woman just convalescing, to be given cold baths, deprived of sufficient clothing and fed with horrible food?

QUIET INMATES OUT FOR A WALK.

On this morning I had a long conversation with Dr. Ingram, the assistant superintendent of the asylum. I found that he was kind to the helpless in his charge. I began my old complaint of the cold, and he called Miss Grady to the office and ordered more clothing given the patients. Miss Grady said if I made a practice of telling it would be a serious thing for me, she warned me in time.

Many visitors looking for missing girls came to see me. Miss Grady yelled in the door from the hall one day: "Nellie Brown, you're wanted." I went to the sitting-room at the end of the hall, and there sat a gentleman who had known me intimately for years. I saw by the sudden blanching of his face and his inability to speak that the sight of me was wholly unexpected and had shocked him terribly. In an instant I determined, if he betrayed me as Nellie Bly, to say I had never seen him before. However, I had one card to play and I risked it. With Miss Grady within touching distance I whispered hurriedly to him, in language more expressive than elegant: "Don't give me away." I knew by the expression of his eye that he understood, so I said to Miss Grady: "I do not know this man." "Do you know her?" asked Miss Grady. "No; this is not the young lady I came in search of," he replied in a strained voice. "If you do not know her you cannot stay here," she said, and she took him to the door. All at once a fear struck me that he would think I had been sent there through some mistake and would tell my friends and make an effort to have me released. So I waited until Miss Grady had the door unlocked. I knew that she would have to lock it before she could leave, and the time required to do so would give me opportunity to speak, so I called: "One moment, Señor." He returned to me and I asked aloud: "Do you speak Spanish, Señor?" and then whispered, "It's all right. I'm after an item. Keep still." "No," he said, with a peculiar emphasis, which I knew meant that he would keep my secret.

CHOKINGS AND BEATINGS.

THE NURSES AMUSE THEMSELVES BY WORRYING THEIR HELPLESS CHARGES.

People in the world can never imagine the length of days to those in asylums. They seemed never ending, and we welcomed any event that might give us something to think about as well as talk of. Anxiously the hour was watched for when the boat arrived to see if there were any new unfortunates to be added to our ranks. When they came and were ushered into the sitting-room the patients would express sympathy to one another for them and were anxious to show them little marks of attention. Hall 6 was the receiving hall, so that was how we saw all newcomers.

Soon after my advent a girl called Urena Little-Page was brought in. She was, as she had been born, silly, and her tender spot was, as with many sensible women, her age. She claimed eighteen, and would grow very angry if told to the contrary. The nurses were not long in finding this out, and then they teased her. "Urena," said Miss Grady, "the doctors say that you are thirty-three instead of eighteen," and the other nurses laughed. They kept up this until the simple creature began to yell and cry, saying she wanted to go home and that everybody treated her badly. After they had gotten all the amusement out of her they wanted and she was crying, they began to scold and tell her to keep quiet. She grew more hysterical every moment until they pounced upon her and slapped her face and knocked her head in a lively fashion. This made the poor creature cry the more, and so they choked her. Yes, actually choked her. Then they dragged her out to the closet, and I heard her terrified cries hush into smothered ones. After several hours' absence she returned to the sitting-room, and I plainly saw the marks of their fingers on her throat for the entire day.

This punishment seemed to awaken their desire to administer more. They returned to the sitting-room and caught hold of an old gray-haired woman whom I have heard addressed both as Mrs. Grady and Mrs. O'Keefe. She was insane, and she talked almost continually to herself and to those near her. She never spoke very loud, and at the time I speak of was sitting harmlessly chattering to herself. They grabbed her, and my heart ached as she cried: "For God's sake, ladies, don't let them beat me." "Shut up, you hussy!" said Miss Grady as she caught the woman by her gray hair and dragged her shrieking and pleading from the room. She was also taken to the closet, and her cries grew lower and lower, and then ceased.

The nurses returned to the room and Miss Grady remarked that she had "settled the old fool for awhile." I told some of the physicians of the occurrence, but they did not pay any attention to it.

One of the characters in Hall 6 was Matilda, a little old German woman, who, I believe, went insane over the loss of money. She was small, and had a pretty pink complexion. She was not much trouble, except at times. She would take spells, when she would talk into the steam-heaters or get up on a chair and talk out of the windows. In these conversations she railed at the lawyers who had taken her property. The nurses seemed to find a great deal of amusement in teasing the harmless old soul. One day I sat beside Miss Grady and Miss Grupe and heard them tell her perfectly vile things to call Miss McCarten. After telling her to say these things they would send her to the other nurse, but Matilda proved that she, even in her state, had more sense than they. "I cannot tell you. It is private," was all she would say. I saw Miss Grady, on a pretense of whispering to her, spit in her ear. Matilda quietly wiped her ear and said nothing.

SOME UNFORTUNATE STORIES.

A FEW OF THE APPARENTLY SANE WOMEN TELL OF THEIR TROUBLES

By this time I had made the acquaintance of the greater number of the forty-five women in Hall 6. Let me introduce a few. Louise, the pretty German girl whom I have spoken of formerly as being sick with fever, had the delusion that the spirits of her dead parents were with her. "I have gotten many beatings from Miss Grady and her assistants," she said, "and I am unable to eat the horrible food they give us. I ought not to be compelled to freeze for want of proper clothing. Oh! I pray nightly that I may be taken to my papa and mamma. One night when Dr. Field came I was in bed, and weary of the examination. At last I said, 'I am tired of this. I will talk no more.' 'Won't you?' he said angrily. 'I'll see if I can't make you.' With this he laid his crutch on the side of the bed and, getting up on it, he pinched me very severely in the ribs. I jumped up straight in bed and said: 'What do you mean by this?' 'I want to teach you to obey when I speak to you,' he replied. If I could only die and go to papa!" When I left she was confined to bed with a fever, and maybe by this time she has her wish.

There is a Frenchwoman confined in Hall 6, or was during my stay, whom I firmly believe to be perfectly sane. I watched her and talked with her every day, excepting the last three, and I was unable to find any delusion or mania in her. Her name is Josephine Despreau, if that is spelled correctly, and her husband and all her friends are in France. Josephine feels her position keenly. Her lips tremble and she breaks down crying when she talks of her helpless condition. "How did you get here?" I asked.

"One morning as I was trying to get breakfast I grew deathly sick, and two officers were called in by the woman of the house, and I was taken to the station-house. I was unable to understand their proceedings, and they paid little attention to my story. Doings in this country were new to me, and before I realized it I was lodged as an insane woman in this asylum. When I first came I cried that I was here without hope of release, and for crying Miss Grady and her assistants choked me until they hurt my throat, for it has been sore ever since."

A pretty young woman spoke so little English I could not get her story except as told by the nurses. They said her name is Sarah Fishbaum, and that her husband put her in the asylum because she had a fondness for other men than himself. Granting that Sarah was insane, and about men, let me tell you how the nurses tried to cure (?) her. They would call her up and say: "Sarah, wouldn't you like to have a nice young man?" "Oh, yes; a young man is all right," Sarah would reply in her few English words. "Well, Sarah, wouldn't you like us to speak a good word to some of the doctors for you? Wouldn't you like to have one of the doctors?" And then they would ask her which doctor she preferred, and advise her to make advances to him when he visited the hall, and so on.

I had been watching and talking with a fair-complexioned woman for several days, and I was at a loss to see why she had been sent there, she was so sane. "Why did you come here?" I asked her one day, after we had indulged in a long conversation. "I was sick," she replied. "Are you sick mentally?" I urged. "Oh, no; what gave you such an idea? I had been overworking myself, and I broke down. Having some family trouble, and being penniless and nowhere to go, I applied to the commissioners to be sent to the poorhouse until I would be able to go to work." "But they do not send poor people here unless they are insane," I said. "Don't you know there are only insane women, or those supposed to be so, sent here!" "I knew after I got here that the majority of these women were insane, but then I believed them when they told me this was the place they sent all the poor who applied for aid as I had done."

"How have you been treated?" I asked. "Well, so far I have escaped a beating, although I have been sickened at the sight of many and the recital of more. When I was brought here they went to give me a bath, and the very disease for which I needed doctoring and from which I was suffering made it necessary that I should not bathe. But they put me in, and my sufferings were increased greatly for weeks thereafter."

A Mrs. McCartney, whose husband is a tailor, seems perfectly rational and has not one fancy. Mary Hughes and Mrs. Louise Schanz showed no obvious traces of insanity.

NURSES WHO SWEAR

PATIENTS HURRIED INTO THE ASYLUM WITHOUT SUFFICIENT EXAMINATION.

One day two new-comers were added to our list. The one was an idiot, Carrie Glass, and the other was a nice-looking German girl—quite young, she seemed, and when she came in all the patients spoke of her nice appearance and apparent sanity. Her name was Gretchen. She told me she had been a cook, and was extremely neat. One day, after she had scrubbed the kitchen floor, the chambermaids came down and deliberately soiled it. Her temper was aroused and she began to quarrel with them; an officer was called and she was taken to an asylum. "How can they say I am insane, merely because I allowed my temper to run away with me?" she complained. "Other people are not shut up for crazy when they get angry. I suppose the only thing to do is to keep quiet and so avoid the beatings which I see others get. No one can say one word about me. I do everything I am told, and all the work they give me. I am obedient in every respect, and I do everything to prove to them that I am sane."

One day an insane woman was brought in. She was noisy, and Miss Grady gave her a beating and blacked her eye. When the doctors noticed it and asked if it was done before she came there the nurses said it was.

While I was in Hall 6 I never heard the nurses address the patients except to scold or yell at them, unless it was to tease them. They spent much of their time gossiping about the physicians and about the other nurses in a manner that was not elevating. Miss Grady nearly always interspersed her conversation with profane language, and generally began her sentences by calling on the name of the Lord. The names she called the patients were of the lowest and most profane type. One evening she quarreled with another nurse while we were at supper about the bread, and when the nurse had gone out she called her bad names and made ugly remarks about her.

In the evenings a woman, whom I supposed to be head cook for the doctors, used to come up and bring raisins, grapes, apples, and crackers to the nurses. Imagine the feelings of the hungry patients as they sat and watched the nurses eat what was to them a dream of luxury.

One afternoon Dr. Dent was talking to a patient, Mrs. Turney, about some trouble she had had with a nurse or matron. A short time after we were taken down to supper and this woman who had beaten Mrs. Turney, and of whom Dr. Dent spoke, was sitting at the door of our dining-room. Suddenly Mrs. Turney picked up her bowl of tea and, rushing out of the door, flung it at the woman who had beat her. There was some loud screaming and Mrs. Turney was returned to her place. The next day she was transferred to the "rope gang," which is supposed to be composed of the most dangerous and most suicidal women on the island.

At first I could not sleep and did not want to so long as I could hear anything new. The night nurses may have complained of the fact. At any rate one night they came in and tried to make me take a dose of some mixture out of a glass "to make me sleep," they said. I told them I would do nothing of the sort and they left me, I hoped, for the night. My hopes were vain, for in a few minutes they returned with a doctor, the same that received us on our arrival. He insisted that I take it, but I was determined not to lose my wits even for a few hours. When he saw that I was not to be coaxed he grew rather rough and said he had wasted too much time with me already. That if I did not take it he would put it into my arm with a needle. It occurred to me that if he put it into my arm I could not get rid of it, but if I swallowed it there was one hope, so I said I would take it. I smelt it and it smelt like laudanum, and it was a horrible dose. No sooner had they left the room and locked me in than I tried to see how far down my throat my finger would go.

LAST DAYS.

ONE GOOD NURSE—SITTING STILL FOR FIVE DAYS—SOAP ONLY ONCE A WEEK.

I want to say that the night nurse, Burns, in Hall 6, seemed very kind and patient to the poor, afflicted people. The other nurses made several attempts to talk to me about lovers and asked me if I would not like to have one. They did not find me very communicative on the, to them, popular subject.

Once a week the patients are given a bath, and that is the only time they see soap. A patient handed me a piece of soap one day about the size of a thimble, I considered it a great compliment in her wanting to be kind, but I thought she would appreciate the cheap soap more than I, so I thanked her but refused to take it. On bathing day the tub is filled with water, and the patients are washed, one after the other, without a change of water. This is done until the water is really thick, and then it is allowed to run out and the tub is refilled without being washed. The same towels are used on all the women, those with eruptions as well as those without. The healthy patients fight for a change of water, but they are compelled to submit to the dictates of the lazy, tyrannical nurses. The dresses are seldom changed oftener than once a month. If the patient has a visitor, I have seen the nurses hurry her out and change her dress before the visitor comes in. This keeps up the appearance of careful and good management.

The patients who are not able to take care of themselves get into beastly conditions, and the nurses never look after them, but order some of the patients to do so.

For five days we were compelled to sit in the room all day. I never put in such a long time. Every patient was stiff and sore and tired. We would get in little groups on benches and torture our stomachs by conjuring up thoughts of what we would eat first when we got out. If I had not known how hungry they were and the pitiful side of it, the conversation would have been very amusing. As it was it only made me sad. When the subject of eating, which seemed to be the favorite one, was worn out, they used to give their opinions of the institution and its management. The condemnation of the nurses and the eatables was unanimous.

As the days passed Miss Tillie Mayard's condition grew worse. She was continually cold and unable to eat of the food provided. Day after day she sang in order to try to maintain her memory, but at last the nurse made her stop it. I talked with her daily, and I grieved to find her grow worse so rapidly. At last she got a delusion. She thought that I was trying to pass myself off for her, and that all the people who called to see Nellie Brown were friends in search of her, but that I, by some means, was trying to deceive them into the belief that I was the girl. I tried to reason with her, but found it impossible, so I kept away from her as much as possible, lest my presence should make her worse and feed the fancy.

TRANSFERRED TO ANOTHER WARD.

SHE IS CURSED BEFORE SHE LEAVES AND GETS NO BETTER QUARTERS.

When Pauline Moser was brought to the asylum we heard the most horrible screams and an Irish girl, only partly dressed, came staggering like a drunken person up the hall yelling, "Hurrah! Three cheers! I have killed the divil! Lucifer, Lucifer, Lucifer," and so on, over and over again. Then she would pull a handful of hair out, while she exultingly cried, "How I deceived the divils. They always said God made hell, but he didn't." After she had been there an hour or so, Dr. Dent came in, and as he walked down the hall, Miss Grupe whispered to the demented girl, "Here is the devil coming, go for him." Surprised that she would give a mad woman such instructions, I fully expected to see the frenzied creature rush at the doctor. Luckily she did not, but commenced to repeat her refrain of "Oh, Lucifer." After the doctor left, Miss Grupe again tried to excite the woman by saying the pictured minstrel on the wall was the devil, and the poor creature began to scream, "You divil, I'll give it to you," so that two nurses had to sit on her to keep her down. The attendants seemed to find amusement and pleasure in exciting the violent patients to do their worst.

I always made a point of telling the doctors I was sane and asking to be released, but the more I endeavored to assure them of my sanity the more they doubted it. "What are you doctors here for?" I asked one, whose name I cannot recall. "To take care of the patients and test their sanity," he replied. "Very well," I said. "There are sixteen doctors on this island, and excepting two, I have never seen them pay any attention to the patients. How can a doctor judge a woman's sanity by merely bidding her good morning and refusing to hear her pleas for release? Even the sick ones know it is useless to say anything, for the answer will be that it is their imagination." "Try every test on me," I have urged others, "and tell me am I sane or insane? Try my pulse, my heart, my eyes; ask me to stretch out my arm, to work my fingers, as Dr. Field did at Bellevue, and then tell me if I am sane." They would not heed me, for they thought I raved.

Again I said to one: "You have no right to keep sane people here. I am sane, have always been so and I must insist on a thorough examination or be released. Several of the women here are also sane. Why can't they be free?" "They are all insane," was the reply, "and suffering from delusions."

After a long talk with Dr. Ingram, he said, "I will transfer you to a quieter ward." An hour later Miss Grady called me into the hall, and, after calling me all the vile and profane names a woman could ever remember, she told me that it was a lucky thing for my "hide" that I was transferred, or else she would pay me for remembering so well to tell Dr. Ingram everything. "You d—n hussy, you forget all about yourself, but you never forget anything to tell the doctor." After calling Miss Neville, whom Dr. Ingram also kindly transferred, Miss Grady took us to the hall above, No. 7.

In hall 7 there are Mrs. Kroener, Miss Fitzpatrick, Miss Finney, and Miss Hart. I did not see as cruel treatment as downstairs, but I heard them make ugly remarks and threats, twist the fingers and slap the faces of the unruly patients. The night nurse, Conway I believe her name is, is very cross. In hall 7, if any of the patients possessed any modesty, they soon lost it. Every one was compelled to undress in the hall before their own door, and to fold their clothes and leave them there until morning. I asked to undress in my room, but Miss Conway told me if she ever caught me at such a trick she would give me cause not to want to repeat it.

The first doctor I saw here—Dr. Caldwell—chucked me under the chin, and as I was tired refusing to tell where my home was, I would only speak to him in Spanish.

THE "RETREAT" AND "ROPE GANG."

SOME OF THE CRUEL ATROCITIES PRACTICED THERE—THE LAST GOOD-BY.

INSANE HALL NO. 7.

A Mrs. Cotter told me that for speaking to a man she was sent to the Retreat. "The remembrances of that is enough to make me mad. For crying the nurses beat me with a broom-handle and jumped on me, injuring me internally so that I will never get over it. Then they tied my hands and feet and, throwing a sheet over my head, twisted it tightly around my throat, so I could not scream, and thus put me in a bathtub filled with cold water. They held me under until I gave up every hope and became senseless. At other times they took hold of my ears and beat my head on the door and against the wall. Then they pulled my hair out by the roots so that it will never grow in again."

Mrs. Cotter here showed me proofs of her story. The dent in the back of her head and the bare spots where the hair had been taken out by the handles give her story as plainly as possible! "My treatment was not as bad as I have seen others get in here, but it has ruined my health, and even if I do get out of here I will be a wreck. When my husband heard of the treatment given me he threatened to expose the place if I was not removed, so I was brought here. I am well mentally now. All that old fear has left me, and the doctor has promised to allow my husband to take me home."

I made the acquaintance of Bridget McGuinness, who seems to be sane at the present time. She said she was sent to Retreat 4, and put on the "Rope gang." "The beatings I got there were something dreadful. I was pulled around by the hair, held under the water until I strangled, and I was choked and kicked. The nurses would always keep a quiet patient stationed at the window to tell them if any of the doctors were approaching. It was hopeless to complain to the doctors for they always said it was the imagination of our diseased brains, and besides we would get another beating for telling. They would hold patients under the water and threaten to leave them to die there if they did not promise not to tell the doctors. We would still promise because we know the doctors would not help us, and we would do anything to escape the punishment. After breaking a window I was transferred to the Lodge, the worst place on the island. It is dreadfully dirty in there, and the stench is awful. In the summer the flies swarm the place. The food is worse than we get in other wards and we are given only tin plates. Instead of the bars being on the outside, as in this ward, they are on the inside. There are many quiet patients there who have been there for years, but the nurses keep them to do the work. Among other beatings I got there, the nurses jumped on me once and broke two of my ribs.

"While I was there a pretty young girl was brought in. She had been sick and she fought about being put in that dirty place. One night the nurses took her and, after beating her, they held her naked in a cold bath, then they threw her on her bed. When morning came the girl was dead. The doctors said she died of convulsions, and that was all that was done about it.

"They inject so much morphine and chloral that the patients are made crazy. I have seen the patients wild for water from the effect of the drugs, and the nurses would refuse it to them. I have heard women beg for a whole night for one drop and it was not given them. I myself cried for water until my mouth was so parched and dry that I could not speak."

I saw the same thing myself in hall 7. The patients would beg for a drink before retiring, but the nurses—Miss Hart and the others—refused to unlock the bathroom that they might quench their thirst.

Hall 7 looks rather nice to a casual visitor. It is hung with cheap pictures and has a piano, which is presided over by Miss Mattie Morgan, who formerly was in a music store in this city. She has been training several of the patients to sing, with some show of success. The artiste of the hall is Under, pronounced Wanda, a Polish girl. She is a gifted pianist when she chooses to display her ability. The most difficult music she reads at a glance, and her touch and expression are perfect.

On Sunday the quieter patients, whose names have been handed in by the attendants during the week, are allowed to go to church. A small Catholic chapel is on the island, and other services are also held.

A "commissioner" came one day, and made the rounds with Dr. Dent. In the basement they found half the nurses gone to dinner, leaving the other half in charge of us, as was always done. Immediately orders were given to bring the nurses back to their duties until after the patients had finished eating. Some of the patients wanted to speak about their having no salt, but were prevented.

The Insane Asylum on Blackwell's Island is a human rat-trap. It is easy to get in, but once there it is impossible to get out. I had intended to have myself committed to the violent wards, the Lodge and Retreat, but when I got the testimony of two sane women and could give it, I decided not to risk my health—and hair, so I did not get violent.

I had, towards the last been shut off from all visitors, and so when the lawyer, Peter A. Hendricks, came and told me that friends of mine were willing to take charge of me if I would rather be with them than in the Asylum, I was only too glad to give my consent. I asked him to send me something to eat immediately on his arrival in the city, and then I waited anxiously for my release.

It came sooner than I had hoped. I was out "in line" taking a walk, and had just gotten interested in a poor woman who had fainted away while the nurses were trying to compel her to walk. "Good-bye; I am going home," I called to Pauline Moser as she went past with a woman on either side of her. Sadly I said farewell to all I knew as I passed them on my way to freedom and life, while they were left behind to a fate worse than death. "Adios," I murmured to the Mexican woman. I kissed my fingers to her, and so I left my companions of hall 7.

I had looked forward so eagerly to leaving the horrible place, yet when my release came and I knew that God's sunlight was to be free for me again, there was a certain pain in leaving. For ten days I had been one of them. Foolishly enough, it seemed intensely selfish to leave them to their sufferings. I felt a Quixotic desire to help them by sympathy and presence. But only for a moment. The bars were down and freedom was sweeter to me than ever.

Soon I was crossing the river and nearing New York. Once again I was a free girl after ten days in the mad house on Blackwell's Island.

NELLIE BLY

Untruths in Every Line

Monday, October 17, 1887

Nellie Bly Contradicts a Recent Article in the "Sun."

She Gives Many Additional Facts About Her Remarkable Sojourn on Blackwell's Island—More Praise for Dr. Ingram—He is the Right Man in the Right Place—The Other Doctors Heartless and Careless.

On my first arrival in New York the editor of the *Sun* said to me in an interview, "There is nothing so valuable as a reporter who gives facts; who, when told that two and two make four, puts it four instead of three or five." I have always been particular in stating only facts in all my work, but never did I confine myself so closely to this rule as in my story of "Behind Asylum Bars." As the *Sun* undertook to prove that I really passed ten days as an insane girl on Blackwell's Island, I would like to correct the many mistakes and misstatements which I counted throughout the six columns recently published about me in that journal.

"On the road to Bedlam," I wore, as I did from the time of my arrest, a grey cheviot dress, trimmed with brown braid; brown undressed kid gloves, black sailor hat, trimmed with grey illusion; a thin brown illusion veil, worn down over my chin. I was silent as we entered the hall, but instead of "despondency and depression being unmistakably delineated upon her countenance" any observer could have detected triumph stamped on every look and movement. I had succeeded in passing the experts and the goal was within grasp. It was more than I could do, in spite of my ability as an actress, to maintain a "despondent" appearance. I had a wild desire to yell "Eureka!" and even Miss Neville and Miss Mayard noticed it.

"I never saw any one change so suddenly," said Miss Neville. "You look really happy and delighted that you have been lodged in an insane asylum."

"I can't see what has cheered you up so," said Miss Mayard. "Ever since we left Bellevue you have looked happy."

"Well, we might as well make the best of it," I explained. "No matter in what position I am I try to laugh and be happy."

THEY WERE SHARPER THAN THE DOCTORS.

Yet with the signs of happiness visible to two women called insane the paper and the doctor say: "Despondency and depression were the outward and visible symptoms that suited the diagnosis under which she had effected her entrance to a madhouse. Dr. Kinier's task is therefore an easy one. There is the certificate of insanity of the type of melancholia from the commission, consisting of Drs. Field, Braisted, and Fitch." Yet would he say I was despondent when I never felt happier and had to hold my handkerchief over my mouth to hide the triumphant smile that would quiver on my lips.

"When asked if she heard voices, she answered 'Yes'" is a statement I emphatically deny. I was asked at Bellevue Hospital if I heard voices, but Dr. Kinier never mentioned the subject to me. "She also kept her hand applied to her head all the time, as though suffering severely from trouble there, and, as a final and finishing stroke, she relapsed into the silence that had marked her advent and refused the grudging 'Yes' or 'No,' or even a mute nod or shake of her head." I kept my handkerchief over my mouth to hide the smile, not my "hand applied to my head." I did not refuse to answer, but refused to tell where I lived. "He is not alone in the opinion that the fatigue and nervous strain of what she had undergone had affected her so that it was a matter of little difficulty for her to seem to be of unbalanced mind," is another statement that will not stand. I was not in the least fatigued, and my nerves are and were always remarkable for their strength. I have faced what seemed positive death, yet I never felt my nerves even twinge. Is it probable, then, that facing a doctor who paid more attention to the nurse than to me would affect me, or that the foolish examination of the doctors at Bellevue could be a strain on my nerves? I certainly had a conviction at first that the doctors could not be deceived, but when I saw that they could I was as easy as if I had been talking over the latest theatrical success.

A THEORY THAT WON'T STAND.

I went to "tea" first and was not bathed until bedtime, as I described in yesterday's WORLD. My "expression of dissatisfaction" at the sight of the table was a mistake. I was only amused, forgetting all else in the sight of the fat woman stealing all the prunes. I did not eat, so if the nurses reported what I ate they made a false statement. I was quite amused at the following paragraph:

"The formality of having her face and hands washed after the meal had been an incident that quite too forcibly reminded her of the loss of her individuality and her position in an institution where the progress of events was independent of her wish or will. This compulsory washing after meals is one of the most rigidly enforced of the institution, and coming, as it does, so soon after the obligatory and preparatory bath of a newly admitted patient, had a very great effect in impressing Nellie, who was accustomed to washing herself." I was there ten days, and in all that time was not once even given permission to wash after meals and I never saw one of the patients given a wash. The bathroom was locked after we were washed in the morning and remained locked until the following morning. Only once a day had we the least chance to wash our faces, so if the "compulsory washing after each meal is one of the most rigidly enforced regulations of the institution," it was taking a vacation during my term as the "Insane Cuban Girl."

HOW SHE TREATED THE NURSES.

The attendants in Hall 6 made no effort to come to an understanding with me. They found I was not crazy enough to afford them any amusement, and they never spoke to me during my entire stay except to yell some command. I never spoke Spanish to the nurses, as I knew they could not understand it, and from their conversation among themselves I knew I could not endure their remarks if addressed to me. There are some things vastly worse than listening to the chattering of insane people. The "white counterpane" said to cover me on my first night, I wish to state, is one of the things only used in daytime for the sake of appearance. They are taken away at night. I did not "toss and tumble upon the narrow couch," passing "the first three hours of the night in a most miserable fashion." I lay quite still on the hard bed, never moving, but listening intently to all the outside noises, and wondering what the newspaper men thought, now they knew I was at last in the asylum and planning a course of action. I did not sleep the entire night, and I did not receive any "sleeping dose of chloral" until three nights later. The "clean but clumsy underclothing" consisted of the labeled slip given to me the night previous, nothing more was added except one skirt and a dress. I asked for more undergarments, but they were refused me. The underskirt was fully five inches longer than the dress, which was not of "blue and white furniture material," but black and white calico. I made no objections to the dress, but when one of the nurses saw it she said it would not do for the doctors to see me in it, and so I was given a longer one. This is different from the statement: "It was much too short. This last objection was fatal. Nellie would have none of it, and shorter had to be got." During my stay I was not once asked to make my bed or any other beds, nor did I see them ask any of the patients who were there with me. Yet the *Sun* asserts: "Nellie refused to do anything, either with her own bed or anywhere else. She was allowed to remain quietly in the sitting-room." I did improve the opportunity to talk with the other patients, and when they complained of the cold I did tell them to ask for more clothing, but they refused to accept my advice, telling me how useless it was.

HER TUSSLE WITH A NURSE.

"Venturing a threat of suicide" was also a very comically and false assertion. The incident, from which the story arose, did not take place on Tuesday, Sept. 27, as the *Sun* states, but after my removal to Hall 7 on Saturday, Oct. 1. It is true I wanted to walk with Anne Neville, and the nurses said I could not because her dress would not match mine in color. I determined, when Miss Fitzpatrick threatened me and said I would be forced to obey, to give her a sample of my strength, which from my slenderness no one would suspect. So I caught hold of Mrs. Finney and held on, letting them both try their utmost to unhand me. When I had given them proof of my strength I told them not to try their beatings on me, as I was sane and the fight would not be an easy one. Miss Fitzpatrick taunted me with my hopeless situation, telling me I had no help and that she could get many to assist her to force me to obey. I laughed heartily and remarked: "Do you know that if I wanted to leave here this instant I would merely go down to the down to the river, jump in, and being an excellent swimmer, swim across. Once in New York you would never have Nellie Brown again as a patient." If this was a threat of suicide I do not know it. I took care to tell each doctor I was not ill, and that, as I was sane, they had no right to keep me there. All my talk was useless. "Nellie, with her companions of Hall 6, took a ride on the carousel that first afternoon, but made no manifestations of pleasure or interest while doing so," is another misstatement. I never once had even a chance to ride on the carousel. When the day came for Hall 6 to indulge in that pleasure it rained and so we were kept in the house. After my removal I found that on Wednesday the hall would have its day. Before the hour arrived I was on my way to New York.

THE CHLORAL EPISODE.

The night the chloral was given me I protested and did not want to take it, but what could I do, with one man and two women insisting that I should? I did take it, but as soon as the attendants left I tried to see how far my finger would go down my throat, and the chloral was allowed to try its effect elsewhere. All the night I did not go to sleep, but I kept my eyes tightly closed whenever the night nurse made her approach. "She asked for warmer clothing and when some clean, but not new, Canton flannel underclothes were offered her she refused to take them." Every day I complained of the cold and asked for additional clothing, not only for myself but for the helpless creatures around me. The nurses and most of the doctors did not listen to my pleas.

HUMANE DR. INGRAM.

One day I shivered with the cold as I was taken out to see the Assistant Superintendent, Dr. Ingram. He asked me kindly if I was cold, and I told him how we all suffered. He spoke to Miss Grady, and asked her if we had enough clothes on. She said we had, but he gave her orders that she give all the patients more. Shortly after we were all called out and given one additional undergarment, which the patients received with thanks. By Dr. Ingram's kindness I was offered an undersuit of red flannel, but I had not the heart to wear it while the other patients had only Canton flannel, so I refused it and accepted the one garment the same as had been given the others. We all felt warmer after this, and many were the blessings breathed on Dr. Ingram.

Through the kindness of Dr. Ingram I was removed to Hall 7, which he thought would be pleasanter for me. I took off the dress belonging to Hall 6 and put on that given to me without a protest. The dress was pink and much too short. I told Miss Finney I would prefer a longer dress, but she said that my feet were pretty and I have no cause to want to hide them. I answered that I was fully aware of their beauty, but that they were not on exhibition. Then I asked, and was allowed, to take the tuck out of my skirt, which made it come to the top of my high-cut boots. As I put on the pink dress, I remarked to Anne Neville, "This is hard on my Cuban complexion," and she laughed and said it was, when I continued, "It doesn't make any difference here. No one cares about the looks of insane women."

MANY DELIBERATE UNTRUTHS.

I must say that I think Miss Finney excels in the line she took, telling untruths about me. She said in the *Sun* that I refused the dress and it had to be changed. I can prove by Miss Neville that she told a deliberate untruth. She again says I would not walk with anyone except Anne Neville, while I never once walked with Miss Neville after being transferred to Hall 7. She does not tell the truth when she says that I tried to excite other patients and ask them why they were not screaming; that I never conversed with other patients; that I repeatedly asked to talk with one of the members of the staff, and that I was saucy, disrespectful and impudent. In the first place, she spoke to me just once after failing, that first night, to make me tell her of my life, and that was when I wanted to walk with Miss Neville. All her other statements are the most fantastic untruths I ever read.

THE WAYS OF DR. FLINT.

Dr. Charles C. Flint is reported as saying I was impudent and listless, among the other charges he makes against me. I will relate all my conversations while on the island, with him, and the public may judge for themselves. One morning he came in and seated himself in a rocking chair near the piano. "Anne Neville, why aren't you sewing?" he called. "Because my eyes are weak and sewing hurts them," replied Miss Neville. "That doesn't make any difference," he said, unkindly; "others have weak eyes and they have to sew. The sewing must be done. Nellie Brown why don't you sew?" "Because I do not want to," I answered, quietly. "That doesn't make any difference; the sewing must be done. Will you sew?" "No," I said, decidedly, and I did not. Mrs. Cotter then asked him if she was to go home, as he had promised, that week. "No, you are not," he said roughly, "and you might as well know it now." Mrs. Cotter burst into tears, and she was still crying when Dr. Ingram came in. He went up to her, with an expression of pity on his kind face, and asked the cause of her evident trouble. Then he cheered her and promised to do what he could to have her released. "Now smile once before I leave you," I heard him say; "I cannot leave you in tears." She looked up and smiled, and he went away content. For the remainder of the day Mrs. Cotter was the happiest patient in the asylum.

In the afternoon Dr. Flint again made his appearance, walking with his hands in his pockets, through the ward. Miss Neville had been needing medical aid for many days, and as it had no effect to speak to the nurses, I determined to speak to the doctor, so calling him to me I told him Miss Neville had an ingrowing nail which pained her dreadfully. "Have you one?" he asked, hatefully. I confessed to being free of any such thing. "Then keep quiet and allow others to speak for themselves," he advised me, in a most insulting manner. Just then Dr. Ingram called to ask me if I was Lottie Peters, of New Orleans. Dr. Flint came up to where we stood, and I said to Dr. Ingram, "This is the most impudent man I ever met." He asked me why and I told him. A few moments after Dr. Ingram, assisted by Flint, gave Miss Neville the aid she needed.

MORE UNHISTORICAL STATEMENTS.

Mrs. Kroener also tells an untruth when she asserts that I made "one patient very noisy and excited for some three or four hours." I am hardly surprised at this, however, as she told Dr. Caldwell, in answer to his inquiry, that I never spoke to anyone, but sat silent all day, only answering when addressed. I was much surprised to hear her say this, as I talked a great deal with the patients. Miss Annie Grupe told a falsehood by saying that I refused to put on additional clothing when offered me. It can be proven by the testimony of other patients, as well as the falseness of Miss McCarten's statement that I tried to make patients disobedient. If I had thought the doctors were not gentlemen, I had no chance to make such a statement to her, and if I had, it's not likely that I would make a confidant of a woman such as I saw Miss McCarten to be. I would not trouble myself to contradict such a cruel and unfeeling person as Miss Grady, but her remark that I "made faces" at the attendants is simply absurd. I would be surprised at nothing she could say. Of the doctors, I have nothing to say, except that nearly all receive pay for work they do not perform. They are heartless and careless and anxious to get through their duties with as little trouble as possible.

MORE PRAISE FOR DR. INGRAM.

On taking my leave Mrs. Kroener, not Lawyer Hendrick, said I should bid the doctors good-by, but I replied, in their hearing, that I only cared to say good-by to Dr. Ingram. Supt. Dent said: "Good-by, Nellie Brown. I hope you will get well." I replied, with a smile, that I was as well as I would ever be, and telling him to bid Dr. Ingram, who was out, good-by for me, I left them. I cannot give too much praise to Dr. Ingram. He is thoughtful and always kind to the patients, and they have every respect for him. He is always ready to listen to their complaints and do what he can to help them. He encourages them to talk to him, and he is really the right man in the right place.

NELLIE BLY

[EDITOR'S NOTE: For the complete reporting surrounding Bly's stay on Blackwell's Island, including the Sun article Bly is here refuting, see the volume entitled INTO THE MADHOUSE*, available now.]*

Trying to Be a Servant

Sunday, October 30, 1887

Nellie Bly's Strange Experience at Two Employment Agencies.

She Pays a Dollar to the Agent and is Guaranteed a Situation—She Has No References—The Agent Knows Nothing of Her Character—Nevertheless, He Declares to a Customer that She Possess All the Virtues in the Calendar—Can a Common Thief Thus Recommended Get Service in New York Homes?—How Applicants Are Treated—The Agency Sure to Make Money Whether the Girls Get Places or Not—The Out-of-Town Trick—A Weary Waiting for Work—Queer Experiences.

No one but the initiated know what a great question the servant question is and how many perplexing sides it has. The mistresses and servants, of course, fill the leading roles. Then, in the lesser, but still important parts, come the agencies, which, despite the many voices clamoring against them, declare themselves public benefactors. Even the "funny man" manages to fill a great deal of space with the subject. It is a serious question, since it affects all one holds dear in life—one's dinner, one's bed and one's linen. I had heard so many complaints from long-suffering mistresses, worked-out servants, agencies and lawyers that I determined to investigate the subject to my own satisfaction. There was only one way to do it. That was to personate a servant and apply for a situation. I knew that there might be such a thing as "references" required, and, as I had never tested my abilities in this line, I did not know how to furnish them. Still, it would not do to allow a little thing like a "reference" to stop me in my work, and I would not ask any friend to commit herself to further my efforts. Many girls must at one time be without references, I thought, and this encouraged me to make the risk.

On Monday afternoon a letter came to The World office from a lawyer complaining of an agency where, he claimed, a client of his had paid for a servant, and the agent then refused to produce a girl. This shop I decided to make my first essay. Dressed to look the character I wanted to represent, I walked up Fourth avenue until I found No. 69, the place I wanted. It was a low frame building, which retained all the impressions of old age. The room on the first floor was filled with a conglomeration of articles which gave it the appearance of a second-hand store. By a side door, leaning against the wall, was a large sign which told the passing public that that was the entrance to the "Germania Servants' Agency." On a straight, blue board, fastened lengthwise to a second-story window, was in large, encouraging white letters, the ominous word, "Servants."

I entered the side door, and as there was nothing before me but the dirty, uncarpeted hall and a narrow, rickety-looking staircase, I went on to my fate. I passed two closed doors on the first landing and on the third I saw the word "Office." I did not knock, but turned the knob of the door, and, as it stuck top and bottom, I pressed my shoulder against it. It gave way, so did I, and I entered on my career as a servant with a tumble. It was a small room, with a low ceiling, a dusty ingrain carpet and cheaply papered walls. A heavy railing and a high desk and counter which divided the room gave it the appearances of a police court. Around the walls were hung colored advertisements of steamship lines and maps. Above the mantel, which was decorated with two plaster-paris busts, was a square sheet of white paper. I viewed the large black letters on this paper with a quaking heart. "References Investigated!!" with two exclamation points. Now, if it had only been put quietly and mildly, or even with one exclamation point, but two—dreadful. It was a death-warrant to the idea I had of writing my own references if any were demanded.

IN THE INTELLIGENCE OFFICE.

A young woman who was standing with a downcast head by the window turned to look at the abrupt newcomer. A man who had apparently been conversing with her, came hastily forward to the desk. He was a middle-sized man, with a sharp gray eye, a bald head, and a black frock coat buttoned up tightly, showing to disadvantage his rounded shoulders.

QUESTIONED IN THE AGENCY.

"Well?" he said to me in a questioning manner, as he glanced quickly over my "get up."

"Are you the man who gets places for girls?" I asked, as if there were but one such man.

"Yes, I'm the man. Do you want a place?" he asked, with a decidedly German twang.

"Yes, I want a place," I replied.

"What did you work at last?"

"Oh, I was a chambermaid. Can you get me a position, do you think?"

"Yes, I can do that," he replied. "You're a nice-looking girl and I can soon get you a place. Just the other day I got a girl a place for $20 a month, just because she was nice-looking. Many gentlemen, and ladies also, will pay more if the girls are nice looking. Where did you work?"

"I worked in Atlantic City," I said, with a mental cry for forgiveness.

"Have you no city reference?" he asked.

"No, none whatever, but I want a job in this city, that's why I came here."

"Well, I can get you a position, never fear, only some people are mighty particular about references."

"Have you no place you can send me to now?" I said, determined to get at my business as soon as possible.

"You have to pay to get your name entered on the book first," he said, opening a large ledger, as he asked, "What is your name?"

"How much do you charge?" I asked, in order to give me time to decide on a name.

"I charge you one dollar for the use of the bureau for a month, and if I get you a big salary you will have to pay more."

"How much more?"

"That depends entirely on your salary," he answered, non-committal. "Your name?"

SHE PAYS THE REQUIRED DOLLAR.

"Now, if I give you a dollar you will assure me a situation?"

"Certainly; that's what I'm here for."

"And you guarantee me work in this city?" I urged.

"Oh, certainly, certainly; that's what this agency is for. I'll get you a place, sure enough."

"All right. I'll give you a dollar, which is a great deal for a girl out of work. My name is Sally Lees."

"What shall I put you down for?" he asked.

"Oh, anything," I replied, with a generosity that surprised myself.

"Then I shall put it chambermaid, waitress, nurse or seamstress." So my name, or the one assumed, was entered in the ledger and as I paid my dollar I ventured the information that if he gave me a situation directly I should be pleased to give him more money. He warmed up at this and told me he should advertise me in the morning.

OUT OF WORK.

"Then you have no one in want of help now?"

"We have plenty of people, but not just now. They all come in the morning. This is too late in the day. Where are you boarding?"

At this moment a woman clad in a blue dress, with a small, black shawl wrapped around her, entered from a room in the rear. She also looked me over sharply, as if I was an article for sale, as the man told her in German all that he knew about me.

"You can stay here," she said in broken, badly broken English, after she had learned that I was friendless in the city. "Where is your baggage?"

"I left my baggage where I paid for my lodging to-night," I answered. They tried to induce me to stop at their house. Only $2.50 a week, with board, or 20 cents a night for a bed. They urged that it was immaterial to them, only I had a better chance to secure work if I was always there; it was only for my own good they suggested it. I had one glance of the adjoining bedroom, and that sight made me firm in my determination to sleep elsewhere.

THE RECEIPT.

As the evening drew on I felt that they would have no more applications for servants that afternoon, and after asking the hour that I should return in the morning, I requested a receipt for my money. "You don't need to be so particular," he said, crossly, but I told him I was, and insisted until he was forced to comply. It was not much of a receipt. He wrote on the blank side of the agency's advertising card:

Sally Lees has paid $1.
Good for one month
use of bureau.
69 4th ave.

On the following morning, about 10.30, I made my appearance at the agency. Some eight or ten girls were in the room, and the man who had pocketed my fee on the previous afternoon still adorned the throne back of the desk. No one said good morning, or anything else for that matter, so I quietly slid onto a chair near the door. The girls were all comfortably dressed, and looked as if they had enjoyed hearty breakfasts. All sat silent, with a dreamy expression on their faces, except two who stood by the window watching the passing throng and conversing in whispers with one another. I wanted to be with or near them, so that I might hear what was said. After waiting for some time I decided to awake the man to the fact that I wanted work, not a rest.

"Have you no place to send me this morning?"

"No, but I advertised you in the paper," and he handed me the *Tribune* of Oct. 25 and pointed out the following notice:

> NURSE, &c—By excellent, very neat English girl as nurse and seamstress, chambermaid and waitress or parlor maid. Call at 69 4th ave., no cards answered.

I choked down a laugh as I read myself advertised in this manner, and wondered what my role would be next time. I began to hope some one would soon call for the excellent girl, but when an aged gentleman entered I wished just as fervently that he was not after me. I was enjoying my position too much, and I fear I could not restrain my gravity if any one began to question me. Poor old gentleman! He looked around helplessly as if he was at a loss to know what to do. The agent did not leave him long in doubt. "You want a girl, sir?"

THE AGENT FURNISHES REFERENCES.

"Yes, my wife read an advertisement in the *Tribune* this morning and she sent me here to see the girl."

"Yes, yes, excellent girl, sir, come right back here," opening the gates and giving the gentleman a chair behind the high counter. "You come here, Sally Lees," indicating a chair beside the visitor for me. I sat down with an inward chuckle and the agent leaned over the back of a chair. The visitor eyed me nervously, and after clearing his throat several times and making vain attempts at beginning he said:

"You are the girl who wants work?" And after I answered in the affirmative he said: "Of course you know how to do all these things—you know what is required of a girl?"

"Oh, yes, I know," I answered confidently.

"Yes—well, how much do you want a month?"

"Oh, anything," I answered, looking to the agent for aid. He understood the look, for he began hurriedly:

"Fourteen dollars a month, sir. She is an excellent girl, good, neat, quick and of an amiable disposition."

I was astonished at his knowledge of my good qualities, but I maintained a lofty silence.

"Yes, yes," the visitor said musingly. "My wife only pays $10 a month, and then if the girl is all right she is willing to pay more, you know. I really couldn't, you know—"

"We have no ten-dollar girls here, sir," said the agent with dignity. "You can't get an honest, neat and respectable girl for that amount."

"H'm, yes; well, this girl has good references, I suppose."

"Oh, yes, I know all about her," said the agent, briskly and confidently. "She is an excellent girl, and I can give you the best personal reference—the best of references."

Here I was, unknown to the agent. So far as he knew, I might be a confidence woman, a thief or everything wicked, and yet the agent was vowing that he had good personal references.

"Well, I live in Bloomfield, N.J., and there are only four in the family. Of course you are a good washer and ironer?" he said, turning to me. Before I had tome to assure him of my wonderful skill in the line the agent interposed: "This is not the girl you want. No, sir, this girl won't do general housework. This is the girl you are after," bringing up another. "She does general housework," and he went on with a long list of her virtues, which were similar to those he had professed to find in me. The visitor got very nervous and began to insist that he could not take a girl unless his wife saw her first. Then the agent, when he found it impossible to make him take a girl, tried to induce the gentleman to join the bureau. "It will only cost you $2 for the use of the bureau for a month," he urged, but the visitor began to get more nervous and to make his way to the door. I thought he was frightened because it was an agency, and it amused me to hear how earnestly he pleaded that really he dare not employ a girl without his wife's consent.

SOME OF THE GIRLS' STORIES.

After the escape of the visitor we all resumed our former positions and waited for another visitor. It came in the shape of a red-haired Irish girl.

"Well, you are back again?" was the greeting given her.

"Yes. That woman was horrible. She and her husband fought all the time and the cook carried tales to the mistress. Sure and I wouldn't live at such a place. A splendid laundress, with a good 'karacter,' don't need to stay in such places, I told them. The lady of the house made me wash every other day; then she wanted me to be dressed like a lady sure and wear a cap while I was at work. Sure and it's no good laundress who can be dressed up while at work, so I left her."

The storm had scarcely passed when another girl with fiery locks entered. She had a good face and a bright one, and I watched her closely.

"So you are back, too. You are troublesome," said the agent. Her eyes flashed, as she replied:

"Oh, I'm troublesome, am I? Well, you can take a poor girl's money, anyway, and then you tell her she's troublesome. It wasn't troublesome when you took my money, and where is the position? I have walked all over the city, wearing out my shoes and spending my money in car-fare. Now, is this how you treat poor girls?"

"I did not mean anything by saying you were troublesome. That was only my fun," the agent tried to explain, and after a while the girl quieted down.

THE OUT-OF-TOWN TRICK.

Another girl came and was told that, as she had not made her appearance the day previous she could not expect to obtain a situation. He refused to send her word if there was any chance. Then a messenger boy called and said that Mrs. Vanderpool, of No. 86 West Thirty-ninth street, wanted the girl advertised in the morning paper. Irish girl No. 1 was sent, and she returned, after several hours' absence, to say that Mrs. Vanderpool said, when she learned where the girl came from, that she knew all about agencies and their schemes and she did not propose to have a girl from them. The girl buttoned Mrs. Vanderpool's shoes and returned to the agency to take her post of waiting.

I succeeded at last in drawing one of the girls—Winifred Friel—into conversation. She said she had been waiting for several days and that she had no chance of a place yet. The agency had a place out of town to which they tried to force girls who declared they would not leave the city. Quite strange they never offered the place to girls who said they would work anywhere. Winifred Friel wanted it, but they would not allow her to go, yet they tried to insist on me accepting it.

"Well, now, if you won't take that I would like to see you get a place this winter," he said angrily, when he found that I would not go out of the city.

"Why, you promised that you would find me a situation in the city."

"That's no difference; if you won't take what I offer, you can do without," he said indifferently.

"Then give me my money," I said.

"No, you can't have your money. That goes into the bureau." I urged and insisted, to no avail, and so I left the agency to return no more.

AT ANOTHER AGENCY.

My second day I decided to apply to another agency, so I went to Mrs. L. Seely's, No, 68 West Twenty-second street. I paid my dollar fee and was taken to the third story and put in a small room which was packed as close with women as sardines in a box. After edging my way in I was unable to move, so packed were we. A woman came up, and, calling me "that tall girl," told me roughly as I was new it was useless for me to wait there. Some of the girls said Mrs. Seely was always cross to them, and that I should not mind it. How horribly stifling those rooms were! There were fifty-two in the room with me, and the two other rooms I could look into were equally crowded, while groups stood on the stairs and in the hallway. It was a novel insight I got of life. Some girls laughed, some were sad, some slept, some ate and others read, while all sat from morning till night waiting a chance to earn a living. They are long waits, too. One girl had been there two months, others for days and weeks. It was good to see the glad look when called out to see a lady, and sad to see them return saying that they did not suit because they wore bangs, or their hair in the wrong style, or that they looked bilious, or that they were too tall, too short, too heavy or too slender. One poor woman could not obtain a place because she wore mourning and so the objections ran.

I got no chance the entire day and I decided that I could not endure a second day in that human pack for two situations, so I resolved to follow the resolution of several of the other girls and try answering the advertisements in the morning papers. How I succeeded in this I shall tell some other time.

Nellie Bly

What Becomes of Babies

Sunday, November 6, 1887

Hundreds and Hundreds of Little Ones Given Away Yearly

Not the Petted Darlings of the Rich, but the Infants Born to Shame—These Are the Ones that Are Given into Alien Hands—Regular Traffic in New-Born Babes—A Money-Making Trade in Humanity.

What name awakens such universally tender feelings as that of "baby?" Last week some philanthropist wrote to The World to suggest that I try to find out what becomes of all the baby waifs in this great city. Not the little ones who are cordially welcomed by proud parents, happy grandparents and a large circle of loving relatives, but the many hundreds of babies whose coming is greeted with grief and whose unhappy mothers hide their little lives in shame. Unhappily there are hundreds and hundreds of them, but it is an impossible task to tell what their fate is.

However, here is a condensed account of my studious inquiries in this direction. I took several Sunday newspapers and made note of many of the medical and manicure advertisements. The following is the result: Dr. Hawker, of No. 21 West Thirteenth street, has a suggestive advertisement. I thought from that he might know something on the subject I wished to investigate, so I called on him. The door opened in response to my knock, and a well-dressed, short man, with a bald head, looked out over his glasses at me. I saw a young man in the office, so I said, with a blush not at all assumed: "I want to speak with you privately, please."

"Oh, yes, yes," he said, stepping out into the hall and closing the office door; "step this way. Wait here, I will see you presently."

He opened the door and I entered a back room. It was already occupied by a man and a woman. From appearances, the bed-lounge, cupboard, table, kitchen-stove and bureau, I think that room answered the purpose of the entire house. No one spoke, so I sat down on the lounge and took in my surroundings.

The front office, into which I was soon ushered, was vastly different from the room in the rear. The floor was nicely carpeted, and the chairs, desks and medicine case all helped to lend the air of the office of a well-to-do physician. The doctor drew his chair close to mine in a confidential manner and waited, inquiringly, for me to begin. My position was a delicate one, and I knew it. So I said: "I read your advertisement, and as you say you give 'advice free,' I thought I would come to you for aid. There is a—a baby I want to dispose of. Can you help me?"

WHAT TO DO WITH IT.

"Yes. How old is the child?"

"It was born on the 5th of May," I answered, with a gasp.

"Yes; pretty good child by this time. Boy or girl?"

"Oh, a girl!" (I hadn't thought of this before.)

"A girl? Too bad. They are very hard to get rid of. Now, if it was only a boy you would have more chance."

I got a little quaky by this time, and I almost felt like assuring him that it made no difference to me, that really if boys were easier to bargain for it might just as easily be said a boy. Luckily I kept still.

"The child is healthy?" I nodded my head. "What complexion?"

"Neither dark nor fair," I replied, as I couldn't tell the complexion of a babe I had never seen. "What shall I do with it?"

"The child is yours?" he asked.

I was almost stunned, for I feared next he would ask me questions I could not answer without disposed of without any questions being asked. "Can it be done?"

"Yes, it is done daily. It is mostly done when the child is born. However, I can advertise for you. Will you make a full surrender?"

"What is that?"

"You give up the child and never know where it goes or anything more about it. I will do this for you for $25; you to pay advertising and all outside expenses."

This was soon agreed on. I did not hesitate at $25 when I was never going to pay it.

"Tell me something about such cases. It is all new to me. What becomes of the babies and how can the mothers tell whether they live or die or are treated well?" I asked, aiming for the news I was in search of.

"After a mother makes full surrender of a babe, which is done at the place it is born, she has no way to tell what becomes of it. Of course, it may be ill-treated or reared in the wrong manner, but it has to take the chance. We advertise and people reply. We never ask them who or what they are. I don't know as much about them as I do about you this moment. Many of the women come veiled and we never even see their faces. If satisfied they take the babe, pay their fee, jump into a carriage and drive no one knows where. The child has no chance ever to find out who it is. The ones who take it have not the faintest idea who or what the mother is; they have never even seen her.

"Of course there are some women who do not make full surrender, but get me to procure boarding places for the babies. I had a woman who lived in Fifty-second street that did all this work for me, but she died a few weeks ago, and I have no one since. I can have your child boarded for $4 a week. No, the care is not what mothers would give. What is the death rate of such children? At the very least eighty out of one hundred. You think it horrible? Well, it's the way of the world. Women who do not want the expense of a child, and who do not wish to make full surrender, leave them at the Catholic Home in Sixtieth street, near Lexington avenue. When the home is not full, a basket is hung on the door-knob at night, and women drop their babies into it. If you are not a Catholic you won't want to do that. Others give them to the Commissioners, who send them to Ward's Island, where there are 800 children. If you dread bad treatment and large death rates you should see that place!"

I pretended that I had some love for the imaginary child, and really I did have, so I said I should take the night to think it over, and if I decided to relinquish it I would return on the morrow.

Mrs Conradsen,
Healing Medium. Hours, 9 to 9,
West 15th st.

BOY BABIES BETTER THAN GIRLS.

So read the next advertisement on my list. I had no idea who she was or what, but somehow the notice seemed to suggest that I would not apply to her in vain. She lived in a large, three-story brownstone house, which had the appearance, from the closed shutters and doors, of being unoccupied. I rang the bell repeatedly before I was shown into the presence of the woman, who was not ill-looking. My first story had been such a success that I decided to repeat it, with a slight difference. As the doctor said girls were hard to get rid of, I determined this time it should be a boy, and so have every chance there was.

"I have a child I want to get rid of, without being known or appearing in the case. Can you help me?"

She then asked the age, health and complexion of the baby boy. Apparently she was satisfied, for she said she could board him out at $4 a week for me. When I told her it was necessary that I cut off all connection with the child, she said for $10 she would get me someone to take it. She noticed my accent and she asked me how long I had been from France. I told her I was a Southerner and she said she knew I did not belong in New York or I would not have to ask so many questions on the subject.

"It seems odd for you to keep the child so long," she said. "I always advertise them in about a day after they are born. I do not charge anything for placing babies when they are born here, but, as yours was not, I will have to charge you $10 for my trouble. That is little enough, and you must bear all other expenses, for I may not be able to place him for a month or so. How do I place them? Well, if the mother makes a full surrender, I advertise them and lots of people answer. Plenty come only through curiosity and many in hopes of getting a trace of news. Sometimes they imagine they can see resemblances in the baby's face to one they suspect. I always know such people, as they ask who the mother is, what she is like, where from, if I have any knowledge of the father, and what sort of a man visited the mother while she was here. I very quickly show them the door. Those who want babies never ask a single question.

WHAT BECOMES OF THEM.

"What do they do with them? Ah, that is hard to say. I have known women to get babies repeatedly, but I don't know what for. Who are the mothers? They are never poor girls, but all come from the middle and higher classes. Not one out of a hundred is a working girl. Do they get rid of the children? Only occasionally. They generally tell me to get a home and they will pay for the keeping. I have a long list of people. They mostly live in flats, who keep themselves on the incomes derived from mothers. Sometimes the mothers know where their children are and visit them, but oftener all the business is done through me No, I do not suppose the best care is taken of babies. What can one expect of a woman who may have twelve to care for? When they die they are buried as the woman's child and no questions are asked."

"Are there many babies?"

"Why, my dear, there is no place that can equal New York. There is a doctor who runs a large place on Sixth avenue for aristocrats alone, and his place is always filled. He keeps all the babies, but I can't say what he does with them. He never knows who his visitors are, and he only asks one question of them; that is, What should he do with them in case they die. I have had girls come to me whose homes were only a few blocks above here and no one was ever the wiser. It is seldom I know my guests. I have no desire to know. They do not see one another. I charge from $6 a week to $25. Do I have plenty? My house is never empty. I have only one room unoccupied now. In connection with this I am a doctor and I give massage and electric baths. There are free homes for children, but if you want the child to live you won't take the chances there. Yes, a number of children die at birth. The mothers are never here longer than two or three weeks."

I had all the news I wanted from her and so I bade her a friendly good-by, promising to bring the babe and pay her $10 for its disposal in any manner, so that I was left entirely clear of all connections with it. She asked me no personal questions.

In West Sixteenth street I called at several manicure parlors, but they were found to be legitimate, as far as I could ascertain, although very few of them seemed at all surprised at the nature of my visit. From an advertisement of Mrs. Stone's I concluded she could give me some valuable information as to what became of all the babies. I asked the woman who made her appearance if she was Mrs. Stone. She said no, that the advertisement was put in for a regular practicing physician of Brooklyn. I wanted the address, but she said she was not allowed to give it, but if I would return in a few hours she would ascertain if I could see the party.

A BROOKLYN "HOME."

I got the address on my return, and I went away over to Howard and Monroe streets, Brooklyn. A commodious frame house, surrounded by an ill-kept lawn, stood directly on the corner. It proved to be the one I wanted. From all indications the house was but recently occupied. To the woman who answered to the name of Mrs. Stone, I repeated my oft-told tale, and asked her prices. She could not think of having the child adopted for less than $50.

"I presume you have plenty of this business to do," I suggested.

"Plenty; why there is no business that can compare with it."

"It is a blessing there is some one to take charge of the babies, else it would be hard on them, I suppose," I suggested, in hopes she would venture some information.

"It would make me sick to try to tell you what is done many times by girls who have not enough money to pay for having their babies adopted. I knew one girl, the daughter of a clergyman in Jersey City, who ran away from home and came to New York. After all her expenses were paid she had not enough money to pay for having the child adopted. When she was able to return home, she rolled up a bundle of clothing and, taking her baby, started saying that she was going home. On the way she smothered the child. That was the last of it.

"What do I do with the babies? Well, I advertise one as soon as it is born. I never allow the mother to even see its face. Sometimes I know who takes the child, but more frequently I do not. Some people are particular and want the child born in wedlock, so I have several marriage certificates on hand to satisfy them. They never see the mother, or she them. We know nothing of the child after it is taken away. Oh, yes, the business pays, for it is only people of the higher classes who are our patients."

"Mrs. Stone, if babies die while in your care, is it difficult to obtain a burial permit?"

"No, it is very easy. We always retain a physician who never asks any questions, but writes out the burial permit according to our instructions. No, we never give the correct name, but assume any we wish. I seldom know who my patients are. If a patient dies she is buried under the name she gave me. In the Potter's Field? Certainly. It is as easy to get a burial permit for a woman as for a child."

I promised to take the baby to Mrs. Stone the next day, and to sign a paper to the effect that I would never inquire after the child after the time I gave her $50 to dispose of it.

A MONEY-MAKING TRAFFIC.

The next advertisement was that of a man who proclaimed himself "ladies' physician," in Sixteenth street. He advertised under the name of Morgan, but the plate on the door bore the name of Dr. Clarke. However, I asked for Dr. Morgan and was told that he was in. The general appearance of the house bespoke good business. Dr. Morgan grew very confidential when he found that I would not hesitate at any price, so the child was taken out of my hands. I had by this time a very tender feeling for this imaginary child. I had lessened his age, as most of them complained it was too old, and I had changed its complexion. I had long ceased to pretend it was my own. It now belonged to a friend of mine. This was a more comfortable position for us. My mind pictured it one of these handsome, dimpled baby boys we read about, and I occasionally felt a mild surprise that the mother could part with it. One's imagination is a wonderful thing when one once gives way to it.

"What becomes of all the babies?" I asked earnestly.

"Most of them die," he replied, "and those that live are given to women who advertise that they will take them. What becomes of them then, no one knows. They procure full surrender and so no one has the right to ask. Or it is very easy to say that some one adopted the child, but they don't know who. It all depends on the mother. If she is willing to spend money she can get a home for it."

Fully eight out of every ten who advertised medicated, vapor, electric or any sort of baths were in the habit of taking children for money considerations. What do they do with them? is a question unanswerable. They all say that the entire year does not bring them a slack week. Of course the majority of children die, but is it supposable that there are rich families enough to be adopted daily without ceasing? Every one said that only the rich adopt the babies. If it is only the rich, then the supply must be greater than the demand.

The gentleman who wrote to THE WORLD said that his wife called on Mrs. Gray in Sixth avenue, who advertises manicure and vapor baths, and while there she found that the house was filled with mothers and babies. I climbed two flights of narrow, dirty stairs and saw Mrs. Gray, who said she would take the baby on full surrender only, for $50. She said the mother could never know what became of the child afterwards.

AFRAID OF DISCOVERY.

"I get lots of children; but one has to be careful, as there are so many schemes going around. I had a woman come here the other day that acted as if she were a detective. I gave her no information. One never knows when they will get caught up."

Mrs. Gray then brought an infant from an inner room and showed it to us. As I grew liberal with my price she grew more confidential, but throughout the interview she displayed a shrewdness and a fear of betraying something.

"I had a woman come to me one day and say that her husband threatened to leave her if she did not part with a child she had previous to the marriage. She got me to take the child and put it in a home. She paid me well and paid the child's board, visiting it every week, while the husband thought she did not know where it was. It is now seven years old. Burial permits are easy to get. I retain a reputable physician and he never asks any questions. Where do all the babies go? Why, rich people adopt them, of course." I promised her the baby and a fifty-dollar bill, and I was never to know anything of it afterwards.

> DR. MAY—W. 24th, graduate of university, Phil., Pa; 25 years' experience, skillful, safe treatment; one interview sufficient, consultation strictly private.

I called on Dr. May and I really thought the man was insane. In order to inspire us with confidence he told of the most criminal actions. He readily consented to take charge of the child for the modest sum of $500, and he told us he could not be asked to do anything that he would refuse.

He showed us diplomas from a New York and also a Philadelphia medical college. He also said he belonged to the Board of Health and was a member in good standing in the Masonic lodge. Notwithstanding all this, he confessed to the most criminal actions, and when we started to go he asked me if I had any money with me. I said no, and then he begged that I give him, if but 25 cents, to retain his services. I shudder when I think of what a horrible creature he is, according to his own confession, yet see the position that at least he claims to hold.

"A physician is bound not to reveal the secrets of his patients," he said. "Once I was taken to court in a divorce case. It was just another story of a jealous husband and pretty wife in love with her physician, but I refused to reveal anything, and the man lost his case. An insurance company also took me upon a case where a man died of hard drink. I treated him for it; but I would not tell, and so the company was the loser. Women always trust me. They know that once they pay me I'm bound not to tell on them."

CHILDREN ADOPTED FOR A PURPOSE.

LADIES can confidently consult Mrs. K. Gollas, ladies' physician, West 29th st.

Mrs. Gollas was at home and ready to be consulted. She would take the child for $35. "I always have children taken away by the time they are a day old. It is a great deal of trouble to have several months-old babies adopted. Why? Well, women want to pass the babies for their own and so they get them young. I have had women come from France and Germany to adopt a child. They have had property that depended on an heir, or they wanted to cheat other relatives out of it, and so buy a child. Customers always say what complexion they want the babe. I think they are all rich people who take the children, for what would poor people want with them? We never know anything about the child afterwards. The charitable homes where infants are taken, are horrible places. Last summer at one asylum the babies died by the hundreds. I keep a physician who gives burial permits for infants or adults who die in my house. The mothers seldom, if ever, keep their children. A short time ago a woman gave up her babe, and the parties who adopted it told me accidentally that they had bought a home on Long Island and from whom. I told the woman, and strange as it may seem, they had bought their home from her father who is a farmer, and would be her neighbor, though they never knew it. So you see the woman can see her child every day."

I visited the New York Foundling Asylum in Sixty-eighth street, near Third avenue. The Sister at the desk kept attending to her finger nails while I was talking to her. "I will only make arrangements with the mother. If she gives us the child, she never sees or hears from it again. We only take full surrender and no one can know where they go."

As I left the asylum I met sixty-two girls in blue dresses and 100 boys in line, crossing Lexington Avenue. I do not know where they were from, but their orphanage was stamped on them.

NELLIE BLY

[EDITOR'S NOTE: For more information about unwanted babies in New York during this era, see two Bly articles in Volume Two of this series, "With The Prison Matrons" and "Nellie Bly Buys A Baby." For more information about the New York Foundling Asylum referenced above, as well as a selection of real notes left with abandoned babies, see my novelette CHARITY GIRL, available now.]

THE GIRLS WHO MAKE BOXES

SUNDAY, NOVEMBER 27, 1887

NELLIE BLY TELLS HOW IT FEELS TO BE A WHITE SLAVE

She Tries Her Hand at Making Paper Boxes—Difficulty in Getting a Job—Must Work Two Weeks for Nothing—After One Learns the Trade It is Hard to Earn a Living—A Fair Picture of the Work.

Very early the other morning I started out, not with the pleasure-seekers, but with those who toil the day long that they may live. Everybody was rushing—girls of all ages and appearances and hurrying men—and I went along, as one of the throng. I had often wondered at the tales of poor pay and cruel treatment that working girls tell. There was one way of getting at the truth, and I determined to try it: It was becoming myself a Paper Box Factory Girl. Accordingly, I started out in search of work without experience, reference or aught to aid me.

It was a tiresome search, to say the least. Had my living depended on it, it would have been discouraging, almost maddening. I went to a great number of factories in and around Bleecker and Grand streets and Sixth avenue, where the workers number up into the hundreds. "Do you know how to do the work?" was the question asked by every one. When I replied that I did not, they gave me no further attention.

"I am willing to work for nothing until I learn," I urged.

"Work for nothing! Why, if you paid us for coming we wouldn't have you in our way," said one.

"We won't run an establishment to teach women trades," said another, in answer to my plea for work.

"Well, as they are born without the knowledge, how do they ever learn?" I asked.

"The girls always have some friend who wants to learn. If she wishes to lose time and money by teaching her, we don't object, for we get the work the beginner does for nothing."

By no persuasion could I obtain an entrée into the larger factories, so I concluded at last to try a smaller one at No. 196 Elm Street. Quite unlike the unkind, brusque men I had met at other factories, the man here was very polite. He said: "If you have never done the work, I don't think you will like it. It is dirty work and a girl has to spend years at it before she can make much money. Our beginners are girls about sixteen years old, and they do not get paid for two weeks after they come here."

"What can they make afterward?"

"We sometimes start them at week work—$1.50 a week. When they become competent they go on to piecework—that is, they are paid by the hundred."

"How much do they earn then?"

"A good worker will earn from $5 to $9 a week."

"Have you many girls here?"

"We have about sixty in the building and a number who take work home. I have only been in this business for a few months, but if you think you would like to try it, I shall speak to my partner. He has had some of his girls for eleven years. Sit down until I find him."

He left the office, and I soon heard him talking outside about me and rather urging that I be given a chance. He soon returned, and with him a small man who spoke with a German accent. He stood by me without speaking, so I repeated my request. "Well, give your name to the gentleman at the desk, and come down on Monday morning, and we will see what we can do for you."

And so it was that I started out early in the morning. I had put on a calico dress to work in and to suit my chosen trade. In a nice little bundle, covered with brown paper with a grease-spot on the centre of it, was my lunch. I had an idea that every working girl carried a lunch, and I was trying to give out the impression that I was quite used to this thing. Indeed, I considered the lunch a telling stroke of thoughtfulness in my new role, and eyed with some pride, in which was mixed a little dismay, the grease-spot, which was gradually growing in size.

Early as it was I found all the girls there and at work. I went through a small wagon-yard, the only entrance to the office. After making my excuses to the gentleman at the desk, he called to a pretty little girl, who had her apron full of pasteboard, and said:

"Take this lady up to Norah."

"Is she to work on boxes or cornucopias?" asked the girl.

"Tell Norah to put her on boxes."

Following my little guide, I climbed the narrowest, darkest, and most perpendicular stair it has ever been my misfortune to see. On and on we went, through small rooms, filled with working girls, to the top floor–fourth or fifth story, I have forgotten which. Any way, I was breathless when I got there.

THE PASTING TABLE.

"Norah, here is a lady you are to put on boxes," called out my pretty little guide.

All the girls that surrounded the long tables turned from their work and looked at me curiously. The auburn-haired girl addressed as Norah raised her eyes from the box she was making, and replied:

"See if the hatchway is down, and show her where to put her clothes."

Then the forewoman ordered one of the girls to "get the lady a stool," and sat down before a long table, on which was piled a lot of pasteboard squares, labeled in the centre. Norah spread some long slips of paper on the table; then taking up a scrub-brush, she dipped it into a bucket of paste and then rubbed it over the paper. Next she took one of the squares of pasteboard and, running her thumb deftly along, turned up the edges. This done, she took one of the slips of paper and put it quickly and neatly over the corner, binding them together and holding them in place. She quickly cut the paper off at the edge with her thumb-nail and swung the thing around and did the next corner. This I soon found made a box lid. It looked and was very easy, and in a few moments I was able to make one.

I did not find the work difficult to learn, but rather disagreeable. The room was not ventilated, and the paste and glue were very offensive. The piles of boxes made conversation impossible with all the girls except a beginner, Therese, who sat by my side. She was very timid at first, but after I questioned her kindly she grew more communicative.

"I live on Eldrige Street with my parents. My father is a musician, but he will not go on the streets to play. He very seldom gets an engagement. My mother is sick nearly all the time. I have a sister who works at passementerie. She can earn from $3 to $5 a week. I have another sister who has been spooling silk in Twenty-third Street for five years now. She makes $6 a week. When she comes home at night her face and hands and hair are all colored from the silk she works on during the day. It makes her sick, and she is always taking medicine."

"Have you worked before?"

"Oh, yes; I used to work at passementerie on Spring Street. I worked from 7 until 6 o'clock, piecework, and made about $3.50 a week. I left because the bosses were not kind, and we only had three little oil lamps to see to work by. The rooms were very dark, but they never allowed us to burn the gas. Ladies used to come here and take the work home to do. They did it cheap, for the pleasure of doing it, so we did not get as much pay as we would otherwise."

"What did you do after you left there?" I asked.

"I went to work in a fringe factory on Canal Street. A woman had the place and she was very unkind to all the girls. She did not speak English. I worked an entire week, from 8 to 6, with only a half-hour for dinner, and at the end of the week she only paid me 35 cents. You know a girl cannot live on 35 cents a week, so I left."

"How do you like the box factory?"

"Well, the bosses seem very kind. They always say good-morning to me, a thing never done in any other place I ever worked, but it is a good deal for a poor girl to give two weeks' work for nothing. I have been here almost two weeks, and I have done a great deal of work. It's all clear gain to the bosses. They say they often dismiss a girl after her first two weeks on the plea that she does not suit. After this I am to get $1.50 a week."

When the whistles of the surrounding factories blew at 12 o'clock the forewoman told us we could quit work and eat our lunch. I was not quite so proud of my cleverness in simulating a working girl when one of them said:

"Do you want to send out for your lunch?"

"No; I brought it with me," I replied.

"Oh!" she exclaimed, with a knowing inflection and amused smile.

"Is there anything wrong?" I asked, answering her smile.

"Oh, no," quickly; "only the girls always make fun of any one who carries a basket now. No working-girl will carry a lunch or basket. It is out of style because it marks the girl at once as a worker. I would like to carry a basket, but I don't dare, because they would make so much fun of me."

The girls sent out for lunch and I asked of them the prices. For five cents they get a good pint of coffee, with sugar and milk if desired. Two cents will buy three slices of buttered bread. Three cents, a sandwich. Many times a number of the girls will put all their money together and buy quite a little feast. A bowl of soup for five cents will give four girls a taste. By clubbing together they are able to buy warm lunch.

At one o'clock we were all at work again. I, having completed sixty-four lids, and the supply being consumed, was put at "moulding in." This is fitting the bottom into the sides of the box and pasting it there. It is rather difficult at first to make all the edges come closely and neatly together, but after a little experience it can be done easily.

On my second day I was put at a table with some new girls and I tried to get them to talk. I was surprised to find that they are very timid about telling their names, where they live or how. I endeavored by every means a woman knows, to get an invitation to visit their homes, but did not succeed.

"How much can girls earn here?" I asked the forewoman.

"I do not know," she said; "they never tell each other, and the bosses keep their time."

"Have you worked here long?" I asked.

"Yes, I have been here eight years, and in that time I have taught my three sisters."

"Is the work profitable?"

"Well, it is steady; but a girl must have many years' experience before she can work fast enough to earn much."

The girls all seem happy. During the day they would make the little building resound with their singing. A song would be begun on the second floor, probably, and each floor would take it up in succession, until all were singing. They were nearly always kind to one another. Their little quarrels did not last long, nor were they very fierce. They were all extremely kind to me, and did all they could to make my work easy and pleasant. I felt quite proud when able to make an entire box.

There were two girls at one table on piecework who had been in a great many box factories and had had a varied experience.

"Girls do not get paid half enough at any work. Box factories are no worse than other places. I do not know anything a girl can do where by hard work she can earn more than $6 a week. A girl cannot dress and pay her boarding on that."

"Where do such girls live?" I asked.

"There are boarding-places on Bleecker and Houston, and around such places, where girls can get a room and meals for $3.50 a week. The room may be only for two, in one bed, or it may have a dozen, according to size. They have no conveniences or comforts, and generally undesirable men board at the same place."

"Why don't they live at these homes that are run to accommodate working women?"

"Oh, those homes are frauds. A girl cannot obtain any more home comforts, and then the restrictions are more than they will endure. A girl who works all day must have some recreation, and she never finds it in homes."

"Have you worked in box factories long?"

FINISHING UP.

"For eleven years, and I can't say that it has ever given me a living. On an average I make $5 a week. I pay out $3.50 for board, and my wash bill at the least is 75 cents. Can any one expect a woman to dress on what remains?"

"What do you get paid for boxes?"

"I get 50 cents a hundred for one-pound candy boxes, and 40 cents a hundred for half-pound boxes."

"What work do you do on a box for that pay?"

"Everything. I get the pasteboard cut in squares the same as you did. I first 'set up' the lids, then I 'mould in' the bottoms. This forms a box. Next I do the 'trimming,' which is putting the gilt edge around the box lid. 'Cover striping' (covering the edge of the lid) is next, and then comes the 'top label,' which finishes the lid entire. Then I paper the box, do the 'bottom labeling,' and then put in two or four laces (lace paper) on the inside as ordered. Thus you see one box passes through my hands eight times before it is finished. I have to work very hard and without ceasing to be able to make two hundred boxes a day, which earns me $1. It is not enough pay. You see I handle two hundred boxes sixteen hundred times for $1. Cheap labor, isn't it?"

One very bright girl, Maggie, who sat opposite me, told a story that made my heart ache.

"This is my second week here," she said, "and, of course, I won't receive any pay until next week, when I expect to receive $1.50 for six days' work. My father was a driver before he got sick. I don't know what is wrong, but the doctor says he will die. Before I left this morning he said my father will die soon. I could hardly work because of it. I am the oldest child, and I have a brother and two sisters younger. I am sixteen, and my brother is twelve. He gets $2 a week for being office-boy at a cigar-box factory."

"Do you have much rent to pay?"

"We have two rooms in a house on Houston Street. They are small and have low ceilings, and there are a great many Chinamen in the same house. We pay for these rooms $14 per month. We do not have much to eat, but then father doesn't mind it because he can't eat. We could not live if father's lodge did not pay our rent."

"Did you ever work before?"

"Yes, I once worked in a carpet factory at Yonkers. I only had to work there one week until I learned, and afterward I made at piecework a dollar a day. When my father got so ill my mother wanted me at home, but now when we see I can earn so little they wish I had remained there."

"Why do you not try something else?" I asked.

"I wanted to, but could find nothing. Father sent me to school until I was fourteen, and so I thought I would learn to be a telegraph operator. I went to a place in Twenty-third Street, where it is taught, but the man said he would not give me a lesson unless I paid fifty dollars in advance. I could not do that."

I then spoke of the Cooper Institute, which I thought every New Yorker knew was for the benefit of just such cases. I was greatly astonished to learn that such a thing as the Cooper Institute was wholly unknown to all the workers around me.

"If my father knew that there was a free school he would send me," said one.

"I would go in the evenings," said another, "if I had known there was such a place."

Again, when some of them were complaining of unjust wages, and some of places where they had been unable to collect the amount due them after working, I spoke of the mission of the Knights of Labor, and the newly organized society for women. They were all surprised to hear that there were any means to aid women in having justice. I moralized somewhat on the use of any such societies unless they entered the heart of these factories.

One girl who worked on the floor below me said they were not allowed to tell what they earned. However, she had been working here five years, and she did not average more than $5 a week. The factory in itself was a totally unfit place for women. The rooms were small and there was no ventilation. In case of fire there was practically no escape.

The work was tiresome, and after I had learned all I could from the rather reticent girls I was anxious to leave. I noticed some rather peculiar things on my trip to and from the factory. I noticed that men were much quicker to offer their places to the working-girls on the cars than they were to offer them to well-dressed women. Another thing quite as noticeable, I had more men try to get up a flirtation with me while I was a box-factory girl than I ever had before. The girls were nice in their manners and as polite as ones reared at home. They never forgot to thank one another for the slightest service, and there was quite a little air of "good form" in many of their actions. I have seen many worse girls in much higher positions than the white slaves of New York.

NELLIE BLY

Wanted—A Few Husbands

Sunday, December 4, 1887

Nellie Bly's Strange Experience at a Noted Matrimonial Agency

---

Some of the Men Were Bashful, Some Were Bold, Some Poor and Some Rich, But All Were "the Favorites of Their Circle"—Queer Letters—Husbands That Cost $100—Quick Proposals—Meeting One's Fate.

The New York woman can hardly have a single desire that cannot be gratified through some bureau or agency of this town. Through them she can get a house, have it furnished, secure new wardrobe, a good form, a clear complexion, the latest shade of hair, and a loan to start the wheels of the concern in good running order. If she desires a husband, and a family warranted to have a marked resemblance, they can be had through the same channels at a nominal price. This husband-getting interested me. I did not want to marry but I was as curious as a little boy with a dynamite cartridge. I wanted to investigate. But how? A woman always hesitates about telling that she wants to marry. She would not confess to the lack of opportunity under any circumstances.

I saved the address of a Matrimonial Bureau which does business now in East Thirty-first street, and late one evening I called. I was ushered into a parlor and was soon talking to a man and woman who professed to introduce congenial spirits. He was a small, nervous man, with light brown hair and blue eyes. His wife was a black-eyed, black-haired, pleasant-looking little woman, with persuasive conversational abilities that her husband fully recognized. I told them I had heard of the agency and was anxious to partake of the bliss of making fires and sewing on buttons. I wanted to try through them to give some lonely man a chance to find his ideal. Knowing absolutely nothing of the running of the concern, I made inquiries very carefully.

"You find plenty of people anxious to marry, I suppose?"

"Oh, yes. We have between five and seven thousand names on our books of matrimonial candidates."

"Not all in New York?"

"The majority live here, although our list covers the greater part of the United States. Who are the people? Well, we have one minister, several doctors and medical students, and all classes of business men down to the laborer. We have not the same variety among the women. They are mostly those who need a home or who are many days past a desirable marrying age. I should think that you would have plenty of proposals and would not need our assistance," he concluded, flatteringly.

"One tires of meeting friends always in the way indorsed by society," I answered, "and it seems possible that, by stepping aside from the ordinary way, I may meet some congenial one that I could never have known otherwise."

He rubbed his hands, smiled and showed me the mammoth album containing photographs of gentlemen. (I was not permitted to see the women.) Such a collection! The Rogues' Gallery is hardly more varied or interesting. By the side of a clerical-looking man, with quiet, hypocritical face, came an ancient Santa Claus, who looked as if, after all his years, he ought to know better. It was all very interesting, and I was longing to take the album away as a souvenir. It may be that these photographs were not all of would-be Benedicts, for I noticed over the mantel a large card announcing that orders would be taken there for photographs.

The woman wanted me to fill out a descriptive blank. I was at that moment in a very tight place. I dared not give my own address, lest they find out that I belonged to a newspaper, and I had no other. I said I was living with an aunt and that she was so conventional that if she ever heard of me doing such a thing she would do all sorts of harm to me. But I wanted a copy of the descriptive blank and had to invent something to get permission to take the blank home. Through a great many imaginary stories I got it and filled it out the next day. Here it is as I filled it up:

THE CATALOGUE OF VIRTUES.

Lady's Description Blank No. 17,244
Registered in Book —, page —.

When you have filled out this description blank plainly write your full address on a separate piece of paper; pin both together and return to us.

Your name will be given in confidence and no person whatever can obtain it from us. All others will know and address you (in our care) by a number only.

For $5 you are entitled to our services until you become engaged (or for $3 for three months) in assisting you to make selections from the description blanks and from the advertisements that may appear, also to the forwarding of post-paid letters and the insertion of a forty-word advertisement during the time for which you engage our services.

1. What is your age? Eighteen.
2. What is your weight? Varies; 120 pounds in sealskin sacque.
3. What is your height? Five foot five inches, including French heels.
4. What is your complexion? Brunette.
5. What is your nationality? American.
6. What is your occupation? Killing time.
7. What is your religion? Very liberal.
8. What is your amount of real and personal property? (?)
9. What is your yearly income? $2,000.
10. What amount do you expect to inherit? $200,000 on the death of my grand-parents.
11. Have you good health? Perfect.
12. Were you ever married? Left a widow two months after my marriage.
13. If so, how many children have you? None.
14. What are age and sex of children? —
15. What are your views and habits in regard to the use of tobacco and alcoholic drinks? Liberal, if not used to excess.
16. Are you accomplished in vocal or instrumental music? Yes, in both.
17. In what State or Territory do you reside? New York, at present; cosmopolitan.
18. Will you answer in some way all courteous letters we may forward to you from our patrons whom we believe to be sincere? With pleasure.
19. Between what ages must your correspondents be? Twenty-three and eighty years.
20. Do you object to one who has been married? No.
21. Do you object if your correspondent has one child? No.
22. Do you object if your correspondent has more than one child? No.
23. State what religion you prefer. Have no preference.
24. State what nationality you prefer. Have no preference.

Your photograph is a very valuable addition to the description, and will be held by us subject to such instructions as you send with it, and promptly returned when requested. In selecting correspondents from our lists, our patrons almost always prefer those of whom a photograph and the most complete description may be seen.

If you give good references it enables us to introduce you more promptly and often to a better class of our patrons. Inquiries are never addressed to your references over our own signature, or in a manner to give them an intimation of your business with us.

Any further description you may desire to give of yourself or correspondent must be written concisely and plainly, without your name or address, upon one side only of a sheet of paper containing no other matter. Names of references should be written on still another sheet of paper.

THE PRICE OF A HUSBAND.

After I had filled out the blank and paid my fee I was requested to sign a check for the amount I would pay on the day I married. Then came the hitch. They wanted my address so as to insure them the money and I could not give it. I pleaded my aunt's displeasure, my disinheritance by my grandparents and at last said I would rather not come than have to give it. They had the $5, and they suggested that I try the agency for ten days and if, at the end of that time, I did not have enough confidence in them to give my address, we would arrange some other way. I was glad to get off so easily, so I signed the check with my assumed name. Here is the check:

$100. NEW YORK, Nov. 11, 1887.

When I marry, or promise to marry a man whose acquaintance I have formed through the influence of, or to whom I have been in any manner introduced by .... either through the columns of ...., or otherwise, I promise to pay .... or order on demand, for value received, in above services rendered, the full sum of $100.

Signed, Mrs. JEAN HASTING THOMPSON.

"How do you get so many people?" I asked, for almost every time I went there I found the three-story house filled and the several clerks always kept busy.

"We advertise for many different things, and when we get the replies we send them our matrimonial paper. Then we have parties who send us names and addresses."

ANSWERS TO PERSONALS.

About the same time a young friend who had more recklessness than discretion answered a "personal," and received the following reply from the agent I was patronizing:

Miss——:

The advertisement which you answered by addressing Burnette, Box 20 *Journal*, uptown, we inserted for one of our patrons with whom we are personally acquainted. As you gave so brief a description of yourself, it is impossible for us to tell whether our client would be suited with your description or not.

If you will call we will give you a full description of him. If you cannot do this and will fill out and return to use inclosed description blank we can then give you more definite information, and if agreeable a personal introduction at our rooms. Respectfully,

H.B. WELLMAN (BARNARD).

This letter, if presented within two weeks from date, will entitle you to an introduction to the gentleman described. If you accept this invitation appoint your own time in the evening or Sunday.

I next bought a box at a downtown office where I could receive my letters. Shortly afterwards I got a little yellow envelope and in it was this strange missive:

A. NO.1,986.

MISS GYPSY HASTINGS: You are invited to be present at your rooms promptly at 8 o'clock P.M. Friday, NOV. 25, 1887. Hoping at that time to make you acquainted with an agreeable gentleman, we are, respectfully,

H.B. WELLMAN.

NOTE—If you desire to be introduced by any other name than the one written above, plainly write it here...

Detach the part of this sheet marked B and return to us in inclosed envelope by return mail. If you accept the invitation, sign and date the printed form B; if you decline the invitation, or if you cannot be present at the time stated, and desire us to endeavor to make arrangements at some other time, state the time and write full particulars on the back of sheet marked B.

On arrival ring the bell nearest our name-plate at the door. You will be shown to a private reception room. Then present the portion of this letter marked A to the one who has admitted you, and you will be notified when the person arrives who is to meet you.

Should the interview continue longer than one hour after the time appointed, an additional charge will be made.

B. NO. 1,986.

It is optional with our patrons to accept or decline these invitations, but if accepted and an unforeseen emergency should prevent your coming, you will notify us at once by telegraph or messenger. The failure to notify us in this manner subjects you to a fine of 50 cents, which must be paid before you can receive another introduction.

.................1887.

MR. H.B. WELLMAN: I will on the terms above stated accept your invitation to be present at your reception rooms at 8 o'clock P.M. on Friday, NOV. 25, 1887.

GYPSY HASTINGS.

THE TALKING CANDIDATE.

It was raining that evening when I started out to meet a would-be husband. Husband-hunting did not appear a very congenial pursuit, as I waded through the mud to a Broadway car that stopped half a block above where I signaled it. Once at the house the agent took me into a small room and lectured me on the good qualities of the man.

"He is not a dude, but he is a good man and would make a first-class husband. He is President of two mining companies and is very rich and aristocratic, so you'll have to be nice. Come now."

With eager expectancy I followed on tip-toe, and French heels, to meet the paragon of perfection. I stopped at the door, took a long breath and put to death an amused chuckle, as the agent rapped gently with his knuckles. There was no response, but the agent went right in and I followed. He mumbled something meant for an introduction, and a great, long figure arose from the sofa at the end of the room. The door closed and I was left alone with him.

He was easily six feet two, loosely built. His clothes, while comfortable, would never make him a rival of the great Berry Wall. He had brown hair, side whiskers and mustache. His movements, except of the tongue, were slow and heavy. He was fully forty-two years old.

"I did not hear your name," I said, after a long pause.

"I was introduced as Mr. Hoage, but my name is Calvin A. Poage. I am President of two mining companies. Our office is 61 Broadway, and I love at the Hotel Barrett."

AN INTERESTING BIOGRAPHY.

Mr. Poage then handed me two certificates in proof of what he had said. They read that they were to "certify that H.C. Gilbert had bought 100 shares in the ——— Mining Company," and were signed H.C. Gilbert, Secretary, and C.A. Poage, President. "I was born in Virginia," he continued, "and my father was a teacher. When I was yet a child he removed to Missouri. He was a very smart man, and master of thirty different musical instruments. I am master of very nearly as many. I was a prodigy when a child. People used to come from miles around to see me. When I was eight years old I could speak and write Latin, and when I was ten I wrote Greek. At eighteen I graduated from Princeton. Yes, I was always wonderfully smart," with a self-satisfied air. "I have gotten all the glory I want in this life, and now I am working for money. I am an eloquent orator, and was owner and editor of a paper called the *Occident*, in San Francisco, for years. I am well known as a writer, and people urge me to sell them letters."

"How lovely to be a writer," I breathed rapturously, and I kicked the table to remind me that a story depended on my self-control. "What do you write for, these horrid daily papers or the dear, delightful magazines?"

"I write for the *Century* and a number of others. I'm very famous as a writer, as well as a lecturer, and if I wanted to devote myself to literature I could make lots of money," with pride.

"Oh, really! How lovely!" I exclaimed, with an accent of wonderment, and not wholly assumed. "How silly I am! I always thought writers got very little money."

"Oh, no," pompously; "there is John Howard, Jr.—he is now senior—he got $25,000 a year from one paper."

It was again necessary for me to exercise my self-control. The assumed knowledge of one he did not know even by his correct name was too much.

"Henry George and I are bosom friends. When he was unknown, out in California, his paper and mine got up the great land scheme. I helped him organize the Anti-Poverty Society, and my name is No. 18 on the list. I am a lion in society and that's why I've left it for this. The young ladies all make such a favorite of me that it bores me."

HIS FAMOUS FRIENDS.

"Do you know Talmadge? Well, he and I are like brothers. When he came to San Francisco his first visit was a complete failure. I took him up and my paper made his success. I am the distinguished literary man he speaks of in his lecture as going with him through Chinatown. I went over to his church one Sunday after I came East. I did not intend to trouble him when the sermon was over but as I started out he called to me: 'Come here, California,' and began climbing over the pews and everything to me."

The minutes dragged into hours and yet he talked. I quit listening to him at last and began to think of other things. When my thoughts returned to earth he was still talking. I was weary and faint from the siege, so I suggested, with quivering lips and a trembling voice, that it was time for me to go home.

"Can't I see you again?" he asked.

"Not so long as oatmeal is cheap and Rough on Suicides only 15 cents a box," I began to mentally swear. Then aloud. "Well, I couldn't see you here again, and Aunt is so queer." That poor aunt!

"What church does your aunt attend?"

"Methodist," I replied, carelessly.

"Well, you tell me her minister and I will get him to introduce me. I know she will be glad to meet me. Everybody is."

"Oh!" I exclaimed, realizing that I was in deep water. I must do something to save myself. "You don't know my aunt's minister. He believes in mission work, and prayers, and sewing and asking blessings over chicken dinners. Indeed he's dreadful," and I gave a little shudder at my narrow escape and the eloquent picture.

He then said that he often met women on the cars, in art galleries, at church fairs and in music stores. I disclaimed all knowledge of how to flirt, and added that even if I did my aunt would never recognize such a man. He left me on the corner without lifting his hat, and so ended my first introduction to a would-be husband. I got on a car, rode several blocks, got off, and made a complete circuit in this way, so that if any one were following me I should know it.

HARD TO SUIT.

On the plea of wanting to make a selection, I got the description book one day and read of its applicants. Most of the men were decidedly original in spelling and grammar. Most of those belonging to New York were commonplace and monotonous, while those from the West possessed at least an amusing sparkle. One man wrote opposite to the questions as to having children or if he objected to a widow with children. "Know;" another, "Now." Very few objected to a widow or to one child, but almost every one objected to more than one child. Several said that if the child was a boy they would not object. One man wrote that he wanted a wife who had money enough to start a drug store. Another wrote: "I am an athlete, a dead shot, am handsome and have a magnificent figure. The girl must be my equal in this." Evidently one man had a better taste in religious matters, for he wrote: "My wife must have a neat, trim figure and lots of vim. She must not expect to turn the house into a Y.M.C.A. hall or a 'Clergyman's Rest.'"

HE WAS ALL FOR LOVE.

The next candidate was a slim little man with black hair and mustache. He looked like an undertaker in costume. He wore a double-breasted black coat, highly polished shoes, a silk hat, light overcoat and carried a large-headed cane. The agent first told me that he did not know much about this man and that I would have to watch out for myself. I told him I felt quite capable of doing that. Mr. Holmes, Miss Hastings, and I was left with him. He sat at the opposite side of the room and appeared quite bashful and nervous.

"Do you think you would always love your husband, Miss Hastings?" he asked bashfully.

I had some doubts on the subject, but I answered confidently in the affirmative. He smiled a bashful smile and gave his chair a hitch.

"Would you marry for love, Miss Hastings, regardless of what the man was?" he queried plaintively.

Again I replied heartily in the affirmative, and he smiled and gave his chair another hitch.

"Do you admire dark men, Miss Hastings?" I looked at his brunette complexion, and, with a soul-stirring sidelong glance, I breathed the affirmative. Again he smiled and gave his chair a hitch.

GOOD AT QUESTIONS.

He was quite an adept at asking questions, and at each favorable reply the chair was slightly moved until I began to see that it was gradually making its way across the room to where I sat. To break the monotony I asked him of those he had met before me.

"I was not much taken with them," he said. "The last one I saw was about forty-five years old, and she was dreadful. She talked all the time about dudes, and I felt offended." I laughed quite heartily, for I wondered if he thought himself a dude. He told me then how much I pleased him, and asked me to meet him again. He got the matrimonial paper and showed me this advertisement of himself:

> 1558. A gentleman of thirty, with $60,000, a fine position, a good character, good health, reputation and habits, wishes the acquaintance of ladies under twenty-eight, highly educated and of unblemished character and social rank. Money no object.

I promised to write to him, so we exchanged addresses. His was B.W. Holmes, P.O. Box 3, 441, city. Before the hour was over his chair, quite strangely, had crossed the room by itself and was close to mine. This made me think of home, so I said "aunt" did not allow me out late and I must go.

In a few days I received quite a thrilling letter from him. It has not yet been answered.

HER THIRD CANDIDATE.

My next candidate was quite devoid of sentiment. When I arrived at the house the clerk told me all the reception rooms were full and so she put me into a little side closet, where there was one table, a chair and an oil lamp. I peeped through the door and saw a young woman, apparently a servant, taken into another room. This was the only time I ever saw any one, although the house was always filled. At last the agent called me and I was brought face to face with a tall, fair-complexioned, sharp-featured man. He was not badly dressed and his manners were short and decided.

"I haven't the least idea of marrying," he said almost instantly, as if he feared I would fall into his arms. "I only come here for the fun of the thing. What do you come for?"

Instantly I thought maybe he was one of the detectives set to find out my purpose, so I determined to balk him. Nothing could induce me to speak ill of the place.

"Of course, people cannot meet for good purposes here. Any one can have friends enough without coming here for more."

I talked softly of fate guiding our footsteps and leading us to our alter egos, and made my eyes look a sentiment my heart was far from feeling.

"Well, my name is J.E. Cassett. I live at No. 152 Lexington avenue and have an insurance agency at No. 155 Broadway. I was born in Cincinnati, O. My people are the first in the place and they just run the town. When I came here I did not know any one, so I thought I would try this place. I think it is a money-making scheme."

"Have you met many here?"

"No, I did the most of it through corresponding, but the letters all slopped over with one idea, and that was marriage. Every one was crazy to marry. I was not, so I quit it."

"Did you meet any of your correspondents?"

"Yes, I met one. She lived in Philadelphia, in a nice three-story brown front. I sent my card up to her, and when she came down she said I must let her folks think that I met her at Asbury Park last summer. She wanted to be married by a minister. I think the most of the people who come here are matured and long past the day of sentiment. It is the matter of money or a home with them."

HE USED TO BE ONE OF THE BOYS.

My next candidate for matrimony was a little fellow with black mustache and eyes and head of gray hair, of which he was quite proud. This time I was in a little hall room with a sofa, a chair, a stand and a badly smelling oil lamp. The little fellow put his light cape overcoat across the chair and sat down on it. He talked a great deal about himself. He said he was quite a noted singer and socially was in the best circles. He longed to find a wife.

"Lately I think of nothing but marriage," he said. "I used to be one of the boys, but now I want to settle down. I want a wife who will be satisfied to love me and me alone."

"As if your wife would ever wish to love another!" I sighed.

"I did not like any of the ladies I met here before," he chirruped sweetly, "but I should like to meet you again. My assumed name is Carl W. Vincent, and I receive all my letters care of Ditson & Co., 867 Broadway.

If you would only let me know what evening I could meet you I would be so happy."

I told Carl he had better meet more women at the agency before he decided on one. I encouraged him in this laudable search for a wife, but I refused my personal aid. One similarity in all the candidates' stories impressed me. With one exception they belonged to the best of families, moved in the highest society and were the favorites of their circles.

HE WANTED A HOUSEKEEPER.

One of the funniest candidates was a man who evidently thought to get a housekeeper for nothing by marrying her. His first questions were: Can you cook and sweep well; have you a good temper; can you make beds nicely; are you a good washer and ironer; will you make the fires and carry the coal, and is your health perfect? Answered in the affirmative, he said: "If you can give me proof of all this I will marry you."

One of the most sensible men I met there was a young Englishman. Barring his lisp, he was nice.

"I want a wife who loves her home and who is of a cheerful disposition. I do not care if she has money or not. I would not marry a woman for money. I went to see a young lady and she asked me whether I would get up and make the fires. 'What's the use of living if one has to make fires?' I replied. So she said she would never marry a man who would not promise to do that. I don't care whether a woman can work or not, but I must have a sensible, amiable, neat, happy wife. I do not know a girl among my acquaintances that will answer my ideal, so I sought this agent's aid to help me find one."

AN OLD WIDOWER.

Among the other candidates was a Mr. Williams, who has a drug store in Harlem. He has been a widower for thirteen years and has a daughter fifteen years old. He was rather timid.

"You are so good-natured and happy," he said, looking admiringly at me, while I laughed at some of his remarks. "I wouldn't be afraid of you. It would not take me long to ask you to marry me. I suppose you think I am old enough to be your grandfather?"

"No, oh no," I replied with a smile. I did not want to discourage him.

"You have such a way about you. I would not be timid if I knew you long."

I laughed at the doubtful compliment and he flushed with pleasure.

"I have a nice home and a greenhouse, and to-day I bought a $300 hot soda fountain. Do you like soda? Wouldn't you like to be a druggist or a druggist's wife?"

I thought he was getting along too rapidly for his own good, so I changed the conversation.

"Tell me of some of the women you have met here," I said.

"With one exception they were perfectly horrible."

"How horrible?"

"Every way; dress, appearance, manners and so anxious to marry. I never saw one a second time."

"You must be hard to please," I suggested with a little pout.

"Oh, no. Really now, don't think that. If I had only met some one like you"—

But I told him my aunt would miss me and left him, and that ended my experiences in a matrimonial agency. I am still in search of a husband and Mr. Wellman has my $5.

NELLIE BLY

Learning Ballet Dancing

Sunday, December 18, 1887

Nellie Bly in Short Gauze Skirts Kicks at a Mark

How it Feels to Go About in an Abbreviated Costume—Making Her Outfit—Holding on a Bar to Practise—Why It Is Healthful—Comments of the Old Professor—It Seems Easy, but Requires Much Hard Work.

I have been learning to be a ballet dancer. I have always had an almost manlike love for the ballet, and when I go to spectacular plays and to the opera I try to get close to the bald-headed row. Breathless with admiration I have watched the ballet twirl on its toes and spring into picturesque attitudes, the very poetry of motion.

It seemed so lovely that I longed to learn the art. Prof. Mamert Bibeyran, of No. 1 Irving Place, advertised for pupils, and I ascertained that for two years he had conducted the ballet of the American Opera Company and that the last success of the Casino ballet was the result of his instructions. I decided that he should teach me what I wanted to learn.

I felt quite brave until I entered the dance hall. Pausing at the entrance I saw at the further end of the hall a young girl in short gauze skirts. She was holding on a bar with one hand and her foot was swinging out into space to the time of a violin in the hands of her instructor. It looked very comical to see her foot go out first front, then to the side and then back, slowly and regularly, while the rest of her body was in perfect repose. She saw me and warned the professor of my presence.

"I want to learn ballet dancing," I said, by way of introduction, when he came up to me. "How much do you charge?"

"Are you a professional?" he asked. "Do you want to learn for the stage?"

"Well, I am not on the stage at present," I replied, evasively. "I want to learn ballet dancing, and if I like it I may go on the stage."

"Yes," he said, with an encouraging smile. "It is a great art, and requires time and patience to learn. My terms are $20 a month for a lesson of one hour daily."

"Very well. I am anxious to begin. What sort of a costume must I get?"

"Come, this young lady will tell you," and he led me to his pupil in short skirts. She was a pretty French girl, with no knowledge of English as it is spoken. She gave me her hand in greeting in a very pretty manner. Her eyes were sparkling, and her cheeks were pink from the exercise. She was well worth looking at.

"Anything will do to practise in," she said. "I bought crinoline," holding up the edge of her dainty little skirt. "It takes twelve yards for the skirt, and this only cost me seven cents a yard. Three yards of velvet or plush is plenty for your bodice, and then you must have ballet slippers made."

After receiving a few more suggestions about my costume, I gave an assumed name and address, shook hands with my new acquaintances and started out on a buying expedition. I first went to a stage costumer, and as she wanted $10 for an outfit, I concluded to make my own. Accordingly I bought twelve yards of black crinoline and decided to make the bodice of an old evening dress do for the ballet. "How much will a pair of ballet slippers cost me?" I asked a man who makes only theatrical shoes.

"It all depends on the material," he said. "I can make you a satin pair that will last you a long time if you care for them, for $1.59." So he measured my foot and I went away feeling sorry ballet suits were no more popular, they are so cheap.

That evening I tried to imagine myself a lonely ballet girl such as I had read of in thrilling romances, sitting in her bare attic room, making her stage costume of gauze and spangles, while the tears coursed down her pallid cheeks. I sat on the floor while I divided my black crinoline into three equal parts. Then I cut them, lengthwise, three different sizes. The longest was a little shorter than an ultra fashionable bathing suit and the third and shortest was—well, it was pretty short.

At 3 o'clock the following day I was at the hall. The Professor showed me the dressing-room and I was left alone. That first dressing was funny! I put on the tights and my black crinoline skirts. I never realized until that moment how short they were and how extremely stiff. My ballet slip-

pers were awaiting my arrival and they were the prettiest little one and a half satin slippers I ever saw. I grew so proud of them I began to feel glad my skirts were quite short enough to show them to advantage.

Dressed at last in a ballet costume I looked at myself and marvelled at the change. There is everything in dress after all. I had entered a quiet, staid-looking spinster, and presto! I now looked like a sixteen-year-old girl and quite flippant and pert. I did not feel as I looked, however. All at once I grew painfully modest. It is not so bad to wear a bathing-suit when everybody else around has one on, but when everybody is in full dress one would feel awfully short in a bathing costume. That was my position. I felt as if I had forgotten and gone to a full-dress reception in a bathing suit.

For an instant I was inclined to put on my street dress, and pleading sudden indisposition, take my leave, but I looked so healthy and there was no powder-puff around, so I was afraid the statement would not bear out. Several times I got up and started and my heart failed. I went back again and sat down. I pulled at my skirts, but they would not lengthen. I began to fear the Professor would soon think I had fainted or committed suicide. "It's a go," I said mentally, and I opened the door and closed it rather quickly behind me, lest I should grow faint-hearted and go back in. The Professor was sitting in the hall playing dreamily on the violin. When he heard the door close he looked up and said:

"Ah!"

That "ah" was meant kindly, but it reduced all my courage to pitiful shakes. I caught my crinoline skirts in and vainly tried to increase their length by bending. The Professor smiled.

"Oh, this is your first appearance in ballet skirts, I see. Never mind, you'll get used to them in a little while," he said kindly. I did. Before my lesson was finished I was sorry to exchange my short, airy costume for the heavy garments fashion says we must carry.

"And now we will begin," said Prof. Bibeyran. "Catch hold of the bar with your right hand." The bar is a long pole fastened firmly to the wall. It is for beginners to support themselves on until they learn to balance on one foot.

"Now, first position," he said, taking hold of the bar and facing me.

"You put heel to heel, with the toes in a perfectly straight line. When I say, 'Bend,' you raise the heels slightly, at the same time bending at the knees. When I say 'Rise,' you pose the heel which is touching them on the floor again, and straighten the knee. You do this movement eight times. Now begin."

I clutched the bar tightly and put my heels together, my feet in a straight line north and south. "Bend," said the Professor. I bent my knees slowly, going out in the direction of my feet. "Rise," and I go to my first pose. "Bend," continued the Professor. "There, do not bend with more weight on the right knee. Keep firm, and bend with your weight full in the centre. Rise." I felt relieved to get back.

"Bend," he called again. "Hold up your head. Never look at your feet; it is awkward. Keep a bold front, the back perfectly straight and stiff; the movement all at the knees, please, the weight on the centre. Now rise, bend, rise. All right; turn."

"Why turn?" I asked.

"Because one side must have the same ease and proficiency as the other. If you learn exercises on the piano with the right hand only you could not play equally well with the left. Just so with dancing. If you would not learn one side as well as the other, I feel you would be a one-sided dancer. Now, again, this time raise the arm that is not engaged with the bar."

I put my right arm up with a sudden movement, very emphatic and according to my master, very ungraceful.

"Keep the little finger straight and the other three lightly closed. Rest the thumb on the index finger—so. It gives the hand a small appearance from the front. Never turn your hand flatly to your audience, but always give a side view. Now, raise the arm out from the body, curved and then slowly open it in a straight line with the shoulder. Keep the elbow turned back—it looks badly in front and will show the bones when there are any. Slender girls must always be more graceful than plump ones, because there is fear of showing ugly angles."

At first it seemed a still, unnatural position, but I persevered.

"When you close," he continued, "bring the arm gracefully down, with the elbow well out from the body. You want to always show the lines of the waist, and you can't do it with the elbows tight to the ribs."

THE TERRIBLE TOE EXERCISE.

My cheeks were burning and I felt as if I had taken a new lease on health and life by the time I had completed my first lesson. I have tried swimming, dancing, driving, riding, fencing, swinging clubs and the gymnasium, but none of them ever equalled the perfect and exhilarating exercise I got during my ten days learning to be a ballet dancer. I felt quite eager for my second lesson, and began to seriously contemplate exchanging literary work for the ballet. I kicked off my long skirts and donned my short ones with much pleasure.

"Do you only have professional people as pupils?" I asked of my ballet master.

"Oh, no," he replied. "I teach deportment and society dancing as well. I have some pupils, society people, who are anxious to carry themselves well, and the best way to obtain it is to study deportment or the ballet. It is not only the key to all dances, but the key to grace and ease. I call this calisthenics instead of ballet dancing."

"Well, they tell me that ballet dancing impairs the health," I said.

"Ridiculous, my dear child. It gives force to the nerves and muscles and develops the body. It throws the head up, the shoulders and arms back and turns the feet out. This is the only exercise which develops all parts of the body. In Boston I have had doctors bring women whose health was impaired to me for care. Now, after our little lecture, we will go to work."

"We will commence at first position, the same as you learned yesterday."

I found my master was going to make me perfect in every exercise before he allowed me to pass it. This would use up all my lessons and I would have seen very little of what's to learn, so I urged that he put me forward.

"This is an art, and if you do not learn the first well, you cannot learn the rest."

"But I want to see what it is like. Rush me on and give me an impression of what it is."

"My dear child, I am not all-powerful. I cannot pass my hands over your head and make you a ballet dancer. How can you take an attitude when you can't balance on one foot, or how can you pirouette when you have not learned to stand on your toe?"

"Take first position." I did, heel to heel. "Slide a point in line with your shoulder." This was done by raising the heel and sliding the foot away from its mate, leaving a distance of fifteen inches between them. "Pose the heel." I let my heel rest on the floor. "Now bend and rise without lifting the heels from the floor and then close front, ankle with ankle, which leaves you in third position."

This was done repeatedly until my master was partially satisfied. Then he told me to stay in third position and bend and rise, lifting the heels. Ankle touched ankle, and I needed the aid of the bar to keep my balance. Fifth position was more awkward still. The feet had to be closed tightly, with heel touching toe, and so without moving I had to bend and rise. It was with difficulty I did it at first, but after a few days' practice I was surprised at my own suppleness.

AN AERIAL KICK.

"Now make very straight point," said my professor briskly.

"What is straight point?" I asked.

"It is to slide along the floor, curving the foot and keeping the toe on the floor, the knee very straight and stiff, allowing movement only to the hip and keeping the rest of the body as firm as a statue. Pose your arms nicely, now batements."

"What does batements mean?" I asked helplessly, standing all the while with my toe posed on the floor.

"It means to do this," and the professor gave a sudden kick way up in the air.

"Oh!" I said; "batements means to kick. All right, here goes."

"No, no; not kick," interposed the master quickly. "That is not elegant; mules kick. Now do this in good time—one, make a point; two, batements; three, down; four, close the front. Well, repeat."

Did I kick? Well, it was the funniest exercise of the lot. I felt a little diffident at first and the kick was very low.

"Batement in line with the nose," said the master. "Longer, longer."

He put out his hand on a level with my chin, I kicked did not touch him. He urged me to kick higher. I did, and my foot touched his hand. He raised his hand to a level with my eyes and I launched a kick that surprised the gentle master and myself. You see, I was so eager to kick that I forgot all about my balance. Well, I did not fall, but I cut one of the most laughable capers one ever saw. Next I had to kick out at the side, always retaining an immovable front position. It was easier than the front kick. The back kick was the most difficult of all.

"The knee must be kept stiff during all the movements at the body. Strike out the foot as if you want to touch the crown of your head. Bravo." I never knew before how much pleasure there was in a kick and I fear had I continued longer I should have become a chronic kicker.

Soon after this I was given a most peculiar exercise. It began by slowly sliding the foot in a half circle to the front, to the side and to the back. The speed was increased until after awhile I was standing on one foot and the other was flying around in a circle like a top. Again I was told to slide a very large circle and let the toe but touch the floor in the rear.

"Raise your foot, curve the knee, bend the body at the waist and turn the face to the raised hand. That is attitude." I did not bend exactly to please him, so he came, and taking hold of my shoulder and toe, tried to make them meet; at least it felt so to me. Afterward I could assume the position more easily. While yet in attitude he called:

"Straighten the knee and arm. Point the toe. Support the leg high. That is arabesque. Close."

Again and again I repeated this, and not for a moment did I feel tired or lose interest. I must confess, though, that the following day I felt as if my bed had been too short. I was very stiff until I began to exercise and then it all left me.

In the next exercise I was told to stand on one foot and raise the other foot, resting the heel on the ankle. Then I had to make a kick with the knee straight. This was done higher and higher, each time with greater rapidity, to develop the muscles and make them firm but elastic. A few more exercises, which are too tedious to tell of, and I had, against my master's advice, who wanted to make me perfect, finished "on the bar."

I was now placed in the centre of the floor without any support, and to the music of the violin I had to move my arms in rotation, first with an outside and then with an inside curve. This was done with my feet in first position, then in second, and so on. If you want to know how difficult it is, place your feet lightly heel to toe and make curves above your head and at either side and in front. It is no child's play. This rotation of the arms is made with the feet in all the different positions in order that one may be sure of her balance. Then all the exercises were gone over again, the only difference, which is all the difference in the world, being that I had no support, but must balance myself or fall. Attitude and arabesque are done. If everybody studied ballet dancing for a few lessons the fine work of the dancers on the stage would be more appreciated. It looks very easy from the front to see the graceful girls fall

A DIFFICULT POSTURE.

into those lovely positions, but it takes years of practice, and hard work at that, to be able to do so.

I began the preparation for the pirouette by standing on the toe of one foot. The heel must not touch the floor. The pirouette, attitude and arabesque are the most difficult things I attempted. It would be folly for me to insinuate that I learned them. It takes years to become an artist of the ballet, and I could not do it in ten lessons. What I attempted was done imperfectly, and much against the wishes of Prof. Bibeyran, but my only desire was to get an insight into the work done by the ballet.

The first thing to strive for in ballet dancing is firmness and a good balance. Another exercise is to take one position, bend, jump with both feet off the floor, and close in a different position. While doing these exercises the master plays the violin, and the dancers count to keep time, changing rapidly from one position to another. But to attempt to tell all about the ballet dancing would take a volume. I know that is a grand exercise, and that while I was learning everyone remarked my healthier appearance.

NELLIE BLY

IN QUAINT OLD ECONOMY

SUNDAY, JANUARY 8, 1888

THERE DWELLS A SECT WITH MORE MILLIONS THAN MEMBERS

Of the Thousand Who Followed George Rapp to America in 1805 Eighteen Now Remain—They Think the World Will End Before the Last of Them Dies—Quiet and Simple Life in a Pennsylvania Village.

Economy is the quaintest village in the United States. It is situated on the Fort Wayne Railroad, eighteen miles below Pittsburgh, yet it is as unlike an American town as if it belonged to another part of the globe. Neither the bustle of the nearby city nor the railroad and steamboat lines ever penetrate the heart of the sleepy town. It is the home of the Economites, a society founded by George Rapp in Germany many, many years ago. What all their beliefs were is more than any outsider can ever tell. Their chief aim was to live as the earliest Christians did, as portrayed in the writings of the apostles. Driven from Germany by religious persecution, they emigrated to America in 1805 and settled in Pennsylvania.

They bought land and built a village which they called Harmony. They dubbed themselves Harmonites, and gave what earthly goods they possessed to their founder and leader, George Rapp, who was their father, banker, adviser and preacher.

At first the members married with the understanding that they were only to live together for a few months every seven years. After several had broken this law, and among them Rapp's own son John, George Rapp decided that it would be more in conformity with the teachings of the disciples to live a life of celibacy. Several of the members who had wives and sweethearts rebelled against this. They were all formally ordered to appear before their leader, where they were told to give up their love and their wives or to renounce the society. Those who were true to Rapp moved with him to Indiana, where another Harmony was founded. Disease attacked the new village and reduced the number of its inhabitants so greatly that the remaining ones fled back to Pennsylvania. In 1825 they bought 2,500 acres of land in a most beautiful valley near Pittsburgh. Here they settled and here those of them who are still alive, live to-day. The misfortunes that befell them in the two Harmony settlements caused them to change the name. They called their new home Economy and themselves Economites. The members who deserted the Harmonites either died out or became as other citizens of the globe. Many of their descendants are well-known people in and around Allegheny City.

THE CHURCH OF THE ECONOMITES.

THE EIGHTEEN WHO SURVIVE.

About one thousand members first settled in Economy, but as their number was never increased by birth or by adoption, and as death occasionally invaded their homes, there remain at the present time not more than eighteen members, the youngest of whom is sixty-two years old. When they first took vows of celibacy they believed that the world was nearing its end, and so they lived simple lives, preparing for the mysterious hereafter. George Rapp, just before he died, told the others the world would surely end before the last member died. They believe it.

On entering the village one sees plain houses, wide, well-kept streets, lined on either side with large shade trees and chickens—nothing else. It is a most unusual sight to see any people on the streets. The thrifty appearance alone prevents a visitor from thinking it a deserted village or imagining that the inhabitants were awaiting the Prince's arrival to awake them from a century-long sleep. The houses are all alike. They are all built with the gable end towards the street and cannot be entered except through the yards. There are no front stoops to fall over in Economy. Grapevines are trained to cover the street side of all the houses, but they are pruned so as not to interfere with the light of the windows. I imagine it would be pleasant to sit at one of those windows during grape seasons.

The men are housekeepers, and so are the women. They never mingle, not even at work. The dress of one is the dress of all. Everything is on an equality. The men wear blue broadcloth long-tailed coats, wide trousers and broad-brimmed black hats. On holidays the broadcloth is exchanged for blue silk attire. The women wear straight, full skirts, gathered on a plain waist of blue flannel, gingham or silk. Their heads, indoor and out, are always picturesquely attired in bright blue silken Normandy caps.

The oldest citizens of this part of Pennsylvania still remember and speak of the wonderful broadcloths, flannels, blankets, Economy whiskey and wine they obtained from the Economites. The factories are all silent and deserted now, and the members have long since grown too feeble for hard labor. It was in Economy that silk culture and manufacture on a large scale were first begun in the United States.

THE SIMPLE LIFE THEY LEAD.

Everything in Economy is run by rule and regulation much as at boarding-school. At 5 o'clock in the morning the bell on the one church rings and every one in the village rises. At 6 o'clock every dweller sits down to breakfast and what is eaten in one house is eaten in all. There is a day for "milk soup" and one for "wine soup" and for every other dish peculiar to the place. The bell rings again at 7 o'clock for all to go to work; at 9 it brings them back to lunch, at 12 to dinner, at 3 to lunch again, at 6 to supper, and at 9 it rings for everyone to put out his light and go to bed. No member ever rebels or disobeys.

There is a wine cellar in Economy famous for its old liquors, but it is never sold except to invalids. None of the Economites drink water, and their employees are given wine and cider. Visitors are all cordially helped to wine and cake, no matter how short their call.

HOW THEY GET THEIR NEWS.

The only paper published in Economy is a novel one on wheels. It is the side of the milk wagon which carries to each dweller, as well as the milk, the work to be done. "The apples will be gathered to-morrow," "The cherries will be gathered to-morrow," or "Such a field will be reaped," is inscribed on the wagon's side, so that when all are supplied with their daily portion of milk they know what labor awaits them.

The store, post-office, hotel, church, town-hall and Rapp mansion are all situated near the centre of the village. The store is a strange-looking place, with little else than needles, thread and a few dishes for sale. Everything is bought and divided just the same as in a large family, even the carpet in one house is the same as in all the others.

No family names are used among the members, "Jacob" and "Anna" and "Dorothy" are sufficient. If there are two of a name, they distinguish them by the locality where they live. Thus, there are a "Dorothy near the mill" and a "Dorothy near the orchard."

One laundry does the washing for the entire town. All the work is done now by employees, as the members have grown too feeble. The workers are obliged to obey every rule of the village. No man is allowed to smoke, chew or be intoxicated within town limits, and not one inhabitant is permitted to leave the village without first having obtained consent from their leader.

NO NAPS IN CHURCH ALLOWED.

On Sunday no excuse is accepted for absence from church. It is a quaint little chapel painted blue and white, and in keeping with the people who gather in it to worship according to their belief. There is no chance to forget prayers there while trying to see what others wear. Straight, uncushioned benches answer for pews. The men sit on one side of the church and the women on the other. Their leader, at present Mr. Henrici, selects a text from the Bible, and, sitting in a high-backed chair, tells his little band how they should live. He never writes out any long and eloquent sermon, but speaks as his heart believes, in a very simple but impressive manner. In the centre of the church is a clear space, with one lone bench. It is the "bench of punishment." If anyone should be so unwise as to nod over the sermon or act otherwise than he should, Mr. Henrici calls him out to the "punishment bench," where he must sit until service is over.

Miss Gertrude Rapp, the granddaughter of the founder, although at least eighty-six years old, still plays the organ and leads the singing twice every Sunday. She is yet a pretty woman, rather petite, has large blue eyes and the whitest of white hair, which, tucked under her quaint little blue Normandy cap, makes her a perfect picture of ye olden days. She occupies the Rapp house—the White House of Economy. It contains many costly, beautiful and curious relics. In the large parlor are vases filled with wax flowers and fruit which Miss Rapp made while a girl, and many other samples of her handiwork. There are two large square

AN ECONOMITE.

pianos, brought from Europe, and some costly paintings, among which is a copy of West's "Christ Healing the Sick," by Otis, with life-size figures, and "The Nativity," by Andrea del Sarto. Among the stellar objects of interest is an escritoire, once the property of James G. Blaine's mother, when she lived on the outskirts of Economy.

The Rapp garden is another beautiful spot. It is surrounded by a high, ivy-covered stone wall and is well-stocked with modern and ancient flowers. The only modern building near it is a costly green-house. Rising out of the centre of a lake is a bandstand and here on Sunday, during the summer months, the village band delights the citizens. Down near the corner is an ivy-covered grotto, built of a variety of stones, many of which were put there by the founder, George Rapp. A heavy door, covered still with the bark of the tree, keeps intruders out. The grotto is handsomely decorated on the inside. Set in the wall are four immense stones on each of which is inscribed:

GEORGE RAPP,
Founder of the Harmony Society.
Born 1757. Died 1847.
Harmony, Pa., 1805. Harmony, Ind., 1815.
Economy, Pa., 1825.

When an Economite dies he is wrapped in a winding-sheet and buried in the white graveyard near the orchard. No tombstone ever marks his resting-place. In the centre of the orchard is a mound where the Indians buried their fallen after a battle with the French. Scientists have in value offered large prices to the Economites for the privilege of opening it, but they have an unusual regard for the dead, even though they were redmen.

TRAMPS ARE TREATED LIKE PRINCES.

The Economy Hotel has many visitors. One large room is always reserved for tramps. They are always treated just the same as the citizens. They are kept overnight, and, after being given some money in the morning, are started on their way. No one ever leaves Economy hungry.

The Economites dislike to be written about, because so many write to them afterwards and want to join them or come to their village, which is as private as any home. They absolutely refuse to take anyone. People often wonder what will become of their wealth, for they are very wealthy. Everything they engage in prospers, and it has become a saying that an Economite is always lucky. The Fort Wayne Railroad travels for miles through their property, and the society owns stock in both it and the

Pittsburg and Lake Erie. The Economites were among the first to find valuable oil and gas on their land, and it is said they have more millions than members at present. Miss Rapp says she has never touched a penny since she was a baby, and that if she saw money she would not know a ten-cent piece from a dollar.

"I have all I can eat, all I can wear and I want nothing, so money is no use to me," she said.

Romantic stories are often told by outsiders about the Economites. George Rapp had a stone chair hewn out of a high cliff overlooking a river at Harmony, upon which he used to sit and watch the men at work in the fields below, and in summer preach to his followers. The spot is still visited by sightseers and is known as "Rapp's chair." It is still well preserved.

The world does not seem nearer its end than it did when George Rapp founded his quaint society, yet his followers are firm in their faith that their last member will see its end. It will not be many years until his disciples will all have followed his footsteps through death's grim portals, as they did through life, and then what will become of Economy and its millions?

NELLIE BLY

IN THE MAGDALEN'S HOME

SUNDAY, FEBRUARY 12, 1888

NELLIE BLY'S VISIT TO AN INSTITUTION FOR UNFORTUNATE WOMEN

A Wicked Girl's Chances for Reformation—How Poor Creatures Abuse a Noble Charity—Matron Burr's Experiences—The Girl Who Befriended an Unlucky Cat—The Toboggan Slide of Sin.

Quite recently the thought was forced upon me by an incident which I witnessed in the street: Do women who have started thoroughly on the downward path ever reform?

I could recall hundreds of cases where men had been pointed out to me as having "once been wild, but had now reformed," but I could not remember an instance of a woman spoken of as reformed. As one thought brings another, I began to speculate on a woman's chances of reforming. I must confess I could not see many, but I knew that in New York there must be some institutions devoted to the good cause. I made inquiries and I learned of several, among them one that had been in operation for fifty-four years. I immediately decided to learn more about it. I allude to the New York Magdalen Benevolent Home, No. 7 East Eighty-eighth street.

Dressed to suit the character I wished to represent, I went late one evening to East Eighty-eighth street. I saw an old-fashioned building surrounded by a high brick wall, and I knew without looking for the number that it was the institution I wanted. The wall looked very formidable, and I felt rather homesick as I gave a strong pull at the bell-knob.

I shivered slightly, as I thought they must surely have a big, brutal door-keeper, and I wondered if I could ever get out when once inside. It is not so droll as it may appear, this being locked up of one's own accord without a surety as to how long it may last.

ENTERING THE HOME.

I heard footsteps. A chain rattled heavily against the gates, a key was turned, and before me, candle in hand, stood a meek-looking, little, bent woman. She viewed me calmly, and I recovered from my amazement enough to say:

"Is this the Magdalen Home?"

"Yes," she answered, still holding the gate but not offering me admittance.

"Well, I came to see if I could stay a few days," I stammered.

"We don't take any one in here for a few days. They must stay six months. But you had better come in and see," she said, noticing my disappointed look.

I stepped inside and waited until she bolted and barred the gate; then I followed her up the steps into the house. She set the candle on a table in the hall, and knocking on a door, told me to enter. A woman and a man occupied the room, and the former rose and came towards me.

"Are you the matron?" I asked.

"No, the matron is out. I act in her absence," she replied.

"I want to see if I can stay here awhile," I said rather timidly.

"Every one who comes here stays for six months," she answered. "There are other homes you can go to for a shorter time."

"Six months is a good while," I said, determined not to hear anything about other homes.

"It is not very long to those who really wish to reform. Have you been doing wrong?"

"Well, I thought it might do me good to get out of the city a while," I answered, non-committal.

"You know, I suppose, that we have here only drunkards and those who have sinned? You should know if it is well for you to be among them, if you have done enough to merit it."

I began to think that for once I had failed in my attempt to dress the character I wished to represent. I had even put whiskey on my coat to create the impression that the color of my nose was not alone due to the weather.

"I think it is just as well for me to flee from temptation," I stammered by way of explanation when she asked me to sit down.

"We think six months is short enough time for a girl to break off from old associates and form new habits. Those that come here know what is before and those sent by parents or Judges are kept whether they want it or not."

"But they always reform?" I asked.

"No, very seldom, I am sorry to say. They come here and what they did not know before others tell them."

"Any one can come here?" I asked.

"Yes, any girl who wishes to reform can come here and after she tells her story and it is decided that she is a fit inmate for the Home she remains for six months. Clothing and food are furnished free to all. We give them every chance to do right. It is a very discouraging work though. I have spent years at it and I find we make very few, indeed the very fewest reformations. If you do not think you would like to stay six months you can stay any way to-night and have a talk with the matron, Mrs. Burr, in the morning. She went to the Florence Mission to-night to attend the wedding of one of our girls."

"They do marry, then?" I said.

"Oh, yes. That girl was in here for six months and when she went out she fell in with bad company again. While intoxicated she met another girl who tried to induce her to go to some place. She replied that she was bad enough and she would not get any worse. The other girl then, who had been persuading her to go to this place, said 'The Florence Mission is the place for you,' and took her there. Just think of a bad girl taking any one to a mission! Well, the girl got converted, and to-night she is marrying a very good man. I will see if I can get you a room for to-night, and by morning you will know whether you want to stay or not."

She went into the hall, and I could hear her talking with the little jailer who admitted me. I think the jailer had taken a dislike to me, and was urging that I be sent elsewhere. At any rate, they talked a long while, and I began to feel weary. Again the bell rang, and I heard them say:

"What did you come back for?"

"I didn't like the place," said the new-comer. "It was in the country, so I wouldn't stay," and then they told her what bed to take, and I heard her go heavily up the uncarpeted stairs. Once more the bell resounded, and this time warm greetings were exchanged. Then the door opened and a very pleasant, kindly faced woman came in. She looked at me with a smile as she said "Good evening," and then sat down on the sofa beside me. It was the matron. She rather urged me to tell her why I wanted to come in the home, but I replied that I would rather not speak on that subject just yet.

"What you tell me, my dear, no one else ever hears, but we must know your history before we can say you are a fit subject for the home; otherwise one might come here and learn more wickedness than they would ever forget."

"Is it unpleasant to meet all those girls?" I asked, to avoid discussing the first person singular.

"Well, they will pounce on you and want to know all your history, and tell you all theirs the first thing. But if a girl really wishes to reform we give her every opportunity. You can think it over and I will talk with you in the morning. We have seventy girls at present, and I will have to put you in with another girl. She is a very good girl. She has done wrong, but I believe she is truly converted."

I was again at the mercy of the little jailer. She walked in advance, carrying a lamp, along some narrow hallways. Fire may be my weak point. I know, anyway, the thought came that if the house caught fire I should never be able to find my out those narrow passages. Entering a room she set the lamp down on a wash-stand as she called out: "Johann, I have brought you a bed-fellow."

The girl turned her face around and, opening her large black eyes, looked at me.

"You get ready for bed," she said to me, as she started to leave the room, "and I'll come back for the lamp."

HOW THE NIGHT WAS SPENT.

This was not much like a prison or any asylum. There were no cold baths. What a difference in the treatment of women who have erred and of the poor creatures who are afflicted through no fault of their own! The room in which I was to spend the night was of good size. A worn Brussels carpet covered the floor. The walls were nicely whitened, and along one side were hooks for clothing. Beside the bed there were two cheap bureaus, a wash-stand and two chairs.

"Were you sent in?" was Johann's first question as I began to undress.

"No; I came myself," I answered.

"Ah!" with satisfaction and relief. "Then there are hopes for you."

"Six months is rather a long time to stay here," I suggested as I unbuttoned my boot.

"What is six months here to an eternity in hell?"

I dropped my boot in astonishment and looked at her. She raised herself to a sitting position in the bed. Her black hair was tossed, and her eyes gleaned unnaturally.

"I really couldn't say, you know," I stammered. "I never spent any time in either place."

At this moment my jailer came for the lamp. As she went out the door she gave this parting salutation:

"Johann, don't throw her out the window before morning."

"Oh, no," replied Johann; "she is a very nice little girl." The door closed and we were left in the dark. She asked me all about myself, and I in turn questioned her.

"I make artificial flowers. I learned the business when I was a child. I need to make $2 per day; now I can only earn $7 a week. We are paid by the amount of work we do."

"Where do you live?" I asked.

"I rent a small room on a top floor in the locality of Hester street for $1.50 a week. It has a single bed in it, and I buy an oil-stove, on which I do my cooking. No, I cannot save any money. By the time I pay rent and for fuel and buy my food I have but little left for clothing myself."

"Why do you not board in some of these charitable homes? I would imagine it pleasanter than to live as you do."

"I am tired seeing misery, and the only people who go to charitable homes are miserable. I want to get it out of my sight and hearing for a while, so I have a room. Cheap boarding-houses are generally nests of vice, so I would not patronize them."

"Have you been here long?"

"I have been here a year now. I had gone to every extent in sinfulness and, as a last remedy, I came here. I am so glad, for I have seen the folly of my former life and am just as anxious to live rightly as I was once to live wrongly. I wish I never had to go out in the world again, but then I am six of seeing the misery in Homes."

A DAY IN THE MAGDALEN.

I was about ready to go to sleep when the rising bell rang. I had passed the night in a restless manner and was glad to find it ended. Johann got up and sat on the edge of the bed, while I put on my gown. We soon were ready to go downstairs. I followed her along the narrow hall and into the sitting-room. It was a good-sized room with white walls, benches and a desk. It looked similar to a country school-room. A large stove occupied the centre of the room, and clustered around it were some twenty girls. They wore plain calico dresses and some wore aprons. They looked at me as curiously as I looked at them. One of the number made room for us and we joined the circle.

"How many new ones came last night?" asked a girl.

"Three," responded several.

"Did she," indicating me, "come herself?" asked another of Johann, who replied in the affirmative.

"What other Homes have you been in?" some one asked me.

"None; this is my first," I replied.

"Hello, Minna!" they called out in chorus to a newcomer with a youthful face and short gray hair. "Why didn't you sleep all day?"

"Sleep! I haven't closed my eyes all the night; I haven't slept for a week, and if they don't soon give me something they'll have to send me to the crazy-house on Blackwell's Island," said Minna, complainingly.

Gradually the circle increased around the stove until the breakfast-bell rang, when all made a rush for the hall. There were no rules or regulations to be obeyed, and every one rushed at will. I followed in the train down to the dining-room, which is in the basement. The matron, Mrs. Burr, was there, and she gave me a place at an end table. When the room was filled the girls began to chant a hymn of thanks, after which they repeated a prayer, and then began on the simple meal before them. It consisted of bread, butter, molasses and a bowl of coffee. One woman who sat at our table would not eat her bread, which she broke in bits and pushed to someone else's plate. This raised a disturbance, and Mrs. Burr sent her from the table as one would dismiss a naughty child. Otherwise the breakfast passed very quietly. Mrs. Burr always spoke in the most gentle and quiet manner to the unruly ones.

HOW THE PLACE LOOKS.

I made a survey of the place. The ceiling was low but nicely whitened. On the walls were mottoes that would not harm people to obey. The women interested me most. There were probably fifty in the room—the youngest a pretty peach-and-cream-complexioned miss of not more than sixteen years, and the eldest a feeble woman who looked not less than seventy.

As they finished eating they left the table without asking to be excused. They were all expected to go to the sitting-room, but I do not think they did. However, the majority went there. Mrs. Burr. Mrs. Hartley and Miss Henscher took their places behind the desk. Mrs. Bartley read a chapter from the Bible and then prayed, after which the girls repeated a prayer in unison. The matrons then went to their breakfast and we were left alone.

"How do you spend the day?" I asked a girl.

"Just as we please," she said. "We read or we can work on mosquito-netting or in the laundry. Some knit or crochet. We generally please ourselves."

"Girls must have it very nice here?" I remarked.

"My aunt says it is an encouragement to laziness and crime," interposed a girl who had been listening to us.

"Well, I would think some are reformed by being here," I said.

"Oh, yes," answered another; "there is one here now who has been here four times, and she says it has done her good every time."

"What makes her come back if it does her good?" I asked.

"Well, when she gets out she falls in bad company and goes back to her old ways; then she gets into trouble and comes back here."

I could not see how the Home benefited her if it did not last after she got out. From the conversation of some of the girls I learned that they had been making the rounds of the charitable homes since childhood, and I don't doubt that their mothers did the same before them. Two of them even spoke of being in Homes in other cities. Johann was the only one I found who had the least remorse for what she had done. The others were as indifferent about it as if it were an honor to them.

They were all very nice to me, and when they saw that I was not inclined to be communicative they did not bother me with questions. They used snuff liberally and offered to share with me. I declined their kindness. During the day several letters arrived and, after being read by the matron, they were given to those for whom they were intended.

At noon we were given fish, bread and tea, and in the evening bread, butter and tea. The food was plain, but there was plenty of it. Several times during the day the girls came into the sitting-room with slices of bread, so that I knew they never suffered from hunger. A large space of ground surrounds the Home, inclosed, of course, by the high wall, where the girls can go as much as they wish. The laundry work is done for the neighbors by such girls as are willing to work. It is done at reduced prices in order that the inmates may have something to employ their time. Each girl does her own washing. They have perfect liberty in everything except to go out the gate. The Home is non-sectarian, although Protestant services are held every Sunday. The girls are offered every chance of reforming, but they seldom accept. This life is like a toboggan slide. Once they start, it is impossible to stop until they reach the end, which is death. They keep up the rounds—from the streets to the courts, to the island, to the Home and to the streets again—year after year.

In the afternoon of my day there the ambulance came to take a sick girl to the hospital. The girls rushed to the front of the house to get a "peep uv de cop an' his brass buttons," they said, and many were the remarks passed about him. One girl won the admiration of the crowd by asserting that she winked at him.

There are many peculiar characters at the Home. The most interesting one is probably a little homely creature whom the girls call Vanderbilt, because she imagines she runs the house. Vanderbilt gets herself up in a comical style, but she is withal good-humored. When she first came to the Home some painters who had been there had painted a white cat green. The poor cat seemed likely to die. It became Vanderbilt's charge. She nursed it and tended it until the paint wore off—and took the hair with it. Vanderbilt would often go to Mrs. Burr and ask for some Vaseline to rub on her sore face, when instead she would rub it on Tom Vanderbilt's (as the cat is known) back. Tom knows who was kind to him, and follows Vanderbilt from one end of the house to the other. When she sits down he jumps on her lap and displays more affection than I ever saw a cat manifest before. Tom looks pretty well now, and his tail gives bright promise of once again wearing fur.

I was rather amused to hear the superstitious girls tell what "sign" the most common occurrence conveyed to them. When spoken to about the absurdity of such beliefs, one said:

"Well, I know they are true. One day I spat on the door, and I said 'That for change of residence,' and the next morning I was in the Police Court." This was convincing.

THE MOTHERLY MATRON.

Towards evening Mrs. Burr took me into the reception room. She asked if I had yet concluded that I would like to stay six months. I did not feel inclined to forfeit my liberty, especially as I had gotten all the information I could, even if remained a month. I had but little sympathy for those women who do wrong and have no inclination to do otherwise. I determined to get out as soon as possible. I said the time was too long, and that instead of being benefited by remaining there, I should learn more wickedness. She told me of other Homes I could go to and stay a shorter time.

"I told you the women here are bad," she said. "We get the very worst. A great number of them have served their terms in the penitentiary and workhouse. We offer shelter to any woman who wants to reform and we teach her all we can, but it is not encouraging work."

"Do they ever reform?" I asked.

"Well, even if they wish to reform they find it almost impossible. We had a woman here who was once of a very wealthy family. She was well educated, but she fell in love and it ruined her. She got to be of the very worst before we got her. She repented and wanted to do right, but she could get no chance. She had no recommendations, and at every place she applied for work we were compelled to tell her history. No one would have her after that. One charitable woman said she would have taken her for a nurse, but she had two sons coming home from college and she could not have the girl in the house. Girls often leave here with a desire to do better, but they have no money, no trade, no character, and in a while they get discouraged and go back to their old haunts. The majority of them do not care to reform. They come here because it offers them refuge when they have nowhere else to go. We endeavor to do all we can for them."

Promising to go to see the receiving committee of the Home or to some other mission I left the Magdalen. I tell you the path of sin is like a toboggan slide; once we start down there is no stopping until we reach the end.

NELLIE BLY

Nellie Bly on the Stage

Sunday, March 4, 1888

She Wears a Scant Costume and Marches With the Amazons

It Isn't Very Hard to Get Such a Job—The Girls Earn $5 a Week—Tights that Did Not Fit—Dressing in a Crowded Room—How She Behaved on the Stage—A Bad Beginning.

I made my début as a chorus girl or stage Amazon last week. It was my first appearance on any stage and came about through reading among The World advertisements one that called for 100 girls for a spectacular pantomime, so I found myself one afternoon at the stage door of the Academy of Music. There were but two men there. I looked at them and they looked at me, and as nobody made any movement to speak, I asked:

"Where do I go in answer to the advertisement?"

"Mr. Kiralfry told me to say he had all the girls he wants," replied one of them. Then, probably noticing my look of disappointment, he added: "But you can step in on the stage and see him yourself."

The stage was bare and cold. A solitary gas jet only added to the dismal aspect of the place. The scenery even leaned up against itself as if it were tired. Near the front of the stage was a row of girls, twenty-four in number, watching the movements of a graceful little Frenchman, who twisted and danced before them. Standing around in rather forlorn groups were other girls, of all sizes, ages and appearances. Some were talking in a lively way, while others stood about silent and sad. A woman who received the least attention of all was a ballet dancer who was practicing.

I saw no one to speak to, so I followed the example of the other girls—

stood and watched the rehearsal. Every two girls in the magic circle had a small gilded chair of mythological design. The Frenchman was teaching the girls to jump on the chair, then down, then to run around it, and up again and so on. It looked very uninteresting and simple, and yet the girls often made mistakes. The little master seemed to have unlimited patience, and at every false move gently showed the correct way. There was a remarkable absence of the "brutality" displayed against the poorly paid ballet girls which one hears so much about. The girls seemed to enjoy the exercise and the man was kind.

At last I saw a man emerge from the gloomy portals at the far side of the stage and come towards me, where I stood on one foot, holding the other, like an elephant, or a goose, as you please, up to rest.

"To whom shall I apply for a situation?" I asked.

"For what?" he questioned, looking at me with a kindly smile.

"In answer to the advertisement in to-day's WORLD."

"Will you please sit down and wait? I'll see you in a moment," he said, and he left me.

I looked around. I could see nothing but the perpendicular scenery and the stage door. My feelings were rather shocked. I remained standing.

"Do you like the chorus?" I asked, turning to a slender girl, with a shabby dress, a careworn face and mournful eyes enclosed in dark rings.

"Yes, I like it. It's as easy as anything a girl can do."

"Does it pay well?"

"I think as well as anything else. Girls in factories and stores work from 7 in the morning until 6 in the evening. They get from $1.50 up to $4. The very fewest number get $5. On the stage we work a few hours every night, and we have two matinees and two rehearsals a week, and we get $5. This is the best place."

"I would like to have that job," said another girl, indicating a woman with a towel around her head dusting the orchestra chairs. "She gets $6 a week, and then when she cleans the actresses' rooms they give her lace and old dresses, and sometimes a five-dollar bill."

"Come with me; I want you names," said the man who had spoken to me, and we followed him in single file across the dim-lit stage and into a little room. Everything here had as barren a look as the stage. Trunks were piled on trunks and a number of odd chairs took up more space. He found a piece of paper and called the first girl to give her name. She gave it and he told her to come next week. He asked the second, "What is your name?"

"I want to know how much you pay, first."

"Five dollars a week," he replied, while he suspended the pen.

"Well, then, we (indicating her companions) won't come."

"All right. Good day. Next!"

"They expected to get $25 a week," explained a girl.

We all gave our names and four of us were told to report for duty at the stage door at 7 o'clock that evening. It was only the rehearsals I wanted, but I decided, as this was all that offered, to see what it amounted to.

At 7 o'clock I walked past the crowd of men who surrounded the stage door into the Academy. I secretly wondered if they were the "eligibles" I had read so much of who swarmed about stage doors with their hearts and fortunes, flowers and diamonds to lay at the feet of their chosen idols. I did not see any evidence of any of these articles, but the crowd was there nevertheless.

There was no one on the stage or anywhere to be seen. The solitary gas jet was yet solitary. I could not find any one, so I took up my stand and stood. Presently from some mysterious part of the stage came the girls who had been engaged at the time I was. They began to complain because they had been informed that there were no extra suits for the extra girls—us.

"Are we to go on without any knowledge of the play?" I asked.

"Yes, we'll have to try to get beside some girls who will be good enough to help us."

I did not see how we could do it and not break up the show, but as I was bent on having fun I did not much care what form it took. The performers began to arrive. Almost all the girls carried little parcels or baskets. These I found contained their "make up." At last, Mr. Kiralfry came and seeing us he came up and spoke.

"There is nothing to do until after the first set so you can go up and watch the play."

He left us and then I saw a long string of men coming in, one after the other. They were making a noise like a cat, and I recognized them as being the men at the entrance whom I mistook for devoted lovers. They disappeared under the stage.

At last I and my friend were called to prepare for the stage. A few garments were given us and we were shown a room to dress in. It was already well filled with girls in all stages of dress and undress. "This room is full enough. Go somewhere else," cried one girl, crossly, and with the exception of the three prettiest girls, they were all angry because we crowded in with them. I spoke to two of three, but they did not reply—simply looked at me with quiet scorn. I had some idea of the dressing but my luckless companion had none.

"How do you get these things on?" she asked, in surprised disgust.

I looked at her. She was trying to get her thin silver tights on over her shoes and undergarments.

"You must take off your shoes," I explained, as no one else offered to.

"Indeed I will not," she said, vehemently. "It's very rude; I will not do it." But in a while she did take off her shoes.

"How do you get the tights on?" she cried again.

"You cannot get them on over all your undergarments," I told her, and even the angry girls laughed as they looked at her. I forgot my own appearance in laughing at hers. She got the tights half on, then she got the little short waist around her shoulders and the shoulder scarf around her waist. She put the band of white hair, which only encircles the head, on, and had no helmet. This allowed her black hair to show and make a queer picture. She got a spear and a shield, and so she made her way down to the stage looking like an Amazon who had been badly whipped in a fight.

I fared but little better. My garments were too large, my ballet slippers were easily four sizes too long. I put the rouge on my face and found I had forgotten my powder. The white wig was too small and would show my black hair underneath. My helmet was too large and would slip back. I was a sad sight.

"You will be too late. The curtain is up," cried someone, and I rushed after a girl down the stairs and to the wing. I was only conscious that there was a crowd of people going out and I was among them, giving a hitch every now and then to my armor. A blaze of light, a crash of music and, with an inward laugh at my own boldness in attempting something I know nothing of, I was facing a New York audience in the Amazon march. I did not feel like an Amazon. Down we swept towards the footlights, while I wondered what our next move was to be.

"You started with the wrong foot," said a girl at my side. I did not know which foot I started with, so I said, "Which foot is it?"

"Oh, any one will do for you," was the satisfactory answer, while I mused on how funny it must look from the front to see one brave Amazon out of step with the whole army. Backwards we went, and my helmet slipped on the back of my neck.

"Your black hair is showing," whispered another girl. This was not reassuring, and did not tend to give me courage to try to do better. I gave a jerk to my helmet while the horrible thought struck me. What should I do if my helmet fell off on the stage and I was left with my sham wig and black crown before the audience? Once again we went to the front, and I congratulated myself on being in step when a girl in a very emphatic manner whispered:

"You have your shield on the wrong arm!" That reduced me again, and I resolved to change it in face of the audience, when she whispered:

"Face about."

I turned my face to her and found every girl had her face turned the other way, and if I kept on I would have to march backward while the rest went forward. I would not do this, so I simply took my time and turned in the right direction. I began mildly to wonder why the gallery gods did not notice my strange action. As we marched in a circle around the stage I changed my shield and poised my spear lightly on my side. (I had been carrying it under my arm.) Again we went to the footlights. A girl whispered for me to "stand at D," and I obeyed. I heard a voice from the wing cry:

"My — — —! What is wrong?"

I look with a smile to see what is wrong, and I see that the other girls are marching to one side; they have divided and I, being in the centre, am left alone in front! I followed with more haste than grace after the nearest girl. Then we did movements which I had not the least knowledge of, so I was more than a little relieved when they marched to the wing. I was glad to get off. I found my poor companion still in a state of undress. Together we sought the dressing-room, and I forgot my own discomfort in laughing at her remarks. I am out of a stage engagement at present.

NELLIE BLY

Some Ladies Who Fence

Sunday, March 11, 1888

Nellie Bly Takes a Hand at Foils and Likes the Exercise

It Looks Very Easy, But Isn't—Women Cleverer Than Men Are—Anybody Can Learn to be Graceful at It—How Members of the Fencers' Club Dress—Teachers Say That the Practice Is Growing in Favor.

I have been learning to fence. It is quite the proper thing nowadays for women to learn how to handle the foils. The craze is not as new, however, as one would imagine. Long ago, twenty or twenty-five years, when Prof. Gebhard opened a gymnasium, he began to teach women to fence. He was the first to introduce it as an art or exercise for women in New York. Laura Keene, an actress, was his first lady pupil, and she became quite skillful with the foils. At first actresses only came to him, but the following summer Prof. Gebhard went to New York, where he formed a class made up entirely of society women who knew and appreciated the advantages of healthful amusement. The other day I applied and was accepted as a pupil of Prof. Gebhard. He has a class composed of some twenty young women and a second class of a smaller number, besides private pupils. The class wears gymnasium dresses, short skirts, loose waist and fencing shoes. They say women learn much quicker than men and enjoy the sport.

"This is a foil," said Prof. Gebhard at the beginning of my first lesson. "You must always keep the broad side up, and remember the point is what you want to strike your adversary with. Now take first position." He placed me facing him with my heels tight together.

"Now salute, putting the foil perpendicularly before your face, then transfer it to the left hand and hold it easily by the side. When I say 'First position,' you catch the foil firmly by the right hand, sliding the left half way along the foil and so raise it above the head, bending the knees at the same time."

The Salute—First Position.

It seemed very easy to do by watching him, but it was not so easy as it looked.

"When I call 'On guard,'" continued the Professor after I had done the first task to his satisfaction, "you loosen the left hand, still retaining the curved position, while with the right you aim the foil at me, at the same time stepping forward with the right foot. Do not move the left. On guard!"

I did what he told me, but my movements must have been exceedingly stiff and ungraceful. He looked at me in some alarm as he called:

"Bend the knees. Keep a good balance on the left foot so you can go back to the other position as soon as I say." Again and again it was repeated, much to my enjoyment.

"You must keep the hand firmly clasped around the hilt, else the one you fight with will disarm you. Always keep the back of the hand down, the nails up."

"Do you have much trouble teaching girls?" I asked, as I stopped to find out where my breath was.

"No, they learn very easily. I consider fencing the very best exercise, for it puts every muscle in motion. Now your next move is to 'strike out,' holding the arm straight, pointing the foil at my breast, and as you do this you must straighten the left arm. On guard, strike out!"

I "strike out," and almost lose my balance, and while fearing every moment I shall topple over, I try to retain the position.

"You did not balance well on your left foot," he explained. "Now your next move is to step out the right foot, and at the same moment strike me with the point of your foil. Now, on guard, strike out, attack. You would never kill your enemy if you struck him in that way."

I think I made a sorry-looking fighter—or rather fencer. I felt much in my own way—as if I was stumbling over myself.

"You must never have a front position," he explained. "Always present a side view, excepting the face. Leave an ample distance between the feet and balance firmly on the left, so at the call you may be able to resume your first position."

For one hour I practised those simple exercises that were difficult to learn. I found as they grew easier I grew more anxious to be able to strike him. I just wanted to learn to fence, so I could strike him once and surprise him. I did not accomplish my desire the first day.

"I thought you would be so stiff from the exercise that you would not come again," said the Professor, when I next reported for instructions. Again I was drilled through the first lesson, and then I was taught to advance and retreat.

"Now I am your enemy; I retreat while you advance, stepping the right foot forward and bringing up the left, always keeping them in the same position."

He retreated and I advanced. I had determined that I was going to strike him, and I smiled as he watched me entirely ignorant of my wicked designs. I made him retreat clear back against the wall of the gymnasium, and he looked at me in a surprised way, but I did not accomplish my object. He must have thought that I had an unusual amount of energy for a new pupil. A quick and double-quick step was taught me before this lesson was finished. I was afterwards taught to attack on the inside and the outside of the foil, up and down, and an above and under movement. The more I learned the more interested I became, until it was with regret I resigned my place as a pupil.

I then went to Prof. Berger, who has a system of fencing which he says is wholly his own. He is a pleasant little man with a shock of white hair and the biggest of blue eyes. Fencing is to him a grace. He glories in the movement and positions of grace which must be assumed as a ballet-master would delight in a graceful pupil or an artist in a model.

"You see on the board? First position, second position, on guard and *a fond*. Now first position: put your left heel against your right ankle, hold the foil in your right hand gracefully in front of you; move it easily to the left hand, by which you catch it half way between and then raise it by both hands above the head. Make a circle or frame of your arms and foil for the face. That looks lovely! This is second position. Loosen the left hand and while keeping that arm still in the curved position bring the foil down with

READY FOR ACTION.

the right hand, pointing it directly to my eye. That is 'on guard.' Now you strike out by straightening the arm at the wrist, and that is '*a fond*.' Is not that easy and graceful?"

Somehow it did seem easier than the other lessons. "Do you have many pupils?" I asked the little Professor, as I rested my foil on the toe of my boot. It was information, not lessons, I wanted.

"Yes, a great number. Every day I get inquiries about fencing lessons. It is so pleasant and pretty; it gives ladies rosy cheeks, straight shoulders and graceful carriage of the head."

"Who is the best fencer you have among the women?" I asked, regardless of instructions.

"Miss Hilliard," he replied, "sister of the actor, Robert Hilliard."

Capt. Nicolas, of the Fencers' Club on Twenty-fourth Street, regards fencing in a very scientific light. It seems very easy to learn by his instructions. During the course of a lesson I asked him what he thought of fencing as an exercise for women.

"There is none better," was his emphatic reply, "Fencing, to be done properly, requires the exercise of every muscle and instinct. It trains the mind in speediness of thought, the eye in quickness of sight, the body in quickness of movement, the instinct in quickness at conclusions."

There are a great number of women at the present time engaged in learning the art of fencing. The Fencers' Club, which is in the same house as the Authors' Club, is composed of nineteen ladies. Admission is procured by sending a letter to Mr. J. Murray Mitchell or Mr. Charles De Kay. The club-rooms are devoted exclusively to the women's class three days in the week, from 10 A.M. to 2 P.M. Pretty and appropriate costumes are worn by the class to allow perfect freedom of movement.

Among those belonging to the Fencers' Club are Mrs. Edward Mitchell, Mrs. L. S. Stevenson, Miss Flagg, Miss Moore, Miss Helen Bancroft, Miss Sara Beldon, Miss Praeger, Miss Sears, Miss Ives, Miss Warrington, Miss Hadley, Miss Ruth Laurence, Miss Lusk, Miss Williams, Miss de Macarty, Miss Haight, Miss Lapsley, Miss Cammann and Miss Mitchell.

Some of the members of Prof. Berger's class are Miss Hilliard, Miss Matthews, Miss Mann, Miss Cochrane, Miss Eveylen and Miss Webber.

One of Prof. Gebhard's classes is composed of Miss Billings, Miss Pagot, Miss Vandervoort and their friends.

Prof. M. Senac has a class composed of the members of the Conservatory of Music on Seventeenth street. In private he has Miss Rose Coghlan and Mrs. Langtry as pupils. He says they are quite handy with the foils. Miss Pauline Hall is practising under the care of M. Louis Trouchet.

Nellie Bly

Nellie Bly as a Mesmerist

Sunday, March 25, 1888

The Strange and Awful Experience of a Certain Mr. Gray

He Consents to Allow the Learner of Mesmerism to Practice on Him and Undergoes Horrible Torture—The Professor Believes Nellie Bly to be a Kind of Feminine Fiend—How She Got Even with Him—Secrets of the Black Art.

For what car fare costs, added to the price of a shave, I can become one of the greatest mesmerizers in the world. This is how I know. An advertisement in a Sunday newspaper a week or so ago attracted my attention. Under the name of "Mesmer" the advertiser offered to teach the art of mesmerism, with satisfactory tests at the completion of the lessons. In a day or two I had exchanged letters with "Mesmer" and had received his price for lessons and minute directions how to reach his place of residence. "From 3 to 6 or 7 to 9 I can see you any day," he wrote, so without advising him I went to Brooklyn. I found his home, No. 227 Court street, to be about fifteen minutes' ride from the bridge. His name was Thompson and his place was on the top floor, rather bare and uninviting. His big wife was the only one at home, so I agreed to climb three flights of stairs again. The next day a little girl of six let me in and took me to her papa.

Mr. Thompson, besides being tall and thin, had long gray hair, combed back from his long, pale face. His eyes were a sharp black. A drooping mustache covered his mouth completely. "Do I think you can learn to mesmerize?" he repeated, in answer to my question. "Yes, I assure you I can make you a first-class operator. My price is $10 in advance and $40 with the final test. What is the test? Well, after I give you two lessons I get a subject and allow you to operate on him. If you mesmerize him you are perfect in the art."

"I am afraid I cannot learn, and then I shall have given my money to no purpose," I urged.

"Oh, you can't help but learn," he reassured me. "I can see that you will make a splendid operator. Everybody does who learns from me. I impart to them some of my power, which, I think, some are born with. I've had men come to me and say that they understood mesmerism perfectly, but could not operate. Yet after a few lessons they could operate as well as I can. I am also a clairvoyant," he went on. "I'll teach you that after you learn mesmerism. It is very easy. One can soon learn how to throw one's self into a trance. There is lots of money in it for a clever person."

After making him guarantee that he would make a good operator of me I paid him the $10 fee and began my first lesson. He sat down on a sofa, facing me, and told me to do everything just as he did.

HOW IT IS DONE.

"When you tell your subject to sit down see that he gets an easy position, for he has to sit perfectly still for ten minutes. Always see that he does not cross his knees or wear overshoes. Why? Because it detracts from the influence you get over him. I want first to tell you always to say 'please' to your subjects and have command in your voice. Repeat what I say and watch every word closely. 'Now, sir, please put the right thumb on the left pulse, press hard enough to feel the beating and think only of that.' All right; you did that well.

"The first lesson is to teach you to get control of the muscular power. In the second lesson, I teach you mental control. When you have the man in this position, with the right thumb on the left pulse, you must close his eyes, so, making a pass with your right hand down in front of his face, the fingertips almost touching him. You say 'Now, sir, please close your eyes.' When you once get a man's eyes closed so that he is unable to open them you can have him in your power."

"When you have the subject's eyes closed," he continued, going back to the lesson, "and he thinks of nothing but the pulse beatings, you go up to him about three times in ten minutes and make passes over him, three passes each time, in this way." He got up and, bringing his arms above my head, passed his hands slowly before my face close without touching. The movement was made as though he was sweeping some invisible thing from before my face. Then he told me to make the passes over him. I did so until it was done to his satisfaction.

"After the ten minutes have passed you take the subject's hands and place them gently one on each knee. Then with your left hand you take his and run your thumb close up between the joints of the little and ring finger and press very hard."

"What do you do that for?" I asked.

"I don't always tell, but I don't mind telling you. There is a nerve called the nerve of sensation between those fingers. You press hard on it and it communicates with the brain. At the same time you place the fingers of your right hand on the subject's head, and with the right thumb you press hard directly between the eyebrows. Then you are touching and controlling the organ of individuality. The nerve in the hand and this nerve connect, and this places the man in your power. While holding him so you say firmly, 'Now, sir, I am going to make you so that you can't open your eyes. Try hard! Open your eyes! Try hard!' and then he cannot open his eyes. After you remove your hold you snap your fingers close to his ears and say, 'All right, sir,' and he opens his eyes."

IN CASE OF FAILURE.

"Yes, but what if he does open his eyes when I say he can't?" I urged.

"Well, then you try it over."

"Yes; but he might open his eyes every time, and I wouldn't like that."

"You must not try him more than three times. If you do not have him under the influence the third time, say 'You are partially under the influence, and at another sitting I can mesmerize you.' Be sure to add a remark about his strong will power. This has the effect of making him more susceptible to your influence the next time."

"Why cannot he open his eyes when I say 'Try hard?'"

"Because you are pressing hard on the organ of individuality. When you say 'Try hard,' which you must always do, he makes a great effort and tries to open his eyes by raising his brows. Your thumb prevents him. If he simply tried to unclose his eyes, which he would do if you did not urge him to 'try hard,' he would have no difficulty in so doing. When you remove your hand and say 'All right,' he quits trying hard and opens his eyes. Once you have done this you have the man in your power. I have sewed together with a needle whole rose of people while they were in this state."

"Beautiful!" I exclaimed, pleased with the idea which brought a vision to me of sewing all objectionable people on one thread. "Can I sew people?" "Yes, I will teach you that. Now, you know how to control the muscular movements and you can make the subject do just as you please, and he can't help himself. You have merely to catch his eye. 'Now, sir, please look at me.' He looks. Hold up your right index finger and move it. He will do the same. Say: 'Faster, sir, faster. Now, sir, you can't stop,' and you suddenly stop and point your finger at him. He can't stop, but keeps on until you snap your fingers and repeat, 'All right, sir.'"

"Yes; but what if he can stop?" I urged. The flesh was willing, but the spirit was very weak.

"Then you will have to try him again."

THE MENTAL POWERS.

The next evening found me ready for another lesson. In this I was to learn the art of controlling the mental faculties of another. Did I learn? Well, just see what a wonderful test-show I had.

"These are very precious secrets," he said, "and so the young girl (referring to the one who accompanied me) had better go somewhere and wait for you."

"To control the mental powers you tell the subject to stand up and face you. You take his hand in the same way as when you closed his eyes, then passing your open hand close to his face, letting it rest for a second before his eyes, you say, 'Now, sir, I am going to take away your name.' Of course you have asked him previously what his name is. You remove your hand and you say, 'Now, sir, what is your name?' and he can't tell you. Ha, ha!"

"Can't he?" I said, dubiously. "What would you do if he could?"

"Try it over. If you want to give an exhibition for your friends I can get you all the subjects you want for a car fare and a shave."

"Can you really?" I asked, innocently. "That would be lovely. How can you get them?"

"Oh, I have a number of young men you can operate on, and they are glad to do it for a car fare and a shave. Then, you know, you generally have a supper. I used to give parlor entertainments at a house in Twenty-third street. I once mesmerized the wife of the editor of the Scientific American there. It made a big excitement."

"Will you give me the addresses of your subjects?"

"When you have given the final test I will," he replied, warily. "One is a young travelling man, and another is in a store over in the city."

THE TEST.

The young woman and I arrived a little late the next evening, but fully prepared for the donkey party. Mr. Thompson looked like a valentine, attired in a "swallow-tail" coat of the cut of forty years ago. He greeted us with a triumphant smile.

"Ah, ladies, let me introduce you to Mr. Gray," he said, as I began in a business-like way to take off my hat and coat.

"He is my subject?" I asked, and after their affirmative reply turned to Mr. Gray and said:

"Are you ready to be butchered?"

I knew that this subject was going to be mesmerized, even if I did not touch him. I immediately decided to do things contrary to what I had been taught and to prove to myself that the subject was shamming. Consequently I merely took hold of his hand and did not press the nerve, as instructed, and placed my right hand on his brow—without any pressure, however.

"Now, sir, you can't open your eyes. Try hard! Open your eyes! Try hard!" I said.

The subject pulled and twisted and jerked at his eyes, which still remained closed. I snapped my fingers, called "All right!" and he opened his eyes, rubbed them, and like the angelic heroine in the novel coming out of a sham fainting fit, exclaimed: "Where am I? What were you doing with me?"

I told him to sit on a chair and, after making passes over him, I told him he was unable to get up. He squirmed all around, but he sat there. I placed his hand on the wall and made passes over it and he pulled and twisted, apparently unable to release himself. Then I ran him all over the room, sometimes on his knees, then bent double and again straining his neck to view my finger as it was held above my head. Mr. Thompson protested that I was not treating the subject fairly, but I said that if he were mesmerized he could not feel it, and kept on. At last, when his face grew red from the violent exercise, I rested my hand on the edge of the piano. He put his head close down beside it. I jerked my hand quickly away and left him standing there.

"Don't leave him in that position too long," urged Mr. Thompson, ever watchful for the subject's comfort.

"I do not intend to take him out of it until to-morrow," I replied firmly. Mr. Thompson looked at me in surprise, and his wife, who had been witnessing the performance through a half-opened door, entered the room.

"Poor fellow! It's too bad to keep him in that position so long."

"Oh, you know," I said sweetly, "he can't feel uncomfortable so long

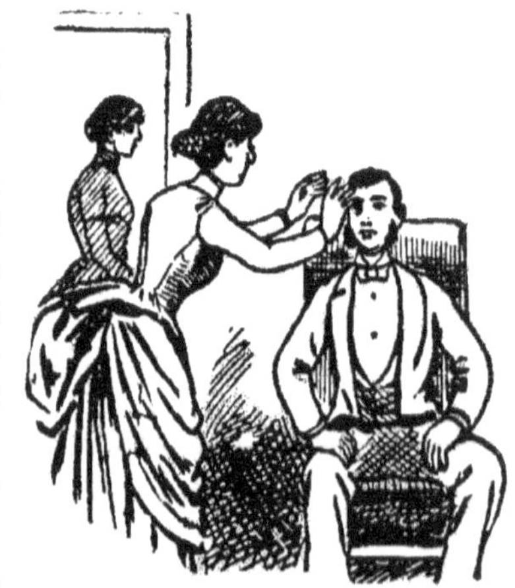

MAKING PASSES ON HER SUBJECT.

as he is mesmerized. I'll be back to-morrow evening to bring him out."

HAVING FUN WITH A SUBJECT.

After a great deal of urging, Mr. Thompson suggested that I would have more fun to make my subject see things, so I consented to remove him from his cramped position. A sigh of relief swept through the room when I changed my resolution. Then he went through another sham performance, in which I made him see snakes, pretty girls and rats. It would be tiresome to tell all the pace I put him through, but be assured I gave that young man more exercise than he would have had in breaking a bucking horse. Once I told him that he was Robert Ingersoll, and he began to address an imaginary audience. Then I made him try to imitate Bill Nye.

"Is there anything you can suggest?" asked Mr. Thompson.

"Yes, I will make him stand on his head," I answered.

"Oh, no; you must not do that," he answered, greatly alarmed, "he might hurt himself."

"Nonsense. As long as he is so thoroughly mesmerized he can't hurt himself," but Mr. Thompson urged me to put the young man in a cataleptic state, so I gave up my scheme of making him stand on his head and leaving him so.

I stood him up, put his feet close together, his hands by his sides and made several passes over him, while I whispered in his ear, "You're a fraud." I gave him a gentle shove, and he fell back right into Mr. Thompson's arms, who lowered him to the floor.

"Now is he just like one dead?" I asked as if I were frightened.

"Just exactly," was the reply.

"Could I do anything to him and he would not know?" I asked again.

"Yes; he is paralyzed—he is in the state of death."

I made a sudden movement and went down on my knees by the subject's side. My movements were noted with surprise and alarm. "Why, his heart beats," I said, as I felt it throbbing.

"Yes," said Mr. Thompson, nervously, "of course his heart beats."

"But you said he would be just the same as dead. I can see him breathe. No one would ever bury him for a dead man."

"Do you want to paralyze his heart?" he asked, sternly.

"Certainly," I replied. "I want to put him in the state you said could not be told from death. This is nothing like it."

"Do you want to kill the man?" said Mrs. Thompson, rushing like a tigress up to me.

SHE DID NOT MIND KILLING HIM.

"Oh, I don't object in the least," I replied, coolly. "Will he stay in this position until I take him out?"

"Certainly," replied Mr. Thompson, making an effort to regain his courage. "No one can do anything with him but you."

"Very well," I said with quiet determination. "I intend to go home now and when I return, a week from to-night, if he is just as I left him I shall believe in mesmerism."

"Oh, no; we can't do that," said Mr. Thompson, but I was deaf to all pleadings and protests.

"I never saw any one act like you," yelled Mrs. Thompson. "That man has a wife and two children, and I won't be responsible to them. I believe you would like to kill a man. I won't have it—now! It's getting late; this has to stop."

I did not answer, but quietly amused myself by pulling the subject's hair and pinching his ears and nose. He stood it bravely, never for an instant moving. Once I moved away and he turned his eyes to see what I was doing.

"Strange to see a dead man move his eyes," I said with a laugh. Mr. Thompson said I was mistaken, and his wife kept up her growl about me.

"I guess I might as well sew men now," I remarked with quiet calm.

"Oh, you must not do that; you'll kill the man. What do you mean, anyhow?" yelled Mrs. Thompson, while her husband joined in urging me to desist.

"I might as well learn to sew men now," I said, taking a needle from my dress, which I had brought along for the purpose, and deliberately trying the point on my thumbnail.

"I won't allow that to be done in my house," yelled the wife, and the little girl, seeing such a turmoil, began to cry. Even the young girl with me said I had better wait, but I was determined to test my subject.

"Say miss, wouldn't you rather sew him when you have him singing?" asked my instructor, coaxingly. "It's much more effective."

By this time I had tried the point several times on the subject's ear, and observed a slight twitch every time. I had no desire to butcher him in cold blood. I knew that if I ran it through the muscles of his ear he would be compelled to yell, but really my heart failed me, much as I despised him for his fraud. I stuck my needle back in my dress and, taking his head between my hands, thumped it up and down on the floor. Again Mrs. Thompson protested, and Mr. Thompson protested he could not have his subjects treated so badly. I must say that the subject filled his position to perfection. I put the needle through the lobe of his ear twice, and he sang on. Of course those who had had their ears pierced know that the pain is comparatively nothing, so I did not regard it as a sure test. Mr. Thompson looked at me in triumph, but I had one more card to play against him.

"I have a final test to make," I said, and going to my coat I took from the pocket a small bottle I had brought along just for this purpose.

A HORRIBLE TEST.

"What is it?" asked Thompson, eyeing me in a frightened manner.

"Assafoetida," I replied, shortly.

"What is that?" he asked in a hushed whisper, as the color left his face. I turned to my subject, who had stopped singing, and saw him watching me intently.

With deliberation I pulled the cork from the bottle. The odor of the beastly stuff filled the room, sickening even me. I slowly poured about two tablespoonfuls into a glass. Placing one hand on the shoulder of my subject and holding the glass outstretched in my right hand I said, in a most determined and solemn voice:

"This, Mr. Thompson, is the terrible drug known to scientists as assafoetida. It is composed by mixing several deadly drugs together. You notice its odor? (I was almost choked and the young girl was buried in her handkerchief up to her eyes.) Well, if this man is mesmerized and I give him this drug, it can do him no harm; if he is not"—

"What will it do?" asked Mr. Thompson, as I made the impressive pause.

"What will it do?" I repeated, as I shrugged my shoulder slightly. "Well, if he is not mesmerized the effects will be fatal."

The door burst open as he sank limp and helpless into a chair, and Mrs. Thompson came in like a detained tornado. "Don't let her give it to him," she yelled excitedly.

"I won't," he answered in a shaking voice, trying to re-assert himself. "I can't allow my subjects to be treated in this manner." But he continued to sit there gazing at me in a helpless, bewildered way. A quiet reigned for a moment and the subject began to sing, which he had left off when I was relating my fairy tale about assafoetida.

"Would you take that drug?" asked Mr. Thompson of me in an insinuating manner.

"This fatal drug? (The subject quieted his song to listen.) No, sir; nothing on earth could compel me to. This drug? Assafoetida? Why, if I were bound hand and foot I would die before I would swallow it."

Mr. Thompson again became limp and helpless, but Mrs. Thompson sprang at me like a tigress. "What sort of woman are you, anyhow? You would do anything. Give me that poison," and she made a rush for the bottle. I quietly took both bottle and glass in my hand, remarking that the deadly (?) drug was my property. I looked at my subject and he quickly turned his eyes from me and began to sing. "When I'm dead let Tom go free; papa, promise this to me." I smiled slightly and resumed my dramatic discourse.

"Now, Mr. Thompson, this man's life is in your hands. If you say he is mesmerized, I will give him this terrible drug—(Little Eva's song is cut short)—and, if you have told me an untruth, then he will die."

"Stop," he pleaded. (Little Eva's song is resumed.) Turning to his wife he asked, sadly, "Did you ever hear of assafoetida?"

"Yes, I have, but I don't know what it is. Don't allow her to give it to him. She would murder; she will do anything. What are you?" she cried, turning to me. "Have you no feeling?"

I made no reply, but gently held the glass close to my subject's nose. He moved his head from side to side to escape the odor. The room was filled with it and I felt that I must soon close the scene or smother.

"Your decision, Mr. Thompson. I can wait no longer," I said impatiently. The order was more than I bargained for and the young girl whispered:

"I can't stand this smell. Give it to him and let's go."

"Won't you just taste it?" pleaded Mr. Thompson.

"Taste assafoetida?" I asked in surprise. "Mr. Thompson, it is easily seen that you don't know anything about the fatal drug you speak of. (Singing ceases.) I tell you honestly I would die before I would allow any one to give it to me."

"You'll be responsible for his death," he almost sobbed.

"Oh, no; on you rests the responsibility. I do not ask you to tell me if this man is playing the fraud or not. I merely show this fatal drug—assafoetida—and tell you its effect. If Mr. Gray is mesmerized it will not hurt him; if he is not it will kill him. (The singing ceases in a little quaver and he pretends to arrange the imaginary strings on the banjo. He is past singing.) "Shall I give it, Mr. Thompson? Yes or no?" and I held the glass out as a handkerchief is held at an execution.

"No," he gasped. I had conquered. I snapped my fingers lightly in disgust and Mr. Gray dropped the cane and flung himself on the sofa.

"I won't take any drugs, only what is mixed and given by a physician," he said.

I laughed, satisfied with my test. Here was my subject, who was supposed to have been unconscious, disclosing the fact that he knew what we had been talking about. Mr. Thompson was unable to speak, so Mr. Gray continued: "I'll stand anything but drugs or burning."

"Mr. Gray, I admire your nerve. I have all evening, else I should have been rougher with you."

Mr. Thompson refused to give me the names and address of any of his subjects. He did not even ask for the $10 to be given after the satisfactory test.

NELLIE BLY

THE KING OF THE LOBBY

SUNDAY, APRIL 1, 1888

EDWARD R. PHELPS CAUGHT IN A NEATLY LAID TRAP

NELLIE BLY'S INTERESTING EXPERIENCE IN ALBANY

HOW THE LOBBY KING CONTRACTS TO KILL BILLS FOR CASH

DEALING WITH LEGISLATORS AS WITH PURCHASABLE CHATTELS

Phelps Furnishes "THE WORLD" Representative with a List of Assembly Committeemen Who Are Bribable—His Agreement to Kill Assembly Bill No. 191 for $5,000—Afterwards Concludes to Take Less—The Check to Be Made Out to His Side Partner, J.W. Chesbrough—"I Pass or Kill Any Bill"—A Revelation of Baseness Which Should Fill the State with Indignation—The Watch Here.

For I'm a Pirate King!
I'm in the Lobby Ring!
Oh! what an uproarius
Jolly and glorious
Biz for a Pirate King!

I was a lobbyist last week. I went up to Albany to catch a professional briber in the act. I did so. The briber, lobbyist and boodler whom I caught was Mr. Ed Phelps. He calls himself "King of the Lobby." I pretended that I wanted to have him help me kill a certain bill. Mr. Phelps was cautious at first and looked carefully into my record. He satisfied himself that I was honest and talked very freely for a King.

He said that he could buy up more than half the members of the Assembly. It was only a question of money. I pretended to doubt his ability to do this. To prove his strength he took out a list of members and put a lead pencil mark against those he swore he could buy. In his scoundrelly anxiety to prove his strength and to get my money he besmirched the character of many good Assemblymen.

Everybody knows Ed Phelps, the Lobbyist. He has been in trouble before, but his assurance has carried him through. During the celebrated Conkling-Platt Senatorial fight I am told that Phelps, in company with Lo Sessions, was indicted for bribing a member, who took the money up to the Speaker's desk and exposed him.

Again, Mr. Phelps had the assurance to sue one Jones, who lives at One Hundred and Thirty-fifth street and Alexander avenue, for $5,000 on a note which Jones gave. The suit was brought in the Supreme Court here. He even tried to get the courts to sustain his wrong-doing. Jones claimed that he had given Phelps the note because the latter claimed to be able to buy certain senators in aid of a bill. He found that the senators were already in favor of the bill and so refused to pay. The suit was afterwards dropped, because Phelps was threatened with exposure.

But enough of Phelps. He is notorious. Anything I can say cannot blacken his character more. I can only tell what I did.

I selected a bill that I pretended to be interested in. It was Assembly bill No. 191. I said that if it passed it would ruin my husband's patent-medicine business. He said he could suppress it.

The bill itself is not very interesting, but here it is:

STATE OF NEW YORK

No. 191, Int. 298.
In Assembly,
January 27, 1888.

Introduced by Mr. J. W. Smith—Read twice and referred to the Committee on Public Health—Reported from said committee for the consideration of the House and committed to the Committee of the Whole—Ordered, when printed, to be recommitted to the Committee on Affairs of Cities.

AN ACT

For the better protection of the public health in relation to the sale of medicines and medicinal preparations

The People of the State of New York, represented in Senate and Assembly, do enact as follows:

SECTION 1. It shall be unlawful for any person, firm or corporation to sell, offer or advertise for sale in this State any secret or proprietary medicinal preparation or any substance, fluid or compound for use, or intended to be used, as a medicine or for medicinal purposes, unless the person, firm or corporation preparing or putting the same up for use shall first file with the State Board of Health a formula or statement under oath showing all the ingredients and compound parts of said preparation, and the exact proportion of each contained therein, which shall be of standard strength, and also the name under which it is intended to be sold. If said Board of Health shall be satisfied that said preparation or its ingredients are not detrimental to public health or calculated to deceive the public, they shall issue a certificate, under the seal of said Board, authorizing the sale of said preparation in this State, setting forth the formula under which the same is to be prepared, and stating the name under which the same is to be sold, and it shall be unlawful for any other or different article to be placed in or added to said preparation, or of a different degree of strength, or to sell the same under any different name than as set forth in such certificate, and there shall be paid to said State Board of Health for each certificate so stated the sum of $1 for the use of said Board.

SEC. 2 It shall be unlawful to sell, offer or advertise for sale in this State any secret or proprietary medicinal preparation of any substance, fluid or compound for use or intended to be used for medicine or for medicinal purposes, unless the bottle or other vessel containing the same shall have plainly printed upon the outside of the wrapper and label thereof, in the English language, statement of each and all of the component parts and ingredients of the same and the proportion of each contained therein, and in addition thereto the name and place of business of the person, firm or corporation manufacturing the same, and also the words "Sale authorized by the New York State Board of Health."

SEC. 3. Every violation of the provisions of this act shall be deemed a misdemeanor, and in addition thereto the person, firm or corporation violating the same shall forfeit the sum of $200, to be recovered by any person who will sue for the same in any court of competent jurisdiction, one-half thereof to be paid to the person bringing suit and one-half to the State Board of Health for the use of said Board.

SEC. 4. Nothing contained herein shall be construed to prohibit the sale of compounds or medicines put up by a licensed pharmacist in accordance with a physician's prescription, delivered at the time of such sale.

SEC. 5. This act shall take effect immediately.

THE TRIP TO ALBANY.

Armed with this little bill and what I had learned, without confiding in any one, I took the train for Albany. The day (last Tuesday) was not bright, so I spent the time reviewing what I had learned. The only thing that amused me was my list of lucky odd numbers. It was the 27th of March, the train was an odd number, my chair was No. 3 and there was an odd number of passengers. Even when I reached Albany this odd streak did not desert me. I walked to Stanwix Hall and was given room No. 15, and there were only three chairs in the room. I did not look any further for odds.

The next day about noon I made my appearance at the Kenmore Hotel, where Mr. Phelps resides and keeps his legislative office. A half-grown boy in uniform met me at the door and politely escorted me through the lobby of the hotel to the elevator. A number of men who sat around glanced at me curiously.

"I want to see Mr. Phelps, please," I said as the boy started the elevator on its upward flight.

"Do you want to send your card up?" he asked. I had intended to send up a card—not Nellie Bly's, of course—until the boy unwittingly let me know that it was possible to get in without the use of that modern passport. I immediately decided to storm his castle.

I followed Buttons along the softly carpeted halls until he stopped at a door which bore on a little china plate the number 98.

At the boy's second knock an invitation to enter was given in a gruff voice. I stood at the half-opened door and saw a gray-haired man busily writing at a desk which occupied the centre of the room.

"He's in the other room," he replied to Buttons's inquiry for Mr. Phelps, without lifting his head. The boy knocked on the door which separated the two rooms, as he said, "A lady to see you Mr. Phelps."

"Very well, show her to the other door," was the answer, delivered in a rather smooth and not disagreeable voice.

THE MEETING WITH PHELPS.

"Are you Mr. Phelps?" I asked, only to make him confess the fact.

"Yes, madam," he replied, smiling slightly, while he offered me a chair, with the request to "please be seated."

I sat down and looked about me. This was not what I had pictured to myself. This self-possessed, smiling man could not be the vampire I had been made to believe him. As he sat in the chair close by me with a reassuring smile on his face he did not look more than fifty-five years old. He is not a robust man, yet he is not of delicate build. He was dressed plainly, but with taste. There was nothing gaudy or loud about him, as one might imagine from his position. His hair and his side whiskers are gray. His upper lip and chin are clean shaven and he has something of the parson in his appearance.

The room in which we sat was comfortably furnished. It was apparently fitted up for an office; the only piece of furniture which looked out of place was a wardrobe which stood against the centre wall.

I thought my surest bait for this occasion was assumed innocence and a natural ignorance—not entirely assumed—as to how such affairs are conducted.

"Mr. Phelps, I came to consult you on a matter of importance," I began nervously, as if afraid of my position. "I—I hope no one can overhear us?" and I looked at him imploringly.

WINNING HER CONFIDENCE.

"Oh, no; you are safe to speak here," he assured me with a pleasant smile. He drew his chair closer to me and adjusted his glasses carefully on his nose, meanwhile looking me over critically.

"I have come to see you about a bill," I began to explain. His face lighted up a girl's will over strawberry soda on an August day. He smiled encouragingly and rubbed his hands together gently.

"What bill is it?" he asked eagerly.

"A bill about patent medicines," I answered. "My husband is ill and he sent me to New York from Philadelphia to place some advertisements and a friend, who also has a patent medicine told me of this bill, so I came up to see if anything could be done."

"Have you the bill with your?" he asked in a low tone.

"Yes, my friend gave it to me when he told me about it," I replied. He got up and walked over to the door, as if to be positive it was tightly closed. Then he came back, and taking the bill, which I held in my hand, he quickly scanned it.

"Do you think you can kill it?" I asked, with a proper amount of enthusiasm.

"Oh, yes," he responded heartily. "Never fear, I'll have it killed."

Excusing himself he went to the other room. When he came back he had a large ledger in his hand and a large smile on his face. He sat down and, resting the book on his knee, he ran his finger down the alphabet. He turned to a page which was filled with data of bills—a sort of a memorandum. He grew very happy after this and closed the book in order to pay all attention to the poor little lamb who had come to be fleeced.

"What made you come to me?" he asked. I hardly knew what was my best reply, so I said:

"Well, I had often read of you, you know; so when my friend told me about the bill I did not want to place the advertisements and so lose all my money. If that bill passes, you know it will ruin our business."

"That is true," he assented warmly. "It will kill patent medicines. But who sent you to me?" he still urged.

"My friend said I might consult Mr. Phelps," I answered evasively.

"Who is he?" he asked sharply.

"I would not like to give his name without his authority," I said, while I wondered what I would do if he pressed the subject.

"I only wanted to know, because we have had lots of people up here paying to have that bill killed. Do you know Pierce of Buffalo? He is trying to get it killed," he said.

"I never heard of the bill until yesterday," which was true. "I concluded not to go home, so I telegraphed my husband and came on here."

"Where are you from?" he asked.

"Philadelphia. We make a patent medicine there but it sells all over New York State. Do you think you can kill the bill?"

IT WILL TAKE MONEY.

"Oh yes; I assure you of that. Now you keep up your nerve," he said, seeing my assumed nervousness. "I'll kill that bill. It will take money, you know."

It was a shock, this cool assertion. I clutched at my umbrella.

"I am willing to pay anything up to $3,000," I said faintly, "if you assure me it will be stopped."

"I can assure you that," he replied confidently. "Of course, you don't need to talk of $3,000. You see there will be my expenses, and then I will have to pay some Assemblymen."

He went to the end of the room and took from there some pages containing the names and classifications of Assemblymen and Senators—a list of committees. Under the title of "Affairs of Cities" he showed me the twelve names of the men who he said would kill or save the bill.

"Mr. Crosby, of New York, is a rich man and can't be bought," he said calmly. "But we can buy Gallagher, of Erie, Tallmadge, of Kings; Prime, of Essex; De Witt, of Ulster; Hagan, of New York, and McLaughlin, of Kings. The rest are no good."

Oh, Mr. Phelps, I thought sadly, you are into the trap with both feet, for he had marked with his lead-pencil the names as he read them off.

"But if the rest are opposed?" I urged quietly.

"The majority gains," he said sweetly. "There are six out of eleven I can buy."

"How much will it take for them?" I asked, innocently.

"You can get the lot for $1,000."

Great goodness! just imagine, the whole lot for $1,000!

"I must never be known as connected with this," I began to cry. "It frightens me. I wouldn't have it known for anything; though," I added, "I'm willing to pay all it may cost to have the bill killed."

"That is nothing," he said lightly. "That's my business. I just stay here to watch bills for railroad presidents, insurance companies, &c. I'm kept here just to do this," he said firmly. "There is a lawyer of the name of Bates in New York who is also assisting me in getting people who want to fight the same bill you are here about. I've had my agents send out hundreds of copies of it."

SHE CAME TO THE RIGHT MAN.

I felt inclined to ask if it were to bleed the public, but I was afraid. I had not finished yet, so I said, "I thought when I came up that I would go to see Mr. J.W. Smith, who introduced the bill, but I did not know where to find him, so I came direct to you."

"It's a good thing you did," he said warmly. I wondered if he would feel so sure of that in a few days. "Smith is a dissipated and unprincipled fellow. He would have taken your money and given you no returns. You came just to the right one to help you this time."

"You are sure then for about $3,000—which I would rather spend this way than lose it in advertising—you can kill the bill?"

"I can have it killed for that amount or near it," he replied confidently. "Now, where can I see you again to make final arrangements?"

"Any place you state," I replied.

"Well, when you come from Philadelphia—could you come Friday? Well, you telegraph me to meet you at your hotel in New York. Where do you stop?"

"Sometimes at the Sturtevant and again at the Gilsey," I answered. "But then I dread exposure in this affair. Could you not appoint a place where it would attract less attention? Have you no place I could see you?"

"You might come to my office," he said, falling easily into the trap I had laid for him. That's where, of all places, I wanted to go, but I said with well-feigned surprise:

"Oh, you have an office in New York also?"

"Yes in the Boris Building. Do you know where that is? Well, when you cross the Cortlandt Street Ferry you cross to Broadway, and it is about two blocks below. No. 115, room 97. Wait, I'll write it here for you on the bill." And he thereupon took the bill and wrote on the margin, "E.R. Phelps, 115 Broadway, room 97, Boris Building."

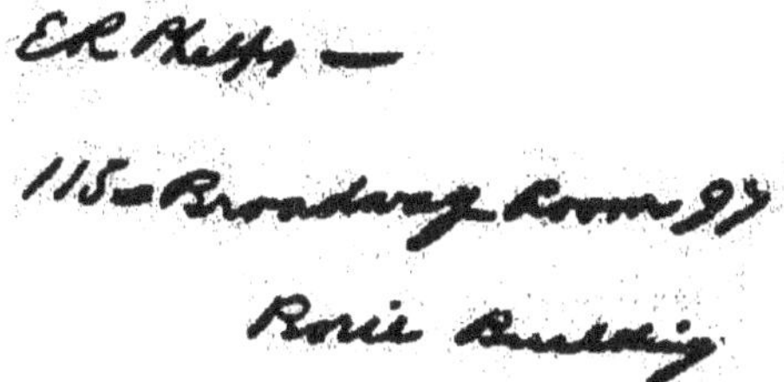

"How very kind of you," I said.

"Now you come down Friday; meet me there between 12 and 1. If I'm not in when you arrive wait for me. I'll be there as soon as possible. I live out of the city. Come down prepared to make final arrangements (this meant pay the price) and I assure you I'll kill the bill afterwards."

"Then I can place my advertisements on Friday, on your assurance that the bill will be killed?" I asked.

"Don't place them until you see me." This was for fear I would resent the price after my advertisements were safely placed. "I assure you, after you see me you can safely place them. The bill will then be dead, or just as good, it will be harmless."

TRYING TO GET RID OF HER.

"Why stay in Albany any longer?" he asked. "Why not take the 1.30 train for New York?" It was close on to that time, and I wanted my dinner, so I told him.

"They carry an eating car," he urged. "Take that train; it will get you in at 5 o'clock"

"That will allow me to go on to Philadelphia," I said, apparently falling into his plans, while I had no intentions of going.

"There is no use in waiting any longer," he urged. "You'll be seen, and that will raise comment. You might as well go now, and be sure to meet me Friday." I began to suspect that he feared if I remained longer some other boodler would get hold of me and rob him of his prey, or that I would discover that which I already knew, i.e., that the patent-medicine bill was really dead and had been for some time. So I promised to go.

"I'll take that list home to show my husband," I said, as I reached for the list he had marked of buyable assemblymen.

"Give it to me," he exclaimed hurriedly, as he took it from my grasp. "Your husband may know some of these men and may tell them. It wouldn't look well for me to cross off those that can be bought. I'll cross out all the names."

THE LIST OF HONEST MEN.

My heart sank. I really believe if hearts could faint mine fainted. Here was my only clue to those who, Mr. Phelps alleged, could be bought. If he crossed out all I could not tell one from the other. I shut my eyes and thought of several nasty things against cunning men and odd numbers. Then I opened them and looked blankly as he started to destroy my clue. He placed the sheet on a book on his desk and made crosses against the remaining names, excepting Mr. Crosby's, and then he handed it to me. I glanced at it, and with a prayer of thanks folded it hurriedly and placed it in my purse.

The rough covering of the book had caused the lead pencil to make a peculiar spotted line against the second lot of names marked by Mr. Phelps.

When marking the original ones the committee list was on a flat, smooth surface, and as it happens that the lines are as distinctly recognizable as though they were in different colors.

Here is a fac-simile of the list just as he marked it:

Affairs of Cities.

Mr. Crosby, of New York;	Mr. DeWitt, of Ulster;
Gallagher, of Erie;	Hagan, of New York;
Burns, of Westchester;	Blumenthal, of New York;
Tallmadge, of Kings;	McLaughlin, of Kings;
Prime, of Essex;	Sullivan, of Monroe.
Cromwell, of Richmond;	

After dining at my hotel I started for the city. I had told Mr. Phelps that the name I gave him—Miss Consul—was an assumed one, taken because my own and my husband's name was so familiar that everybody would recognize it at once So I went under my maiden name.

As soon as I got to New York I sent a telegram to a friend in Philadelphia, instructing him to forward it from there to Mr. Phelps. It was done to ease any doubts he might have. This ran as follows:

PHILADELPHIA, March 28.

E.R. Phelps, Room 96 Kenmore, Albany, N.Y.

Have made satisfactory arrangements with husband. Will see you as agreed.

MISS CONSUL.

THE SECOND MEETING.

Friday came and with it the disquieting intelligence that the bill I professed to be interested in had been reported adversely by the committee on Thursday. Would my story be without a climax? How would Mr.

Phelps act under this news? However, I borrowed a long sealskin dolman to give me a matronly look, and hiring a hansom I was driven to No. 135 Broadway, the Boris Building.

Mr. Phelps's name was on the door of No. 97, and before I could knock the door was opened, and he, smiling sweetly, stood before me and invited me in. "My son," he said, introducing a rather handsome young man who sat behind the solitary desk the office contained. I was wondering how Mr. Phelps knew I was at the door, when I glanced out and saw that from his window he could see everybody who came up on the elevator. The door of the office was darkened.

"I suppose you know about the bill?" he inquired sharply.

"Oh, no," I said, in assumed voice of alarm and ignorance. "Can't it be killed?"

"Yes, that's it," he said smiling, "it has been killed."

"So soon. How clever you must be!" I remarked flatteringly.

"Well, I saw that you were anxious to kill the bill and I told you that it should be killed. It's done. That will never bother you again." Mr. Phelps's son here took his silk hat and left the room.

"How did you ever manage it?" I asked simply, with a world of admiration in my eyes.

HOW CLEVER MR. PHELPS WAS.

"Why, you see"—he talked in a confiding whisper—"I went to work on it right away. You see I had it transferred from the committee that first had it. As I told you, Mr. Crosby could not be bought, and I knew he and some others determined to pass it, so I went to the ones I told you I could get and told them I wanted that bill killed. They said they were anxious to get rid of it, so I had it reported back to the Committee on Public Health. I knew I could get them easier."

"Oh, how very clever!" I breathed rapturously, "and they did not refuse?"

"No, they asked me what it was worth," he said boldly, "and I told them $1,000, and so they promised to do it."

"They did not dare refuse," I murmured again.

"No; I should say they did not," he said laughingly. "You see that's my business. I'm the head of the Lobby."

"Oh, indeed! What a good thing I went to you. How can you ever do all the work?"

"Why, I keep a lot of runners who watch and know everything that happens. I am head. They report to me, and I have books in my rooms where entries are made of every bill and notes of every incident connected with it. You noticed when you gave me the bill in the Kenmore I went into another room and got a large book? Well, by that book I at once saw all about the bill and knew just what to say to you."

"What did you say to the committee about the bill?" I asked, curiously.

"I just told them the bill had to be killed, and I told them it was worth $1,000. I had to give my check for it right off, but I told you that I could have it done for $1,000 for the committee, with my expenses extra."

"My husband could not understand how you could buy the whole committee for $1,000. It seems so little," I suggested.

"I couldn't if that was my only case, but you see this is my business. I spend all my time at it. I pay these men heavily on other bills, so that makes some bills more moderate."

"Then you can have any bill killed?"

HE OWNS THE HOUSE.

"I have control of the House and can pass or kill any bill that so pleases me," was Mr. Phelps's astounding reply.

"Next week," he continued, "I am going to pass some bills and I'll get $10,000 for it. I often get that and more to pass or kill a bill."

I was stricken dumb. I did not know what to say. The brazen effrontery of this appalled me.

"You can take this," handing me the Albany *Journal*, "to show your husband that the bill was killed. You will also see an account of it in today's WORLD."

"I would like you to tell me who sent you to me," continued Mr. Phelps. "Not that I want to pry into your affairs, but it may be one of my agents and I want to pay him."

The only agent had been my own sweet self, so I demurred and said I feared to give the name without the man's authority.

"I have to pay the money for killing the bill to the committee this week," Mr. Phelps began, returning to the subject of money, "and as I got it done so quickly I thought I would deal honestly with you and only charge you $250 for my expenses. That will make a total of $1,250. Could you write a check here for that amount?" he asked boldly.

FENCING ABOUT THE MONEY.

"I—oh, dear, I'm dreadfully frightened," I exclaimed, to give myself time to think. He smiled, as if well pleased. "You see, my husband told me not to do anything that would connect me with this affair." I breathed easier. "For that reason I do not want to give a check."

"Well, you could write out a check payable to J.F. Chesbrough. He is a relative of mine, and it's just the same as giving it to me; or you could make it out in my son's name."

"No, I don't want it made out to Phelps, I'm afraid," I said; "but if you send your son up to the St. James Hotel, where I am stopping, I will give it to him there."

"That will do," he said carelessly, and then he called "Johnny! Johnny!"

"Aha! Johnny is waiting on the outside," I thought, and comes at the call when the poor lamb is fleeced. I began to fear that really, somehow, they would compel me to pay the money.

"I'd rather make out a check," I began, hastily.

"Very well, I'll write the name for you," and suiting the action to the word he took from his desk a white envelope, smaller than the ordinary envelope, and made the check payable to. He then wrote in the corner the amount, $1,250.

"My son will go up with you and get the check," he said, and again began to call "Johnny."

"Oh, then I might just as well get the money and hand it to him," in half hopes of getting him to abandon the idea of sending someone with me. I wanted a chance to escape. He took the envelope from me and tore the ends and back off it. I wanted to save that name, so I said quickly: "Give me that, I'll write the check after all and give it to your son."

He handed it back. The name was yet clear, but the numbers were partially torn away, only "50" remained. Here it is:

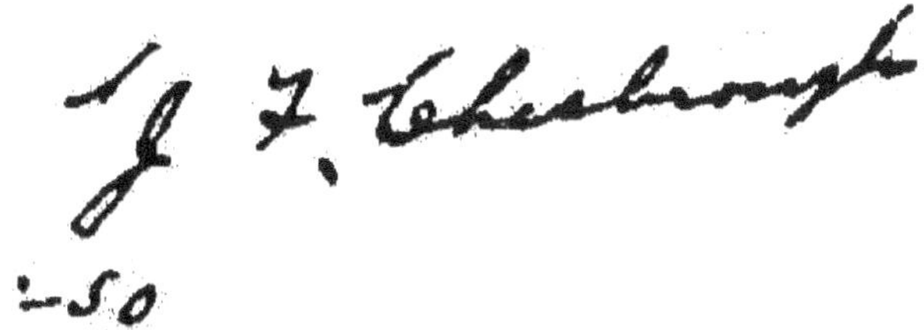

Mr. Phelps showed me the telegram, which purported to come from me in Philadelphia, after he had called his son in to tell him to accompany me to my hotel.

SUCH AN HONEST LITTLE WOMAN.

"I felt queer about you at first," he said. "It is the most unusual thing in the world for a woman to come to me for such work. First I thought it was a trap to catch me." I looked at him and then at his son in a hurt manner. "But then I saw how innocent you were and how honest. I must say I was surprised though."

"Well, you see, I did not know what to do," I urged, as if I had blundered. "I was so ignorant of it all."

Mr. Phelps, jr., leaned on the desk and glanced at me admiringly. My cheeks began to burn and I began to long for freedom. Would I never escape them.

"Madam is going up to the St. James," Phelps, sr., explained to Phelps, jr., "and you are to go with her. She will give you a check there for some work I have been doing for her."

"Can't you come along?" I asked Mr. Phelps, sr. "I hate to have your son connected with this; besides I am better acquainted with you." I was getting deeper and deeper into it and I didn't know what to do.

"Father, you go," urged the young man. "You might as well. You would leave the office in a half hour, anyway."

I said I had a cab at the door, but that I would not like to be seen taking Mr. Phelps away in it. They urged, but I was firm, and at last Mr. Phelps said his father would go up on the Elevated Railway and would get there about the same time I would.

FAREWELL WORDS.

"He can wait for me in the parlor," I began, joyously, now that I could escape. Wait for me? Well, he would wait years before I would come. "I'll get the money, and when I go in the parlor I will hand it to you. No one will see me there." He could be sure, no one would ever see me give him money.

"Where will you get the money?" he asked, impudently.

"Father, that's nothing to you, so she gets it," the young man remarked, for which I looked my heartfelt thanks.

"In a half hour, in the parlors of the St. James Hotel?" said Mr. Phelps, as I arose to start.

"Yes," I replied, and walked smilingly with the young man to the elevator.

"I was extremely nervous over this," I said, half apologizing for my hesitating manner.

"You'll get over that by the time you have had more bills to kill," he said, encouragingly. I laughed and said that I thought I should.

I got into the cab, gave the driver instructions to go a thousand different ways and to stop at THE WORLD office, where I could write my story. He was a man who knew his business and I felt confident in a short time that I was not followed.

So far as I personally know, Mr. Phelps is still waiting my arrival in the parlor of the St. James Hotel.

NELLIE BLY

[EDITOR'S NOTE: For the complete follow-up reporting to Bly's exposure of Phelps, including a full transcript of sworn testimony by both Bly and Phelps before the New York State Legislature later that month, see my novella CLEVER GIRL, *available now.]*

Nellie Bly's Odd Letters

Sunday, May 27, 1888

Queer Communications Written by All Kinds of Strange People

She Began Getting Affectionate Letters at the Tender Age of Four—Of Late Her Mail Has Not Room No Loving—Cranks Who Want Her Aid—Delightful Notes from Girls—A Singular Collection.

If there is anything for which I have a special weakness, barring a fine horse and chewing-gum, it is letters. My mania for them has been the growth of years—I don't dare say how many. It began when I was about four years old and still wore bibs and such juvenile apparel. The seed which implanted this mania was the receipt of a letter addressed to my full Christian name which crossed the envelope twice. The writer was a boy of twelve, so I have been told. I had formed his acquaintance while he was visiting his grandmother in the country. We got up the flirtation by peeping at each other through the crevices in the back fence. He soon called, and many long summer days we spent "keeping house" under the east piazza. Cupid's cousin, Miss Sudden Fancy, made a dent in our baby hearts. So my little lover wrote me many misspelled love letters after cherry time when he had been taken home.

As my number of birthdays increased so increased my mania for letters. I cherish a tender respect for the gray uniform, and the sound of the postman's shrill whistle arouses more blissful thrills in me than the first blood does in an amateur pugilist. Since my debut as a mad girl last October my mail has been of generous size and my collection of letters unique. People of all classes have written me, and their letters come like a friendly hand from the dark.

I turn over my parcel of unknown letters, and I feel a sense of happiness that in so many different lives people think of me. First comes a dainty, scented thing which betrays the happy school-girl, who writes:

> "We girls think you are just too lovely for anything. It must be perfectly beautiful to go around just as you please and to catch all the bad people." I turn from it with a smile to another just as sweet and girlish—and, say, what is sweeter than a girlish girl?
>
> "Please won't you tell me if you are a man or a woman? My chum's brother says you never existed at all, and I say you are a girl. Please decide for us. Inclosed find stamp for reply.
>
> "P.S.—Do you play tennis?"

School children write me for a favorite maxim or quotation; working people write on every subject; reformers write to enlist me in their cause, and, in short, I think my letters very interesting, even to the autograph hunters. Do I answer them? Why, certainly, those that require answers. Let me show you a few samples of my queer letters.

> CITY, NOV. 26.
>
> *Nellie Bly,*
>
> DEAR MADAM: As you are a friend to the working class, I take the liberty to address you, thinking you would help me. I would like two ladies employed during the day to board. They could have a clean, comfortable home, good board, washing included, at $4 per week. I have advertised, but, receiving no reply, I decided to write to Nellie Bly, as I know she can do anything, and I know she can get me some boarders. Come up Tuesday A.M. And judge for yourself, and I will be glad to see you, as I may not be home in the afternoon of Tuesday, and I expect to be out Wednesday.

I am sorry to say, as I was the only homeless girl I knew, I could not assist her in getting boarders.

> DEAR MISS BLY: I have an old lady with me who is going to die soon and wants to see you. She is poor and has no money, and as you do so much good I thought you might give her some. The old lady is kept to her bed, so when you come be sure to bring not less than $5. Come soon or she may not live to see you.

I do not like to be referee in family quarrels, so I did not answer the following unique note:

> MY DEAR MISS NELLIE BLY: Do you believe in wearing bustles and

> do you wear one? My husband says no sensible woman will, and I have heard him say, when reading your contributions to THE WORLD, that you are the cleverest woman he ever heard of. Please write that you wear a bustle so I can show him. It will be a great favor to me.

I often receive suggestions, and I think that they are the most agreeable letters a press writer can get. Most letters are from people who have been swindled. Often I should be able to investigate it, and so save others from a like fraud, if the writer would only have enough confidence to tell the whole story and give addresses. Such things are always treated in confidence.

Ever since I wrote my experience in the Blackwell's Island Insane Asylum I have received scores of letters on the subject. The majority are from people claiming that they are or were unjustly incarcerated. Others are from doctors and nurses wanting to expose in inner workings of the institutions. Oh, the tales they tell make one's heart sick! Never, since I mentioned the brutality shown the insane, have I been able to allow myself to study the subject. The hopelessness and horror of the patients' lives rack my nerves. Nor is this confined to our country. Here is a letter I received from Scotland:

> SCOTLAND, NOV. 25, 1887.
>
> As a friend sent me THE WORLD newspaper, date 16th October, I was interested in Miss Bly's experience in the lunatic asylum. I have been interested in that subject this twenty years, and if I could write, a thing I am not accustomed to, I would surprise you with my experience. One time I had the misfortune to be laid up with what was thought brain fever. I was sent off to a Royal Asylum, not a charitable one, for we had to pay well. The first night a cowardly brute of an attendant attacked me with a candlestick, and then for three days I knew nothing. When I got better I found a cut on the crown of my head and one of my hands cut to the bone. I asked him about his first night's performance and he told me I tell out of bed and cut my head, and cut my hand fight with the door. That's the way they always get off. After eight days my face all broke out and my hair had to be cut off. The attendant had washed me with a sponge, as I was not able to wash with my cut hand. Well, I looked in a bedroom one day and saw a man in bed with bad legs, and I was horrified to see when sponging his legs with the same sponge as they had washed me. I told the doctor I got this from the dirty sponge, and he said it was all bosh and that he was very glad my face was broke out, as my friends would not be allowed to see me for weeks. The doctor had only two words for us. He just when through the wards once, in the forenoon, and if one asked any-

thing, it was "All right," or "By-and-By."

As so his letter runs, a repetition of asylum brutality. A patient wrote me from a New Jersey asylum asking me to correspond with him. "It is a privilege for which women have beseeched," he wrote, "and which I grant only to you. You must first send me your photograph and complete description of yourself, else I will not answer your letters, though your heart break. I am god of the sun and have lived 10,000 years and shall bestow on you life everlasting."

Still another wrote that he had been searching for hundreds of years for me and that I had been given him as wife by six kings and four emperors. Had not the doctors stolen his money and made him a prisoner we would be King and Queen of England. He begged that I have him released, that we might regain our rights. Victoria tottering on her throne?

A letter written in the city was a most peculiar thing. It began so:

> *Nellie Bly,*
>
> MOST RESPECTED MISS: You have hunted me out. Now tell me why you want me. I was not fit to be sheltered by the roof that covered you, so I fled without causing you any trouble. Take advice of poor friends and never see me again. I saw you the other night and know you had hunted me out. Tell me when and where you want me and why? You must tell me and then never again will you behold this watcher in life, must not be followed. I never believed any fair girl, still know that I am determined I shall not fight.

There was a lot more to it, in the same style, and a name and address, written in a plain business hand, was given. I did not hunt him out and have not heard from him since. This rather startling letter was from a woman:

> *To Nellie Bly:*
>
> Perhaps you will be able to appreciate my sincere thanks (and it must be the thanks of many helpless, tortured, innocent prisoners of a free nation!) for the abuse you endure, risk and expose.
>
> The free press is the only hope for the people as a truthful weapon.
>
> Asylums and manufactured lunatics are the invention of late years.
>
> The glut in the lunatic market is kept up by artificial means, which is brutal and a disgrace to the nation.
>
> There is no such disease as insanity; it is poisoning!
>
> I have made this known almost daily for several years to those who were convinced and to those who did not wish to be convinced.
>
> Yellow fever is bilious fever, brought on by too much acid.
>
> Some doctors say that arsenic poisoning is sometimes mistaken for

cholera. *(New-Times.)*

I inclose two articles for you to republish.

One of the clippings referred to was entitled "Who the Gods Destroy They First Make Mad," and the other was a short notice headed "A Drugged Nation."

A young man in the West wrote that for fifteen years he had loved and been true to "Nellie Blythe," but since she had gone on the stage he had lost her, and he begged to know if I were the same girl. I had the letter answered, and told him that Miss Helen Blythe was on the stage at the present time and that my name is minus "the."

Many letters of which I take no notice consist of a few lines of command, such as "Come to — at such an hour," without a word of explanation. Others say: "I would be pleased to have an interview with you at such an hour. Call." I am not even curious enough to wonder what they want.

Among my latest received was this:

> DEAR MADAM: I know your time is precious, but if I could see you for a few minutes I think you would take an interest in my trouble. As you are so good at exposing bribery you could do a great deal of good and save life that is in danger, for money. Money is my tempting, and a large sum at that. They have carried it to such an extent and put up so many jobs to get it that with your tact to help I could stop it. For the sake of all that is good and just grant me an interview as soon as possible, telling me where to see you.

Who could resist "ministering to a mind diseased" at such a plea, although they knew they could do nothing to really benefit?

Do I ever get anonymous letters?

No, I never did until recently, that is since the publication of my last article, April 1. As I have known where they came from they have not bothered me, especially since I have such a contempt for anything that is too cowardly to sign a name and address. A letter unsigned never hurts. The last one received was rather unique. Here is a reproduction of it. It was made up of words cut from different newspapers and read:

> "WARNING!—Last Edition.—NEVER sign Nellie Bly AGAIN to any ARTICLE printed in THE WORLD or any *other* NEWSPAPER printed in ENGLISH.—Business."

NELLIE BLY

Why Don't Women Reform?

Sunday, June 17, 1888

Nellie Bly Asks This Question Of Police-Court Prisoners

She Spends a Day at Jefferson Market Court and Jail—Drink Seems to Be Responsible for Most of the Evil—Missionaries Apparently Can Render Little Aid—What the Women Have to Say for Themselves.

I went to the Jefferson Market Police Court on Wednesday. It was a beautiful bright sunny morning outside. Within the contrast was not a pleasant one. The courtroom was dark and forbidding. On an elevated platform, inclosed by a high board partition, sat Judge Ford, a pleasant-faced silver-haired man, who seemed to judge rightly the accused brought before him. Directly in front of Judge Ford's desk topping off the board partition was a wide shelf furnished on either end with a gas jet and Bibles. This is reached by a small platform mounted by two steps. In couplets, like the gas jets and Bibles, an officer occupies either end. Their mission is to direct prisoners in swearing—on the Bible, of course—and to restrain their emotions during examinations. On this and at its base the prisoners relate their tales of trouble.

Three colored men were called. One was accused of moving another's trunk, free of charge, and forgetting where he left it. It had been left by the owner at George Washington's house. The defendant said George complained that it was in his way and asked him to remove it. The Judge did not seem to think "cherry-tree-hatchet" tales fellow the name, and George had to swear and kiss the Bible just the same as if he had been

John Smith. George swore, in true Southern dialect, that he had never seen the prisoner before he called for the trunk.

"What did you do with the trunk?" asked the Judge.

"I dunno, sir: I think I left it at 127." He was sent back to jail until further evidence could be procured.

A woman clad in a calico dress, with a shabby shawl over her shoulders, tried several times to get out of the iron gate. She evidently did not want to appear against her husband, a short, cross-eyed man who, were he as square as his face, would be a sure delegate for wings. He had taken a clock, among other things, and was trying to pawn it to get money for drink, she said, mildly, and he did not deny it very strongly. She left sadly, bearing the clock under her arm, while he was sent back to jail. I wondered how much she would here to suffer for it when he gets out.

Then came two boys, who had run off from home to join the Wild West. The mother of one broke down completely at the sight of her son in charge of an officer. Next came four women who made some display in dress. "I have nothing to say," was the stereotyped reply of each to the Judge.

"Ten dollars or ten days," he said. They walked quickly down, paid their fines and quitted the room. Benefited? Taught a lesson? No, with a capital N and an accent. They may be there again the very next night.

IN THE PRISONERS' WARD.

The most interesting part of my visit was the talk I had afterwards with the prisoners. The big man who opens the door to the jail had a kind face but no manners. "This is my friend, Miss Hamilton," said my escort, and the tall man politely turned his head aside and said something about us being without passes, but still we got in. First we saw a long, narrow room with high barred windows. On one side was a slanting board table where the prisoners sleep their first night. Of course there are no pillows or bed clothes. The softest thing in sight is the board. The women's side was empty, but the men quite filled their room. Some came boldly up to the grated door when I came in sight. Others rested carelessly on their board beds, using their coats for pillows. Those I spoke to were quite unlike other prisoners I have seen. They were guilty! That is, they acknowledged their guilt.

"My wife put me here," said one comely looking fellow, "because I drank."

"Why do you drink?" I asked.

"Because I have too much money. Buy clothes? Why, I have three suits. You wouldn't want me to buy more. You'll be getting married some day and putting your man in here."

WHAT THE MEN EAT.

We mounted the iron staircase, taking care not to rub against the white-washed walls, and were soon in the ward, or whatever they may call it, where the male prisoners were. It looked the same as any public building for punishment. The walls were all white washed, the floors were all stone and everything marvellously clean. I walked along the iron balconies and talked with a few of those confined behind the barred doors. James, the newsboy-bootblack arrested on the charge of robbing an express wagon, rose, pale and worried, from a reclining position on his cot.

"It's lonely in here," he said. "Do you know when I will get out? I don't know nothing about it" (referring to the robbery). "I black boots for the Mayor's secretary, and was there the time they said I did it. If I could only send him a letter he'd come to see me and sell them. Read this," handing me a paper. "They say I'm a legged tief, which means an old tief."

I read in the newspaper notice "an alleged thief" and explained to him the difference much to his relief.

"I never took nothing, and I never was 'rested cept for playin' ball," he said. "I know they can't do nothin' with me 'cause I'm innocent, but it's a long time to be sent up."

In the next cell was a frank-looking young man.

"What are you in for?" I asked.

"For stealing a watch," he said, getting up on his cot and looking at me with a smile.

WHY HE STOLE.

"Why did you steal it?" I asked again. He looked at his hands as they lay clasped on his knees and then up to me rather sadly. "I don't know why. The man in the next cell—that's his wife and baby visiting him—was with me and we got drunk. I don't remember how it was, but we got in a fuss on the street and the watch was found in my hands. I must have taken it, of course, but I was too drunk to know anything about it. When I get out I'll keep sober. I hope the other man will get out. You see he has a wife, and the watch was in my hands." As he talked the delicate young girl swayed back and forth in her endeavor to hush the mournful cries of the babe whose father stood behind the iron bars quietly watching them.

A man, said to be "Weeping Lawrence," but who told me his name was Campbell, was next seen. He had been sitting despondently on the cot until I spoke to him. He rose a tall, well-built man, of probably forty years, and removing his plain straw hat, stood with uncovered head. Of course he said he was not the "Weeping Lawrence" who had been gathering subscriptions for twenty years to bury his dead wife. His wife was alive and he was a stonecutter by trade. He had me write a card to notify his wife of his imprisonment and then I left him.

The little runaways were confined in one cell. They lay on the cot building a future for themselves. They were not in the least ashamed of their Wild West escapade, nor of the money they had purloined. I think had they been confined in separate cells, with no one to speak to, that their punishment might have made an impression. Confinement is not so hard when one has congenial companions.

WITH THE WOMEN.

I then left the men and talked some time with Mrs. Byrnes, the matron of the female ward. I really think no one could fill the position better. She is a delicate-looking refined little woman, anxious to do what she can for the poor creatures in her charge. They all spoke of her kindness. "I get to know them all," she said, "they became regular guests. I never knew any to reform. They start in looking very well and go down, down to the very lowest. The cause? Drink. But they have good hearts. They often use horrible language to me, but I do not mind it, I know they are in drink. When sober they are nice. I have done little favors for them that came within my power, and they always repay them."

She escorted me into the ward, which is exactly like those below. A motley crew of women were sitting about on the benches and a few were walking up and down the ward. What pen could ever describe the pictured misery? The pencil of Doré might have got a sketch of Hades from such a scene, so lost, so hopeless were their expressions. Is there no remedy for this? Is there no punishment that will teach these creatures to do differently? Who is more competent than themselves to say? I decided to ask them.

"I want to speak to you," I said placing a detaining hand on the shoulder of the awning-maker. She passed in her walk, looked at me inquiringly from beneath the black straw hat and red reeds while she folded her arms in her shawl across her breast. She was better dressed than the others and looked like an honest working girl.

WAS SHE INNOCENT?

"What brought you here?" I asked. "The policeman," she answered, looking with cold, gray eyes at me. "His story was false. I was returning from a friend's and it was only 8 o'clock. What brought me here first? Drink, of course. I lost my husband and then my only child—a girl of eight years. I commenced drinking, and here I am. There's no use trying to do differently. Once the police know you they have you out all the time drunk or sober."

She started off in her short, nervous walk and I spoke to others. A colored girl had fallen to the floor in a fit and the majority grouped around her. Two women in "ticking" dresses, with their hair combed back smoothly and their sleeves rolled up, attracted my attention. "What brought you here?" I asked the larger.

"Drink," she answered, looking up with a smile. "I took two glasses of beer while out marketing. The lady scolded me for it and I felt ashamed. So I went out and drank more. The police brought me here and I've got ten days," and she began to roll her sleeves up higher, without any pugilistic intentions, however.

"And how did you get here?" I asked of the girl beside her.

"Same thing" she said. "My time's up, though, and I get out to-day. I don't drink much. I went in and took a glass of beer and it set me off. It was fixed."

"That is true," said Mrs. Byrnes, who, having come) in, had overheard the girl's story. "There are many, many places run quietly, having the appearance of a private house, and when girls go in there they are drugged and their little bit of money taken from them."

THE POLICE POWERLESS.

"Why don't the police raid them?" I asked.

"I do not know. I suppose the majority are unknown to them."

"You won't drink again when you get out?" I said to a battered-up creature in a cheap calico.

"Oh, yes I will," she said earnestly, "just as soon as my three months are up I'll get drunk."

"It only makes me worse," said a colored girl who sat next, while several others joined in saying it did no good.

"What shall we do with you, then?" I asked in bewilderment.

"Why, they should build a place and put in the ones who keep it up for life. It's no use putting them in and out all the while. They never reform."

"We are not so bad at first, but every time we go back we get worse," said another. "Then, you see, the police get to know us, and it's no use trying. They run us in just for the sake of having a case. Then they lie about us."

"What brought you here?" I asked an old woman, whose face was bloated almost out of shape.

"You know, same thing as brings us all," she replied, lifting her bleary, bloodshot eyes to me "Do different? Who wants to? It's no use. I've only been out three weeks, about as long as I ever stay I've got my position on 'The Island.' I get discharged. I take a holiday, and then I always go back."

THE MISSIONARY.

Just then a gray-haired woman, in a little black poke bonnet, came in. She placed a pair of black-rimmed glasses astride her, and from the satchel on her arm distributed tracts. "I am sorry to see you here," she said to me, taking me for a prisoner. "But he sends us here to soften our hearts. He took all my loved ones from me to soften mine, and he brings you here to soften yours. If I was not too old I would lift up my voice and sing for you all. I must give you a tract that tells of his kingdom."

"Thank you, madam," I said gravely, taking the little blue paper, entitled "Looking unto Jesus." This incident amused the prisoners very much.

"We can't laugh at her, for she is an old woman," explained a pretty, dark-eyed girl who sat in front of me. "She has been twenty-five years visiting here, but missionaries do no good here. What prisoner will need such talk at such a moment? Their whole thought is on how they will get out, or how they can put in their 'time.' There are moments when one thinks of religion as they do of home, but it isn't on such an occasion. I know such talk hardens us instead of doing us good."

"How can we reform you people, then, when persons and religion have no effect?"

"You can't reform us so long as we don't want to reform," she said, toying with the long, slender purse she carried. "A missionary talked with me for an hour one day. I kept silent because she was an old woman. She wanted me to go to a charitable home to reform. 'Madam,' I said, when she had ceased, 'what's the use of going to that home, when I have one of my own to go to, if I want to reform!' "

"Why doesn't imprisonment reform people?" I asked curiously.

"Because we have congenial companions. We get board fee and altogether it's a pleasant change or rest from the streets."

"Why did you leave home?" I asked.

REFORM IMPOSSIBLE.

"My parents were too strict with me," she said, with a sigh. "I was between fifteen and sixteen and they would not allow me any companions except of their own choice, whether I liked them or not. I ran off one night to a hall and my father beat me for it, so I ran away. I have regretted it since, but it's useless now. Indeed, many parents drive children away by being too harsh."

"Why don't you reform?"

"It's an impossible thing to do. Even if I were to try, the very police who have pulled me in would jeer me on the streets, and if I were returning from work they would ask if I were up to my old tricks. They have done it. Once the police know you, you are done for. They pull you in and tell stories, and the more you say to the Judge the more you hurt yourself."

"Try to reform; it's worth making a trial," I suggested. She looked at me with a twinkle in her soft, black eye, while she said a little warningly:

"Don't turn missionary."

"I won't," I replied, feeling utterly helpless; "but really you understand the subject and the subjects so well you should be a missionary yourself. But go to work. It seems so hard after a while."

"There are things hundreds of times harder than work," she replied, a shadow coming into box eyes.

"Then you don't want to reform?" I said, sadly. She pressed my proffered hand. We gazed a moment at one another and parted. I tell you it is useless!

Another girl, who was imprisoned on the same charge, said:

"Why don't the police pull men, who are worse than we are? They insult helpless working women. Why don't the police protect us instead of protecting men, who are simply able to care for themselves? When a woman is insulted on the streets she must endure it unless she wants to appear in a court-room. There are many men who lounge around the streets at night just to insult timid women. I have known plenty of them. Are they ever pulled? If the officers were half so diligent in protecting women you would see more men brought up in the mornings that you new see women."

I believe such to be the case and I think the girl's suggestion a good one.

What made the greatest impression on me?

First, the utter uncleanness of the modern form of punishment.

Second, that the majority of misery results from cheap drinks.

NELLIE BLY

How to be Cured by Faith

Sunday, July 1, 1888

Nellie Bly Has Some Experience With A "Mind Healer."

No Woman Is Really Ill, She Only Thinks She Is—Even Beauty Can Be Had for the Thinking—As for a Stomach, the Faith Curers Will Take That Away Entirely—A Queer Eye-Closing Séance.

Faith and a dollar bill. That is all that is necessary to procure the "influence" of a mental healer for any of the maladies which beset the human race. Of course the faith must be unlimited. So must the dollar bills. With the proper amount of both the ailment will either grow better or worse, as the century passes away. What do mind healers doctor? Everything—from lovesickness to a broken leg—and all by faith and influence. The pull on nature held by doctors and druggists is over, say the healers, and in the near future the former will be day laborers and the latter's income will be derived entirely from the fizzing soda-fount.

My first experience was with Miss Bell, of Broadway, who calls herself a "mental healer." Her flat is shady and cool. The reception-room, with a lounge, some easy chairs and bric-à-brac, has an air of comfort and of cleanly keeping. A green palm, standing in a fancy vase near the window, moved the tips of its long, graceful foliage sleepily in the lazy wind. The girl who admitted me said Miss Bell was at home, yet I waited quite a time for her appearance. It caused me to wonder if mental healers, like ordinary women, had to devote some time to their gowns before they greeted their early callers. However, I played pleasing airs on the keyboard of my patience and endeavored to find comfort in my situation.

Presently the sliding doors at my back were opened. On turning around I saw a delicate-looking woman being ushered from the inner temple by one I instinctively felt was Miss Bell. She told me to sit down, pointing to a rocker near the window, through which the light fell on my face. I felt that this position was given me so that she might study her subject. She leaned against the desk, shrewdly "taking me in" while she asked me questions about my assumed complaint.

From Miss Bell's appearance I would say that she could easily sway the will of weak and sickly women. The extremely heavy brows which overshadowed her dark eyes lent a severity to her strong and not unkind face. Her black hair showed in the slight streaks of gray that age was coming on. She was closed in a thin, loose wrapper, appropriate for the warm morning.

"Is anything wrong with you?" she asked, pleasantly.

"I am troubled with insomnia," said I, trying to make my eyes have a dreamy, half-awake expression.

"Why, you don't look sleepy," she replied, smartly. That's one for her, I thought as I mentally gave myself a brace. I then explained that, though I could not sleep at night, I did not feel drowsy until the afternoon. This appeared to satisfy her, for she began to search for a cause.

"Have you any trouble?" she asked.

"Nothing of a serious nature," I replied, easily.

"Have you nothing on your mind now?" I might have mentioned dressmaker bills, a search for a summer resort that filled the qualifications of its advertisement and other similar things which silver the hair and implant crows'-feet in conspicuous places. But I did not. I only made her easy on the subject. She brought a book and pencil from the desk, and, giving her one of the names I have in reserve for such occasions, she wrote it down.

"Married or single?" she asked.

"Neither," I answered thoughtlessly. Glancing up I caught her look of—I might say, apprehension—so I added, "Widow."

"Oh," she sighed, sympathetically: "how long since?"

"Very nearly three years, I guess," was my careless reply. Whew! I was positively stupid. A widow! and forgotten how long since I had entered such a delightful state! Where's the woman that could do such a thing? I concluded it would be wiser to add hastily, "'Twas three years last February."

"Does that weigh on your mind—prevent you from sleeping?" she asked, soothingly.

"No, madam," I answered, emphatically. Then followed a moment's silence in which we looked at one another.

"No children?"

"No."

"When did you first find it coming on?"

"The wakefulness? I could not say," I answered, truthfully.

She then inquired how I spent my nights. I told her I read a great deal, and mentioned what books. She asked if I had been treated by a physician, and when I said I had and found no relief, she assured me that it was wasting time and money; that it was useless to take medicine, and she could cure me in a short time if I would take her treatment and have faith. My faith in unknown and untried things is not one of my strong qualities, but I would at least allow her to make a test of her powers.

A SLEEPING MATCH.

"Make yourself perfectly easy in this chair," she said. I did so. The chair was roomy, and yet it was one of those chairs that fit one so well that it's bound to bring a feeling of ease. It is policy for mental healers to own comfortable chairs. "When you get a position that is perfectly easy sit still, do not move, and keep your eyes closed."

She sat down in an easy willow chair that stood by the side of and facing mine. Her elbow rested on the arm of the chair and she covered her eyes with her hand. I closed my eyes. I had imagined all forms of treatment employed by mind curists, but this was entirely different from any of them. I had heard that they sat back to back while the influence accomplished its mission. I was rather relieved to find there would be no back-rubbing.

NELLIE BLY SHUTS HER EYE.

I wondered, lastly coming nearer my mortal self, what sort of people would come here and give a dollar to have a companion in an eye-shutting séance. I smiled when I thought what an eye-shutting business it was any way. How funny it would be, I thought, if her eyes were open and she saw that smile. Would she not think my faith was weak? I concluded to make a survey. If she had seen my amused grin I would hatch up some explanation to justify. I opened my left eye, the furthest from the healer, and peeped. I was saved! She was all right. Her eyes were as snuggly shut as a two-day-old kitten's. I closed my eye again.

I began to get warm. The downey upholstering of the chair recalled childhood lessons about a fiery furnace, and I dimly speculated on my coming out unscorched. My new boots began to make my feet feel like muffins. At last, when I had given up all hope of living to see the fall styles, she got up. I gave a sigh, stretched my stiffened body and opened my eyes.

FEELING THE INFLUENCE.

"You felt the influence?" she half asked, half asserted. I was bewildered. I did not know there was any "influence" being exerted. I began to wonder if it gave me the muffin sensation inside my boots. I was forced to answer truthfully that I felt no influence, or if I did it was so new to me that I could not recognize it.

"You won't feel it the first time," she said reassuringly. Why did she ask the question if she knew this? "My price is $2 for the first treatment and $1 each visit afterwards. Now, I want you to go to bed at 11 o'clock this evening. Lie down in a comfortable position and I will use my influence and take all your wakefulness from you. Yes, my influence is sometimes better away than near. Distance makes us lose some things which make us stronger. Before 11.30 you will be asleep."

I made an appointment for another "treatment" and left her surrounded by half a dozen sickly looking women.

The next morning the girl, whose brown, sharp face and keen, dark eyes glanced from beneath a shaggy crop of short black hair, gave a twist on her run-over heels and a fling of her knee skirts, as she told me Miss Bell was out, but would return in a few moments. I had waited only a short time when a slender woman, with grayish short hair, brown eyes and a challie wrapper, came in. Miss Bell had been suddenly summoned to the bedside of her mother in Nebraska, she explained, and the patients were to be left in her charge during the former's absence. I followed her into the room where I had sweltered the previous day during the closed-eye séance.

Miss Allen, so she informed me was her name, said she had been told what my trouble was, and she also wrote my name down, in order to better remember it, she explained. After we had discussed my pretended affliction I concluded to make an effort to get some information about the business.

NO ONE NEED BE ILL.

"I think if I understood it better I would be more quickly benefited," I suggested feelingly.

"You could not understand," she said evasively. "It's like a patient asking a doctor how he knows what is wrong with him and how he ever learned what would work for a cure."

"But you claim all doctors are wrong and medicine fatal; only healers and faith are right," I insinuated.

"Indeed we do," she answered firmly. "People need to never be sick. They only are responsible for all their ailments."

"Are you never ill?" I asked boldly, for her face bore indications of illness.

"Certainly, healers can be ill in a few hours if they wish, or they can never know an unwell moment. It all depends on them."

"How?" I demanded.

"Oh, that's what I can't tell you," she replied shrewdly.

"Why?" I again demanded shortly.

"Because I would tell it subjectively and you would understand it objectively. It can't be explained, but if you accept the treatment you will never be ill. Some healers will not say one word to their patients, for they think if they explain too much there would be no occasion to give treatment."

That is the theory of all frauds. So long as they can contrive to keep the people in the dark as to their method of business so long will they have followers and make money.

"Then it's the work of the mind or imagination that cures or kills?" I suggested.

"Yes and no," she replied with a smile. "I can't explain it to you. It's the truth. We teach thought and truth, and with them no unhealthiness can come. Why are people sick? Just because they know no better. As Christ said on the cross, 'They know not what they do.' It was and has been forever, but we have only lately learned the truth."

"Who started it?"

"Women," she said, with pride. "We are indebted to women for this blessed truth. You know it was a woman Christ first spoke to after rising from the tomb, and he said, 'Go tell the brethren."

"Do you have men healers and believers?"

"Men?" She looked disdainfully. "We make no distinction between the sexes. There are no men and no women—no sexes. It's all one family; all children of our great Father."

HOW TO LEARN THE BUSINESS.

"How did you learn all this wonderful knowledge?" I asked, with a show of admiration I was far from feeling.

"We have a class in which we received twelve lectures a year. How much does it cost? Only $100 for the course. The increase of the believers is rapid. If I were told that I had lost my nice little home and income and that I should be given $1,000,000 to live on and enjoy if I would renounce this faith, I would say, I keep the truth, I refuse the $1,000,000," with a disdainful but majestic sweep of the arms, "but truth is life."

Miss Allen told me that the mental healers have no special church. The eye-closing of the day previous was again indulged in. After a short time she announced that it was finished and asked if I had not "felt the influence," as she had "put it on unusually strong." Of course I failed to detect it.

"Go to bed to-night at 11 o'clock," she said; "make yourself very easy, then count out ten red-letter days of your life. Let them be the happiest days you know. Live them over slowly, one after the other. I will meanwhile exert my influence and take your insomnia from you, and you will gradually slip off to sleep as peacefully as a child."

"But I have tried such things," said I. "Once I was told, in order to coax the God of Sleep, to imagine I saw a flock of sheep jumping, one after another, over a fence into pastures new. I pictured the scene. I saw the black woolly sheep with a bass 'maa!' nimbly jump the old rail fence into a nice, untouched meadow of stylish green grass dotted with no less stylish daisies and clover. I saw him followed by a white contralto. 'Maa!' and she was over. I saw in the rear the sportive lambkins elevating their heels and frisking around like a group of girls at a Sunday-school picnic. I noticed in the distance a brown bushy-tailed squirrel sitting on a post nibbling something in his tightly clutched forepaws. I even saw the comical shakings of their funny little tails by a group of gossiping sheep."

"Did you go to sleep?" she asked, with interest.

"Sleep! I was told to count the sheep. I counted. They jumped; I counted. Some would clear the fence by a yard; others would graze it with their heels; still others would turn like acrobats over the elephants in a circus, and always light on their feet amid the loud approving 'maas' of the flock. I counted, but I did not sleep. Why? Because the more I counted jumping the fence, the more there came to jump the fence, until I concluded they were working the double racket, as in a stage street scene—walking off at one end and coming back on the other. Ah! it was a sad experience."

"Well, you try what I tell you," she said. "I'll use my influence and you will sleep. When you come down to breakfast—(How could I, living in a flat?)—and they ask you how you slept, say, "Splendidly." If you did not sleep, say it anyway. It won't be a lie, for you will sleep, even if you don't know it. I'll keep your wakefulness for you. I have taken it away. You have left it here. Now, my dear sister, you will soon learn the truth and be happy."

I paid my dollar fee, and she walked with me to the elevator.

In the same house with Miss Bell, in the flats above and below, Mrs. Day and Miss Church hold forth as healers of the same faith and secure a nice income from a large circle of believers.

During my visits afterwards I heard some things which were to me most amusing. My next complaint was dyspepsia.

"You haven't dyspepsia. It's only your thoughts, "said Miss Allen. "Now go home, eat everything you want and as much. You'll be rid of all dyspepsia, for I'll have your stomach here; you'll leave it with me."

"I should be most happy," I answered, warmly, although I could not see how it was to be done. There wouldn't be much use of healing my stomach when I had reached a shore where hunger cometh not.

"You won't know that you have left your stomach here," she assured me. I didn't. I went experimenting and ate a welsh rarebit that night, and I had a faint suspicion that my stomach still occupied its old site and was with me more than ever before.

BEAUTY CAN BE BOUGHT, TOO.

"Everything that ails us arises from some thought. But our thoughts we control our bodies," she said on another occasion. "You deny any worry except that you want more money. Now, when you learn the truth and how to think you will get all things. You won't have to try for it; money and everything will come else come to you."

"Will beauty come?" I asked, waiting breathless for her answer.

"Yes!"—emphatically. I think back with a sigh of relief. "I had a girl come to me, thin and far from prepossessing. I taught her how to think, and to-day she is a beautiful girl, perfectly proportioned, a dream of grace and with an exquisite complexion and charming manner."

"Give me that priceless recipe," I pleaded in thrilling tones.

"Think beautiful thoughts," she answered. "Do not envy your friend, do not quarrel; be careful to cherish no feeling of discontent or malice. Don't use your mirror; forget what the body you knew as yourself looked like, and sit down and sketch in your mind the picture you want to represent. Think, my arm is white and soft and round, my face is bright and intelligent, my complexion is clear and my body is erect, my movements are grace, my conversation is pleasing. I love the world, I love life, I love God. And in a few weeks your friends will tell you of the improvement."

I looked at her. I recalled my mirrored self. I wondered.

"Our mind and body are like a magic lantern," she continued, as I silently tried to estimate the amount of faith it would require to work the transformation she suggested. "Our mind is the lantern, our thoughts the slides and our body the wall of reflection. If we slide in an ugly thought it reflects on the body; if we slide in a lovely thought it reflects, and so we make ourselves.

"To show you an example of how our minds govern our bodies, I will tell you what I did. In company with two friends, Miss Church and Mrs. Day, I took the boat last Saturday a week and went to Newburg, up the Hudson. The heat was almost unbearable. When we reached Newburg, in the parlor of the hotel was a crowd of people sweltering. They talked of nothing but the heat. At last I suggested what a sad thing it must be to be cast on an iceberg: how cold and hungry we would be. Then I talked of the blizzard, and one large, fleshy woman, who had been mopping her flushed face, said: 'Why, dear me, I feel cool; you have made me forget the heat.' See, I had turned her thoughts into a different channel and she was no longer sweltering. While on the boat I saw a white cloud way over the mountains. I pointed it out to her, suggesting that it looked exactly like a snow cloud and was doubtless bringing a cooling rain. She actually shivered."

What more is to be said?

NELLIE BLY

GIRLS OF THE WILD WEST

SUNDAY, JULY 8, 1888

NELLIE BLY GOES DOWN AND MAKES FRIENDS WITH THE RIDERS

The Lassies of the Show Are Just Like Nice Girls Everywhere—Miss Hickok Has a Bridle Made from Hair Taken from Scalped Indians—How They Learned to Ride and Shoot Out West When Young.

Whew! But can't they ride? Buffalo Bill removed the gray sombrero from his handsome head in languid surprise, quite English, while I explained that I didn't want to see any cowboys—although they are a jolly lot—or red chiefs in green paint, trousers and rooster-tail crowns, but just the women folk. He did not object. He said he would be pleased to present me to them as soon as they came off. Just then Nate Salsbury, a hundred handsomer since his marriage, loomed in sight and proffered to relieve Buffalo Bill of the task. We "juked" under the rope which enfences the camp and wandered down to the white tents where live the girls I sought. They were having a little meeting under one of the big trees, and so when Salsbury said: "Ladies, this is Miss Bly, from THE WORLD," I just blushed and said, "Ladies," and wished I had a plate of cream, a palm-leaf fan and a fizzing soda. "Won't you come in and sit down?" one said kindly, and we all followed her into a tent on which was printed in big black letters "Lillian Smith." We talked about the weather and the recent rain and then one excused herself in order to change her habit, she said. Two more wanted to fix up, so I was left alone with two.

"Tell me all about yourself, beginning with your name," I said, generously, to the one nearest the entrance.

"I don't think there is much to tell," she replied, taking off her sombrero and displaying a handsome lot of auburn hair. (She rides a sorrel.) "My name is Mrs. Georgie Duffy."

"Where are you from?"

"Wyoming." She crossed her feet, displaying a pair of jaunty, high-heel boots.

"How did you learn to ride?"

"I always knew how to ride; I never learned." This was not encouraging. "How did I get with Buffalo Bill? Well, he was traveling out our way and I heard he wanted a rider. He had none then, so I went to him and he gave me a place. For two years Della Farrell, the young girl who has just gone out, and I were the only riders with the Wild West."

"Of course, you like riding?" I half asserted.

"Yes, I like it," she replied, warmly. "Well, I wouldn't do anything else. I don't call this riding, going around a ring. Out home, where we used to canter for miles through the country, is what I consider riding."

"How much do you do here?"

"I have the race with Della Farrell, and then I ride in the dance. Twice a day I do this; that's all."

"Does nothing ever happen?" I asked, half desperately.

"No, indeed. I think it's a tiresome world; it's all the same. My husband is one of the cowboys. He joined the show when I did. Any children? No, thank heaven."

Mrs. Duffy put on her sombrero and went to her tent, so I turned to the hostess. She was bright-faced, clever girl, and her fingers nimbly constructed a thread lace while she talked with me. She understood what I wanted without making me ask questions.

LILLIAN SMITH.

"My name is Lillian Smith. I do the shooting," she said in a pleasing, unaffected way. "This is my house."

"It is quite pleasant," I replied, as I surveyed the neat interior. Over the entrance was draped a mosquito netting, which gave a certain privacy to her tent, although it did not keep out mosquitoes. The place literally swarmed with them. The white sides of the tent were relieved by dozens of photographs of Miss Lillian's friends. A centre table, some soft rugs and easy chairs gave a very cosy and homelike look. In the rear was her dressing and bed room.

"I see you have a mirror, anyway," I said, noticing the large one above a table.

"Yes, that's the one thing I can't do without," she replied with candor; "I always want to be sure my dresses are on straight."

"It is not strange that I should shoot," she said, dropping her knitting for an instant to kill, with a sound smack, a mosquito that was imprinting a kiss on her round cheek. "I was born in Coalville, Mona County, Cal. My father was a trapper, or hunter, as you may call him. He shot game for the market. The only other child—my brother—was ten years older than I, so you see I had to find some amusement to fill the place of playmates. My father gave me an old rifle and taught me to shoot."

"What did you shoot at—marks?"

"First at game," she replied, turning in place a gold watch bracelet, "and then at balls in the air, as I do here. After one month's practice, when I was but eight years old, I broke 323 glass balls without missing, and out of 500 I only missed five. That's my dog," she said, referring to an exquisite little dog terrier that came nosing around me in a friendly way. "I brought her from England with me. Her name is Beauty. I brought two other dogs—a Scotch collie and a Hardale terrier. They are out in the stables."

A young Indian lad in gay attire came quietly in and seated himself as if very much at home. He listened to us with dark eyes wide open.

"How did you get before the public?" I asked, while I quietly murdered a mosquito that had tested the thickness of my unfinished kid.

"I got quite a local reputation and one day my father met the manager of Woodward's Garden, San Francisco, Cal., and he offered me an engagement. I was to give two exhibitions a week for $100, and in all I was to give seven exhibitions. I was only nine years old then and had never been in a city in my life. The largest crowd of people I had ever seen at once time was composed of six people; imagine, then, what must have been my feelings when 7,000 people witnessed my first exhibitions and an increased number those following. Afterwards I travelled with my father, giving exhibitions, until I came with Buffalo Bill. Does it pay? Well, I should say so."

"Have you never shot yourself?" I asked after she had called my attention to her gun-rack, holding a half dozen rifles, in the corner of the tent.

"My rifle has never gone off accidentally, which is due to the fact that I was taught rightly at first. You see that rifle?" pointing out one not remarkable in any way. I gazed at it steadily. It did not go off. I replied that I saw it. "Well, in London the Queen called me to her and asked me my age and how I liked to shoot, and then she held the rifle, saying, 'This is quite a heavy rifle.'"

There were no finger-marks on it.

"I own a horse also," she continued. "He is the only horse in the world, I guess, that has a mane the whole way down his spinal cord. I call him Nigger. Yes, I like to ride, and do quite a lot of it for pleasure. Do we ever get letters from mashers? Well, rather. I got one from a policeman in Newark last week. None of the girls with this show ever care for such things." Miss Smith is the wife of Jim Kidd, the cowboy.

"Come in, Miss Bly, and sit down," said pretty Della Farrell, as she held open her mosquito-bar portals. "Bessie will be here in a moment. Take off your hat and be comfortable."'

DELLA FARRELL.

Della Farrell, the young girl who rides the race with Mrs. Duffy, is quite pretty. She had her slender, girlish form tastefully clothed in a white-embroidered blue dress. Her large, blue eyes with long, curled lashes, gaze on one with a truthful, frank candor, and her wavy brown hair, which hangs in artistic looseness around her head, is charming. In the V-shaped vest she wore several gold medals which she has gotten by winning races. One, especially pretty, given her during her first season, is engraved with herself on horseback. Just then Bessie Farrell came in and we all went into the room at the rear of the tent, where it was cooler.

"I could not say when I rode first," said Della. "I have been riding ever since I can remember."

"We were born and raised in Denver, Col.," said Bessie, with a smile. "There were our father and mother, our brother and we two girls in our family. We always had lots of horses and, children-like, we were always romping with them. We were never taught to ride, but just hammered it into ourselves by hard experiences, which is the best way after all."

"I was never inside a riding-school," said Della, looking up from the popcorn she was dissecting, "and from what I have seen of women who learn riding so I think it better to learn outside."

"Della learned outside," Bessie said with a laugh. "We had a pony"—

"Dolly was its name," Della interposed, with her mouth filled with popcorn.

"And we children always fought over it, rode it turn about, or stole it from the other," Bessie continued, "just as children will. We had our own saddles and bridles, that's one right we religiously kept. I never liked horses half so well as Della did, but I had a mania for stealing away—when I got any money—and hiring a horse from some stable."

"We never used riding habits," said Della. "We just jumped on and rode in our short skirts. If we had learned in long skirts we would never have lived to give exhibitions."

BESSIE FARRELL.

"No, I should say not," Bessie said, as she vigorously used her fan. "Dolly ran off with Della at last—("She was a little divil," from Della)—and so father sold her, because Della was badly hurt."

"I had the worst old saddle," explained the charming Della. "It only had one horn."

"We would never have been in a show," said Bessie, "if old Dave Cook, the great Rocky Mountain detective, hadn't told at our house one evening that Buffalo Bill was in town and that he wanted a lady rider for his new show. Della got wild to join him—("I had to coax a long time before my mother would consent," said Della)—and she went down to the theatre and made an engagement with him. Then I came on and joined them at the Madison Square Garden. It is not hard work, and the pay ranges from $50 to $100 a month, with board."

EMMA HICKOK.

Bessie Farrell is quite as nice as Della. She wore a black lace skirt, a cambric blouse closed with gold buttons, a pretty pin, several handsome rings and a large white hat covered with red roses. She has blue eyes, light hair and a lovely expression. I bade them good-by and went to see Miss Emma Hickok, who does the fancy riding, making her horse go through all sorts of movements at the touch of her whip.

Her eyes are dark and her hair, which

is short and curly, match them in color. She is rather petite. She wore a white lace dress, caught at the throat with a handsome pin and at the waist with a dozen silver pendants, even as the fashionable women of to-day carry. Heavy silver bracelets encircled her wrists and her fingers glittered with costly rings. Her tent is quite handsome and two vases of fresh flowers enhanced the whole. She is always at ease and did the honors of her little home in a pleasing manner.

"My life has been spent among horses," she said. "My father was a famous horseman and since I can remember I have known how to ride. I was born in Cincinnati, but I can't say that I belong to any one place. My life has been spent on the road, so I really have no home. When five years old I began my career as a rider. All I know about training horses I taught myself. Is it hard business? Yes, very. It is dreadful for a woman to keep it up long. Of course I like it, having spent my life at it. The way I got with Buffalo Bill was through my step-father, Wild Bill, who was once Col. Cody's partner. The work I do now I call rough work. I don't do any fine business. The big bay which I now ride I only rode three weeks before we arrived in London. I call him 'Caprice,' because he is such an ugly-tempered brute. While in England I bought a little black Arabian horse. I call him 'Kismet,' and now have him home with me."

"I notice that you do not use a saddle in your exhibition," I said. "What do you use instead?"

"I use what is known as a 'sway.' It is a pad about six inches wide, and has three horns and a wide girth. My stirrup is a patent one, which I bought in London for a pound. It is arranged so I cannot be dragged. If I fall, the spring flies open and my foot comes out. I always ride with a spur, and I'm the only woman I ever knew who does. You see, if the horse gets stubborn, I have my whip in my right hand and the reins in the left, so, with my spur, I can control both sides. If he jumps one way to avoid punishment he gets it on the other side."

THE GRAND SALUTE.

"Why do you use a sway instead of a saddle?"

"Because it is more attractive. It is much more difficult and so, in the eyes of professionals or those who understand the art, my performances are much superior. There is another thing I do which no other woman does. I ride with a stirrup as long as a man's. Why, because if the third horn should break I am perfectly independent, having firm footing. As an exercise for women nothing can excel horseback riding.

"I want to show you something which has no like," she said, and, going to the interior, she brought forth a bundle. "When Col. Cody first saw me ride he said: 'You are the finest rider I ever saw and I will send you the finest bridle I ever saw.' Several weeks later I received notice that a package awaited me at the express office. It was an exquisite bridle made of finely woven hair, with buckles of solid silver and tassels of hair.

"This is made of human hair," she said, "from scalps of Indians taken by Buffalo Bill, and the buckles are made from chunks of silver given him at different mines. It is not possible that you will ever see the like of it again. August Belmont, the New York banker, offered Col. Cody $1,000 for it"—

"Break away, thar—break away!" shouted a deep, good-natured voice, and a great, monstrous fellow, stooping almost double, entered the tent. "Break away, now," he repeated, and I looked apprehensively at the chair he threw himself into.

He was immense! He wore a bright red shirt, crossed at the front with a gold chain heavy enough to tie down an elephant. He removed his black sombrero and tossed back his long black hair carelessly, while he glanced at me with his bright black eyes in a boyish, teasing manner.

"You are mistaken. This is a different lady," said Miss Hickok, hurriedly, whereupon she added:

"Mr. Buck Taylor, Miss Bly."

"How du du?" said I.

"How are you?" said Buck.

We smiled and shook hands.

"Now, look here," he said. "I'm going to kill the next one. ("Please don't, she may be nicer," I inserted.) You're the third that's come here and talked us to death and we haven't seen a line of it printed yet. I shall kill the next."

"What will you do with yourself when the Wild West is no more?" I asked, in order to divert his mind from his murderous threats.

"Go back to Texas."

"How do you make the un-English Indians understand?" I asked at random.

"Club them into it," he replied, with a laugh. "Say, why don't you try to ride one of the bucking horses? Now, that's what would make a story."

"But I might get my neck broken," I protested.

"That's what would make the story," he replied, coolly. "Then there would be something to write up." He followed me out as I started home. I stopped to bid Col. Cody, who was dictating a letter, good-by.

"Come down some day and take a ride," he said, cordially. "The girls have lots of habits. You look just the right size to ride. I hate these big women who want to ride. Do they? Well, the bigger the woman the worse she wants to ride."

NELLIE BLY

THE INFAMY OF THE PARK

SUNDAY, AUGUST 5, 1888

NELLIE BLY UNEARTHS A SCOUNDREL FAVORED BY THE POLICE

Charles Cleveland, a Man of Leisure, Debauches Central Park to His Own Vile Uses—He Drives There Daily and Invites Young Girls to Ride—The Police Smile at Him and Assist in Getting His Prey.

There is one man in this city who, with the sanction of the Park Police, debauches Central Park to his own infamous uses.

Many complaints have come, from time to time, to THE WORLD touching Park policemen. Women complain that they dare not go to the Park alone because of the familiar and offensive manner of these officers—those paid guardians of propriety and quietness. Young men complain that if they stay in the Park after dark these same guardians blackmail them, and that rather than be subjected to the disgrace of taking their companions before a magistrate, they accept the officers' offer to compromise and give up their money.

A few days ago a young married woman sent THE WORLD a letter, the startling contents of which suggested the necessity for an investigation. She said she went to Central Park every morning for a walk and she had noticed particularly the peculiar actions of one man. Regularly every morning he drove through the Park. Whenever he saw a girl sitting alone on a bench he would draw up and ask her to take a drive. One morning he asked a girl—who was to all appearance a working girl—to take a spin with him around the Park. She did so and when he brought her back the young married woman went to the same bench and, sitting down, began to talk to the girl. First they talked about the weather and then the girl, yielding to the subtle inquiries, told the story of her drive.

The man, while driving around, spoke to every officer and in return received familiar salutes. Several times he drew up and spoke in a whisper to some, who would continue on their beat with a smile, while he resumed his drive. He told the girl that every policeman knew him, and that they would solicit girls for him to take driving. Every day between 10 and 11 A.M. he took to the officers their beer, which they drank behind the trees. This insured his safety, and he could do anything he wished, from robbing a man to cutting down a tree or stealing flowers, and they would not molest him. He repeatedly referred to the "madam" who he said owned the team which he drove.

This was about the substance of the letter, which, in addition, contained a description of the man and his turnout, so I decided to see if the Park policemen, who are paid to protect, were capable of abetting crime. I dressed myself like a country girl and went to the Park. I sat down on a bench fronting the drive which leads from the Fifty-ninth street entrance to the Seventy-second. I opened a book and awaited developments. I had not long to wait. Among all those driving I saw only one who answered the description of the man I wanted, and it required but a few moments to be convinced by his actions that I had made no mistake.

When he saw me sitting alone he endeavored to attract my attention. Although he never once glanced at the other women around who were accompanied by escorts. Four times he drove past me, coming within a few yards and repeating. He gave little whistles, coughs and smacking of his lips to make me look, but I still gazed at the top line in my book, which allowed me, without raising my eyes, to see all that was going on before me.

THE MEETING WITH THE SCOUNDREL.

When he passed the fifth time, going towards Seventy-second street, I lifted my head and gazed steadily at him. He nodded his head for me to follow him, and though I made no move and did not look pleasant, he kept on making motions with his head for me to come after. An officer on the path, who could not but see the man's performances, merely looked at me lazily. I walked down along the path, going in the direction he had driven, and turning a bend I saw him a few yards distant talking to a woman. He held his team close by the path and she stood on the green sward which divided the path and the drive, talking to him. A guard was standing beside his horse, on the opposite side of the road. I sat down on a bench facing the guard and pretended to read.

Just then the man and woman saw me. She laughed and went back to a bench, while he drove direct to me. He drove as closely to where I sat as the road would allow and then stopped.

"Good morning," he said. I made no reply, but kept my eyes fastened on my book.

"I would like to take you for a drive," he said, "if you will go down the path while I turn."

I got up without replying and looked at the officer. He was watching us.

"Which way?" I asked the man.

"Down towards Seventy-second street," he replied. I walked past the officer, who turned his face, on which rested a broad smile, towards his horse, presenting his back to us. I passed the woman with whom the man had been talking and she looked at me in an amused way. I stopped where the first path crossed the drive and the man came up.

SOLID WITH THE POLICE.

"Aren't you afraid to do this?" I asked as I got into the vehicle with him.

"Why, there's nothin' to be afraid of," he answered, as he arranged the lap robe.

"The officers," I suggested, "aren't you afraid they will arrest you?"

"No, I'm solid with them," he answered, laughing, as if the idea was a good joke. "They wouldn't touch me, no difference what I do."

"You are sure of that?" I asked. "Then they allow men to do such things in this park?"

"They wouldn't allow everybody," he answered, "but there are men who come out every day just to pick up girls and the police never bother them. They are only too glad to do something for me," he added. "Just notice how respectfully they salute me when I drive past them."

That's just what I intended to do, so I kept my eyes open. His boast was not a vain one. Every officer we met or passed, on foot or mounted, spoke to him, and in every instance smiled. Whether the smile was but pleasantness or had a meaning I do not know.

"This is a handsome team you drive," I said, "Yours, I suppose?"

"Oh, yes, they're mine; I've got lots more. I own a livery stable," he replied.

"Oh indeed. Then you come to the Park frequently, I presume," I insinuated.

"About four times a day."

"What do you call your horses?" I asked.

This seemed to stagger him, for he was silent some time; then he answered that he had no names for them. I smiled and said that seemed strange, as I never knew any one who owned horses to have them unnamed. He then asked me if I liked to drive and if I could ride. When I gave him an affirmative reply he said he had a phaeton he would allow me to drive, and he had a good saddle-horse I could have any time. I told him his kindness was overwhelming.

REGULARLY HUNTING FOR GIRLS.

"Do you often get acquainted with girls this way?" I asked.

"Every day," he replied.

While we drove around he asked me all about myself. I told him that I was a country girl and had come to New York as a governess. He told me it was lucky that all my relatives were dead, and asked me if I would not like to go on the stage. He could easily get me on, as he had lots of friends among the profession. Lest the man be given to telling untruths I shall not publish the names of the managers whose friendship he claims; however, he told very strange stories concerning their treatment of the girls. He said he received lots of complimentary tickets and asked me to go with him to the theatre.

"Who was the woman you were talking to in the Park?" I asked him.

"She's a friend of mine," he answered.

"Why didn't you take her driving, then, instead of a stranger?" I inquired.

"Oh, I never take her driving," he said, with a laugh. "She understands it."

"Understands what?" I asked, but he would not answer.

"Does she often come to the Park?" I asked, and he answered that he talked with her there every day—of what I could not learn.

"I go away in a short time to visit all the summer resorts," he said. "I always take several horses along and I have a good time driving. Will you come along?"

"I?" I exclaimed, in my simple, country manner. "Oh, that would be impossible. Is your livery-stable far away?" I asked, artlessly.

URGING HER TO GO WITH HIM.

"Down on West Fifty-eighth street, and I live on West Fifty-seventh street," said he; "and where do you live?"

I named a street—the first one I thought of—and refused to give a number simply because I was afraid of giving wide of the mark, which he would find out. I endeavored to tell the avenues it lay between but got mixed up in that, which was due, I explained, to my country simplicity.

"You will go with me, then, to the summer resorts," he urged.

"Oh, you shouldn't ask me so soon; wait until we are better acquainted. Maybe we will not like each other then," I said evasively. "What is your name?" I asked coaxingly.

"If you meet me to-morrow I tell you my name," he said cunningly. "You can call me Charles until then."

Determined to hunt him down, I made an engagement to meet him the next morning at 10 o'clock, at the corner of Seventy-second street and the Boulevard. If it rained I should not come until the following morning.

WHAT HE LOOKS LIKE.

The man, who is about 5 feet, 8 inches, usually wears a gray pongee duster, which is buttoned up closely to his chin, hiding his clothes entirely. He wears a white straw hat of cheap grade with a black band around it. His gloves are a snuff-brown lisle thread with brown leather inside, rather the worse for wear. His entire clothing is cheap and coarse. His face does not bespeak refinement or culture. His black eyes, deep set and rather close together, are overhung with heavy black brown. His nose is long and very red, the redness which looks more the work of the sun than drink. His drooping black mustache, in which are many gray streaks, covers his mouth completely. His chin and cheeks wore the stubbled beard of many days' growth. His collar, which accidentally got above his gray ulster, was a straight band, very much soiled. His hair is rather white on the temples and above his ears. His conversation is conducted without regard for any grammatical rules. The team he drove was above reproach. One was a bobtail sorrel and the other a bay whose tail almost touched the ground.

A reporter was instructed to follow me the next morning and to track the man to his house, while a photographer was waiting in the Park to get a picture of the man and his rig. Although it rained we were all on the watch for Mr. "Charles." I had found a place where I could watch without being seen. A few minutes before 10 the rain ceased and the sun came out—so did the man. He drove to the place where I was to meet him and round and round, as though expecting that I would yet come. At last he gave up in despair, and about 10.30 went to the Park, closely followed by the reporter. Here he met and talked with the woman he had met the day previous, and, after a consultation of some length, he resumed his drive. The woman went down a side path, and though the reporter followed after as quickly as he dared, she was lost to sight, and he was unable to again find her.

HIS NAME AND ADDRESS.

A photographer from THE WORLD office got a view of the man and his team and the reporter followed him to the stable. There it was learned that his name is Charles Cleveland, and that he is said to be foreman of Lovell's boarding stable, No. 230 West Fifty-eighth street. The team he was driving is said to be the property of Judge Hilton, who is boarding it there during the summer.

In hopes that he would throw some light on the business with the woman and his "pull" with the policemen, I was to meet him the next morning. It was a bright, sunny morning. I was there at the hour named, and Mr. Cleveland came a few moments afterwards. He wanted to go to the Riverside Drive, but I insisted on going to Central Park, where I knew a reporter was waiting for us. He refused to drive over the road where he found me the first morning; why, I do not know. He wanted to go out on the road, but I told him I was to go downtown with a woman and I must return in a few moments. He roughly told me the story was manufactured and kept on his way. He spoke to all the officers, as he had the other day.

Driving out the road on the occasion of our first meeting, he proffered the information that he intended to stop at a road house kept by a widow—a particular friend of his—for drinks. I told him I never drank and insisted on his returning. It made no difference, he drove up to a one-story frame house on One Hundred and Sixteenth street, speaking to the two mounted guardians on the corner, and we got out. The horses were taken around to the stable, and he came into the reception-room, pulling off his gray ulster. He had on a clean collar, and his hair couldn't have been slicked tighter to his head. His trousers were the worst bagged at the knee I ever saw and were quite short, plainly showing the new heavy shoes he wore. After removing his ulster he looked at me in a self-satisfied way, as if he felt sure in all this "get-up" he would completely capture, as well as awe, the simple country girl.

IN THE ROAD HOUSE.

He told me to "sit down and give us a tune," and when I declined he said: "I seen my friend ——, of Wallack's Theatre, and he sez he'll take you on, so I want to hear your voice. Come, give us a tune!"

Finding that I would not he went out to order drinks. I had at last consented to drinking a lemonade. The waiter, in white jacket and apron, followed Mr. Cleveland in with two glasses, which he placed on the table. The lemonade was a deep amber shade to the depth of an inch on top.

"That doesn't look like country lemonade," I said, as I stirred it around with the straws until it all became an amber tinge. "What is in it?"

"I only had him put some sherry in it," he said. "Go ahead and drink it; it won't hurt you; it will brace you up."

"I don't want to drink it," I said.

"Drink it; it won't hurt you; you're mighty particular," he growled.

"All right, I don't intend to drink it," I said, firmly.

"You drink it, now. I have to pay for it," Mr. Cleveland said, coarsely. "You think I put something in it, don't you? That's why you won't drink; you're afraid."

"Probably I am," I answered, slowly. "I could not trust a man who has done as you have."

THE SCOUNDREL'S PLAN.

"I've been better to you than most men would be," he hurled at me. "When they bring girls out and they refuse to do what the men say they put them out and they have to get back to the city as best they can."

I gave him a gentle hint that it would save him trouble to take me where he got me, and so he made me go to the back of the house to where the team was standing beneath a shed. We drove back to the Park.

"You will get into trouble if you go around hunting up girls in the Park all the time," I said, after a long silence.

"Will I? I'm safe enough. I ask the girls to take a drive and if they make any fuss the police will pull them in. They wouldn't touch me. I'm solid."

"How do you get solid?" I ask.

"That doesn't make any difference. It's only the girls that get into fusses," he said. "I never ask regulars to get in; I always take girls who are strangers. Now, I knew you were a stranger the first moment I saw you."

"How did you know?"

"Well, I'm in the Park all the time, and I know everybody by sight who comes there. The moment a strange girl comes in I can pick her out. I'm no fool. I'm not picking up the ones that know the town. Anyway, you can't say that I used you badly."

"It's according to what we call badly," I said. "Any man who will try to entrap a girl because she looks innocent deserves harsh treatment."

"I don't want to talk about it. You can get out here," he said, gruffly.

I refused to get out because it was too far from any station, and compelled him to drive me nearer to Seventy-second street. Mr. Cleveland let me get out, and whipped up the borrowed horses without a word of farewell—almost before my foot reached the ground.

NELLIE BLY

Editor's Note: Belva Ann Bennett Lockwood was the first woman to make a legitimate run for the office of President of the United States (Victoria Woodhull, the first woman ever to run, was a year shy of the Constitutionally-mandated age of 35 at the time of her attempt).

Lockwood was already a breaker-down of barriers. She attended the National University Law School (today George Washington University Law School), but was refused a diploma. Unable to join the bar without one, she appealed to President Ulysses S. Grant, who intervened, and the university relented.

Moving to Washington, D.C., she lobbied for the right to argue cases before the United States Supreme Court. This required an act of Congress, and she spent five years making her case. In 1879 President Rutherford B. Hayes signed the bill, which allowed all qualified women lawyers to practice law in any federal court. Lockwood was sworn in as the first female member of the U.S. Supreme Court bar on March 3, 1879. A year later she nominated Samuel R. Lowery to the same court, making him the first Black man to argue before the Supreme Court.

Bly interviewed Lockwood three months before the election of 1888, which saw the Republican nominee, Benjamin Harrison, beat the Democratic incumbent, Grover Cleveland. Harrison's victory was the first time a candidate won the Electoral College yet lost the popular vote.

This was Lockwood's second run for president. She was first nominated in 1884 by the National Equal Rights Party. Since women were barred from voting at the time, her candidacy was often mocked and derided, the press warning of "petticoat rule." Nevertheless, she persisted, fighting for equal rights and world peace until her death in 1917.

As Bly notes, her interview with Lockwood took place in the apartment of Cynthia Hicks Van Name Leonard, a remarkable woman in her own right. At the time Leonard was running for Mayor of New York. An author and activist, she was also the mother of actress Lillian Russell, hence the reference to photographs of Russell. The little girl who greets Bly is likely Russell's daughter Dorothy Soloman.

Woman's Part in Politics

Sunday, August 12, 1888

Mrs. Belva A. Lockwood Talks About Herself to Nellie Bly

The Feminine Candidate for the Presidency of This Great Country Thinks She Has a Fighting Chance—Mrs. Cleveland, However, Is Stronger—Something About Her Home Life—Her Washington Office.

> Equal Rights.—We, the undersigned, citizens of the State of New York, believe in woman suffrage, prohibition, arbitration, money and labor reform and the control of railroads and telegraphs by the Government.

This is the platform, as well as the plank, on which Mrs. Belva A. Lockwood stands during her campaign for the Presidency of the United States. Does she really expect to be elected? Certainly; why shouldn't she? Remember the old adage about certain folks falling out, in which event Mrs. Lockwood might reasonably expect to get her just dues.

The other day I called to see Mrs. Lockwood at the home of Mrs. Leonard, No. 136 West Twenty-third street. Mrs. Lockwood had come from Washington, D.C., on the Saturday previous to lecture in Brooklyn and New York. A girl—pretty and plump—invited me to enter an artistic parlor, where portraits of Lillian Russell predominated. I was lost in the contemplation of Lillian's beauty in various poses and costumes when a lady entered noiselessly, gracefully, and with an ease few women acquire. Her hand clasped mine and held it while she asked if I had called to see her, and I replied that if she was Mrs. Lockwood, I had.

"What is your name?" she asked easily.

"Bly," I replied hurriedly.

"Nellie Bly!" she exclaimed. "My goodness! sit down. I'm glad to see you."

How much there is in a handshake! It bespeaks every passion known to the human mind. I verily believe a handclasp can make or unmake a man. Now Mrs. Lockwood's handshake was delightful. Her hand closed around mine firmly, softly, warmly, not with the vulgar shake, as if testing the strength of the arm, but with a clasp. It seemed to rouse and inspire one with good humor, strength and good-fellowship. If Candidate Harrison's handshake can be compared to Mrs. Lockwood's one might safely bet on him.

"I am very sorry you did not come sooner, Miss Bly," Mrs. Lockwood said, as she leaned back in her chair. "I had a visitor I would have liked you to meet, Sister Agnes, as her name is, came here and founded a school. When it became prosperous it was taken from her, and when she tried to regain it she was sent to an insane asylum. Not being insane she was at length discharged from the asylum. I advised her to go to THE WORLD, as it always stands ready to defend the oppressed."

"Do you have many such visitors?"

"Numbers of them," she replied with a smile. "I have been overrun with visitors wanting advice since I came here. One of the most prominent was a man who came to consult me in regard to the Panama Canal."

"Do you really expect to be elected President?" I asked curiously.

"Certainly," she replied, as she looked at me with an amused smile which allowed several interpretations of her answer.

There have been worse looking Presidents, or I might say, there have been few as fine looking. There is one thing, if Belva Lockwood gains the day she will go into the White House with a reputation that will bear discussion in the family circle. Mrs. Lockwood does not look like the cuts newspapers have published of her, still less does she answer to descriptions of her. She is a womanly woman; what greater praise can one give her. She is firm and intelligent, without being manly; and gentle and womanly without being frivolous. She is the beau ideal of a woman with a brain. She is of good height, neither tall nor short, and of strong, but not flabby, build. She wore a blue tricot skirt, braided in black up the sides. The drapery was not conspicuous for bustle, nor for the ugly flatness which follows the absence of one. A fine white muslin house sacque looked comfortable and was becoming. A certain trimness about the waist proved that Belva Lockwood, Presidential candidate, has not abolished stays. Six large diamonds, set in a square, caught a webby lace scarf about her throat, and from the coils of gray hair glistened a diamond comb. Her curly bang allows a space of broad forehead to show between it and her sparkling brown eyes. A few pinks and sprigs of mignonette were pinned close to her throat.

AN INTERESTING TICKET.

As she talked with me, twirling her black-rimmed eye-glasses, her changing expression echoing her conversation was interesting. I dislike to talk to people with dead faces! It always struck me as uncanny for a tongue to be running inside an unchanging face.

"Isn't this the second time that you have been nominated for President?" I asked.

"Yes. I was ill in Washington at the time," she answered. "The convention which was held in Des Moines, Ia., was attended by some six hundred people, among whom were as many men as women."

"I suppose you depend entirely on the vote of the men to put you in office?"

"Certainly, women have no vote," she replied with a smile. "We are coming to it, though. It is the universal opinion of all thinking men that women will eventually vote. I delivered a lecture not long ago at the Delaware Institution, Franklin, N.Y., in reference to women voting. President Cleveland, in congratulating me afterwards, said, 'It has got to come; we all recognize that.'" "Have you any regular course of canvass?" "Oh, yes, we would accomplish little without plans. We have both men and women to lecture. What women? Well, there is Mrs. Nettie Sanford Chapin, Marshalltown, Ia.; Mrs. Catherine Denning Clark, Lexington, Ky.; Mary Ata L. Stowe, San Francisco, Cal.; Mrs. Mary Anna Munger, Worcester, Mass.; Dr. Rachel Davidson, Flint, Mich.; Margaret Berg, Chattanooga, Tenn.; Alma M. Mitchell, Salem, Ia.; Mrs. Emma Beckwith and Mrs. Cynthia Leonard, of New York. Dr. J. G. Lamber, of Chattanooga, is one of the men who is to lecture and—as I cannot easily recall strange names, I can only say the others are prominent men from Alabama, Mississippi, New York, Vermont and Tennessee."

"Have you any newspapers devoted to your cause?"

"No, not that I know of. There is nothing to make it worth their while," she said with a jolly laugh. "However, I am Vice-President of the Woman's National Press Association, of Washington, and the members are united in favoring me. They will help all they can in their correspondence, but they can't vote. I had been nominated as delegate to the Union Labor party," she continued, "and expected to leave for Cincinnati to lecture the very day Mrs. N. S. Chapin, Chairman of the National Committee, notified me of my renomination for President."

"Have you had any money offered for the aid of your campaign?"

"We receive many private donations, besides having an offer of $25,000 to carry on the campaign; but you know, as we have no big places to offer, we'd not get the help other political parties get. I have just received correspondence which may show you how our work is starting."

BOURBON, IND., 7, 2, '88.

Hon. Belva A. Lockwood,

DEAR MADAM: Your standard was thrown to the breeze this P.M. by our citizens, 'mid wild huzzas of enthusiastic votes. From now to November the good work will go forward until the vote for fair citizenship shall be counted, when you may expect to hear from old Bourbon.

With prayers for your success and the triumphant victory of the cause we all hold sacred, I am, very respectfully yours,

A. C. MATCHETTE, M. D.

"Mrs. Lockwood, if you do not reach the White House this time," I said, "what good do you expect to result from your campaign?"

"It educates the people to the idea," she replied. "If we always talk and never work we will not accomplish anything. Men always say, 'Let's see what you can do.' Now we are trying to show them."

"What class of women support you in your Equal Rights ideas?"

"Thinking women and working women. Society women never go outside of society. It is all in all to them, so they give us no support, and the very poor—the masses—are no better. One is the slave, the other the doll, and equally useless to us."

"Do you mind telling me something of your home life?" It's a question I always feel delicate about asking, but it's always the most interesting thing about prominent people.

"Certainly not," she replied without hesitation, "but it is a little like a writer once calling to get something from my mother to write about me—something I had done in my baby days; but mother said I never did anything. Rather rough on me, wasn't it? I live in Washington, at No. 619 F street Northwest. My mother, my daughter, my granddaughter, my niece and my grand-niece all occupy the same house. This is my card." She handed me the following business-like card:

BELVA A. LOCKWOOD & CO.,
Attorneys and Solicitors,
No. 619 F street, Northwest,
Washington, D. C.
Practise before the United States Supreme Court and Court of Claims. Pension and Bounty Claims a specialty.
Patents obtained.

HER LAW BUSINESS.

"My husband, Dr. Lockwood, was an invalid," she continued, "and so I taught school for fifteen years. It was very poor pay and hard work. I had my family to support, besides the niece I have spoken of, whom I adopted and raised. There were then no respectable paying positions open to women as there are now, so I began to read law. I was admitted to the Bar in September, 1879, and have been in active practice for fifteen years. My husband died in 1877."

"Have you made much money?"

"Well I have run a large house and kept a large family. I never make less than $3,000 a year. Lura M. Ormes, my daughter, is a skilled lawyer. She takes charge in my absence. She also manages the house and looks after her three-year-old daughter, Inez Ormes, who is a wonderfully clever child. Lura likes to do fancy cooking, but none of us waste time scrubbing or making beds. Yes, I can work. I was once a good chambermaid and seamstress. Why don't I do housework? Because servants are cheap and I can earn more in a month at my desk than I could at housework in years. My niece, Clara B. Harrison, is also a lawyer, but her regular duties are attending to the correspondence, at which she is very skillful, and keeping the accounts. She is a widow, with one boy, four years old, Warren L. Harrison. My daughter's husband is interested in getting up a stock company in New York for the telautograph. My office is in the first floor of my house."

"Do you feel encouraged in your work—political work, I mean?"

"Yes, we are making great progress. It is only by practical work that we can show what we can do. People are less wedded to party, and do some thinking. Once it was considered a disgrace to change one's party; now it is a sign of progress. If I don't gain the Presidency, we expect to get in as Governors and legislators. Linda Gilbert, the great prison worker, was nominated for Lieutenant-Governor of New York, in Brooklyn, Saturday night."

"Do you expect to carry any State?"

"Yes, Iowa," she replied.

"Do you favor tariff?" I asked.

POLITICAL VIEWS.

"I favor a reduced tariff. A great number of American industries need protection," she answered positively. "I don't believe in the absence of tariff of the Democratic platform, nor the high tariff of the Republicans. What do I think of immigration? I heretofore thought that America should be the asylum for all foreigners, but now, since they have made our land a dumping ground for paupers and criminals, I think it is the President's duty to suggest reform. What of the Chinese? Their labor is not more harmful than that of the other foreigners. Keep one nation out, do the same with all."

"What exercise would you suggest as best for women?" I asked.

"Tricycle, by all odds," she answered. "I rode one for five years, and there is nothing that can equal it for healthful exercise."

"What do you think of Harrison's chances?"

"Well," she mused, smilingly, "if every man who shakes hands with him is going to vote for him—but that's what you can't tell."

"What are Cleveland's chances?"

"Cleveland?" in surprise, "he is not a candidate. It's Mrs. Cleveland."

"What is your latest work?" I asked, curious to know all that this woman with a mother's face and a man's intellect is doing.

"I am interested in trying to establish a court of international arbitration between America and foreign lands. The trouble over the fisheries treaty with Canada helps to prove how much we have need of it. I am beginning with France—others will come later—and have just sent some papers on the subject from Washington to the Peace Minister of France."

"So, Mrs. Lockwood," I said, "you expect to be elected President of the United States?"

"I do," she answered.

"Next to you, who stands the best chance for the Presidency?"

"Frances Folsom Cleveland."

NELLIE BLY

A New York Voudoo Knave

Sunday, August 19, 1888

Nellie Bly's Encounter with the Famous Dr. Bass

A Negro Scoundrel Who Claims to Tell Fortunes and Sell Love Charms—How he Came to Practise Voudooing—He Has a Fine Practice Among Superstitious Blacks and Ignorant Whites.

Voudooism or "hoodooing," whichever you please, is practiced right here in New York City. Of course the people who believe in it are numerous. Even in this, the century of railways, telephones and telegraphs, a tinge of superstition courses through the blood of the most intellectual. It is almost an impossibility to find any one, if one will acknowledge it, but has some "sign" in which they religiously believe. So it is not surprising that a voodoo doctor not only exists, but prospers in this city.

A little weather-beaten signboard bearing the name James A. Bass, M.D., hangs over the door of 181 West Thirtieth street, about three buildings east of a police station. The large window serves as a showcase for some half-dozen snakes, of as many sizes, curled very comfortably inside of big jars. Over the door hangs a bunch of twigs and roses which, judging from their dusty and worn appearance, must have seen as many summers and winters as the circus clown's jokes.

There were a few old chairs, a bare, unswept floor, two showcases stuffed with scraps of paper and bottles, and long rows of shelves on which the accumulation of dust proves that they are never used and that the jars on them, containing few liquids and many roots, are only for ornamentation and a blind. On the wall hang two mounted diplomas, proving that James A. Bass has a legal right to add "physician and surgeon" to his name. This shop is presided over by a strong young negro. He never has anything to do except to touch the bell and tell a visitor to sit down, for "the doctor's busy." He has not much fear that any envious soul will want to carry away the store, so he spends a great deal of his time on the shady side of the street with a group of negroes.

I sat down and waited. I wanted to see Dr. Bass and engage his services in voudooing something or somebody, or rather I wanted to see how he went about it. A World reporter had investigated the voudoo business here in New York, and among other unenviable things he learned that a woman had been driven crazy by a powder which a doctor had caused to be scattered where she lived. I had not waited long before Dr. Bass came from the back room.

"Do you tell fortunes?" I asked.

"Yes, Miss, sometimes," he replied, with a lisp. "I will be at leisure in a few moments."

"Just come this way," he said when he returned. "I am kept so busy that I can hardly attend to all my customers."

From the shop we went into a small room, partitioned off at one end, which contained a stove, table, bureau and a curtained bed. The next and last room made some attempt at comfort, but it lacked cleanliness. The floor was covered with a good Brussels. A walnut folding-bed, draped with a fine lace curtain, faced a long pier mirror at the other side of the room. A number of sketches, biblical in design, and a few photographs of colored people in various stages of idiocy were hung around the walls. The mantel was covered with a lambrequin, the fire-place was closed, but a parlor stove stood ready to answer for the same purpose. Two large windows opened out into a high boarded space. At once of them stood a leather chair, like those always found in a surgeon's office. A little leather-covered stand, plush-upholstered sofa and chairs, completed the adornment of the room. There were three doors in the room—the one by which I had entered, one up by the mantel, which opened to a wash-sink, and one at the side of the room, which I learned later opened out into a hall.

HE TELLS FORTUNES.

"I don't like to tell fortunes if I am going to work for any one," said Dr. Bass, as he bustled about giving me a chair and gathering up a pack of cards. "It rather hurts the influence of my work, and then one can't trust entirely to fortune by cards, because they change so. One day they run one way, and the next day, except for the main facts, they run entirely different."

I sat down in a chair on one side of the table, and he sat in the operating chair opposite.

"Take off your glove, he said, as he shuffled the cards. "A glove will detract from the current of magnetism, and it makes the cards less liable to come right."

I knew this was but a ruse to get my hand bare, so that he might judge from it my occupation. It was an old trick of fortune-tellers. I determined to keep very still and let the doctor take care of himself. The story of my wrongs or rights, as the case may be, I should unfold after. He cut the cards in three parts and placed them on the table.

"Now, miss, tell me what day and month you were born?" he said.

"The 5th of May," I replied.

"Very well; now draw seven cards and lay them down face upward."

I did so. He shuffled the remaining cards again, and once more I drew seven. Then he made me shuffle the remaining ones. He afterwards scattered them on the table and I again drew seven.

LOTS OF LOVE IN IT.

"M'eh," he said, thoughtfully, through his nose. "It appears, miss, that there is a woman, fair and husky, who is trying to injure you with a man who, away from her influences, would care for you." I heaved a heavy-weight sigh and drooped my head in maiden-like confusion. "There is also a man, with blue eyes and dark hair, upon whom your affections appear to be centered. (That's news, I thought.) He is a source of grief to you. He has no stability, no ambition, no energy, and is very fickle. (Whew! I thought, when I find that individual I'll steer clear of him.)

"There appears yet another," he continued, looming over the cards. "He is tall and fair. He comes in diamonds, so his eyes are blue and his hair is very light."

"Yes, yes," I said, impatiently, as he stopped. "What of him?"

"He has been separated from you," he said dolefully. "He longs to return, but he is weak and he fears your anger. Every time, though, that he makes up his mind to come back those persons who took him away get about him and he weakens. He is weak, but his heart is naturally good and he would make you a splendid friend. I can bring him back to you."

"Thanks, awfully," I said sweetly, while I was running over the list of my acquaintances to find the one he meant.

"Now make a wish and choose a card." I closed my eyes and wished Belva Lockwood would gain the Presidency and drew a card. "Oh," he said, as he held it up. "That's the Queen of Hearts. You have drawn yourself."

"How did you know me?" I asked as I drew again. This time it was the Jack of Clubs, who, he said, was a man I soon would meet. Then came the King of Hearts, and so on until at last he said that cards did not run well for me and that he would go into a clairvoyant state.

HE GOES INTO A TRANCE.

"It will only take two minutes," he said, as he placed a dirty old skull beneath his feet and leaned his head on his arms, which was braced on the table. I smiled and wondered what on earth I wanted to ask.

I looked at the clock and then I looked at him, as he sat with his feet on somebody's skull. I wondered where the rest of the body was and what the poor thing had done that it came to such base uses. The feet weren't very big, and they were incased in fine shoes, yet the footstool was too peculiar to affect one pleasantly.

I glanced at the doctor. He was a small man, not more than 5 feet 5 inches. He wore a black-and-white striped vest and trousers and a black coat. A large watch chain spanned his vest. A white standing collar; a black tie, in which was embedded a large gold pin, was up with the times. His face was a ruddy brown. His straight nose and not over full lips bespoke an alien blood. His capillary adornment was woolly, but it was carefully parted in the centre, and his side-whiskers and mustache were trimmed close. The hand on which he rested was very small, and a circle of diamonds on his little finger glistened and sparkled the more from the contrast to the bronze skin. Yes, he looked prosperous.

"Shall I be lucky in lottery?" I asked quietly.

Ugh! The feet shifted on the skulls, and then the answer came, slowly and methodically:

"No. Lotteries and gaming of all kinds hold only blanks for you."

"What are lucky numbers for me?"

"All odd numbers; seen, five, thirteen, twenty-one, twenty-seven. Your most lucky day is Friday and next is Wednesday," was the reply, which from observation I have learned is true.

"How shall I succeed best in life?" I ventured again.

"By surrounding yourself with business men," was the reply, "and giving your entire attention to business."

HE PROMISES TROUBLE.

"Will I be successful in what I undertake?" I asked.

"You will do something in about four days from now that will cause you lots of trouble (I wondered if it would result from writing about him), but you will turn your back to it and it will all pass away, leaving things brighter than ever. You pass through many strange things; you try to do much good; you worry over other people's ills, and life has grown very wearisome to you. You would be more than satisfied to die, but life is going to be brighter soon than it ever was."

I felt my will weakening. I felt myself believing more and more. I was being swept away and a superstition, which I thought foreign to me, wakened and leaped forth to believe this man who sat there with bowed head telling me such strange truths. I endeavored to arouse myself and to think of the absurdity of it all, but it was some time before I could.

This did not end the business. It was but the beginning. He was now to "hoodoo" some one for me. I determined to put it to him strong in order to see if he would do anything for money.

"What can you do?" I asked during our first interview, "to set matters right?" I did not explain what matters.

"Well, I can bring this man who has no stability back to you, and make him so much under your control that you can do as you wish with him. I can also give you a luck charm to wear which will protect you from all harm. Then I can cast ill-luck on your enemies."

THE HOODOO CHARM.

"That is very nice," I asserted. "Say, now, you don't mind if this one man is married?" I asked coolly, and smiled, "and that I want you to rid this world of his wife and bring him to me? You don't mind all that?"

"No, certainly not," he answered, looking sharply at me; "I conduct all these affairs personally, and I know the people who pay me will not tell, and it is to my interest not to tell."

"Besides this, there is one who hates me," I continued; "now, can you bring on him all the ills flesh is heir to and wipe him off this earth?"

"It can be done," he answered, firmly.

"That is well. You are the person I have needed," I said, flatteringly, as I left him.

I was not to go for the charm until an odd day, and I was to take with me a love-letter written by the weak man, and any other article of clothing which he might wear.

"Cut the letter in small pieces," he instructed, "and bring it to me. Then get one of his stockings if you can—"

"Well, I can't," I exclaimed with energy. "Name anything else. Good heavens! Love and hosiery in one breath!"

"Well, then, a handkerchief that he has been wiping the perspiration on. These two things I will work on and make him your slave."

Armed with a handkerchief and an old letter cut into the smallest possible bits, I went back. The clerk was out, so I walked to the door leading into the first room, which I have already described. A girl, white and beautiful, sprang up in alarm and rushed to the curtained bed in the corner. Putting her head through the opening in the curtains she informed me that the doctor was busy, so I went out into the shop, where I sat down and wondered.

A WORD ABOUT SNAKES.

At length the doctor came out and told me he would be ready to see me in a few moments. Taking some water-like liquid, which smelled like carbolic acid, from a large jar, he disappeared again into the inner room. The time seemed very long and the day was very warm. I grew tired of waiting. At last I was amused by some laborers who were fixing a drain at the doctor's door. Then one caught sight of the snakes in the window and he dropped his pick and began to talk.

"Der yer see this 'er cut o' my thumb?" he said to his companions. They dropped their picks and shovels and replied that they did. "Well, one summer as I was a' livin' in the country I picks up a big stone, an' under it was a—snake. He sees me afore I sees 'im, and 'e takes me 'ere thumb intur 's head. Well, sir, I just takes 'im by 'is—tail—say, that biggest one in ther' is shucks to 'im, he 'us as big round as me leg, but I takes 'im by 'is tail and I jerks his head off. Then I goes to the doctor and he cuts the piece out."

The rest of this interesting conversation was lost by the appearance of the doctor, who took me out and in through a hallway to the back room. This allowed his other visitor to get out unseen. I gave him the letter scraps and handkerchief.

"Here is the charm I made for you," he said as he handed me the finger of a gray Lisle thread glove. It was filled with something and was sewed up at the end with white thread. "Take this home and sew it on the edge of the right side of your corsets. Wear it always and nothing can harm you, and you will always be lucky. When you sleep at night put your corsets under your pillow. It will make you have great social successes."

THE CHARM WAS WORMWOOD.

I took the absurd thing, gave him $5 for it and went home. I opened it, of course. It was not filled with cats claws and such things, but merely a dry green herb ground almost into a powder. This I took to a druggist. He said that it was wormwood, as near as he could tell from the state it was in. So much for my $5 charm.

The next odd day, the 15th inst., found me there again, with faith in my speech and ridicule in my soul. He had three visitors this time, one colored and two white.

"Now we begin to work," he said, cheerfully. "Won't that man wonder what struck him though? He will commence to think of you now, and he'll have no peace until he is at your feet. Sit down at this table and write what I dictate."

I sat down. He made me take off my hat and gloves, and then he put a page of a druggist circular before me, a stub pen and a bottle of lurid red ink. He sat opposite me in the operating chair with a satisfied smile on his face. At my feet was somebody's skull, with the lower jaw missing, but I had too much respect for somebody to touch it; at my other side was a queer iron figure, and standing on the floor near the door was a small cross about a foot in height.

Dr. Bass leaned his elbow on the table. I dipped the stub pen into the lurid red ink and carefully dropped a drop to the floor.

"Why do you use this paper?" I asked.

"Because we must use printed paper and write as it reads," he replied. "Now begin." This, toned down somewhat, is what he dictated and I wrote:

AN EXHORTATION.

"We hereby demand, in the name of the Father, and of the Son and of the Holy Ghost, that—put in the name and address of the young man."

Goodness! I did not wish to put any of my acquaintances in such a position, so without lifting my head I quickly invented a name and wrote on:

"Mr. Fred White, 236 East Twenty-third street, New York City, shall be compelled to come under the complete control of."—

"Now write your name and address," he said.

I was getting into hot water, not having any name prepared. I knew I must set on the instant, so I continued:

"Mrs. A. N. Brown, 169 East Ninety-sixth street, New York City. We demand until then that he shall have no peace of mind or body by day nor night, nor in his whole life; and we further demand that he be worried until this comes to pass. For what is right is right, and what is just is just, and to this end we invoke and conjure all the spiritual powers on the earth, above the earth and under the earth that this must be as it is written, so all the ruling powers of this day and hour, come forth! Also do we bind and burse the chief spiritual power of this day and hour to the bottomless pits of hell until the last day of judgment, unless this demand shall come to pass as it is written. Furthermore, we demand in the name of the ruling spirits, and of Him who said the word and it was done, that Mr. Fred White, of 236 West Twenty-third street, New York, shall have no friendly feeling, nor passionate desires, nor any love whatsoever for any other person than Miss A. N. Brown, of 169 East Ninety-sixth street, New York. This we demand of all spirits, good and evil, and so it shall be, so it shall be, so it shall be."

A FINISHING TOUCH.

"I will finish it," he said as I glanced at the red writing standing out so boldly on the black type. We exchanged chairs, he put his feet on somebody's skull, and wrote:

"By the powers, communicating unto me, do I demand that they shall come from the North and the South, the West and the East, and united shall labor in this cause as it is written and bring it good luck and success. So it shall be, so it shall be, so it shall be."

To this we both signed our names and addresses. He made me write two more, copying line for line, on a page of *Harper's Weekly* and a page of THE WORLD. When done, he wrote his little say beneath and signed them.

Now he put them out on the table and covered them with a white powder until the lurid red ink was lost to sight. Then he folded them and sealing them up in a square package he made me address it to Mr. Fred White, as I would do a letter.

When this was done he lighted a paper at the gas jet, put the sealed package into an iron kettle on the hearth and set it on fire. It burned with a sparkle and hiss into an angry blue flame. He poked the stuff with a curiously twisted stick and threw in more whitish powder.

"How did you learn all these queer things?" I asked.

LEARNING THE BUSINESS.

"I learned it from my father. He practised it in this city. He was one of nine who were given these secrets by an African brought as a slave to this country. He had been a great power in his own country. We can do anything that is not actually among the impossibilities. I can bring people together or separate them; I can cause marriages and death; I can bring ill luck and good luck, but I couldn't raise the dead. Almost all the original nine who were taught the hoodoo are dead, but they have handed it down to their children, and we are, by experience, reaching further than they did."

"Have you much business in the voudoo line?" I asked.

"More than I can attend to."

"How do you work harm to people?"

"About on the same plan as we work good, except we use different powders and I do different things. I can curse people so they are always unfortunate."

"Do you ever teach any one the business?"

"Yes, but not often. I charge $300 for teaching the whole thing, but I would teach you to separate and to draw people together for $50."

"How long would it take me to learn?"

"About a month. Come in Monday and we will fix that enemy of yours."

I still have Dr. Bass's love charm, and he has my $5. I am waiting to hear what will happen to that imaginary young man White.

NELLIE BLY

Candidates' Wives

Sunday, September 9, 1888

Nellie Bly's Interesting Interviews with Them

She Goes Out to Oak View to See Mrs. Cleveland

At Columbus Mrs. Thurman Talks in a Kind, Motherly Way

Mrs. Harrison, at Indianapolis, Tells of Her Happy Girlhood.

And Mrs. Morton Gossips with Her at Rhinebeck About Housekeeping

---

A Symposium of Four Women in Whom Everybody Is Interested Just Now—The Wives of Candidates for the Presidency and Vice-Presidency Tell About Themselves—The Routine of Their Daily Lives—All of Them Seem to Be Women Who Typify Some of the Best Qualities of American Womanhood—Mrs. Cleveland, by Virtue of Her Public Position, May Not Talk—Kindly Mrs. Thurman Say that She Used to Make her Own Dresses and Enjoyed Doing It, Too—Mrs. Harrison First Met Her Husband When Both Were at School—She Learned to Bake Good Bread and Has Literary Tastes—Mrs. Morton Was in Society in New York Before She Was Married—She Looks After the Housekeeping and Her Family of Girls—A Peep Inside the Homes of Four Famous Women.

WASHINGTON, AUG. 29.—I came here yesterday under instructions from THE WORLD to prepare a series of interviews with the wives of the Presidential and Vice-Presidential candidates. It was naturally assumed that every woman in the land would be interested in knowing something of their home life. Naturally I elected to make my first call upon Mrs. Cleveland. I had a great idea about the democracy of the White House before I called there, and I had but little doubt of my reception, even though I was only a little newspaper woman without a vote. I met some well-informed people here who scoffed at me because I expected to tell Mrs. Cleveland the truth—it being one of my first rules never to obtain an interview without the knowledge and consent of the party interviewed, and then be allowed to meet her.

"But why? why will I not?" I urged.

"Because," they replied, "President Cleveland is a very shrewd man, and he does not permit Mrs. Cleveland to meet any correspondents lest she should unintentionally say something which might embarrass him politically."

MRS. CLEVELAND.

I was credulous, however, and I was happy in my belief that I would find things as they had been repeatedly presented in the prints. So, armed with an explanatory letter from a mutual friend, I went on my way rejoicing.

I engaged a carriage yesterday morning and drove out the road to Oak View, Red Top or Pleasant View, whatever Mrs. Cleveland's house is called now. The roads were dusty, but I met a number of people riding and driving, and I even began to look expectantly for the often described phaeton and the bay ponies Mrs. Cleveland drives. I felt that I should recognize them and that I could almost speak to their fair driver without giving offense, as she with her reported tact would instinctively recognize my friendly feeling. Happy in my day-dreams I leaned back in my victoria taking little note of the handsome residences, the green trees and the beautiful views on the way to Oak View.

The two miles or more seemed pitifully long. I began to think the driver did not know the way when I caught a glimpse of a bright red roof gleaming in the warm sun through the foliage of intervening trees. Then we whirled in a little gate which bore a signboard about the penalty dished out to trespassers, and over a little curved road, the color of brick dust, to the house.

The house is quite pretty, but the grounds do not show much care. As I entered I had a clear view of the veranda. On it was a chair, and a small, longeared dog, I believe of the species known as the dachshund. A larger dog lay in the shade of the house; but my whole attention was given to the hammock and the figure it contained. There I knew was the woman the newspapers had raved over, the woman people longed to see, the woman of unsurpassed beauty, tact, culture—the mistress of the White House.

The carriage drew nearer. Mrs. Cleveland sprung out of the hammock. I caught a glance of a startled face, like and yet unlike that made so familiar to us through publications; a glimpse of a blue silk sash and some sort of a light gown, and Mrs. Cleveland disappeared in the doorway. A half-grown boy in a rough gray suit came out, and as I stepped from the victoria he extended the silver salver which he carried. I put on it the explanatory letter from my introducer and a card and followed the boy in.

I sat down in the parlor and waited. I heard a feminine voice and the boy's replies in the room across the hall, then I heard the faint rustle of dress skirts and a cautious step come out into the hall and creep up the stairs. Then I heard the same steps in the room above my head; then all grew quiet.

I waited. The times seemed to stretch in a very uncomfortable way. The short-legged dog came in and walked around me and smelled of my russet shoes, then he wagged his tail in a greeting of good-fellowship and I responded heartily by smoothing down his coat and caressing his long ears. Then he walked off and again I waited. (I never wait only when I am severely alone.) All was quiet. I looked at the hallstand, which held some hats. I counted them by way of occupation. Three feminine, one masculine. On the shelf at the foot of the hat-rack mirror was a life-size crayon of Mr. Cleveland. The hall was carpeted. The parlor was finished in hard wood and covered with rugs. The furniture was very light in color and quite rich. The curtains to the French windows were a thin baby-blue brocade.

In the room back (evidently the library) were a centre table and one low bookcase. On this bookcase was a life-sized terra cotta bust of Mr. Cleveland. Rather strange to say, but a large wax candle stood on each side of it as though it was the figure of a favorite saint.

There was a bunch of fresh-cut flowers on the mantle and the perfume was very sweet, but was not sweet enough to make me forget that time was dragging out most horribly. Could it be that I was forgotten and left to sit here, or had the so-called first lady, like common people, to change her gown before greeting guests. But I heard footsteps above and then I heard the electric bell ring.

Some one scampered up the stairs and then down again. It was the gray-clad boy. He handed me a note for our mutual friend and said that Mrs. Cleveland could not see me and would I please see Col. Lamont.

I was astonished. And yet this was just what I had been told—that all news came through Col. Lamont, that he was the key to the White House and—well, I hated to allow anyone to say, "I told you so." Afterwards I learned that the wives of Senators and Cabinet officers who wished to see Mrs. Cleveland had to notify her in advance, or else they would not be received.

Had I used my ordinary ingenuity as a newsgatherer and not relied on common report that Mrs. Cleveland was accessible and democratic and tactful and kindly, I could have told the readers of THE WORLD more about her appearance and her history.

During my brief stay here I learned that Mrs. Cleveland is virtually cut off from all society. Her intercourse with the people is confined to her receptions, which we all know never lead to friendships. Her only intimate friends in Washington are Mrs. Greely and Mrs. Gilder, and when Mrs. Cleveland wants to visit she always goes to some little place where there is no society to worry her.

All this is enforced, they say, by the publicity of her position. There are no pleasant little tea parties, no social circle of good friends, no informal little dinners.

She has no intimate friends. The school-girl friendships which go so far towards making life pleasant are not for her. Because of her position as Mistress of the White House she is cut off from all those girlish confidences which most young married women know. An external watchfulness is on her lips. Her husband's interests are her own.

Even among the wives and daughters of the cabinet officers and of those closest to Mrs. Cleveland, I am told she has no really close friends. No young people come to Oak View and sit about its broad piazzas and gossip about dress and bonnets and all that feminine finery which all of us women love to talk of. She is separated from those lighter frivolities by the publicity of her position as mistress of the White House. Even shopping is a lost art to her. They tell me here that she dare not linger long over bargain counters—and what woman does not love a bargain-counter—for fear of the crowds which gather and stare her out of countenance. A hurried run up to New York, a furtive dash into some of the big stores there, I hasty selection of what is absolutely necessary, is the best she knows of the pleasant art of shopping.

When she drives out it is over conventional roads, nearly always alone, or with an acquaintance rather than a friend.

I tried to get from acquaintances who knew her well some characteristic saying of hers or some quaint conceit that might throw a better light upon the daily life she leads, but the lips of her friends, like her own, were sealed.

Sweet and lovely as she is, I do not envy her her place as "first lady in the land," shut off as she seems to be from common contact with humanity.

MRS. ALAN G THURMAN.

The Dear Old Lady Made Her Own Dresses and Likes Housekeeping.

COLUMBUS, O., AUG. 31.— "Is there no hotel conveyance here?" I asked a man who had braced himself against a post and was standing there busily doing nothing. I have just arrived in Columbus, 2.30 P.M., and had looked in vain for a vehicle of some sort to take me to the hotel. My impatience was partially due to the fact that I had been unable to get anything to eat since a light breakfast at 7.30 in Pittsburg. But in spite of my aching desire to reach a hotel I had to stand on the platform and long for a carriage.

"Ye-es, sometimes, but they've all gone now."

"So I see," I said dryly. "Well, how can I get to the Nell house?"

"It's a pretty good step to walk; you might go over to that street and take a car, only if you don't take the right car you won't get there."

MRS. THURMAN.

Just then I saw a coupé coming rattling down towards the station. I called to the driver. He drove up, jumped down off the box, touched awkwardly, without removing his battered gray felt hat; relieved himself of the tobacco juice which was bulging out his cheeks, and was ready. After dinner at the hotel he drove me out to Judge Thurman's.

The Thurman house is No. 517 East Rich street. It is a pretty but unpretentious two-story double building. Rich street deserves its name. All the houses, as far as I could see, were set back from the street and surrounded with grassy plots, and the pavements were boarded with well-trimmed shade trees. On the smooth and spacious green lawn which surrounded the Thurman home several pretty children were romping. They gave me one careless glance as the gate closed behind me with a snap and continued their play.

"Is Mrs. Thurman at home?" I asked of a neat woman who answered the bell.

"Yes, she is in next door. Be seated in the parlor, please, and I will tell her."

The first thing about the house which impressed me particularly was the excessive cleanliness of everything. The lawn, the entrance to the house, the hall, the parlor, even the woman servant, were immaculate. The next thing I noticed was that, while everything was comfortable, there was an evident distaste for the thousand and one useless things which crowd the houses of the present day. Everything was plain, and it gave me such a feeling of rest that I wanted to close my eyes and go to sleep. But I didn't, because just then I heard a sweet voice call: "Children, when you go in close the door which I left open." Their response, "Yes, grandma," and the glimpse of silvery hair I had between the shutters told me Mrs. Thurman was coming.

Before she comes in I want to describe the parlor. The walls and ceiling were covered with paper, quiet and modest in tone, and the carpet, deep and thick, harmonized with it perfectly. The mantel, directly opposite the folding doors, by which I had entered, held a life-size photograph of Grover Cleveland, with his name inscribed beneath it in gold script. A tapestry screen hid the fireplace. The furniture, and entire parlor suit, was protected by white covers; a small table in the corner had several books and photograph albums placed on it in a methodical way. There were no curtains, but the closed shutters made a dim, cool shade in the room, and a bunch of freshly cut flowers, bright in color, added a perfume that was pleasing. Almost back of the door hung a life-size oil-painting of Judge Thurman.

"Where is she?" I heard Mrs. Thurman ask, and she looked at me inquiringly, as she came in, so I hastened to say:

"Mrs. Thurman, I hope you will not think of me intrusive"—

"Pray, be seated," she interrupted gently.

"I am writing up the wives of the presidential candidates for the NEW YORK WORLD."

"Oh, indeed; we get THE WORLD."

"I have come out here to write something about you, if you will allow it," I broke in quickly.

"Well, well!" and she gave the prettiest little indulgent laugh, as if I were a sick child that must be humored. "I am such a quiet old lady that there is absolutely nothing to write about," and she laughed again. I have heretofore considered it a blessing that laughing is confined to the human race, for it is generally so peculiar, to say the least, but Mrs. Thurman's laugh was pleasing, unaffected and musical. I am sorry I cannot reproduce it in print.

"Tell me when you were born and what you did as a girl," I suggested.

Sitting down in a willow chair, quite near to Judge Thurman's portrait, and folding her hands in her lap, she said: "Well, I was born in Chillicothe, O. My name was Mary Dun," and smilingly added, "with one 'n.'

"My girlhood days were spent in the same way as those of every girl at that time—vastly different from to-day. The State was then quite unsettled; we did not even have roads. I went to school in the winter; made my own dresses, a thing we were compelled to do then, and which was a pleasure to us; read what novels I could get and generally managed to be very happy."

"What amusements had you then?"

"We had dances, and I was a great rider," and her blue eyes sparkled at the remembrance. "I was a very lively girl in my day, very lively. I was a splendid rider—we had no good roads then, and everybody had to ride. I liked it and excelled in it. I never learned to like driving. I imagine it would look very funny to see me on horseback now." And she smiled again as if the recollection was almost a temptation to try a canter.

"Where did you meet Mr. Thurman?"

"Oh, we were almost raised together. He was born in Virginia, but his parents moved to Chillicothe when he was a baby. We went to school together and were always friends. And now we have lived happily together as husband and wife for forty-five years.

"Yes, forty-five years we have been together," she repeated, as she twisted the thin wedding ring on her finger, "and I just thought the other day when Mr. Thurman returned from the Illinois trip so very ill, that it would be hard to part now. Of course, if I were twenty or thirty years younger I might enjoy this campaign business, but now I hate anything to disturb our quiet life. I am too old for it."

"Does being the wife of a candidate make much difference in your life?"

"It does not bother me much. Mr. Thurman has to see and attend to everybody, but it takes him away, and—well, I am too old to like any changes," and she added a little apologetic laugh.

"Tell me something that you have done?"

"I have done nothing but keep house and raise a family. I am a plain, uninteresting old woman. I never painted, or played, or had any love for fancy needlework. I think when a wife attends to her household affairs properly she has no time for anything else."

"Tell me about your children then?"

"Well, I have two daughters, both married and residing in New York. They are Mrs. McCormick and Mrs. Cowles. I have one son, Alan W. Thurman, who lives in half of this house. I always called him a farmer, for that was what he was taught to be, but he does not farm now. He attends to his father's business almost entirely, and has done so for a long time. My two daughters are childless. I have a grown grandson in Kansas, the only child of my eldest daughter now dead. Allen has six children, two girls, Virginia and Katherine with a K, and Albert Lee, who is 19 years old; Alan, Dan and Stalling Loving."

"Are you concerned with any churches or missions?"

"I do not attend church now because I am a Unitarian, and we have no church in Columbus. I once was interested in missions, but I leave that now to younger women. My home and family are all that have any charms for me. I like a quiet life and dislike anything to make a break in it. I have always been and I am yet my own housekeeper."

Just then the sounds of severe coughing were heard in the room above, and Mrs. Thurman, noticing my start, said in explanation:

"That is Mr. Thurman. He has been ill since his return from Illinois. It has been a long time since he has done much speaking and the strain was too much for him. He has a severe attack of muscular rheumatism and has not been able to see any visitors for several days."

Despite Mrs. Thurman's idea that she is a "very uninteresting old woman," she is a very handsome one and I am going to describe her just as she sat there talking pleasantly and easily to me.

She is of about medium height and build. Her face is unusually handsome for a woman of her years and what imprints time has left are pleasant ones. Her eyes are blue, bright and expressive; her mouth is small with very agreeable lines. She wore a black cashmere gown, plainly made, with basque, skirt and overskirt. A broach, round in design, fastened to the collar about her neck and plain white and black cuffs finished the sleeves. On the third finger of the left hand Mrs. Thurman wore three plain narrow gold rings. Her hair is one of the greatest charms and I believe always was. In her younger days it was a reddish brown. It is now the whitest silvery white, with not one dark thread in it. It looks very soft, is arranged in two little curls that fall artistically over the ears and are held there by black combs. The back hair is twisted and coiled high on the head. The style is most picturesque and very becoming to Mrs. Thurman. She has an easy, unassuming manner and talks freely.

She has never had a photograph taken, and the picture given above is taken from the sketch.

"We do not have any set hours for sleeping or eating, because Mr. Thurman is so irregular. I always get up at 6 o'clock, and we eat at any time Mr. Thurman is ready. I look after the house and see that everything is in order; then, when I am tired, I rest myself by reading."

"What do you read?"

"That depends. If I am very tired I read novels, yes, often trashy novels and they rest me. At other times I like to read biographies. I want to read a great many newspapers, but now I confine myself almost entirely to local news."

"What style of dress do you like best?"

"I never cared for dress; although I was a very lively girl, dress was always a tiresome subject to me. I have worn black almost all my life. What did you say is your name?" she asked suddenly.

"Nellie Bly."

"Oh, yes; I remember now of hearing the name before. But you are too young to be going about the country alone."

"It is easy for girls to travel alone now," I said, answering her smile, but she shook her head unconvinced.

"Do you know anything about Washington?"

"Yes, yes, I know the city perfectly," she replied. "We lived there for twelve years while Mr. Thurman was in the Senate. I liked it very much, although I lived there as quietly as I have done elsewhere. I know all the drives and I knew many people there, but I would be a stranger now, for every new administration makes a complete change in the society. We have lived here for seven years now."

Mrs. Thurman accompanied me to the door, and as she held my hand in a good-by clasp she repeated what I think I have proven to the contrary:

"There is nothing to write about me, dear, I am a very uninteresting, quiet old woman."

MRS. BENJAMIN HARRISON.

She Can Bake Fine Bread and Belongs to Several Literary Club.

INDIANAPOLIS, SEPT. 5.—No. 674 North Delaware avenue is a comfortable two-story red brick house. It is set back from the street, a little to one side of the green lawn which surrounds it. At the rear is a frame stable, and a few bushy trees break the sod. Under one of these a collie put in his time sleeping and snapping at bothersome flies. There is nothing remarkable about the house; in fact, it is the most unpretentious of any along this way, for North Delaware avenue is a beautiful street of artistic buildings.

A grassy track and rows of trees divide the street, smooth and clean, from the sidewalk. The houses are all set back some distance, and the lawns are smooth or broken by flower beds. Tennis grounds and swinging hammocks show that pleasure and ease are both given some thought.

I had waited several days for Mrs. Harrison's return from Put-in-Bay, and it was with some trepidation I called the next morning fearing she would be too weary to see any visitors. However, there was no hesitancy about admitting me, no mysterious running about as if they had something to hide. The woman showed me into the parlor and returned almost immediately to say that Mrs. Harrison would be down in a few moments.

MRS. HARRISON.

"Mamie," I heard a clear, musical voice call, "come take the baby; I want to go down stairs."

"Yes, mamma," and a slender, girlish figure, in a neat morning gown, ran lightly past the door upstairs. I heard the soft rustle of skirts, and then a little lady with large brown eyes and grayish hair stood before me. "I am Mrs. Harrison," she announced, and held out her hand and looked at me inquiringly, while I told the nature of my visit.

"I think it is rather embarrassing to ask one to talk of themselves," she said with a smile. "You would get a better story, either favorably or otherwise, by going to some one who knows me; yet if I can give you anything that will help you, I shall be most happy."

"I was afraid that you might be too tired from your trip to see visitors this morning."

"I am not in the least tired," she asserted, with a bright smile. "It was a trip for rest, and has been of benefit to Mr. Harrison. I am proud that I have a great deal of vitality. I am never ill, and since the nomination I have not had an hour, I can say, to rest. A little baby girl has come to my daughter since then, and I have had the entire care of them both and of my grandson Benjamin added to my other duties. With it all I am well and happy. I have always taught myself not to fuss and worry; that it only increases discomfort and never deducts from it; so I think that the secret of my perfect health."

"With all these duties it must be necessary to have a housekeeper," I suggested.

"No, indeed," she laughed merrily. "That's what I never had. When I was a girl my dear old mother made me learn to work. It used to make me angry. 'I will never do this when I am married,' I would assert petulantly. 'Very well,' mother would answer quietly, 'the knowledge will be no trouble if you don't, and if you are ever compelled to, it will be invaluable.' So I was taught everything and became quite an expert, especially as a baker. My bread was beautiful. I don't know how nice it would be now, for it is years since I have made any. My knowledge has served me well in making me a skillful housekeeper. I have always attended to my own household matters and think it a great pleasure. I often get up at 6 o'clock in order to go to market. I always take Benjamin, my grandson, with me because the early morning ride does seem good. Do my own marketing? Why, certainly, always; how else could I expect to have things to please me?"

"Will you tell me of your girlhood days?"

"Yes, they were my happy ones," she said, feelingly. "I was born in Oxford, Ohio. My father, Dr. John W. Scott, was professor of the Miami University at the time of my birth and was afterwards president of the female college in the same town, which position he held at the time of my marriage. I received my education at the seminary there and was a happy girl. We village girls were very simple in our wants then. We had driving and sleighing parties, but we did not dance. It was considered a great sin then, but we managed to have just as much fun without. We would put on our newly starched calico dresses and sunbonnets and we were grand and content. Isn't it wonderful how the lives of girls have changed? Imagine any girl during her graduating year wearing a sunbonnet, yet we all did so and were proud of them when newly laundered."

"Where did you meet Gen. Harrison?"

"At Oxford. He was a student at the university and I at the seminary. We were friends and we were graduated the same year. When he was twenty years old and I almost that we were married. So we started in life young and we have never been sorry."

"Are your parents living?"

"My father, who will be eighty-nine years old in January, is living in Washington with my widowed sister, Mrs. Russell Lord. I have also a brother living."

"What family have you?"

"I have a son in Montana. He is married to the daughter of Senator Saunders, the old War Governor. My son has a cattle ranch and is somewhat of a journalist. He has one child, Marthina, a little daughter. I have a daughter, Mrs. Mary—we call her Mimi—McKee. She lives here with us, and her husband is a tradesman in a boot and shoe house in the city.

They were married when Mr. Harrison was in Washington, so we had them take charge of the house for us, and since our return they have lived with us. My daughter has two children, Benjamin Harrison McKee, eighteen years old, who is the ninth Benjamin Harrison directly down, and the baby, Mary Lodge McKee, who is but eight weeks old, but is a jolly, plump little fairy."

"What is your regular routine of the day?"

"It does not differ from any one's," she said. "I get up at 6, do my marketing, breakfast at 7.30, bathe and dress the babies and have a romp with Benjamin, lunch at 1 and have dinner at 6. Except in the summer months I devote to mornings weekly to painting lessons, and one morning to a literature class, of which I am a member. By the way, this is a very literary city. We have three literary classes as well as literary clubs; and we have a woman's club, which is most entertaining and instructive. Besides the Woman's Club we have the Fortnightly Club and the Merrill Literary Club, named in honor of our teacher, Miss Katharine Merrill, a remarkably gifted woman. Our success is due to her teaching."

In addition to all this Mrs. Harrison is quite a musician, understanding music thoroughly and being very fond of it. And now I have not told you what she looks like, but as her face is already familiar to the reading public there is not much to tell. Suppose I describe her as she looked the morning I called on her. She is small, probably not more than five feet two, and has a plump figure. Her hands and feet are baby-like in size and her little dimples fingers display a marriage ring and three diamonds. She wore a plain gray cloth skirt and plaited jacket, belted at the waist. Her sleeves were tight and plain, showing the outlines of a finely moulded arm, and enameled gold bracelets clasped the fair wrists. Her eyes are large and a soft brown and her hair contrasts beautifully, being gray. Her mouth is the right size for beauty. She wears a soft, fluffy bang and her hair coiled low on her neck. Her pictures do not do her justice, as they cannot show how her face lights up, how the soul comes into her eyes and how the expression foretells every thought. She is a brilliant conversationalist and indeed a most cultivated as well as a beautiful woman.

Mrs. Harrison is devoted to the babies in her household. Little Benjamin is her treasure. She pets everything that comes her way, from her husband down to Dash, the collie, which lies snapping flies in the sunshine. She carries sugar and apples in her pocket for her horse. It rubs its nose gratefully and affectionately against her shoulder and begs for more as well as gives thanks for that received. She did own a mockingbird that followed her about the house and perched on her shoulder when she sat down, and the neighbors do say it could almost talk and that the understanding was perfect between them. It died not long since, so it is not mentioned now. A beautiful young fawn, a gift to grandson Benjamin, is just now the newest pet.

Mrs. Harrison is a diligent and studious reader, but does not find much interest in the novels of to-day. She is a member of the Presbyterian Church, and until she removed to Washington taught a class in Sunday-school. She is also one of the most useful and tireless managers of the Orphan Asylum. She is passionately fond of music and has quite a brilliant performer in her daughter, Mrs. McKee. Moreover, with all her brilliancy, Mrs. Harrison enjoys a good joke, and can tell in an inimitable manner very funny anecdotes.

"I want to show you a souvenir we have just received from Germany and which we prize above all things," said Mrs. Harrison. Going to another room she returned with an old-fashioned china cup and saucer. On the side of the cup was a small hand painting of a fine old face and an old-styled collar and neck-scarf. Beneath it was painted in small black letters, "William Henry Harrison."

"This was found in Germany, away in some remote corner by some tourist," she explained. "It was bought by them and sent to Mr. Harrison. You see it is a painting of his grandfather and was one of the articles in use at his time. How it got to Germany they could not learn."

But Mrs. Harrison's home? It is not extraordinary in any way. One enters the unusually wide hall by double glass doors. On one side of the hall, which is at the side of the house instead of the centre, is a large, dark leather settee and two high-back leather chairs. On a small inlaid-top table near the parlor door are a few brightly colored asters in a large antique jar and a basket of ripe pears. Above hangs an old painting by Inman of Gen. Harrison's historic grandfather. It is draped with the Stars and Stripes of the United States. A large silk flag is also hung midway in the hall. The parlor is large and not crowded. The furniture is easy and of a variety of designs. A piece of rare old tapestry hangs above the mantel, on which are some antique china ornaments. In the back parlor is a piano, an easel holding the life-size photograph of Mr. Levi P. Morton, and many pretty things which go to make a house homelike. That is it—Mrs. Harrison's house is homelike all over.

"I want to show you some pretty things which the people kindly send us," said Mrs. Harrison, and I went around with her looking at one dainty campaign article after another. Perhaps the most peculiar was a log cabin made by an old colored man in Virginia, who walked eight miles to Richmond to send it to them. It is about two feet in length, and is a typical Southern log cabin. It has a long chimney, and the door and window will open and shut. Between them on the outside of the cabin hangs a miniature coon skin. On a shelf by the door is a wood piggin and a gourd.

A barrel which lives by the side of the cabin is marked 'Hard cider.' A long pole goes up from the end of the cabin, and on it is a Harrison and Morton silk banner, on which is also inscribed, "Americans for America," and the Stars and Stripes wave from the end. It is a perfect thing, and much valued by Mrs. Harrison.

"I lived in Indianapolis all alone with my two children while Mr. Harrison was in the war," said Mrs. Harrison, still showing me around. "Those were my sad days, but I forced myself to be cheerful and looked after my home and little babies until merciful Providence restored my husband to me."

"Carrie Scott, as Mrs. Harrison was known in youth, was a beautiful girl," said Mrs. Miller, a neighbor, who has been acquainted with Mrs. Harrison for many years. "She was always well-bred, has a lovely disposition, makes friends everywhere and changes in fortune never leave any mark on her. She is always dignified and yet cordial. She never holds herself aloof and is very sympathetic. I have never known her to grow impatient and she meets everyone who is anxious to see her. She is very discreet, and her worst enemies, if she has any, could find no fault. One beautiful thing in her disposition is charity for human faults. She always speaks softly of the erring and finds excuses for them. As for dressing she prefers plain gowns and keeps to quiet colors—dark shades for street, and white, pearl and gray for evenings. She dresses becomingly and properly as befits her society; outside of that she does not care. She does not like much jewelry and especially dislikes a display of large diamonds.

MRS. LEVI P MORTON.

She Never Danced nor Painted, and Likes Plain Gowns.

RHINEBECK, N.Y., SEPT. 8.—"Do you know Mrs. Morton?" asked the driver as he shoved his elbow familiarly into my ribs. I looked at him steadily for a moment, but the very sight of his jolly, sun-burned face, his innocent blue eyes and bright red hair scattered my anger and left instead an inclination to laugh. Although I was conscious of smiling I replied stiffly:

"I have not that pleasure."

"On business then, eh?" he suggested, with a grin and another familiar nudge.

"Rather," I answered shortly, and then to turn the subject, said: "What a beautiful country and what lovely roads!" I had just arrived at Rhinebeck an hour before, and the first thing I saw at the station was a mammoth Harrison and Morton banner.

MRS. MORTON.

"This is Ellerslie, Rhinecliff, Mrs. Morton's home," said the driver as we whirled past the stone gate-posts. "Everybody drives through here. There are other gates to go out of which lead to other fine homes. Mr. Morton has built a large, new house. He had the old Kelly house pulled down." Large old trees completely shaded the perfectly smooth road. We whirled along beneath them, across an artistic bridge which spans a little lake, then a sudden turn showed the conservatory high above the road on a grassy knoll and reached by white marble steps. The thick foliage of a group of large trees hides the house until one is close to it. It is a large, artistically designed house, with a carriage drive at one side and a piazza at the other. The piazza was rendered cool and shady by green Venetian blinds. A servant in livery answered the bell and I walked up a flight of stairs into the large reception hall, which is a model of architectural beauty. Directly opposite the entrance are wide glass doors leading to the piazza. The broad stairs, with their carved balustrade, wind up from the left side to the upper floors, and in the alcove is a white marble bust and an antique clock. Next to it is the door to Mr. Morton's library, which faces the parlor. A marble bust of Mr. Morton rests on a pedestal opposite the stairway, and there is an old-fashioned high mantel in the same hard wood as the floor. A number of easy chairs, two centre tables strewn with magazines and bric-à-brac, and a variety of warm, soft rugs on the floor made up the room.

Two little girls in red cambric gowns and large rough straw hat, trimmed with a thin white material, went past and out the door. Then a lady came down the stairs and coming up to me asked if I was Nellie Bly and announced that she was Mrs. Morton. She invited me to go with her to the parlor. I told her the object of my visit and she laughingly said:

"Really now, there is nothing to write about me; if there were I would give it."

"There is always something," I said, "and the public likes to know something of the wives and homes of candidates."

"Well, this is our home; I shall be pleased to show it to you," she said. "We have been in it only a month and we are all very happy. Since Mr.

Morton bought it, two years ago, the children and I have dreamed of it night and day and now our dreams are verified. It was built just for comfort and I can say we have it. We went over the plans ourselves with that object and everything is satisfactory."

"How does being the wife of a candidate affect you?"

"I don't notice that it makes any difference. Everything goes on just the same, except that Mr. Morton has more to do. Mr. Morton has a great number of newspaper people to see him, but you are the first who has thought me worth while to visit," she said, with a laugh that disclosed the prettiest little dimples up close to the corner of her beautifully shaped mouth.

Mrs. Morton is handsome—undeniably handsome. She is about 5 feet 6 inches in height. She would be a little too heavy for a girl—although there are many girls as heavy—but she has a tapering waist and beautifully moulded neck and arms. Her eyes are large, bluish-gray and very expressive. Her complexion is a healthy white. She can boast of her nose, and her mouth is exquisitely aristocratic. Her lips are curved and full, and every smile awakens the most babyish and bewitching dimples I have almost ever seen. Although Mrs. Morton's face has not one wrinkle, and her years scarcely seem to warrant it, her hair looked quite gray in the dimly lighted room. Gray hair is always an attraction, even when combined with a youthful face. It was dressed very neatly, twisted to the crown of the head and there rested in heavy, smooth coils, met by a wavy fringe on the forehead.

Of course, every woman will want to know how Mrs. Morton was dressed. Well, she wore a gray cotton gown, with a waist which fitted to perfection, the skirt trimmed in white, open-work embroidery. A straight gold bar fastened the color, and there was no other jewelry except a large solitaire and a large emerald on the third finger of the left hand. A gray cotton gown, the material of which couldn't have cost more than $5! Think of it! and a woman, too, whose husband is quoted at some $20,000,000.

"Do you receive many begging letters, Mrs. Morton?"

"Yes, but that is not new. I received just as many before Mr. Morton was nominated as now. I think that comes into every one's life more or less.

"I was born in Poughkeepsie, N.Y.," said Mrs. Morton, when I urged her to tell me of herself. "My name was Anna Livingstone Street. My father was a lawyer in practice there, and so there we lived and I received my education. After a while we removed to New York, and I was in society quite a while before I met Mr. Morton. So, you see, there's nothing to tell."

"What did you do as a girl?"

"I can't recall much of anything. I never rode or danced and I never painted, but I was something of a musician. I used to and do yet," pointing to a work-basket filled with yarn, "crochet for missions. Other fancy work I do not like."

"What do you like best in dress?"

"Something plain, always plain," she answered hurriedly. "I never cared for dress; but you know when one is in society one must obey certain rules or be conspicuous for eccentricity. I wear nothing but cotton or flannel gowns during the summer, or for very extra affairs foulards. My preference in jewels is for pearls, and I have some fine ones, but I am not fond of much jewelry of any kind."

I cannot describe the parlor in which we sat because it would take many visits to become familiar with all its beauties. I know the carpet was pleasing to the eye and soft to the touch, that the daylight came in through the wide French windows with a gentle, subdued effect, produced by the green Venetian blinds. I know the walls were hung with fine paintings, that the chairs were snug and of variety, and grouped so easily that they fairly coaxed one to sit down and talk. I know that the little tables were strewn with photographs and rare knick-knacks, and that the breeze from the Hudson came creeping in, rattling stray papers and twisting the colored yarn. I know that it was all as perfect and sweet and comfortable as it could be and not one bit stiff or formal. In short, the entire house and its occupant seemed agreeable and unconventional.

"I love America and everything American," said Mrs. Morton warmly, "so much so that my friends tease me about it. I have very many friends abroad, and I like to go across occasionally, because really the only way to get a man cut off from his business is to take him abroad where he can't get to work. I think a trip always does Mr. Morton good, but I am always glad to get back to my dear old land. I just think it is so perfect that we cannot introduce anything foreign that will excel or even equal what we have. My household is strictly American."

"What do you do all day?"

"My days are very busy, as is every mother's when she does her duty," she said pleasantly. "I have always been my own housekeeper, and, although I am not a practical cook, I know what to order and when things are right or wrong. I see after everything of a domestic nature. I get up at 7 o'clock and give my servants orders for the day; then I see to every detail about my children—that they are bathed, what they shall wear and eat. At 8.30 o'clock we breakfast. Since we have been here the children eat with us, and the first thing discussed is the news. We take all the newspapers, as we wish to read both sides of the political question. The governess reads them to the children, who take as much interest in it as I do. Then I keep up an extensive correspondence. My literary efforts are confined to voluminous letter-writing, but my uncle, Alfred Street, who died some years ago in New York, was a poet."

"Will you stay at Ellerslie all the fall?"

"I hope to. My mother is with me now and later I expect a number of friends. When I told them I was coming to live here they all said I would die of the heat and loneliness, but I have felt neither. I never was happier in my life. Just step here until I show you the grand view we have."

A broad, clear space of rolling green going down, down until it is lost in a dark, heavy wood that seems to touch the water's edge, leaves unbroken a perfect view of the great Hudson, which looks in the sunlight like a mirror on which the quicksilver has been slightly ruffled; above the canopy of blue sky over which white, airy clouds are slowly drifting, while on the right bloomed up as if all-powerful the dark mountains which stretch further and further away until they become but a black line. Down below graze cattle, and coming along a distant lane are cows, stopping occasionally to get a mouthful of grass from along the wayside.

"How many children have you?"

"Now you will laugh when I tell you that I have done nothing but raise a family and keep house since I married, but it constitutes my whole happiness," she added hastily, as if fearing I would infer otherwise. "Edith, my eldest, is a tall, handsome girl of fourteen; Lena is thirteen, Helen is twelve. Louis Parsons, my eldest boy, died while we were in London. Alice is next and is nine, and Mary, the baby, is seven. They have a French governess, and they keep up their music and drawing during the summer; all other lessons are put by until winter. They are very happy children, too. They have their tennis grounds, their pony and dog-cart, in which they take long daily drives about the country; they ride and they do fancy work, and then each has her little duty to perform. One looks after the poultry and brings in the eggs; another sees to feeding the dogs, another to the flowers, and so on. They are busy children. They have formed a sewing class of the farmers' children, many of them from among our farmers, and others from the outside. Every Saturday morning they meet here, and Edith, Lena and Helen teach them sewing. Then they get up picnics and invite us to attend. They have one for to-morrow, I think. Mr. Morton has had tables put in the grove and it is now a very pleasant place for picnic parties. They come from all quarters with their baskets and spend whole days down there. It makes us happy that we can give a little pleasure to others."

"I suppose you will return to the city this winter?" I said.

"Yes, in the late fall. We live at 83 Fifth avenue; but we do not own the house. We are Episcopalians," she replied in answer to my question.

"I do not talk politics," she said with a laugh, "and I do not want any more rights than I have, but I am a politician for my husband's sake. Everything that concerns him is my interest, and I do all I can to aid him in every way. I have no interests that are not concerned with my home. My husband and my children are my whole thought and care. I did not tell you, I believe, that Edith, my eldest daughter, gives bright promises of being an able violinist."

"Have you any brothers or sisters?"

"I have no sisters, but I have a brother in London. He is a partner of Sir Roderick Cameron in Australian shipping business. My father has been dead some twenty years."

"What do you read, Mrs. Morton?"

"Well, I don't do much reading now except the newspapers. We get both Republican and Democratic journals, and I read them all, as we do not like to take a narrow view of anything. Occasionally I read novels, but I do not get much time aside from my duties to devote to reading. I am just now in the midst of 'Robert Elsmere,' and I think it is very interesting. Did you ever see such a display of campaign articles?" asked Mrs. Morton, with a little laugh. "We have so many sent us, and I value them quite highly. I intend to keep them all together as souvenirs."

She took me across the hall to Mr. Morton's library, a very model, where she showed me some of the articles they had received. On the low bookcase, which in circles the room, on either side a bronze figure, were leather plaque busts of Harrison and Morton. There were engraved and hand-painted pictures bearing their photographs, satin banners of different designs, one of very fine work framed, satin ribbons for the lapel, a Harrison and Morton Waterberry watch and all sorts of things, from the finest of work to Turkish towels with "Harrison and Morton" woven in colored letters.

"The children claim the right to all the balloons, which come by the dozen, and they go about wearing several at a time. Well, Chick, why are you not out?" she said, putting her arms around a little girl in a big straw hat, who had caught her skirt.

"I was studying," she replied. "The others are out."

"What a busy child it is," she said tenderly. Then: "The day is too fine to be indoors; go, you must take a drive. Our overseer wanted me to see some of the cows that he intends to send to the fair," she said, as we stood on the stairs waiting for my driver; "he is very proud of them, so I must go."

And then we shook hands and with a few pleasant words parted. I found Mrs. Morton the most informal and approachable of any woman I ever interviewed.

NELLIE BLY

Gay Times Among the Hops

Sunday, September 16, 1888

Nellie Bly Spends A Week With Fun-Loving Hop-Pickers

Home Workers Make Money, but "Foreigners Are Full Of Sport"—Love Among The Vines—At a Hop Dance—Good-Natured Country Gaying—Boarding and the Beds—Babies and Invalids.

Sangerford Centre, Sept. 14.

HOP-PICKING over? Well, hardly. Do ye see that horse? Well, it's hard driving to hop dances that's made him what he is."

I looked at the animal referred to and quietly counted his ribs. I had come to Sangerford Centre, Oneida County, the centre of the hop district, with the intention of joining the crowd of pickers. However, after some investigation I decided that it would take quite a useless amount of time to learn the ins of hop-picking by being a picker, so I selected the easier and surer way of driving about and visiting the pickers at work in the different yards.

"Hop dances are held frequently, then?"

"Every night. But if you want a lively time don't go among home pickers," advised my driver.

"Why?" I asked curiously.

"There is no sport in them," he said. "They are working for money, and there is no sport in home-pickers."

I laughed quietly, but decided to keep away from home pickers. I had no trouble in finding the hop-pickers, for hops seem to be the main product of Oneida County. At any rate, every farm has its large hop-yards and kilns. A small meadow, darted with haystacks, lay between the road and the hop-yard, but through the clear air I had a distinct view of the pickers at work. The first glance impressed me favorably. The hops are planted in perfectly straight rows like corn. Poles of uniform height almost—ten or twelve feet—are put in the furrows about one foot apart. Up these the vines are trained, and from the top the hop hangs in great bunches, grape-shape and light green in color. These contrast with the dark green of the vine very beautifully. So dense and thick grow the hop vines that a large hop-yard looks like a young forest.

We allowed the horse to have a rest as we drew rein to watch the pickers. They were men, women and children, and they seemed quite merry in their work. Indeed I thought too merry, for they called "hello!" to us repeatedly and said our horse was hump-backed, and we should give it a rest, which we were trying to do, and so on until under fire of their would-be funny remarks we drove on to see other pickers. There was no mistake about these. They were not home pickers. They had sport in them. I began to think if they all saluted us as did the first that I would not dare to enter a hop-yard, so we drove some distance, contenting ourselves with a look at distant yards.

After awhile I felt more courageous and decided to stop at the first large farm and enter the fields, even if I lost my hat in a race for the fence afterwards. One does not use any ceremony about going into the fields. We merely tied our horse, which had drooped his ears ever since he had been called "hump-backed," to the fence, and then, climbing over it, made our way to the workers. Winding in and about the covered poles, guided by the sound of voices, we soon found the workers. At times little spaces apart were queer contrivances under which the people worked. The first group we saw seemed the most proper for me to address. There was more chance to win a race than if I had to begin it in their midst, and the hump-backed incident made me a little uneasy in my mind.

A HOP-PICKER.

HOW THEY WORKED.

"Good-morning," I said boldly to a blue-eyed man who lifted his head and looked at me.

"Good morning," he responded, his eyes resting on my face while his hands continued busily at their labor.

"How's the hop-picking this season?" I asked in an off-handed manner.

"It's poor," he replied with a friendly smile, "ain't much to be made this season."

"What's the reason?" I asked, with a great show of interest.

"I don't know," he said, dropping his head. I concluded I was going too deep for him, so I added:

"Dry weather, I suppose. What do you call these things that you pick in?"

"These are hop-boxes," he said, brightening up, "we get 40 cents a box for hops when we board ourselves."

"Then you are a home picker?" I said.

"Yes, I have picked hops in these yards for thirteen years. I met my wife here, and now our three children pick here with us."

"That is nice," I said sympathetically. "How much can you earn in a season?"

"Last season only lasted eighteen days, and my wife, my boy, two girls and myself earned $125 in that time."

"I suppose that the season is almost over now?"

"Yes, this week ends it up. There is no work given out now and some have had to stop already for want of work."

The hop-boxes into which they pick are quite sensible arrangements. They are made in groups of four, which allows four people to work together. Each box is about 22 1/2 feet wide and 8 feet deep. They hold about twenty-six pounds of green hops, which equals probably twelve pounds dried. Each set of boxes is covered with a canvas awning, which serves in the daytime to protect the pickers from the sun and at night it protects any hops remaining in the boxes from possible rain.

"POLE-PULLER" AND "BOX-TENDER."

A man called indifferently "box-tender" or "pole-puller" is paid $1 a day to pull the poles and lay them beside the boxes. This leaves the pickers nothing to do except pick. They lean one side over a projecting pin in the box and pick with both hands from the vine. In a wonderfully short time they clean a whole pole, and throwing it down replace it with another. It is also the box-tender's duty to remove the picked vine from the pole. The vine is left to decay on the spot and the pole is set up with others in a tent-like form.

When a box is full a timekeeper empties the hops into a sack and credits the picker with the amount in his book. The picker also keeps a tally sheet, so that when the day of payment comes he knows that he gets all that is coming to him.

"Where are you from?" called out a gray-haired man at the next box.

"New York," I replied, and he gave a grunt and kept on at his work. I saw a pretty girl, so I made my way to her. She was tall and slender, her eyes were dark, and the curled lashes gave them a winning look of innocence. She wore a straight chalice gown, a broad-brimmed black hat and old kid gloves.

"Have you ever picked hops?" she asked me, as I stopped by her side.

"No," I replied, "but I imagine it is very jolly."

SHE JUST PICKS FOR FUN.

"Well, I pick just for the fun that's in it," she said, with a roguish smile, "but we don't find it in the hop-yards. It all comes at night, after the work is over. You see here we are confined to our own particular boxes, and after you stand picking all day with the same people for two weeks it grows tiresome, and there is not much left to talk about. We can't go from box to box talking, because the yardmaster has rules which must be obeyed. So in reality hop-picking is tiresome, but it is healthy, and the evenings repay us for all the rest of it."

"What do you do in the evenings?"

"We go to hop dances at different places, and we take quiet walks along the road, and many other things we find pleasant to do."

"How much can you earn in a day?"

"I can't make much, as I am not a fast picker, but some times I can pick two boxes and a start."

"'A start'?"

"Yes; some over two boxes to begin on the next morning."

"That means, then, 80 cents a day?" I said.

"No; I get my board, so I am only paid 25 cents a box. Only those who board of themselves get 40 cents."

"How is the boarding?"

"It's very good, but the beds are a sight. Go up and have a look at our boarding-house," and I promised to do so.

IN A DRYING KILN.

We next went to the kiln where the hops are dried. It is a plain little frame building, which looks like a barn. On the roof is a queer, funnel-shaped thing, open at one side, through which the brimstone-smoke escapes. We opened the sliding door and went inside. On the first floor was the furnace and on the second floor, piled three feet deep, were hops. The kiln is directly above the furnace. The bottom of it is made of slats, and through these the brimstone, which is used because it preserves the hops, comes teeming up. The hops are piled in here several feet deep. Two kilns full are dried every twenty-four hours. When the hops are dried the tender takes a large wooden rake and pushes them out into the second room. Then he opens little trap-doors and the hops go tumbling down with a soft rush to the floor beneath, where they are put in sacks ready for market. Drying hops requires the most skillful care. They must be of a certain degree of whiteness, and the least bit too much of brimstone will make them yellow and lessen their value.

As many stories are told of hop-growers holding their stock for a raise in price as is of brokers. One time they held their crop until hops went up to $1.25 a pound. Some sold at this figure and others held in hope of a higher rate. Prices went down, and one grower shot himself and others went crazy.

Invalids live in Oneida County during the hop harvest and spend some time every day in the hop yards inhaling the aroma from the hops in the kilns. It is said to have the most beneficial results.

FULL OF SPORT.

When we left the hop-yard we found the harness all tangled up over our horse and the reins put under the forelegs and buckled over the back. As we started to set things to rights the roars of laughter which came from the hop-yards convinced us that this was an example of the pickers' "sport."

I found the pickers in the next yard I visited "full of sport," as my driver said. Long before I entered the yard I could hear several voices, remarkable for their loudness, joined in singing:

> Say you love me, Mollie, darling,
> Say you love none else but me, do.

As the peculiar refrain re-echoed from hill to hill it started several crows from midday slumber and they flew low over the hop-yards, flapping their black wings ponderously and crying mockingly, "Caw! caw! caw!"

"Hop-picking is great times," said a friendly-looking man to whom I had begun to talk. "They are the life of the whole year and the wealth of Oneida County."

"Where do all the pickers come from?" I asked.

"Well, we have home pickers, who have picked here in childhood, made their matches here and have children and grandchildren doing the same thing over. Other pickers come from everywhere, mostly from Syracuse and down Utica way. One grower brought on some ninety Italians from New York, and they are ruining the business. They do not get as much a box as we do, and then they board themselves, but the hop-growers have an extra expense in keeping policeman to maintain order."

"Is it only the very poor people who pick hops?"

HEALTHY WORK.

"Not altogether. Invalids come here for their health; shop-girls consider it a good way to spend their vacation; some come for fun, some for money and some for health. That's about the size of it."

"Have you ever been to a hop dance?" asked a pretty little girl who was blushing under the gaze of a stalwart fellow-worker on the opposite side of the box. "They are lots of fun. I go to them every night almost. Tired! no indeed. I was ill when I came here from Utica. I was clerking in a store there and had been ill for a long time. Now I think I must be gaining three pounds a week. I pick all day, dance until 12, sleep until 5 and eat—well, I just can't eat enough, and I sleep so soundly that I don't think an earthquake would wake me up. You know hops make one sleep. Invalids send here for hop pillows for that purpose, but they should just come here if they want to be cured."

"Does the work hurt your hands?"

"Not now; it did some at first, even through my gloves, but I don't notice it now. We girls all rub our hands with tomatoes before we wash them and it takes away all the stains. I never had as jolly a vacation in my life and I shall never forget it," she said, as she cast a tender look into the watchful eyes of her handsome opposite. He looked back something which I pretended not to see or understand, and I left them happy. Funny, isn't it, how the god of love strays everywhere, even into hop-yards?

HAPPY BABIES.

It looks very strange to see the babies in the hop-yards—fair babies, dark babies, fat babies, lean babies, dirty babies, clean babies and all sorts of babies except crying ones. In all my visit I did not hear one cry. They roll in the soft earth, they straddle their mother's and father's boxes and watch them pick, they make mud pies and balls and they sleep on shawls in the shade of the hop vines and poles.

"I get up at 5 o'clock and bring my babies with me every day to the yard," said a pretty young mother. "They never cry and they never fuss, although they are here all day, and they never quarrel with other children in the yards. You see I could not leave them at home alone and it's very easy to bring them along."

The fat, dimpled baby looked up at me with its mother's blue eyes from the edge of the box on which it sat. Dirt and all, it was happy and it kicked his chubby legs against the side of the box in great glee. It was but a sample of the colony of babies.

IN THE BEDROOMS.

The houses in which the pickers live are long two-story buildings of the plainest kind. Doors open into either side of the kitchen, which divides the house. On each side of it are rooms containing long tables, bare or sometimes covered with oil-cloth, and long benches answer for chairs. The floors are uncarpeted and not extra clean, but it is an impossibility, with the pickers coming from the soft-earth fields, to keep them otherwise.

The beds are arranged on the top floor in long rows, like in a hospital ward. The bedsteads are purely homemade, being out of boards. Husk bed-ticks and pillows and skimped, dirty bed[;

clothes complete the sleeping outfit. There are no chairs or stools. Two people sleep in every bed, and their satchels are slid under the bed and their extra clothes hang on the wall at the head. All men as well as women make their own beds. If the estate is large enough to have several buildings one is kept for married people, and separate ones for men and women. The smaller the estate the more promiscuous the mixing.

A single tallow candle lights the workers to their beds, where they are expected to be at 12 o'clock, and here they sleep and mingle their snores just as musically as if they were occupants of suits in the Fifth Avenue.

THE COOKS WORK.

"I get up at 3 o'clock," said a cook, whose complexion was of milky whiteness, cheeks a dainty pink and eyes large, blue and sparkling. "I have breakfast ready at 5, when the bell, which is in a bell-tower on top of the house, like a church bell, rings and they all come down. I have one assistant and I get $1 a day for my work. The pickers are not hard to feed. They all say, so long as I give them pie, that they are satisfied. See, it takes baking," and she pointed to the long rows of steaming custard and pumpkin pies, just from the oven. "Everything is cooked wholesale and every house does its own cooking. I boil potatoes by the potful and make puddings by the gallon, as well as coffee. We have dinner at 12 and supper at 6. Home pickers can come about when they please, but borders must be in the hop-yard at 7. I was raised in hop-yards," she continued. "My father owned some, I met my husband hop-picking, and now, as I am left a widow, I am back at it again. Only this year I am in the kitchen. It's too hard, though, and next year I shall go to the yards."

After the 5 o'clock bell rings the pickers, men and women, all walk out back of the house and their wash their faces in buckets and tin pans. The boarding-houses have no looking-glasses, and if the maidens wish to see themselves trim, they are compelled to gaze long at the reflection in somebody's eyes or seek the clear waters which are found occasionally stealing through the valleys. Rainy days are spent indoors, gossiping, flirting, dancing. Sundays they spend as they please, so long as they are quiet. But the evenings!

THE HAPPY, HAPPY GLOAMING.

When the cool shade of night had wrapped the hills and valleys and one deep gloom we started for a hop dance. The drive was a pleasant one. The air was biting and laden with the odor of the drying hops. Occasionally as we flitted by the hop-kilns we would get a flash of light from the furnace. Then yellow gleams amid dark trees would grow brighter and brighter until we would get a view through open doors or windows of pickers in their boarding-houses. Sometimes the horses would shy to one side, and by the flash of the lantern on our wagon we would see devoted couples sitting along the wayside. This grew so frequent that we knew just what every shy indicated.

Then we began to pass young girls in white gowns tenderly escorted by young men along the roadway. They, too, were bound for the hop dance. We usually exchanged some greetings as they stepped to one side to let us pass, some of which were rather unique.

"Ah, there! my sister-in-law," called one young fellow, and I cheerily responded. Everything was evidently meant in the kindliest humor.

HOP DANCE IN A BARN.

Our first hop dance was held in a barn. A few tallow candles and one smoky oil lamp lighted the barn floor, which had been cleared for dancing. We tied our horse to the fence and went in. A group of girls, all in white gowns, stood near the door; the set was just over and they were waiting for another to be formed. I endeavored to make a comfortable seat of a large yellow pumpkin and my driver leaned against a rake.

The orchestra was neither large nor expensive. Three men composed it. One played a violincello, another an accordion and the third a mouth organ. I don't profess to be a musical critic, but I have heard of music awakening tears. This brought tears. A man with very sleek hair, very high, white collar and a huge bouquet of different colored flowers, the ends of which were done up in tinsel, in the lapel of his coat, got on an upturned bucket and cried:

"Ladies and gents, please form for the Money Musk. This way—step up smartly. One more set this way."

Too dumel de dum, ah rattled de lum! and whew! but the whirls! White skirts took a direct angle from the waist, coat-tails ditto, and couples spun like tops; feet flung sideways, twisted and rattled to bang! and everybody seemed to be doing his level best to make things hum.

I endured it as long as I could and then I concluded, except for personal enjoyment, I was wasting my time, for the secret of those dances, the figures called out by the man on the upturned bucket will never be known. They were simply indescribable, but I can vouch for their being the most violent exercise.

A SWELL HOP DANCE.

The next place I went to was advertised in large posters, of which this is a reproduction:

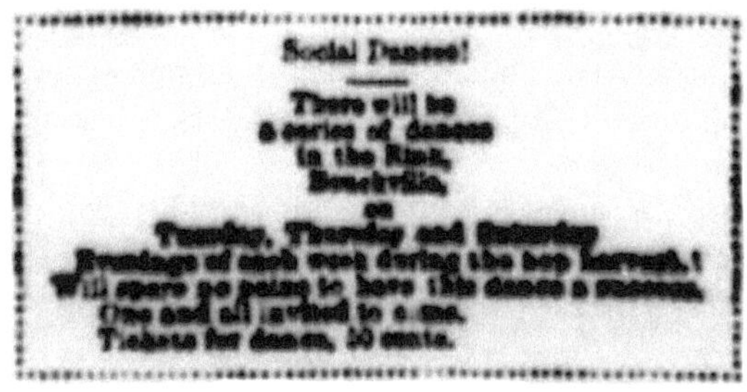

Social Dances!

There will be
a series of dances
in the Rink,
[illegible],
on
Tuesday, Thursday and Saturday
Evenings of each week during the hop harvest.
Will spare no pains to have this dance a success.
One and all invited to come.
Tickets for dance, [illegible] cents.

The large rink was well filled with pickers when we reached our destination. They did not differ much in appearance from those hop-dancers in the barn. The majority of the girls looked very neat in white gowns and the young men were gay in their best attire. The rink was large and lighted with oil lamps, with reflectors. An orchestra of several pieces occupied an elevated platform at the end of the hall. Prominent among the dancers were gay young men who had come from Utica and surrounding towns to enjoy the festivities of the hop harvest. Several boasted of having come from Rome and Paris. I think the fair hop-pickers, among whom were many pretty girls, held their own with the frivolous youths of those wicked cities.

The figures of the dances were called out and the young people danced very well to the even-time music. An adjoining room proved to be a lucrative ice-cream parlor, and the hotel bar made the men quite lively and flushed. All in all, it was a very amusing dance, and in the words of my driver, "there was lots of sport in the foreign pickers." At 12 o'clock the girls got their wraps, the men their hats, good nights were said, and arm in arm the happy couples walked along the dark country roads to their hop boarding-houses.

INDIAN DANCING AND LOVEMAKING.

More peculiar and more picturesque still are the hop dances held by the Indian pickers. One hop-grower has 200 Indian pickers and another 180. They do their own cooking and, according to their employers, are quiet, steady workers, except when they can get fire-water, when they get beastly drunk. The dances held by the St. Regis Indians who used to come from Canada in the hop season were beautiful. They dressed in their feather and bead finery, and to the music of their own strange instruments danced the most weird dances. However, they do not come over now, and the Indians here do not put on much wild finery, but their dances are entirely original and very odd.

Love even scurries around among the Indian tribes. One day the rumor came that a solid squaw of 270 pounds had been stolen—or we would say eloped, with a bold, bad Indian of the tribe on the other farm. It is not easy to understand how a squaw of that solid weight could be easily stolen, but at any rate the chief put in a complaint to his employer. He must have the stolen squaw back in his tribe or there would be an old-fashioned meeting of tomahawks and scalps, and the quiet hop-yards would be turned into gory battlefields, and the hills would resound with the bloodthirsty cry of red men. The hop-grower tremulously ordered his fastest horses harnessed, and in hot haste drove to his neighbors. The message of war was given and a consultation was held with the bold, bad Indian who had stolen the solid squaw. He proved not to be such a child of nature but that he knew the value of money, and compared to the love of the solid squaw, it had weight. He named the price he put on his damaged affections and his blighted hopes, and he held to them with the pertinacity of his race. Nothing would move him. In holy fear of the threatened war, the hop-growers paid him about 10 cents a pound for the release of the solid squaw and gave him extra a ticket to his home. He left, the squaw was returned and all are happy, so far as I can see.

Another farm has had an elopement. A young girl from the village of Sangerford Centre and a strange young man who had worked beneath the same canvas in the yards, sat at the same table in the house and strolled the same path after dark with her, assisted her in disappearing one night when they went out for their usual hour's stroll. That was the first of the week, and they have not been heard of since.

Hop harvest and love harvest somehow seem to come together.

NELLIE BLY

HANGMAN JOE AT HOME

SUNDAY, SEPTEMBER 30, 1888

NELLIE BLY HAS A GHASTLY TALK WITH THE CITY EXECUTIONER

He Has Legally Killed Fifty-Two Men and One Woman—How the Various Victims "Went"—It Costs from $75 to $300 to Hang a Man—A Horrible Scrap-Book—Opposed to Electrical Executions.

"THERE goes the hangman!"

That sentence forever sounds in Joe Atkinson's ears. As he walks the streets to and from his daily work, the children from a safe distance point him out; men nudge each other in warning of his advance; women glance at him timidly, and every one of them whispers, "There goes the hangman!"

Yes, he is a hangman. He has conducted fifty-three hangings since 1853. Only one woman in all this time has suffered the extreme penalty of the law, and she met death as coolly as any man. I went to see Joe Atkinson last week. I knew, in common with everybody, of his successful record as hangman of New York. Now that death by electricity has become the law, Mr. Atkinson's work of seeing that the sentence is carried out is virtually at an end.

"Joe excels in his work," said Sheriff Grant, as he stopped in his work to give me a moment. "He has never bungled an execution, and one can rely on him to give the least possible pain to the condemned."

"I suppose you favor electricity as a means of execution now?" I asked.

"I did indorse it," he replied. "The scheme was laid before me, and the whole working of electricity made so fair a showing that I used all my influence to have the bill passed. I never for an instant doubted that there was a way to carry it out, and now Mr. Gerry has sent a communication to Albany, asking that electricity be prohibited because no apparatus is perfected by which it can be used with certainty. I had hoped never to have another hanging. It is hard to have a man beg for his life and then in the next instant swing him into eternity. No matter how hardened a criminal is, it's hard. I always have an arrangement with Joe to give me a moment after the signal so I can get around a corner out of sight.

"There is one thing I ask of you," said the Sheriff, as I started to go. "Don't give Atkinson's address, and please leave his family out of your story. They are refined people, and reference to them is unpleasant and painful."

"I am Nellie Bly, of THE WORLD, and I want to see Mr. Atkinson, please," I said to the man who met me in a very cosy and homelike house in Brooklyn.

"Well, I am Joe Atkinson; you can look at me," he replied as he stood before me.

"But I want to do more than look at you," I said with a smile, as I glanced down on the little man, the top of whose head did not more than reach my shoulder. "I want to talk to you and have you talk to me."

"What for?" he asked, shortly. He was getting interesting. Nothing is very good that is easily gained.

"To tell to the readers of THE WORLD."

"Hm! The newspapers have published enough wrong things about me. Get some back numbers and you'll get enough tales about me, but no true ones."

"It's the true ones I want," I said, smiling at his bad humor. "I never write untruths; that is why I came to you for a talk."

"I understand it all. It is not that you want to justify me, but it's to get new glory for yourself."

"Doubtless. So I can accomplish two things at one stroke—justify you and gain a story. Who is that pretty boy?" and I crossed the room to examine a photograph.

THE HANGMAN'S HOME LIFE.

"That is my son," said Mr. Atkinson, bringing the lamp so that I could get a better view. "You see what a boy he is—only sixteen and just graduated—that is his diploma there, and the newspapers all said that he was going to take my place as hangman. Why, the boy has always been at school and he never saw a scaffold in his life. It was hard on the lad, because he hates the very mention of it."

"It was a shame," I said.

"They make it hard on me and they make the penalty of crime lose its force," said Mr. Atkinson. "They call me everything that is hard when I am really tender-hearted. I would never hang any one if I could change the laws. But am I evil-hearted because I go at the work to finish it as soon as possible and with the least pain to the condemned man?"

"And how do newspapers make an execution lose its horrors?" I asked.

"Because they take a man who probably has always been a ruffian and who is hardened to the last minute, and they weave a romance about him until the better class of people say, 'Poor fellow! he wasn't half so bad as we supposed,' and doubt the justice of the law, while the lower classes look on and say, 'Well, he died game,' and in their minds to kill their man and die game marks the highest order of heroism. So you see hanging does no good, but it would—it would, if the public did not make heroes out of criminals."

HIS FIRST JOB.

"When was your first hanging?"

"Jan. 28, 1853.—River Pirates William Saul and Nicholas Howlett. Of course I was shaky over it, it being my first and two having to go at once"—

"Did they weaken?"

"Not a bit. They had two priests with them until the last, and they thought they would go straight up. They all do that."

"Didn't you have bad dreams, nightmares and all that sort of thing after your first hanging?"

"No, I felt very sorry for the pirates and would have saved them if I could, but it had to be done, and I braced myself and did it well. Since then I have had so many that I have lost all nervousness. It is just the same with a surgeon. The first time he amputates an arm or sets a leg it hurts him as much as it does the patient, but after a while he performs his work without feeling, because he knows he is doing a merciful act. I am in the same position. I know these people must die, and I think I am doing an act of mercy to complete the end as quickly as possible and as painlessly. Sheriff Grant's the best Sheriff New York ever had."

"How so?"

"He doesn't allow any fooling on the scaffold. It used to be that the criminal was pinioned and fixed all ready to go, and then when he would get out under the beam there would be speeches and long prayers, which must have made the man suffer ten thousand deaths, and then there would be a double-breasted line of 'deputies' reaching from the Tombs to Mail street presenting their little black-bordered cards for admiration, and there would be policemen clubbing them back from the scaffold to give us room to send the criminal off. There would be cursing, yell-ing, fighting among the mob as the condemned went. It was beastly, but

Sheriff Grant"—

"Does he do it better?"

"I should say so. He manages everything himself. He sends to each newspaper for one of the best reporters, and then one or two deputies from his office—the doctors—himself, my assistant and myself are the only ones admitted. All the praying that is done is done before the prisoner is brought out. After he is led from his cell, Grant will not allow anything to prolong his suffering. I have seen him touch a priest on the shoulder when he knelt to pray and say: 'Not here, Father; we can't allow it,' and Grant is a good Christian himself. No prisoner ever incurs additional suffering through carelessness or thoughtlessness on his part."

INITIAL PREPARATIONS.

"What is the first thing you do when a man is to be hanged?"

"Put up the scaffold. I am a carpenter and I get some assistants, and together we do the woodwork. The rope is of extra quality Italian rope, made especially for the purpose, and I never use the same rope twice. I always make sure to have no mishaps. The iron weights are the same that have been in use from the first. One weighs about two hundred and thirty-two pounds. I get the scaffold up, which is just a beam with two braces. At one side is a little frame box in which the rope runs on pulleys. There is a sharp axe in the box and a little hole through which an eye peeps to see the Sheriff's signal. A man is in that box. No one sees him, no one knows who he is. It takes him a week, working ten hours a day, to earn as much as he does for the one stroke of the axe in that box. The prisoner is brought out. His arms are tied by placing a rope from elbow to elbow across his back. In this position it is impossible for him to get his arms up to his head."

"Do you tie his legs?"

"No; once we did, but that is seldom done now. We put the black cap on the head just to come around the forehead, and a rope with a six-turn noose knot is put about the neck."

"How long is the rope?"

"About eighteen inches. This is finished at the end with a sister-hook. From the beam dangles a rope which just comes above the man's head."

"You measure the man, then?"

"Certainly, we get his height, else the rope would never be the right length, and hanging would be a ghastly thing. It is one of the most important things to have the rope exactly the right length. The last word is said, the black cap is pulled down, with a swift movement the rope about the neck is hooked on to the one above, the Sheriff gives the signal, the man in the box gives one quick, sure blow with the axe, and the criminal is gone." Mr. Atkinson gave a sigh and leaned back on the tuffed sofa.

WHAT THE BLACK CAP IS.

"How is the black cap made?" I asked, ever ready for something new.

"You never saw one?" He looked at me as if surprised at my ignorance. "Oh, they are simple things," and he slid forward to the edge of the sofa and spread his hands on his knees. "They are cut about the shape of a bag, and are made of black woollen material. They have little ribbon bows on top."

I felt a shivering laugh choke in my throat as I pictured to myself the ghastliness of little bows nodding in the air on the head of a dying man. Ugh! "At the mouth of the cap is a rubber band which holds the cap up on the head until it is time to pull it down, and then the rubber keeps it close about the throat."

"What is the object of the black cap?"

"It keeps the spectators from seeing unpleasant things, such as twitchings of the face and the bulging of the eyes, and then it makes us lose all feeling in the matter. So long as the face is visible we suffer with the man, but the moment the face is covered we lose all that feeling and can look at the hanging object very calmly."

"How did you learn to make the knot?"

"I first learned with George Isaacs, who used to be a hangman. I came in after him and I have always tried to improve on everything. I have it down as fine now as hanging can be done, and I think we should let a good thing alone; no new-fangled ideas for me."

HANGING WOMEN.

"Did you ever hang a woman?"

"Only one in my time."

"Did she tremble and cry?"

"No; she was just as cool when she went as any man I ever handled. She was Bridget Dugan. She had poisoned a woman in New Jersey. That was in 1867, and we haven't hanged a woman since."

"I suppose that is because they are a little better than the men," I suggested.

"You know what Beecher said about a bad woman?" he said, pointing to a china plaque on the table which bore a good likeness of the dead clergyman. "'A bad woman is worse than ten bad men;' but New York is too tender-hearted to hang women."

"How do the condemned generally die?"

"In New York they go off pleasantly," he said, leaning back thoughtfully. "They are not treated as martyrs in New Jersey. They are put in a small cell and no one gets back of the bars to them. Here they are given a large room, the best of everything to eat, plenty to smoke—"

"And to drink!" I interrupted. He winked his eye and continued:

"Flowers, letters of sympathy, and the way to the scaffold is a regular path of roses. Why, there was Driscoll, he had everything and the newspapers made him a martyr and a Sister of Mercy gave him her silver watch and chain to wear when he went so he might look fine. And there was Chastine Cox, the negro, who murdered Mrs. Hull. The women sent him flowers and fruit and called on him, prayed, cried and sang with him and sat on his lap—"

"Impossible!"

"Yes, they did, but Cox had to hang, and he went on July 16, 1880."

"Do you always see prisoners before they are hanged?"

HE HIDES FROM HIS VICTIMS.

"I try to keep out of their way, but they get me sometimes. The morning Danny Lyons went he said to me just a few moments before: 'Say, Joe, do you think you can break my neck?' 'That's all right, Danny,' I replied. 'Well, it's a tuff neck, Joe.' Then he called me back and he says: 'Look 'ere, Joe, when the job's done you see that this 'ere tie is put up so as to hide the mark, for there'll be a crowd to see my corpse.' He wore a white satin scarf and he thought more of his looks than what was coming to him. And the next moment he went."

"Do you ever have any trouble with weak ones?"

"No, they all have a certain bravado which makes them want to be considered brave. I had one fellow, though, who was wicked—Angelo Cornetti. He was imprisoned in Sing Sing for some one's death, and while there he cut to pieces a fellow-convict who worked with him in the kitchen. He howled horribly when we took him to the scaffold; then he laid down, and we had to carry him, and when I went to fix the black cap he caught my finger in his mouth and almost bit then end off it. He was the worst we ever had."

"What do they usually say last?"

"Oh, nothing much. Danny Lyons said, 'Good-by, Joe.' One man went with the stump of a cigar in his mouth. Almost all protest their innocence. Wait until I get my scrap-book."

Mr. Atkinson walked to a desk in another room and took from it a large book. He sat down close beside me. "This is the first and only card of merit I ever got at school," he said, pointing to a quaint little colored card which was pasted in the back of the book. "There," he continued, touching with his right forefinger some black bordered cards, "are the invitations they used to get out which gave people admission to the hangings. Here," turning the page, "begins the list I keep of all the hangings, with the dates."

I looked and read what was written there in an old-fashioned hand. Some names had faded so I could not tell what they were, some were dim, some were bright-blue and some a deep black. It ran, as nearly as I can reproduce it, in this style:

LIST OF THOSE HE ASSISTED.

William Saul and Nicholas Howlett, river pirates, Jan. 2d, 1853.

Joe Clark, Feb. 11, 1853.

Jim Rodgers, murdered Mr. Swanton going with his wife to market, Nov. 12, 1853.

James L. Hoare, Jan. 27, 1856.

John Dorsey, July 17, 1854.

James Stephens, poisoned wife, Feb. 6, 1860.

John Crimmons, March 30, 1861.

William Henry Hawkins (colored), June 27, 1862.

Nathaniel Gordon, Bedlee's Island, Feb. 21, 1862.

Barney Friery, killed Lazarus, Aug. 17, 1866.

Frank Ferris, Oct. 19, 1866.

Bridget Dugan, poisoned Mrs. Dr. Coriel, 1867.

Gonzales and Palasier, 1867.

George Wagner, March 1, 1867.

Jerry O'Brien, Aug. 2, 1867.

Jack Reynolds, April 8, 1870.

John Real, killed policeman, Aug. 6, 1870.

John Thomas, March 19, 1871.

John Delaney, Hempstead, 1871.

Henry Rodgers, Dec. 7, 1872.

William Foster, March 21, 1873.

Mike Nixon, May 16, 1873.

Isaac Suckhout, July 16, 1873.

John Staunton Goshen, soldier, 1874.

Jacob Mcchella, murdered United States Marshal Stephenson, Jan. 7, 1874.

Jackson and Jarvis, killed farmer, 1875.

Michael Sullivan, April 9, 1875.

William Ellis, William Thompson, Charles Wernd (colored), 1875.

John Dolan, April 21, 1876.

Chastine Cox (colored), killed Mrs. Hull, July 16, 1880.

Pietro Balbo, wife-murderer, Aug. 6, 1880.

Edward Rheinhardt, wife-murderer, Jan. 14, 1881.

William Sindram, killed landlady, April 21, 1882.

Augustus D. Leighton (colored), May 19, 1882.

James F. Walsh, killed sweetheart, July 21, 1882.

Pasquale Majone, murdered wife and mother, March 9, 1883.

Michael McGloin, killed saloonkeeper; hanged same time and same gallows, March 9, 1883.

Angelo Cornetti, May 11, 1883.

Edward Hovey, murdered sister-in-law, Oct. 19, 1883.

James Graves, Jan. 3, 1884.

Theodore Hoffman, murdered peddler, April 18, 1884.

Alexander Jefferson (colored), murdered Henry Hicks and Emma Jackson, Aug. 1, 1884.

George H. Mills, wife murder, April 10, 1885.

Charles H. Rugg (colored), strangler, May 15, 1885.

Miguel Chacon (colored), July 9, 1886.

Peter Smith, May 7, 1887.

Daniel Driscoll, Jan. 23, 1888.

CAPITAL PUNISHMENT ABOLISHED.

"There was a space between 1857 and 1880 when hanging was abolished," said Mr. Atkinson as soon as I had made as good a list as I could. (Mr. Atkinson will not allow his book out of his keeping.) "A woman of the name of Hartford murdered her husband in 1858, and the law was abolished so that she would not be hanged. After the war it was again enforced."

The entire book, which Mr. Atkinson was showing me, is made up of articles touching the executions he has conducted, with a full history of the crimes for which the prisoners died. It is very peculiar, and I don't suppose there is its like in existence.

"Do women ever witness executions?"

"I don't think they do, although they often want to. There was a colored girl one time who peeped through a crack in the fence and saw the hanging of two negroes. She was in for poisoning her employers. They say she went crazy afterwards, although I have my doubts as to that."

"Do you think that any crazy people are ever hanged?"

"No; you yourself know how easy it is to play crazy and fool everybody. They sometimes pretend insanity to escape punishment, but they are sane enough."

THE COST OF IT.

"You don't cut the rope then which lets the criminals swing?"

"No, I superintend everything and I pay a man to do the cutting."

"What does it cost to hang a man?"

"It costs from $75 up to $300."

"Give me a general idea of what is needed and the cost?"

"Well, it takes ten pounds of nails at eight cents to build the gallows; a black cap, noose and pinion rope cost $10; four assistants get $3.50 a day. Then there is canvas to close up places from inquisitive eyes, and the boards cost."

"And that space marked 'cutting, $20,' does that mean the price of the man in the box with an axe?" I asked, as I examined an old "OK'd" bill.

"Maybe," he said, with a laugh. "There, you see I got $57 for all my work. I couldn't buy a home on that, could I? Here, you see that everything for the execution of Majone and McGoin cost only $321.87. That was the highest price ever paid me.

"You see all this," continued Mr. Atkinson, showing me brackets, carved tables and other handsome articles of furniture. "I make all these myself. I am a carpenter. I have no gallows nor ropes nor black-caps about my home, as some newspapers said I have."

"It is the age of exaggeration, you know," I said, and shaking hands with the little hangman I bade him good-night.

NELLIE BLY

Mrs. Warner Miller's Home

Sunday, October 7, 1888

Nellie Bly Chats with the Republican Candidate's Wife

She Lives Very Simply in a Magnificent Farm-House at Herkimer—Fond of Books and Music—Does Not Care For Jewels—Her Children and Guests—Objects To Photographs of Herself and Has None.

[Special correspondence of The World.]

Herkimer, October 6.—Mrs. Warner Miller has no rival, for Mr. Miller's rival in politics, Gov. Hill, is a bachelor, and pleased as I should be to write an account of Mrs. Hill, I fear I shall never have that opportunity, if rumor may be trusted. They do say that no bachelor ever loved bachelorhood as well as does Gov. Hill and that no man with equal chances of meeting fair women was ever so indifferent to their charms. But enough of bachelors.

Mrs. Miller, the wife of the Republican candidate for Governor of New York, seems to be loved by all who know her. That much I learned soon after reaching Herkimer. Everybody here is proud of Warner Miller, because he first saw the light as a humble farmer's son in this quiet valley of the Mohawk. Since honors have rested on his broad shoulders he has not been too proud to still make the valley of his birth his home. Naturally Mrs. Miller came in for a share of the good feeling of the townspeople, first because she was Mr. Miller's wife, but it was not long until she was loved for the sweet ways and the admirable qualities the neighbors found in her. And now I can hear no words save of praise.

"I will give you all I can, Miss Bly," Mrs. Miller said, as she reached out her hand and took mine in greeting, "but really, there has been so much written that I can't believe there is anything left to say."

"You can tell me of your home and family," I replied, encouraged by her kindly smile. "What do you call your home?"

"We call it Oak Hill Farm," she replied, resting her elbow on a small table. "We have some three hundred acres here, and enjoy all the pleasures of a farm without any of the work."

"How so? You don't know anything about chickens and eggs, then?"

"Nothing, except in the consumption of them. We have a farmer, whose house is just over the brow of the hill, and he has charge of everything."

"So you like country life?"

"I love it," she replied enthusiastically. "I grow perfectly wretched when confined in the city. I never grow tired of the country. I search for flowers and I am devoted to the study of nature in the trees and shrubs and birds about me."

"Where do you spend your Winters?"

"The last eight Winters I have been in Washington with Mr. Miller. Like it? Well, yes. I am fond of the society there and like it very much. We never had a house there. Last Winter I spent in Georgia, as I have a slight affliction of the throat, and for this Winter I have no plans. I want to stay here as long as I can, but the house is so unprotected that the cold always drives us away."

OAK HILL FARM.

Oak Hill Farm is a beautiful place, and even a less ardent admirer of nature than Mrs. Miller must find it a pleasant spot. The house is situated on a great hill. It is surrounded by an unbroken lawn of rolling green. Except for a hedge of trees at the right of the house, the view of the Mohawk Valley, with its green meadows and quiet river, is unobstructed. The dwelling itself looks inviting and homelike. It is a farm-house of pretty design, with large windows, cupolas and a broad portico at the front, half shaded by vines. On one end of the portico hangs a red and yellow hemp hammock, as if just ready for some weary one to take a lazy swing. The entrance hall is wide and very comfortable, with rich rugs and portières and lounges. On the right of the hall is a library filled with handsomely bound books, and there are tables and easy-chairs. On the left is the reception-room. It is of comfortable size, giving one the feeling of spaciousness, and one can move in it without stumbling into or crushing anything.

HOW THE HOUSE IS FURNISHED.

The furniture is also comfortable and adds to the impression that nothing is skipped. It is a silk plush, light yellow in color. In one corner of the room, between the hall entrance and the fireplace, is a piano with a red plush cover carefully embroidered. The little ornaments on the mantel bespeak a refinement in selection. In the little niches down by the open fireplace, which is now hidden by a panel, are several little figures representing the Aztec Indians in their various pursuits of life. On a corner table are several books on flowers, trees and birds, while on a marble table by the front window are albums and autograph books.

"Where were you born, Mrs. Miller?" I asked.

"In Gloversville, Fulton County, N.Y., and that is where I first met Mr. Miller. He came there on business."

"How many children have you?"

"I have four. Max, my oldest boy, is at Cornell University; Augusta, my only daughter, is at school near Philadelphia; Berr and Guy, my two younger boys, are at a preparatory school in Lawrenceville, N.Y."

"How do you spend most of your time?"

"Well, in the summer my children demand a great deal of attention, and then I am also fond of congenial society, or, rather, the society of my intimate friends. When one's house is filled with guests one has not much time for much else. I am and have always been my own housekeeper."

PERSONAL APPEARANCE.

Mrs. Miller is of medium height and rather full informed. Her face is round and her eyes are as clear as crystal and blue as speedwell. Her expression is pleasant and her manners easy and unconventional. She wears her dark hair, which has some silver threads, combed high from her forehead in—well, a fold describes it better than anything else—and twisted in a knot at the back of her head. Her dress fitted beautifully. It was of soft woollen material, pinkish in color, with a full front of pink-striped goods and cuffs, collar and lapels of crimson velvet. She wore no jewelry.

"I do not like dress," Mrs. Miller said in answer to my question. "I wish I were a Quakeress, so I could confine myself to one style. Fashion is too fickle and demands too much of one. Life is too short to follow its dictates. I wear colors because Mr. Miller does not like black. I don't like jewelry. Of course I appreciate fine gems, but for my own use I do not like them."

"You like music as it must come in the list with your love of flowers?" I suggested.

"Yes, I do like music, and was a musician when I was younger. Now my daughter takes my place in that. My dancing is also a thing of the past."

"I suppose you go to church?"

"Yes; I attend the Methodist Church in Herkimer, but I do not belong to any mission societies, although I have often been urged to take part."

"Of course you drive?"

HER DAILY DRIVES.

"Oh, yes, daily," she said, with a smile, as she rested her sunburnt cheek daintily on one hand. "We have a stable full of horses and every style of carriage. The drives about here are beautiful. We often drive to Richfield Springs and other pretty places."

"And then I suppose you read a great deal?"—glancing towards the handsome library.

"A great deal," she replied, with a smile. "My early taste was for Scott; now I read history. I should say that the newspapers and magazines come first. Besides, I always read the most desirable of all the late novels. I am not very fond of theatres," she continued, "and only enjoy things that are particularly rare and beautiful. I was educated in Hartford, Conn., and have never done anything wonderful in my life."

"I don't think that you have told me your maiden name?"

"My name was Caroline Churchill, and I was raised in Gloversville."

"And is there nothing to say of your girlhood days?"

"No, there has been too much already printed about that."

"I suppose you favor the temperance ideas?"

"Yes, I indorse them most hardly."

"I should like to have a picture of you, Mrs. Miller, to reproduce in THE WORLD?"

"I have always had a great aversion to having photographs taken," she said, with a smile. "I never had any that were satisfactory. I like handsome pictures, and like to have them of all my family, but I cannot endure my own. I have none in the house. I do not think I have had three taken since my marriage."

As I drove away from Oak Hill Farm I noticed the American flag floating high above the wide lawn.

NELLIE BLY

Our First Ladies

Sunday, October 28, 1888

Women Who Have Graced the White House

The Living Widows and Wives of the Presidents

Personal Sketches of Seven Mistresses of the White House

Nellie Bly Visits Their Homes and Learns the Story of their Lives

---

The Trials and Consolations of Social Leaders at the National Capital

---

Interesting Bits of Personal Reminiscence Told for the First Time—Mrs. Tyler Narrates How She Met President Tyler and Her Engagement—Prophetic Dreams—Her Children—Mrs. Polk's Interesting Recollections of Three-Quarters of a Century—A Day at the Famous Polk Mansion—Tomb of the Dead President—Passing Her Declining Years in Seclusion and Beloved by All—Mrs. Harriet Lane Johnston, President Buchanan's Niece, and Her Sad Afflictions—Mrs. Grant Gives an Insight Into the Private Life of the General—Incidents of His Long Public Career That Have Never Before Been Written—Mrs. Hayes in Comfortable Retirement—Mrs. Garfield's Quiet Life—Her Children—Entertaining Talk with Mrs. McElroy, the Mistress of the White House During President Arthur's Term.

I.

There are now living, besides Mrs. Cleveland, but seven women who have held sway in the White House as the First Ladies of the Land. I have visited them at their homes in the various parts of the country and listened to their narratives as they frankly told me little bits of their personal history which have never before been written.

These representative American women would without exception grace the throne of any monarchy and their history should not be allowed to fade out of mind. They are Mrs. Tyler, the widow of President John Tyler, whom I saw in Richmond, Va.; Mrs. Polk, the widow of President James Knox Polk, now living at an advanced age at the historic "Polk Place," Nashville, Tenn.; Mrs. Harriet Lane Johnston, the niece of President James Buchanan, and a resident of Baltimore, Md.; Mrs. Grant, the widow of President Ulysses Simpson Grant; Mrs. Hayes, the wife of President Rutherford Birchard Hayes, living at Fremont, O.; Mrs. Garfield, the widow of President James Abram Garfield, residing at Mentor, O., and Mrs. John S. McElroy, the sister of President Chester Alan Arthur, living now at Albany, N.Y.

Of these former mistresses of the Executive Mansion not one now resides at the National Capital. They have nearly all returned to the scenes of their earlier life, where they spent quiet but happy days before their public lives began. They are still revered and cherished in the communities in which they live quite as much as in former years when they held sway in the White House.

II.

MRS. JOHN TYLER.

She Tells the Romantic and Thrilling Story of Her Eventful Life.

I had quite a search for Mrs. Tyler, but at last was fortunate enough to find her at the Exchange Hotel, Richmond, Va. I had heard many people say that she was one of the most agreeable women in the world, and I was not disappointed when I met her. I sent my card up from the hotel parlor, and the colored man soon returned and directed me to Mrs. Tyler's room.

There was but the one woman in the room, and she advanced to meet me, and yet I could not think that it was Mrs. Tyler. She was tall, and walked with easy grace. She was well-formed, and dressed in a long black travelling gown. Her heavy black hair, sprinkled with a few gray lines, was parted in the middle, and the thick braids covered the back of the head while one rested on the top like a crown. It was an odd fashion, but very becoming. I was struck with her complexion, which was clear, and the cheeks were so pink that a sixteen-year-old girl might envy the tint. Above all were her wondrous gray eyes. I caught all this in an instant, and then heard:

"I am Mrs. Tyler and you are Miss Nellie Bly?" And then I found voice as well as ease and explained the object of my visit to her.

NO HOME TO CALL HER OWN.

"I am a bird of passage almost," she said, "I hardly have what I call a home. I travel a great deal and visit among my children. The old plantation, Sherwood Forest, on the James River, is the old home, but I have never kept it up since the war, when it was almost ruined."

"Won't you tell me how you met President Tyler?"

"Well, to begin at the first. I was born on Gardiner's Island, three miles from land. I was a descendent of the first white child born of British parents in the state of New York, and the child of the first white child born in Connecticut. My name, as you know, was Julia Gardiner—with an i," she added. "Gardiner without an i is like Thompson without a p. There I grew up until my schooling was finished and then my father took my sister and me to Europe for the finishing touches as it were. While we were in Paris we heard of the death of President Harrison and we American girls all wore crape around our wrists in mourning for a long time. President Tyler we knew was the successor and I had a little canary which I brought back with me, that I had named Jonny Ty, in honor of the President, John Tyler."

"Did you not know him then?"

"No. But on our return my father took my sister and me to Washington that we might have the benefit of the society there. We met the President and became great friends, but I never thought of loving him then. I was not yet twenty and he was easily thirty-five years older than I, but I thought him very nice and I was very gay and frivolous and of course was flattered by his friendship."

"How did he propose to you?"

"You will think of me very foolish when I tell you about it," Mrs. Tyler said, her gray eyes beaming at the recollection. "I often think now how frivolous I was then. There was a grand reception held in the White House on Washington's Birthday. All people of note were there and it was very brilliant. I had been dancing with a young man who was not pleased with the attention the President had been paying me. We had just stopped and were walking about when the President came up, and drawing my arm through his, said to the young man: "I must claim Miss Gardiner's company for awhile." The young man drew off and looked as if he would like to say, 'Well, you are impudent,' but he didn't. I walked around with the President and he proposed then. I had never thought of love, so I said: 'No, no, no,' and shook my head with each word, which flung the tassel of my Greek cap into his face at every move. It was undignified, but it amused me very much to see his expression as he tried to make love to me and the tassel brushed his face. I did not tell my father. I was his pet, yet I feared that he would blame me for allowing the president to reach the proposing point, so I did not speak of it to any one."

"How were you dressed the night the President proposed?"

HER FATHER'S TRAGIC DEATH.

"I wore a white tarleton. It was very pretty and very becoming. On my head I wore a crimson Greek cap. I was very gay and young or I never would have dared to toss the tassel in a President's face. On the 28th of February Commodore Stockton gave a party on the Potomac. Everybody was there, and we had a lovely time. I told my father when we started that he must keep with me all the time, but I did not tell him that it was to keep the President away. I was with my father, and the young man who I told you was jealous of the President, when a gentleman came to me and said, 'Miss Gardner, the President wishes to take you in to the collation which is just served.' 'I suppose I will have to obey orders,' I replied with a laugh, and, asking my father to follow me, I started down. Just then the wind caught my veil and blew it up. Father caught it with his cane and brought it down, saying, 'Take care of your streamer.' They were almost the last words I ever heard him speak.

MRS. TYLER.

"When we got down to the President seated me at the head of the table with him and he handed me a glass of champagne. Father was standing just back of my chair, so I handed the glass over my shoulder, saying, 'Here, Pa.' He did not take it, but he said: 'My time will soon come.' He meant his time to be served, but the words have always seemed prophetic to me. That moment some one called down for the President to come and see the last shot fired, but he said he would not go as he was better engaged. My father started with some other gentlemen and I turned to the young man who had followed me down.

He whispered to me and asked me to marry him, and when I said more noes to him than I had to the President he said he feared I was ambitious. Just then we heard the shot and the smoke began to come down the companionway. 'Something must be wrong,' I said to the young man, and he started up to see. He got to the door, and he turned around and gave me such a look of horror that I shall never forget it. That moment I heard some one say 'The Secretary of State is dead!' I was frightened, and I tried to get upstairs. 'Something has happened. Let me go to my father!' I cried, but they kept me back. Some one told me that there had been an accident, the gun had exploded, but that there was such a crowd that it would do no good for me to try to get there. I cried that my father was there and I must learn his fate. I was told then that he was wounded. That drove me frantic. I begged them to let me go to help him; that he loved me and he would want me near him. One lady, seeing my agony, said: 'My dear child, you can do no good. Your father is in heaven.'

HOW PRESIDENT TYLER PROPOSED.

"Yes," Mrs. Tyler continued, "he had been killed. There were five killed, among whom were the Secretaries of the Navy and State. I fainted and did not revive until some one was carrying me off the boat, and then I struggled so that I almost knocked us both off the gang-plank. I did not know at the time, but I learned afterwards that it was the President whose life I almost consigned to the water. All the five who were killed were buried from the White House in the Congressional Cemetery. I remained at the White House until after the funeral, and then I returned to our city home, No. 43 Lafayette place, New York. The President and I corresponded then and he paid me many nice little attentions. After I lost my father I felt differently towards the President. He seemed to fill the place and to be more agreeable in every way than any younger man ever was or could be. He composed a very pretty song about me then—'Sweet Lady, Awake.' At last he proposed again and I wrote him I was willing this time, if my mother would consent. She told him that she would never consent to my marriage, but if I was determined she would not object.

"I was in deep mourning. So the President told only one member of his family, Gen. John Tyler, and I told my immediate family. We were married very quietly on the 26th of June, 1844, in the Church of the Ascension, New York. I was dressed in pure white liane, with a veil of the same which was not even hemmed. I wore a wreath of orange blossoms, but no jewelry. I never liked jewelry, yet I always wore a diamond star on my forehead, with a slender gold chain encircling my head. It was called the 'Feronia.' After my father's death I replaced it with a black stone. We left for Washington the same day we were married. I took off my wedding dress and put on a deep-black travelling gown of baize and wore no ornament. During my time in the White House I wore black during the day, and white, or black lace over white, in the evening."

"My life was very happy in the White House and everybody was very kind to me," said Mrs. Tyler, thoughtfully. "When we left there we went to our plantation, Sherwood Forest, on the James River. The war came on and the President, who was getting quite old, was very much excited over it. He was a member of the Confederate Congress and was staying in this very hotel in Richmond. I was going to start from the plantation for a three weeks' visit and then join the President in Richmond, when I had a very strange dream. I dreamed that I was with the President and that I had awakened and risen to dress. I looked back to the bed, and there lay the President, pale and worn. I thought, 'My goodness! he is ill and he never called me.' Just then I saw him open his eyes and he said, 'Oh, dear, have you awakened? My head is very bad. Will you hold it?' As I went to hold it Nancy, the maid, came in and I said, 'Your master is very ill.' At that moment I awakened with a dreadfully heavy feeling, and, surely enough, the door opened and in walked the real Nancy. She told me that it was time to get up and dress for the boat. 'I cannot go,' I said. 'I have had a bad dream and I am going directly to the President.'

"When I got to Richmond, with Pearl, my baby, and Nancy, it was night. As I drove up to the hotel a gentleman was coming out. He saw me and recognized me and expressed surprise at my arrival, as he had just left the President, who was not expecting me. The first thing I said was, 'Oh, how is the President?' And he replied, 'Never in better health.' He showed me to Mr. Tyler's rooms, which were in this hall, and then went to announce my arrival. Soon I heard Mr. Tyler's footsteps coming hurriedly over the bridge which connects this hotel with the other part on the opposite side of the street. He kissed me and told me how delighted he wants to see me, and he picked up Pearl and she smiled at him as he said, 'Why, the baby knows me.' He did not think she would because she was so young.

HER DREAM WAS PROPHETIC.

"About midnight I wakened with the worst headache I ever had. I felt that my head would burst, so the President arose and went downstairs to get some morphine. It was not weighed, and he brought it up and weighed it for me himself, and then he held my head for me, saying—I had told him my dream—that it was I instead of he who was to suffer. So I fell asleep. In the morning when I awoke he was standing leaning on his leaving his elbow on the mantel, and he looked very pale. I asked him if he was ill, and he said that he had taken a chill. He said he would go downstairs and get something for it. So, quite drowsy from the morphine, I turned over to sleep again. I was aroused again by his coming into the room, and I was startled to see that he had his collar off and his shirt disarranged, while he looked like death. He told me that he had fainted at the breakfast table about an hour before, but he would not allow them to carry him to our room for fear of frightening me. The others followed him in, accompanied by a doctor, and after fixing him up on the lounge they left.

"Mr. Tyler was in a weak condition for several days and did not leave his room. One night he seemed very much better, and he asked me to turn the gas low and he would take a good sleep. Robert, his son, who had just come in, begged to sleep on the lounge in the same room, and I threw myself down on the side of the bed, but did not undress. About midnight the President jumped up in bed, and, tearing his night robe loose from his throat, called for more air. We sent for two physicians, yet we did not fear the worst. When one of the doctors entered I was making some mustard plasters. The President opened his eyes, and, recognizing the doctor, said, 'I am going, doctor.' When I heard him say this I dropped everything and sprang up on the bed beside him. He leaned his head on my shoulder and said, 'I leave my wife and children to my country,' and then he quietly went to his long sleep.

"And you can see," Mrs. Tyler resumed, after a long pause, "that that circumstance would make me a firm believer in dreams. If it had not been for my dream I would not have been with him during his last hours."

"You were left, then, during the war alone with your children?"

A SON TO BE PROUD OF.

"Yes. I got a pass, though, and returned to my mother at Staten Island, by the way of Bermuda, taking all my children with me save Gardiner Tyler, who was attending Lexington College. Gardiner was too young to join the army, but he joined what was known as the Reserve Guard and was with the Rockbridge Artillery until the close of the war. I had taken John Alexander, the second son, home with me to Staten Island. He was wild to join the army to defend his fireside, he said, but he was too young, being only fourteen. However, he ran off from Staten Island and returned to the South by way of Bermuda. Although they would not take him into the ranks, he followed the army, seizing every opportunity to be of service. He went with the soldiers to Appomattox, and while there held Gov. Gordon's horse while he made a speech. It was very sweet in Alex. The little chap was barefooted by this time and he walked from Appomattox, every step of the way, to this hotel. When he entered the parlor and told the girl that he wished to see Mrs. Ballard the servant looked at the little ragged boy in surprise and then she said, 'Are you little Alex Tyler, the President's son?' We always stopped there, and as she recognized him and all his rags, Mrs. Ballard fixed him up and then I sent both of the boys to Europe. They were two little rebels, you know," and she laughed, "so I sent them out of the country.

"Gardiner returned after a few years, but Alex remained abroad for eight years. In that time occurred the Franco-Prussian War. He practiced lance-throwing for six weeks and then offered his services to the King of Saxony, making known whose son he was. He was excepted and was one of the Uhlans. I was helpless and could do nothing. You can imagine my constant worry, but the lad came through it safely, and was afterwards received by the Kaiser and given a gold medal for bravery and skill.

"On his return to America he married his cousin, Sarah Gardiner, of Gardiner's Island, a handsome woman, whom he had loved as a child. He was sent by the Government as a civil engineer to New Mexico, and there he contracted an illness and died. He would not give up until he fell from his horse. He was dead before we could reach him. He sent a message to me: 'Tell my mother I died an honorable man.' His wife had presented him with a gold watch on which was inscribed, 'Do you remember?' And he said to tell her, 'I remember.'

"She brought his body back and had it buried on the east end of Long Island, where she can see the grave from her window."

MRS. TYLER'S CHILDREN.

"How many children had you, Mrs. Tyler?"

"I have Gardiner, the eldest, who lives on the old plantation, Sherwood Forest, on the James River. He was one of the Presidential electors and is now speaking for Cleveland. He is a lawyer. Then came John Alexander, who died. He left a wife and two children—Gardiner and Lillian. Julia was my third child. She married William H. Spencer, of Geneseo, Livingston county, N.Y. She died at the birth of her first child—Julia Spencer—whom I have raised and who is now sixteen. My daughter's remains were brought to Hollowwood and placed beside those of her father. Lachlan Tyler, my fourth child, is a physician, residing in Washington. He married a Miss Georgie Powell, of Richmond. They have no children. Lyon Gardiner, the fifth son, is President of William and Mary College. He married Miss Annie Tucker, daughter of St. George Tucker, the poet and wit of Virginia, and niece of John Randolph Tucker, of Washington. They have three children—Julia Gardiner, Lizzie Gilmore and John Tyler. Quite a strange coincidence is that my son's wife's grandfather and my son's grandfather were both killed in the explosion on the Potomac. Robert Fitzwalter, the youngest son, has farming proclivities and is near Ashland,Va. He is the perfect image of his father. I never saw a son so like his father in appearance as Robert is like his. He is unmarried, as is also Gardiner, the eldest. Pearl Tyler, my baby, married Mr. W.H. Ellis, a member of the Legislature. They live at Madison, Montgomery County, Va. She has three dear little babies—Pearl, Tyler and Lelia Juliana. The latter is named after me. That name has some very pleasant recollections for me, because in all the poetry that was written to me in my youth that name was used."

A VERY SIMPLE TASTE.

Mrs. Tyler spends most of her time at the homes of her children. She is always accompanied by the grandchild, Julia Spencer, whom she raised from early childhood. Mrs. Tyler will probably spend the Winter in Washington, when she will introduce her granddaughter into society. In addition to being a constant traveler Mrs. Tyler is a great reader. The newspapers and the political news she prefers, and after that she read the magazines. She is not only noted for her beauty, but she is bright and clever as well. In every respect she is a most charming woman. Mrs. Tyler never wore much jewelry. Two great solitaires sparkle in her ears in competition with the sparkle of her great gray eyes, and at her throat she always wears one brooch. She has worn it constantly since she received it as a present from a stranger while she was in Washington. It is a painting on ivory of her husband. I looked at the back of it and I read there inscript:

"Mrs. President Tyler, from Dr. Hitchcock, of Boston."

In another place I read what Mrs. Tyler had inscribed on it herself:

"John Tyler, Jan. 17, 1862. Thou art mine and I am thine for ever."

III.

AT THE POLK MANSION.

Interesting Reminiscences of Mrs. James Knox Polk at Her Historic Home.

If one can imagine a home of a century ago set down in the heart of an enterprising and live city, with modern buildings and improvements of all kinds surrounding, yet itself untouched; with electric light flickering down on a silent old mansion which fifty years have found unchanged, then one can picture the Polk place at Nashville, Tenn.

The Polk mansion stands on an elevation, and the surrounding garden is at least 900 feet square. One might almost say it has four fronts, as it faces Polk avenue, Vine street, Union street and Spruce street. It is all inclosed with a little iron fence, but the gates stand open as if inviting visitors to enter. I looked up the long pathway of pebbles and shells, edged with rose bushes, on which still hung some frost-bitten roses, to the mansion. Despite its age, which shows in the crackled and discolored paint and the upturning shingles, it has a look of stateliness and dignity. In this green garden of rose bushes, small trees and shell-walks, is the tomb of ex-President Polk. Four large white pillars sustain a massive top covering the vault. On a square cenotaph, rising from the vault, are inscriptions which in few words give the record of the man whose remains have rested beneath it for nearly forty years. A white iron railing and a bed of green ivy keep visitors from trespassing too near that sacred spot.

MRS. POLK.

INSCRIPTIONS ON THE TOMB.

I took out my pencil and copied the inscriptions from the three sides, and I looked at the vacant fourth and marvelled at the faithful wife who had waited all these years for her name to break it smoothness:

I.

The mortal remains of
JAMES KNOX POLK,
are resting in the vault beneath. He was born in Mecklenburg County, North Carolina, and emigrated with his father, Samuel Polk, to Tennessee in 1806.

The beauty of virtue was illustrated in his life. The excellence of Christianity was exemplified in his death.

II.

His life was devoted to the public service. He was elevated successively to the first places in the State and Federal Governments; a member of the General Assembly, a member of Congress and Chairman of most of the Congressional Committees; Speaker of the House of Representatives; Governor of Tennessee, and President of the United States.

III.

By his public policy he defined, established and extended the boundaries of his country. He planted the laws of the American Union on the shores of the Pacific. His influence and his counsels tended to organize the National Treasury on the principles of the Constitution and to apply the Laws of Freedom to Navigation, Trade and Industry.

I walked up on the shell path to the long veranda where the massive pillars, although still firm, show their age more than the rest of the mansion. I was almost afraid to pull the bell. I had the same feeling which comes over me when I visit a cemetery. I wanted to walk on my tip-toes and I lowered my voice to a whisper. The influence of the place was on me and I felt that it would be almost disrespectful to sound the doorbells. However, I summoned up my courage and gave a timid pull. At the same instant, as if the bell, which I heard resounding in the hall, had wakened the inmates to life and youth, a clear, girlish voice sang out several notes and a soft touch swept the strings of a banjo. I felt guilty as if I were a fairy prince and had not known it, and I did not know whether to make my escape or to await the result.

THE POLK HOMESTEAD.

Before I had time to decide which course was the better, the door opened at a pleasant-faced woman stood before me.

"Is not this the Polk mansion, or have I made a mistake?" I asked, still mystified.

"This is the Polk mansion," she replied, with a smile.

"And Mrs. Polk—is she in?"

"Yes, Miss, but Mrs. Polk is feeble and seldom sees visitors. Are you acquainted with her?"

"No," I replied, as I gave her my card. "I am Nellie Bly, of the New York World, and I am writing up the ladies of the White House. I have come from New York just to see Mrs. Polk, and I shall be very much disappointed if I must return without doing so."

"Just sit down, please, and I will see if she is able to see you this morning," and the woman left me.

INSIDE THE FAMOUS HOUSE.

I was in the hallway, yet I can hardly call it the hall. Of course that is what it was meant for, but it is larger than most flats in New York and was comfortably furnished. There was a stove at one side, in which was a bright, soft coal fire. There were easy chairs and lounges about, and a centre table of mosaic with the American eagle in the centre. On it were autograph albums, fresh flowers, books and magazines. There were warm rugs on the floor and fine oil paintings on the walls. One, I afterwards learned—a life-size painting of Cortez—was a present from the Government of Mexico to Mrs. Polk years and years ago.

A tiny black dog came out and looked at me inquisitively and then I heard a pleasant voice say:

"Show Miss Bly into the parlor and tell her that I will see her in a few moments."

"Come in here, please," said the pleasant-faced woman on her return. "It is pleasanter here. Mrs. Polk will be pleased to see you in a few minutes."

There was nothing ancient about this room and its modernism surprised me almost as much as had the young voice. There was a grand piano in the corner stacked with music, there were real lace curtains at the windows and portières at the doors. A soft velvet carpet covered the floor and the little black dog came in, and after turning half a dozen times, lay down on a fur rug at the foot of a small table filled with dainty bric-à-brac. There was a bevelled plate-glass mirror between the wide windows, and in its depths was reflected a life-size water color on a brass easel of a beautiful young woman with wondrous black eyes and golden hair. I looked at it, admiring the curve of the eyebrow and of the turn of the lip, and I decided that the original was the owner of the clear voice and banjo and the mistress of the modern niceties in which the room abounded. I heard the bell ring again and two Catholic priests were shown in. I felt almost annoyed—it was very ungracious, I must admit—that any one should interfere with my visit. They were followed by a handsome woman with large, dark eyes and heavy dark hair. She approached with an ease that was very pleasing and held out her little hand.

"You are Miss Bly? I am pleased to meet you. I am Mrs. Fall. My aunt will see you in a few moments and"—and then she introduced me to the priest.

ABLE TO SEE BUT FEW CALLERS.

"It is a great privilege—indeed we think it a great honor—for any one to see my Aunt Sarah now," said Mrs. Fall. "She is not strong, and it's too much for her to see many visitors; we have so many, you know. Everyone who visits Nashville calls here to pay their respects to my aunt, but she does not attempt to see any of them. My daughter Saidee"—with a slight motion towards the picture—"and I try to do what aunt would do if she were younger. We receive them and try to the best of our ability to have them enjoy their visits. Aunt Sarah caught a slight cold and for some days has been unable to leave her room. I am so glad she is better this morning and able to see Miss Bly, who has come from New York to see her."

Then we heard the soft, slow patter of feet in the hall, and somehow we all rose to our feet and turned towards the door. There, on the arm of the pleasant woman who admitted me, framed, as it were, by the door, stood the lady who forty-two or forty-three years ago was the brilliant mistress of the White House. She held out her hand to me—the woman still supporting her—and said in such a sweet way:

"Miss Bly, I am pleased that I am able to see you," and then she spoke to the priests. The faithful woman, Winnie, helped her to a crimson plush sofa, where she sat down. "Come here, Miss Bly, and sit beside me," she said, indicating the place beside her on the sofa with her slender hand, and when I obeyed the others formed a little circle about us.

"I cannot see many now," she said in a clear, distinct voice which gave no evidence of age, "much as I would like to, for I am growing very old"—

"But you grow old so gracefully, Mrs. Polk, that we hardly notice it," said one of the fathers gallantly.

"I do not repine, sir," she said, with a bright smile. "The evening of my life is very happy and peaceful, and I feel very much the kindness of the people to me. I am very grateful for it. I do not know what I have ever done to deserve all the kindness they show me, but it makes me very happy.

"There is one rule I always had," continued Mrs. Polk. "I never refused to see ministers. I never yet refused to see one, and will not so as long as I am able to walk. But you see," and she gave a cheerful laugh which took away what sadness her words contained, "that age will leave its traces. I never attempt to walk now without the aid of Winnie and my cane, but, thank God! my memory is just as good as it was forty years ago. Go with Mrs. Fall and see the paintings in the other parlor," said Mrs. Polk to me, "while I send Winnie to get some photographs I want to show you."

HUNG WITH FINE OLD PAINTINGS.

The other parlor is directly across the hall and is just as it was arranged by President Polk and Mrs. Polk forty years ago. The room is very large and looks bare compared with the furnishing of the other apartment across the way. The furniture is rosewood, with maroon plush upholstery. It was selected by Mrs. Polk in New York while she was still mistress of the White House, and was sent on to their Southern home, which was bought about the same time, and here it has stood ever since. Around the walls are oil portraits of Jefferson, Madison, Jackson and Monroe, painted by Stuart from the originals—the old Madison collection. There were also portraits of President Polk and Mrs. Polk—excellent ones—painted while they were in the White House. Directly above the mantel is a full-length painting of Mrs. Polk. This is a copy by Dury of the original by Healy, which was sent by the ladies of Tennessee to the White House. It is a most beautiful work, showing Mrs. Polk in a maroon velvet and black lace, with several strings of pearls about her pretty throat and wrists. On one side of the mantel is hung a copy of verses sent to Mrs. Polk on some anniversary, and beside it hangs a photograph of the first law office of ex-President Polk. It was in Columbia, Tenn., in 1820, and was nothing more than a log cabin, one story, under a forest of trees. The other room of the cabin was occupied by a boot-maker, who had an ill-shaped hand, cut from a board, nailed to a tree, pointing to his door. At the other door was a tiny sign which read:

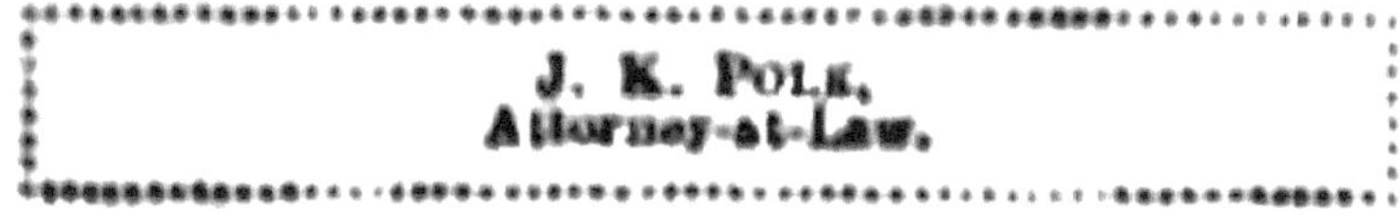

The proprietors of these establishments had placed themselves in position to have their pictures taken. Mr. Polk stands in his doorway with a large law book open in his hands, and the boot-maker is conspicuous at his side.

And now of Mrs. Polk. Mrs. Fall bade me good-by as she was going to church, so I was left to enjoy my visit alone with Mrs. Polk. She sat on the sofa and I beside her while we talked.

"As you see me dressed to-day I have dressed ever since the death of my husband, almost forty years ago," said Mrs. Polk, and she laughed as she added, "I have not followed the fashions closely."

A PEN PICTURE OF MRS. POLK.

Somehow her dress did not look out of fashion. It was made of black cashmere in such a way that it sweeps the floor just a little at the back.

A very fine embroidered shawl was wrapped about her shoulders and she wore a very becoming headdress of white tulle and black lace. Her slender hands, which toyed with the gold-headed cane she carries, were covered with black kid gloves. Her brown eyes sparkle and her laugh is musical indeed. I cannot help adding one note. Mrs. Polk was eighty-five years on the 4th of September last, and the gray—not white—hair, which is worn in curls across her forehead, is her own, as are her white teeth, only two of which are missing.

"In my day," she said after speaking about her hair, of which she has good reason to be proud, "women grew gray, but now they get white. I think it is strange and I have wondered why."

Mrs. Polk showed me the photographs which Winnie had brought her. One was of the Polk mansion, another of Mr. Polk's first law office, which I have described, and photographs of Mr. Polk and herself. Hers—the last she has had taken—was made when she was seventy-three years old. It is only a reproduction of what she is today at eighty-five.

"I am very happy, and have been blessed all my life," said Mrs. Polk. "I went to Washington with my husband when I was but a girl, and I saw him rise from one position to another until he reached the highest. He filled every position for his State but one. He never was in the Senate. I still have the Bible upon which my husband was sworn as President of the United States. During his administration the Mexican War occurred and California, the Pacific coast, New Mexico and the State of Texas are living monuments to my husband's administration. He worked too hard. He was completely run down, and when his term expired and we came here he lived only three months."

It was the custom before the war for Southern gentleman to be buried in their own grounds, so they tell me, and so Mr. Polk asked his widow to bury him in the garden, where he rests to-day. They say that Jackson set the fashion, and it was followed by Calhoun and Polk.

FORTY YEARS OF SECLUSION.

Mrs. Polk, who was Miss Sarah Childress, was born near Murfreesboro, Tenn. She met Mr. Polk when he had his law office in Columbia. They loved and married and moved to Washington, where she spent the best eighteen years of her life. According to report she was not only a beautiful woman, but one of the brightest conversationalists and the best entertainers the White House ever had. She was witty and eloquent and is yet. It is only her expressed wish that keeps me from reproducing her entire conversation. Her life since her husband's death has been spent in waiting a summons to join him. For forty years she has lived at Polk Place, and in all that time she has not accepted an invitation to visit anywhere. She has never been back to Washington since she was in the White House. She has had no wish to return, for, as she says, she had accomplished all there was to accomplish, and she wanted nothing more. Besides, if she returned, it would be proper that she should call on the present mistress of the White House. Now everybody calls on her. Mr. and Mrs. Hayes have called to see her, and Mr. and Mrs. Cleveland. No one of any distinction ever visits Nashville without calling on Mrs. Polk and feeling honored to see her. In every entertainment that is held there she is remembered and a complementary delegation is always sent to her. The only place to which Mrs. Polk ever goes is to the First Presbyterian Church. She has attended this church for sixty years, she tells me, and she never misses a communion.

"I never forgot that God was good to me," she said, "and many times while I was in Washington, when I could not kneel because I was dressed too much, I would bend my knee and thank him for his goodness. I never left my room without doing so."

In Mrs. Polk's day wine was only used in the White House at State dinners, and during her husband's terms she did not permit dancing, as she was a rigid Presbyterian and considered it an improper amusement. All the people of her time are dead except Simon Cameron and Historian Bancroft.

"I had a delightful visit from Mr. Cameron several days ago," she said, "and two years ago Mr. Bancroft the elder, the only remaining member of my husband's cabinet, came all the way here to see me. I considered it quite an honor. We had a lovely time recalling old days. He is eighty-eight now and I am eighty-five."

We can only imagine the conversation these two noted people would have, and feel sorry that it could not be public. During the Centennial the President of the Pennsylvania Railway sent a special car to bring Mrs. Polk to Philadelphia, but she did not go. As all readers of the newspapers well know, Mrs. Polk opened the Cincinnati Exhibition. The electric apparatus was fixed in the hall which I have described, and the box where she was to touch the button was on the mosaic eagle table. Mrs. Polk calls it the National table. Two operators were there, and the minister read the messages until the one which said "Ready" arrived and Mrs. Polk touched the button.

CONVERSANT WITH PASSING EVENTS.

"It was very nice," Mrs. Polk said, "and what wonderful things we can do in this day! Just to think I touched that little button and set into motion the machinery so many miles away! One young man who was present said to me, 'Mrs. Polk, we can never let you go down. When nature gives out we will keep you up with electricity.' I keep up with the times. Although I have never left the spot for forty years, I know how the world is advancing. Everybody is so kind to me, I receive so much reading matter that I always tell Winnie to say to book agents that I want nothing, for if I would live to be a hundred I could never read all that is sent me."

"But you don't read yet?"

"Oh, indeed I do," she laughed, "by the aid of my glasses and a magnifying glass I read, and when you send me The World, if it is a bright day, you can be sure that I will read it. Mr. McLean, of Cincinnati, sends me his paper always, and he says as long as I live my name shall be on his list. Now what do you suppose I read first and mostly?"

"I cannot imagine, "I said, answering her smile.

"Political news; and I have seen my husband's speeches referred to frequently of late. I was a great reader in my youth. Girls are not what they were then. They never seem to read now. I read all the poets then, and committed selections from all so I could refer to them in conversation. We never drove then. It was not becoming or dignified for young ladies to do such things, but now they jump into their dog-carts and drive off like men."

"How did you dress when you were in the White House?"

"I always had rich gowns, but never gaudy. I always liked subdued colors and I never wore diamonds. I did not like them. I wore a brooch, which I wear still, with my husband's portrait painted on it, and my wedding ring. If I had a queen's tiara, I suppose I would wear it, but nothing less in diamonds. I never wore white lace, always white tulle, as you see now, and black lace. I have some lovely gowns upstairs which I never wore. I had ordered them in Paris—where I got all my dresses—and then my husband died, so I never wore them.

HAPPY IN HER DECLINING YEARS.

"Life has given me everything," said Mrs. Polk, "and now I am willing to grow old. I am thankful that I have been spared the infirmities that usually come with old age. I suppose I should, but I can't withdraw my interest in things. I keep up with the times just as if I were out in the world, and I love company. I was always used to it, and when Saidee's friends are here they sometimes want to talk low or walk softly for fear that I shall be disturbed, but I always tell them their noise does me good. I like it. We spent all our money in Washington in entertaining, and now I am repaid by having these events to live over in my mind. I don't know what it is to be sad or melancholy or lonesome. And now in the evening of my life I want nothing. I just keep myself comfortable and I'm happy. I have a moderate appetite and a good digestion."

"What do you do with all your visitors?"

"I regret that I cannot see them so much. You see my spirits are better than my strength," she said with one of her sweet laughs. "I used to send to the door a card with my compliments and regrets and they would send back, 'Please send more,' until I quit it. I am nursing all my strength now. I don't even send my autograph to people who write for it any more. Come and see my room now, Miss Bly, and then as I am unable, Winnie shall show you the house."

Faithful Winnie took Mrs. Polk's arm and led her gently to her room, which is at the front door and across the hall from the parlor. Everything in the room is ancient. The high rosewood bedstead surrounded with curtains has long posters which almost touch the ceiling. The dressing case matches the bed. A single bed in the corner is for Winnie. All the chairs in the room are of cane with arms. The one most used is the one at a wide window which commands a view of President Polk's tomb. There are wide arms on this chair to hold her books, basket and glasses.

"There is my magnifying glass with which I read," Mrs. Polk said, "and that is the chair I always sit in. You see the oil painting of Mr. Polk above the mantel? He hung that there himself a few days before his death and it has never been touched since. Now, Winnie, show Mr. Polk's study to Miss Bly."

JUST AS PRESIDENT POLK LEFT IT.

I followed Winnie up the wide stairs and into the great halls, the pattern of those beneath. Directly above the parlor in which we had been is Mr. Polk's study. Everything looks ready to crumble with age, even the old-fashioned wall-paper is hanging loose and all is covered with dust, as Mrs. Polk will not allow anything to be touched. Winnie opened the cupboards and showed me the letters which Mr. Polk had done up in careful packages. We closed the doors and turned to an old hair trunk that has never been unpacked since Mr. Polk left Washington. We looked at some Indian bead and feather work, which was crumbling to pieces where it lay, but we did not touch it. Then we went out on the upper verandas and viewed the city; first the Capital, from the front where the tomb is, and then the churches from the Polk avenue front.

Mrs. G.W. Fall, the handsome woman I have already spoken of, is Mrs. Polk's niece and was adopted and raised by Mrs. Polk after her return from Washington. She has always lived with Mrs. Polk, even since her marriage, and has entire charge of household affairs. Mrs. Polk never had any children. Mrs. Fall's daughter, Miss Saidee Polk Fall, is considered the beauty of Nashville.

"I am glad to have met you," said Mrs. Polk, when I bade her good-by, "and I hope if you ever return to Nashville that you will come to see me, or, if you wish to write anything more of other days, and I can be of any service by giving you facts or dates, I should be pleased to have you call on me."

And then I left the gracious, graceful lady who was the brilliant mistress of the White House over forty years ago.

IV.

MRS. HARRIET LANE JOHNSTON.

The Saddened Home of President James Buchanan's Niece.

I called at the saddened home of Mrs. Harriet Lane Johnston, at 518 Park ave., Baltimore. Mrs. Johnston met me with the kindness which comes from thorough breeding. Death has robbed her of all those dear to her, leaving her entirely alone. First her parents died. Then followed in succession her sister, her brothers, her uncle, James Buchanan, her two sons and only children, and her husband. Her grief made me feel that she should not be made the subject of a newspaper article at this time. I think that every reader of The World who has ever known sorrow of this kind will agree with me that under the circumstances I should not bring her and her surroundings into public view.

All are familiar with the history of Harriet Lane, whose life was so closely identified with that of her uncle, James Buchanan. She came of Pennsylvania ancestry on her mother's side and of aristocratic Virginia blood on her father's side. Her earliest days were spent in Mercerburg, Franklin County, Pa. When twelve years old she was sent to Charlestown, Va., to be educated. After a course there her education was completed in the Georgetown convent. Even before her school days were over her perfect and commanding figure, her deep violet eyes and heavy golden hair, her exquisite complexion and perfect profile gave her the reputation of great beauty. Her wonderful musical abilities, in addition to her wit, and unusual culture and wonderful conversational powers, made her a brilliant woman. When James Buchanan went as a minister to England Harriet Lane accompanied him. Her entrance into society awakened the utmost admiration for her beauty, grace and humor. She became a favorite with the Queen and was greatly admired by the royal family. During her stay she was one of the foremost ladies in the diplomatic corps at the Court of St. James.

HER MARRIAGE TO MR. JOHNSTON.

When James Buchanan became President, Harriet Lane was the loved mistress of the White House. She was in the White House when the Prince of Wales visited America and became President Buchanan's guest for five days. In January, 1866, Miss Harriet Lane became the wife of Henry Elliott Johnston, a wealthy banker of Baltimore and a member of an old and aristocratic family. On their return from a wedding tour in Cuba they went to their home, No. 518 Park avenue, Baltimore, which Mr. Johnston had caused to be furnished in an elegant and luxurious manner, to be a fitting nest for his brilliant bride.

Harriet Lane Johnston was the devoted mother of two of the noblest boys. The eldest, James Buchanan Johnston, was a remarkable child from his birth, and the marvel and admiration of all who saw him. He died when fourteen years of age, in 1881. Death has entered the home twice since then, taking the husband, Henry Elliott Johnston, and the only remaining child. Harriet Lane is to-day a beautiful woman. Her deep, violet eyes reflect the sadness of her heart; her heavy golden hair has turned to silver white; her perfect mouth has sad, sensitive lines; her figure, just as perfect as when she was the loved mistress of the White House, is always clad and sombre black; her luxurious home in Baltimore is as quiet as the grave. Much of her time is spent in Washington, where she expects to reside this winter.

"Wheatland," James Buchanan's home, is her country home, but she seldom stays long in one place. Despite her deep afflictions, Mrs. Harriet Lane Johnston is ever thoughtful of others, and the hearts of all who have ever known or heard of Harriet Lane beat in sympathy with her in her sorrows.

V.

MRS. GRANT'S EVENTFUL LIFE.

Many Interesting Facts in Gen. Grant's Career Told For the First Time.

Mrs. Julia Dent Grant, the only living woman whose husband served two terms as President of the United States, resides at No. 3 East Sixty-sixth street, New York. The house is within a stone's throw of Central Park, on a wide residence street, and is historic as the place where ex-President Grant spent many of his last as well as saddest days.

I was somewhat nervous about my visit to Mrs. Grant. I only knew of her as the wife of the famous General; the successful hostess for eight years in the White House; the woman who had, in making a tour of the world, been received as a queen in every civilized land. Would any one wonder, then, at my apprehension, when women of so much meaner light so often try to parry all attempts at approach? But I was wrong.

"My son tells me," Mrs. Grant said, with a pleasant laugh, after greetings have been exchanged and she had a drawn me by the hand to a chair and seated herself on a lounge, most cordially near, "that Nellie Bly is a little scamp"—

"Oh, no, no," I broke in, but holding her finger up playfully, she continued:

"That, not being content with exposing the Blackwell's Island Insane Asylum—yes, and benefiting it wondrously—and exposing Phelps, the great Albany lobbyist, she needs must go to Central Park and allow herself to be 'mashed,' and then tell all about it in The World, so that now none of the men dares wink at a girl while driving there, lest she be Nellie Bly."

"Why, that's a shame," I replied, and we both laughed, I fear not altogether in pity of the men.

"I will tell you anything I can of the White House," she continued more gravely, "but it seems such a routine story. Life there always seems to have the same duties. I can only say I loved the White House and everything connected with the dear old historic place. The eight years I spent there were the happiest of my life. I remember the entire time as a series of dreams of happiness, and it broke my heart to leave.

REGRET AT LEAVING THE WHITE HOUSE.

"Indeed, I know," she continued, with a tremulous break in her voice, "that if all the tears I shed of the day we left Washington could have been gathered together in a reservoir the ship of State could have safely anchored in them and escaped all the shoals it ran on the following winter. It seemed just like home and I never wanted to leave it."

MRS. GRANT.

"Were you at all nervous when you first went there?"

"Oh, no; you know it was different with me from what it was with most of the ladies who have been hostesses there. Ulysses, as the successful General, had received ovations everywhere and I had grown very used to them, and then, as head of the army in Washington, our receptions were as brilliant as any held in the White House. Why," she added, with an absurd laugh, "Harper's used to have cartoons of Grant's house on reception day. You never saw them? Well, they pictured ladies sitting on the opposite curbstone putting on their slippers, and the entrance jammed, and people crowded out of the windows. They were very funny. So the White House did not have any terrors for me. I don't think anything ever had. I always thought of my husband so much that I had no time to think of my own feelings. And forgetfulness to self is death to fear."

"What did you do first when you went to the White House?"

"Put things in order. It was just dreadful the state things were in. A green lounge and bright blue chair would be in the same room together, and the shabby carpet had roses on it as big as a wash bowl, and I gave my undivided attention to toning things down until the house was in perfect order. Then I spent several weeks in changing servants, and at last got them right, and they remained with me all the time we were there."

THE EXECUTIVE MANSION EASILY MANAGED.

"Is it difficult to manage household affairs at the White House?"

"Indeed, no; not so much so as elsewhere. For large receptions I gave suggestions to the steward and when everything was ready he would ask me down to inspect the dining-room. That was the extent of my worry. At first they tricked me in the flowers. My eyes trouble me and I do not see very well, so the sly rogues would put fresh flowers at my plate and ones not so fresh and other plates. I think there is nothing so shabby as wilted flowers; don't you agree with me? At last my sister told me of their tricks, so I watched them carefully afterwards. I had the pleasure of entertaining two former ladies of the White House during my term. One day Fred came up to my room and told me that Mrs. ex-President Tyler, with her granddaughter, was downstairs and wished permission to visit the greenhouse. I told him by all means to show Mrs. Tyler through the house and afterwards tell her that I wished very much for her to come to my rooms, as I had a surprise for her. When he had gone I ordered a nice little luncheon served in my room, and when Mrs. Tyler came I took her by the hand and insisted on her lunching with me. She told me that she had come back to Georgetown so that her grandchild might have the advantages of the schools, and I thought how sad it would be to come back unknown, you might say, to the White House where you had once been the honored mistress, so I did everything I could to make her feel thoroughly at home. I showed her her old rooms, and at last took her out into the hall where the paintings are. 'Now, Mrs. Tyler,' I said, 'here is the surprise I have for you.' She looked a long time and she was very much affected. It was a splendid painting of herself which I had found in the garret after I went to the White House among a lot of rubbish. I had it cleaned and hung where it should have been, and the sight of it moved her to tears."

CONKLING HER MOST DISTINGUISHED GUEST.

"Who was the greatest man you entertained at the White House?" I asked.

"Roscoe Conkling."

"But, Mrs. Grant, of all the foreign nobility"—

"Roscoe Conkling was the greatest man in every way, title or no title, we ever entertained at the White House," she replied in a decided manner. "It would be tiresome to attempt to name you even a part of the people we entertained. Of course everyone of note, both visitors and Americans, was entertained by us. We loved company and we were never without it. I always had some relatives with me during the whole time. In our eight years I don't think the dinner was ever laid for less than eighteen. The General loved company as well as I did, and I wish I could reproduce some of the conversations that were held at our table. They never were excelled. Are, those were happy days.

"Unhappiness touched me also when we were there," she continued after a pause, wiping away a tear. "My dear father, Col. Dent, who had been our guest, died. His body was taken to St. Louis on a special train and he was buried at his old home. Then my Nellie was married in the White House, which, although being the most brilliant of weddings, was sad because it took away my only daughter. Fred's wife, Mrs. Honoré, was our guest afterwards, and was introduced into Washington society.

"Ulysses loved horses and he always attended to them himself. We always drove four. I never knew anything about them and he gave me plenty and plenty of money and never asked what I did with it. Our evenings were spent very informally and pleasantly at the White House. After dinner Ulysses and Senator Conkling and Hamilton Fish and others of those old-time friends used to play 'Boston.' I doubt if you ever knew the game. It was played with cards. Ulysses was very fond of it," she added with a laugh, "and it did not please him to be interrupted. But he was very often, for visitors would drop in informally sometimes on business, but our evenings were delightful."

"Did unpleasant talk ever reach you from the outside, or did the world seem very far away?" I asked.

HOW MRS. GRANT CRUSHED A SCANDAL.

"It seemed very close, as if all the world's ills were mine," Mrs. Grant replied, "yet I never allowed any one to carry me scandal and make me nervous over it. I never listened to unpleasant things about myself. One time, however, I did hear a scandal. A Senators wife—I will not tell you her name, for I hope the unpleasant talk as long since forgotten—came to me one day with tears in her eyes and told me that she had received two anonymous letters, warning her that if she came to the White House on reception days with a certain clerks wife I would slight her. Why? Well, the Senator was very poor, Senator's pay, you know, is small and will hardly keep up expenses, at any rate it will support no luxuries. The clerk, whose wife was concerned, was poorer still, and existed on a marvellously small income. His wife's father had given her a coupé when she was married, but she had no horse, nor could she afford either to buy or hire one, so the coupé was a useless thing to her. Now, the Senator owned a horse but was too poor to buy a carriage, and his wife and the clerk's wife being acquainted made an agreement so that both would be benefited. The Senator was to furnish the horse, coachman and bear all expenses, for a share in the use of the coupé. This would enable both women to go driving or make calls in the coupé, which otherwise they could not, and if the Senator wanted to go to dinners in the evenings he was to have the coupé. Now, you see how nice this arrangement was. It gave all a happiness—a luxury, I might say—which could not be theirs without the partnership. But people will talk! They began to say unkind things of the clerk's wife; that she was using the Senator's carriage, and calumniated the poor thing shamefully until at last it reached public print.

"The Senator's wife explained the partnership to me and she added: 'If there was any truth in the scandal do you think I would not be jealous? The poor little wife is so pure and innocent and she is afraid to come to your receptions because of the letters I have received.' I told her to come my next day and bring the clerk's wife with her and I would give them special attention, and that the next day she should assist me in receiving, but I could not ask the clerk's wife to do that, much as I would have liked to, because her position did not warrant it. Well, on the next reception day the Senator's wife came, and back of her, with drooping head and burning cheeks, was the clerk's wife. The poor child looked frightened almost to tears. I looked into her sweet, pure, innocent face and her timid, suffused eyes raised so beseechingly to mine. My heart went out to her and I held out my hand and took her little trembling ones and held them and patted them while I said: 'My dear child, I am so glad to see you. It is so pleasant that you and Mrs. Senator —— can pay calls together. I hope to receive you here often.' I held her hand then and talked with her, keeping the whole line waiting for quite a while. I never heard any more of the scandal, and the Senator's wife and clerk's wife continued to use the same carriage.

VISITED BY HER RIVAL.

"Then one time I had the pleasure of entertaining Mrs. Seymour, whose husband, Horatio Seymour, ran on the Democratic ticket against the General. I heard that she was in Washington, so I invited her to dinner. Afterwards I showed her my room, the big one over the private dining room, and I said: 'This would have been yours had your husband been elected instead of mine.' 'Why yes, and how beautiful it is,' she replied. She was, indeed, a lovely woman."

"Were you annoyed much with cranks at the White House?"

"Not very much. I always, if possible, saw everybody who wanted to see me. The General and I were especially fond of bridal couples, and whenever we caught any we had them to dine with us. But speaking of cranks, I shall never forget one man who came to see me. I was at breakfast and he sent word that he wanted to see me on a matter of importance, so I got up from the table and went to him. I remember yet what a tall, fine, scholarly looking man he was. He talked and talked to me. He was an Evangelist. I made a movement every half hour to go, but he begged so earnestly for a few moments more that I would sit down again. Luncheon was announced, and yet he talked. He said that he intended to talk until he accomplished the purpose of his visit. He had come there to convert me!"

"Did he ever return?"

"Indeed he did," she laughed, "but I had had as much as I could endure. So they kept him away from me. But what foolish things I am telling you," she said, "I let my tongue run away with me."

"It is very interesting to me. Now tell me something of your life while Gen. Grant was winning his honors as a soldier during the Rebellion."

RECOLLECTION OF THE WAR.

"I was like one in a delirium all during the war," she said with enthusiasm. "I love the army and I was the first to urge Ulysses to go to the war, and after that I don't think I was very patriotic. I was a Southerner, born in Missouri, and when I was married my father gave me six slaves for my own property. All my relatives, and my brother, Judge Dent, were on the rebel side. But I did not care for them or for the Union men. All I thought of was my husband—that he should win and gain new victories."

"Did you ever think that he would lose his life?"

"Never once. When he first started from Galena, our old home, he took Fred with him. Fred owned a little pony, and I urged his father to take him along. When Ulysses was ordered on to Memphis I begged him to take Fred, but he replied that the boy was too young. 'Alexander was not older when he accompanied Phillip,' I wrote, which I thought was sufficient to make Ulysses obey, but he replied: 'Fred is not Alexander nor am I Phillip,' and Fred was sent back home. Ulysses was never happy unless we were together, so most of the time that he could have me with him he always sent for me. When he was in Memphis I was with him. I remember one morning there was a great shooting and noise over a victory somewhere. My Nellie came running into my bedroom in her nightgown, with her pretty hair flying over her shoulders and her big eyes stretched their widest, and bright with excitement. 'Oh, mamma, mamma,' she cried, 'the rebels are very nice people. Listen to the shooting. They are celebrating my birthday.' It was her birthday, and the boys for a joke told the poor child that the rebels were celebrating it. And so she thought them very nice people? I had everything prepared for a long Winter—fruit canned, beef smoked and enough wood cut to last the whole Winter at our home in Galena—when Ulysses sent for me to come to him at Cairo. I turned the lock in the door, leaving everything as it stood, and I never went back.

A PEEP AT THE REBELS.

"I want to show you a picture that I value very highly," and she brought up a little water color in a gold frame. She stood it on her knee, and pointing with her finger she said: "You see all these tents? This way to the end is the General's headquarters. This is City Point, where we were encamped, and this," pointing to a blue stream at the edge of the painting, "is the James River. There was a nice flight of steps led down to it, but it has been cut off by the frame. Now, one Sunday, a lovely, clear day, we all got on a boat— I think it was the Mary Powell—and went down the James River. We landed, and climbing a hill, took our field-glasses to view the rebels, when we found they were doing the same with us. We all laughed, and some were afraid of their firing on us, but the General said the ladies' bonnets would keep off the shot. It did, too. On our return trip, when just about here," pointing to a place distant from the camp, "we found a string of boats had been fastened together to make a bridge for our soldiers to cross over the James. I will never forget Gen. Sheridan that day. When we saw him he was lost in what looked like a letter. He would read a few lines and the red would creep up in his cheeks like in a girl's. He was so blushingly happy that I said: 'I'll wager that you have received a love letter.' He blushed the more and smiled. A few moments afterwards I learned that it was not a love letter but an order to go to a battle.

"The second Sunday following one could not tell that lovely City Point was the same place we had been in on the day of the excursion. The women had been put on the Mary Powell for safety, and it was lying at anchor right in front of the steps of City Point, which I told you led down the bank to the shore. A number of other vessels were also anchored here. The men had gone to take Richmond or to die. The General said to me in parting: 'If Lee surrenders I will return and we will go to Washington together. If he takes to the mountains make your way back home—you will be alone.' 'I will wait for you,' I replied. That Sunday was one of suspense. We had no news and were all sitting in a group waiting—waiting. At last a messenger boy came running out and said, all breathless and gasping, 'Mrs. Grant, may I speak to you?' 'Certainly, my dear,' I said, and I patted his cheek, which was as dainty as a girl's. We went into the cabin and he whispered: 'You mustn't tell; it's as much as my head is worth to tell you, but I caught it as it was going over the wires. Gen. Lee is just surrendering to Grant.' I went on deck, and everyone wanted to know what the boy said, but I would not tell. I just laughed, and while they were urging me we heard the dull roar of voice is shouting away down the river. Closer and closer it came, and swelled in volume until it was on City Point, opposite us. Then the cannons were fired, and the steamers blew their whistles in chorus, and every tongue was crying: 'Lee has surrendered!'"

"What did the General say when first you met afterwards?"

"He did not say one word. We just kissed each other in silence, but there was a great deal in that kiss."

EARLY DAYS IN A LOG CABIN.

"When we were married Gen. Grant was then an officer in California. We farmed for three years afterwards at a place which belong to our family. My father had been reading Eliza Kellogg's book, entitled 'Hardscrabble,' so he called our place that and it afforded us lots of amusement. You know it was just a log cabin we lived in, of two rooms, with an attic above, and I had only one girl and she did all the work better than the number I have to do it now. Just after our wedding, before we went to Hardscrabble, we spent some time at my brother's villa, Wishtonwish, just in the suburbs of St. Louis. It has been burned down since. We were very happy at Hardscrabble, and Ulysses never enjoyed anything so much as raising vegetables. He would be immensely pleased with the melons and onions and potatoes he raised. The children all had the measles there and they were very good. Jesse fished out of the window with a spoon and Nellie played with her dolls, while I read to them and told them stories. My children were always so lovely and agreeable. They never were quarrelsome or rude. While full of spirits and eager to romp outdoors, they always seemed to feel that it was unkind to their parents to be boisterous in their presence.

MRS. LINCOLN'S HARD LOT.

"You were asking if it were difficult to fill the position of the mistress of the White House," she continued, after a pause. "At the present time I can assure you not, for even the papers make the mistress everything that is charming and pleasant. No woman ever had it so hard as Mrs. Lincoln. Poor lady! I often think of her. She went in just after a long reign of Democracy, and everything combined to make her life unpleasant. She was a country lawyer's wife, as well as the wife of one of the greatest men that ever lived. When Mr. Lincoln was elected President she ordered some dresses at Cincinnati which she thought befitting the White House. In Washington they made fun of them. She was a perfect lady in every sense, but all the ways of the city were unknown to her. The first reception day she dressed in her finest and was in the parlor promptly at 2 o'clock to receive. The room was empty; no one was there, and she waited. It was 3, and yet no one came, 4 and 4.30, and the poor little woman, thinking that she was cut—for they had tried to treat her rudely—went up to her room and cried herself sick. At 5 o'clock her parlors were jammed, and she wasn't able to come down, having wept herself into a horrible state, so everybody went away scandalized. I tell you my heart aches for her when I think how she was calumniated. One day while she was out driving a Count, an adventurer, sitting in one of the clubs, boasted that he would take a drive with her. So when her carriage came along he motioned for the driver to stop. If the driver had known his business he would have driven on, but he stopped, and the Count, who had been received at the White House, stepped to the carriage window and told Mrs. Lincoln that he had a message of great importance to deliver to her. Poor, unfortunate woman, she did just as she would have done at her country home. She invited him to get in. So he accomplished his boast, and all Washington was shocked. Fate seemed to dog her footsteps and make every little move one of misfortune.

WELCOME WELCOMING MRS. HAYES.

"When the time came for us to leave Washington my heart was broken. When Mr. Hayes was elected I invited Mr. and Mrs. Hayes to come directly to the White House, but they refused. On the Sunday previous to the inauguration I gave a dinner for them, so that Mrs. Hayes would not feel a stranger. The dinner was lovely and everything was arranged splendidly. There were seventeen of my own family at the dinner and a large number of prominent guests and the Legation and Cabinet officers. I shall never forget Mrs. Hayes when she entered. The large doors were thrown open and the General and I advanced to meet them. She was walking by Mr. Hayes, but did not hold his arm. She was dressed in white silk and her dark hair was combed smoothly over her ears. Her soft, black eyes showed like diamonds and her cheeks were as red as roses. I took her hand in mine—it trembled a little—and said, 'Welcome, Mrs. Hayes, to the White House,' and then my guests surrounded us and she was soon at home. After dinner the Chief Justice administered the oath of office to Mr. Hayes in the parlor. On Monday I did not go to the inauguration, because I was too busy burning old letters and the papers that my father had owned, some bearing the date of 1400. I had seen two inaugurations, those of the General, and I did not care to see any more. I had a lovely luncheon ready for them on their return, and I also ordered the dinner and the breakfast for the following morning, so Mrs. Hayes would not have that worry the first thing. Then I told the steward he must go to Mrs. Hayes for orders after that. After dinner, as I was still hostess, I said to Mr. Hayes: 'Shall we return to the parlor?' and he gave me his arm and Ulysses took Mrs. Hayes. When we got in the parlor I said, 'I hope, Mr. Hayes, that you will be as happy here as we have been for eight years,' and then I said 'Good-by,' and we drove away. I told Ulysses as we were driving away that I had intended to say to Mrs. Hayes what General Buckner said to him when Buckner vacated Fort Donelson: 'My house is yours,' but I forgot it. Ulysses just put his arm around me and said he was glad I had not. All the servants who have served me during our term gathered in the hall to say farewell, and they were crying and I cried with them. After two weeks of hourly festivities, I might say, we left Washington on a special train. My car was filled with flowers, and after we had been escorted to it a Senator made a speech thanking me for so successfully filling the position of mistress of the White House. Then another Senator, a dear friend of mine, said it was wrong that we should ever leave it, and somehow I began to think it was. They went out and left me and I began to cry. All my pent-up feelings burst forth at one bound, and, as I tell you, my tears would have floated the ship of State if gathered in a reservoir. I cried for easily forty miles, and then the General came in and said:

"'Why, Julia, my dear, what is wrong?'

"'I feel like a waif, Ulysses,' I sobbed; 'I have no home.'

"'Never mind, we will soon have another one. Remember what a relief it is to me to be released from that position. Now we can do what I always wished to do—visit Europe and maybe travel around the world before we return.'

"And so he cheered me, and I never felt a regret afterwards. It washed itself away in the flood of tears."

TRIUMPHAL TOUR OF EUROPE.

"And he had his wish?" I said.

"Yes, we travelled around the world and were received everywhere with an ovation. What was the most interesting place to me? The crypt where lay the bodies of Ferdinand and Isabella. 'Every school child in America knows the story of Ferdinand and Isabella,' I said to the dear old priest who was our guide, and it seemed marvellous to him that it should be so. I went down into the crypt where they lie. 'Just think, Ulysses, they have been here for 400 years'. 'Julia, come away,' he said, for he always hated to think of death. 'But think, Ulysses, 400 years'—'Julia, I will leave you,' he replied, making for the door. 'But, Ulysses, I want you to think'—'Julia, I'll shut you in,' he said, so I flew to him. Then the dear old priest showed us the jewel-box containing the jewels which Isabella pawned in order to send Columbus to America, and some of the party thought it looked suspiciously new. Then he took down a heavy silver crown which was dotted with jewels. It was heavy and not at all pretty. He said: 'Now, it is only right that the Queen of America should wear the crown of the Queen who was instrumental in finding America.' So I bowed my head and he put the crown on my bonnet and Isabella's scepter in my hand, and I waved it at our party. I soon got him to take it off, and right glad I was to be clear of it, for it was very heavy and not at all pretty."

Mrs. Grant has four children. Col. Fred Grant, the eldest, with his pretty wife and children, lives with Mrs. Grant. His children are named respectively, Julia and Ulysses. Ulysses Simpson Grant (better known as "Buck"), the second son, has three children—Mariem, Chaffee, and Jula Dent, the last in honor of her grandmother. Nellie Grant Sartoris, Mrs. Grant's only daughter and third child, resides in England. She has three children, Algernon, who is preparing to enter Eton; Vivian and Rosemary. One son, Ulysses Simpson, named in honor of Gen. Grant, is dead. Jesse Grant, the baby of the family, is also married and has two children, Nellie and Chaffee.

Mrs. Grant is a small woman, the top of her head hardly reaching my shoulder. She is heavy for her size. Her eyes are hazel, and her brown hair, slightly gray, is banged and worn high in the back. She wore a beautiful black silk morning gown the day I called. On her plump little fingers, whose nails were most carefully cared for, were several diamond rings all of which she called "love tokens from the General and from Nellie."

WRITING HER MEMOIRS.

"I will never wear colors again," she said, in speaking of dress, "but I love bright dresses, and I love to have those about me well-dressed, especially young girls. I like to wear bunches of violets in my belt and I am fond of lace. I dread black so much that I have said in my will that I wish no one to wear black for me longer than six months. I do not think that it is right. I do not read much now because my eyes are so poor, but I am writing my life, which is one of romance and history, for my children."

"Will you publish it?"

"I cannot say. If the children think it advisable after it is finished I will not object."

"Did you wish Gen. Grant to be buried where he is?"

"Yes. He and I never could never speak about death, it was so hard, so he left me a letter in which he said it would seem proper that he should be buried at West Point or at the Soldiers' Home in Washington, but he said it was against the law for a woman to be buried at either place, and he begged me not to allow him to be put where I could not be with him. After awhile I will lie with him out on the Boulevard.

"My life is very quiet now. I received my friends, but I do not go out. I cannot." She paused to wipe the tears which are ever ready to spring forth at the remembrance of her loss. "It doesn't seem right for me to go. I have Fred and his family for company, and I get such sweet, cheerful letters from Nellie. She does not speak of coming home this year, although some newspapers stated that she was; in fact, some have said that she is already in America. I am my own housekeeper, and I write every day of my life, which I have told you about."

"Have you any intention of moving from your present home?"

$400,000 FROM GEN. GRANT'S BOOK.

"I have thought of selling, for the house is very much larger than I need, and buying in Washington. I have not, however, decided definitely. Our Winters are very severe here and my health is not very good."

"Do you belong to any charitable society?"

"No. I never had any ability or taste in that direction. I remember the first one I ever attended was here in New York during the war. They asked me to vote for a sword to be given the most popular General, so I paid my dollar and voted for Gen McClellan. A gentleman in the party protested and said: 'Why, Mrs. Grant, why didn't you vote for Gen. Grant?' 'Well,' I replied, 'I never voted except before except at May fairs, and then we always considered it dishonorable to vote for one's self. The General and I are one, so I vote for another.'"

"You received quite a handsome sum for General's book, I believe?"

"Yes; I received $400,000 for it—quite a large sum, but then I paid most of it out immediately. There is one subject I cannot talk of, but I will explain to you. You see the General was never a successful business man. He was too honest. Why, Miss Bly, do you know that he could not believe that any man was dishonest? Often when I sought to warn him of any one he would say that he did not think any man could deliberately steal. This house was given to me by some Philadelphia gentlemen, and Mr. Ward persuaded Gen. Grant to mortgage it and allow him to invest the money. I was always ready to aid the General and everything, so I consented.

FERDINAND WARD'S RASCALITY.

"When the failure came we had, all together, $84 and some cents in the house—all the money we had in the world. When the General got ill he felt that he wanted to leave something to take care of me. 'I don't care for myself, Julia,' he would say, 'I don't want money, but it's you I think of.' Then he felt so keenly about my losing my house through him; and oh, Miss Bly, it was pitiful to see him while ill work so hard to finish that book before he had to die."

Mrs. Grant sobbed, and I silently sketched a mental picture—the grand old warrior fighting off death until he should satisfy a debt which he felt he owed a faithful wife. Grimly working—forgetting the pangs of the flesh or stifling them and working—working with Death waiting at his elbow; and then the book is finished! The pen drops from his worn fingers; his task is done and he turns to answer Death's summons.

"It was finished," she continued, "and he gave it to me to pay for the house. I paid off the mortgage, $56,000 and interest, and then paid back several relatives of the General all the money which they lost when the firm failed. They were poor, and so I paid them. I knew that Ulysses would want me to do so could he have been here."

I will not write more of Mrs. Grant, but I will always have two pictures in my mind. The one I have described—Gen. Grant's greatest fight—and a true wife waiting the summons to join her husband.

VI.

AMONG THE COWS AND CHICKENS.

Mrs. Rutherford B. Hayes's Quiet Home at Fremont, Ohio.

A large two-story brick house, with wide windows and long, broad verandas filled with green and red cane chair, down in the heart of a twenty-acre grove of the very handsomest old trees, is the home of Mr. and Mrs. Hayes. It is just within sight of the village of Fremont, O. I do not think it is more than twenty minutes' walk from the very centre of the town. I waited several days for the return of Mrs. Hayes from New York, and then, as I could not wait any longer, I decided to see the much talked-of farm and chickens. I had heard so much about the sweetness of Mrs. Hayes and the genial manner of her husband that it was a disappointment not to meet them.

"Why, they have hundreds of visitors," said a gentleman in the town, "and they are most kind to everybody. They show everyone over the farm and all through the house. No one is ever refused admittance. Even travelling men go out there after having finished with their customers, and frequently miss their trains because they get so interested and forget to leave. And then Mrs. Hayes. Why, she is as sweet and unaffected as a child. She will stop on the street and speak to the poorest in the town. And charitable! Let folks who talk about what Mr. Hayes spent in Washington compare their charity list with that of the Hayeses. His whole life is devoted to charitable work, and he never gives away less than $10,000 a year for the benefit of humanity. Yes, and the chickens. I don't think that Mr. Hayes ever looks at the chickens except to please Mrs. Hayes. She loves animals and fowls and she has all kinds. Sell chickens! Why, bless my soul, no sick person in town ever wants for fresh milk or tender chickens. She just gives the chickens and milk away all the time until she has to buy when they need either for themselves. Yes, they can talk, but I'd like to compare the charity lists, bless my soul if I wouldn't."

THE HOMESTEAD WAS A LEGACY.

The homestead is known as Spiegel Grove. It was named by Silas Birchard, who was the owner of it. At his death he willed his property to his nephew, Rutherford B. Hayes. Outside of the grove is a good Ohio farm where vegetables and corn are raised, where there is a cultivated blackberry patch and hotbeds and roses. The site of the grove is very pleasant for its historic memories. In 1812 a famous battle was fought by William Henry Harrison, grandfather of Presidential Candidate Harrison, where the town library now stands in Fremont. While going into camp here Harrison made a cut through Spiegel Grove, and so they point out the way, which is always kept clear of growth, called "Harrison's Walk."

MRS. HAYES.

And then they will take one away across the grove, towards the southwest, and point out "Grandfather Webb's tree." Grandfather Webb, Mrs. Hayes's grandfather, as one may rightly suppose, belonged to Harrison's regiment. He, with another man, was sent out to find provisions. It was most bitterly cold, so cold in fact that they could not make their way back to camp. They built a fire at the foot of this great oak and kept themselves warm. All the soldiers in the camp had their feet frozen that night, but Grandfather Webb and his companion were saved by the fire. The great oak stands there as if proud of the part it has played, wholly unmindful—or bearing it as a brave soldier bears his scars—of the large hole in its side, the result of that night's fire.

After they have finished with this oak they will take you to another, much larger, much grander—one whose bark is rough and seared. People who understand such things say its age is easily four hundred years, and it looks good for a hundred more. And then there is a tiny shoot to see, a sprout of the Magna Charta oak. Near by is a slender young willow with its drooping, graceful branches flying in the breeze. It is the Napoleon willow from George Washington's grave. They say the willow was transplanted from Napoleon's grave to Washington's, and this is the product of a branch of it. And one cannot return to the house without having seen the mossy knoll, away to the south, which is the famous burial-ground. All the pets are given a resting-place in this quiet nook and a large slab on their graves. Among the most notable there are two pet greyhounds, General Hayes's old war-horse Whitey, Miss Fanny's riding horse Pompey, who strayed into the orchard, and, like the bad boy, ate too many crab apples—result: a place in the famous graveyard. Nimrod also lives there. He died last year. He was a great, wise, old white horse that Mrs. Hayes drove everywhere. When any of the townspeople would catch a glimpse of Nimrod they would say "Here comes Mrs. Hayes," so much were they together.

A VISIT TO THE HOUSE.

I went to the house and two little dogs came running out, barking frantically and almost upsetting me in their enthusiasm. They soon saw that I was a stranger and looked very much disappointed, yet kept close to me, as if not altogether averse to making friends provided I was received. I met Mrs. Hayes's niece, Miss Lucy Keeler, and she kindly consented to show me the Hayes homestead.

The house is of ultra Southern style. The halls are in the centre of the house and are very wide. The floors are of hardwood, covered with Rich rugs. The first thing, almost, that met my eye was a large Stuart of George Washington, and beside it was a silver-plated log cabin, which was presented to Mrs. Hayes during the celebration of their silver wedding in the White House in 1877. On the left wall was an old oil portrait of Silas Birchard. The cane he always used was hanging to the edge of the frame. Back of the arch, where the carved balustrade winds up to the other floors, is an open fireplace, where a natural-gas fire burns brightly. Above the mantel, artistically placed, is a collection of weapons. In the centre is a brass Venetian plaque bearing the date of 1400, and above it hangs an English cap, Don Quixote shape, which was taken at the battle of Lexington. Surrounding these are old flint-lock pistols, quaint Japanese swords with chop-sticks conveniently attached, Mexican and Indian swords and pipes, and tomahawk and swords taken by Gen. Hayes. The solitary ornament on the mantel is a solid cast of Lincoln's hand in bronze.

In the corner near this attractive mantel is a chair made of deer horns. It was made by an Indian scout and trapper who, they say, makes one for every President. Above it is framed the General's coat-of-arms and a small portrait of himself when a beardless boy.

EX-PRESIDENT HAYES' HOUSE.

IN THE LIBRARY.

To the right is the large library. I wish I could convey the feeling of comfort and homelikeness it gives. The room is very large and fine portières hide the hall from view as well as keep out the draft. At the other end is the fireplace, made in the deep old style when there were nothing but great logs to burn. It is natural gas however, that twinkles and burns blue and red in its dance over the quaint brass bed. The beautiful bric-à-brac on the mantel is reflected in the large mirror at its back.

All around the room are low open bookcases holding costly and rare books. In one corner, near the cheerful fire, stands upright piano. Tables are set around conveniently on which are books, magazines, photographs and some few fresh flowers. On either side of the entrance door are life-size oil-portraits of Mr. and Mrs. Hayes, painted by Andrews while they were in the White House. It represents Mrs. Hayes in a white flowered silk and lace and shows her to be a very sweet, lovely woman. Mrs. Hayes inherits her beauty from her family, as shown by a portrait of her grandmother—a very handsome woman—which hangs close by. Its companion piece is a portrait of Gen. Hayes's only sister Fanny, who had the reputation of being a wondrously beautiful girl. She died while still quite young.

Miss Keeler then showed me some rare books and souvenirs belonging to Mrs. Hayes. The most beautiful souvenirs are the six volumes of American autographs of all the people, poets and writers of note. It is dedicated to the total abstinence cause and was presented to Mrs. Hayes by the ladies of Illinois. Throughout the volumes is exquisite pen ornamentation. The first name in the volumes is that of Mrs. James Knox Polk and the second, if I mistake not, is that of Schuyler Colfax. One of the tables, a fine rosewood, in this library was bought at the auction in the White House during Garfield's time.

A THRILLING EXPERIENCE.

One painting Mrs. Hayes values very highly. It is a scene on the rapids of the New River, in West Virginia, a wild spot, beautiful in its very raggedness. One time during the war the Governor's regiment was encamped nearby, and Mrs. Hayes started off for a ride with her brother Joseph, a surgeon in the army. On their return they found the picket line had been removed, and they were pursued by rebels. It was a ride for liberty on one side and a ride for a valuable prize on the other. Several shots were fired, but Mrs. Hayes and the surgeon escaped.

A room directly at the back of the library is Mr. Hayes's study. It is a regular student's or rather scholar's den. The open bookcases reach to the ceiling and are piled full of books. A small table is covered with papers, letters and pens. A leather lounge in one corner makes a good thinking spot. In this study Mr. and Mrs. Hayes spend the most of their life. They read and study together. War tales and reminiscences are their chief topics in reading and conversation. Among other things, on the mantel, or I might say in the position of honor, is a full figure in bronze of Lincoln. It represents him in the position so familiar to the public—sitting in a chair. Gen. Hayes says, so Miss Keeler told me, that he thinks, next to Christ, Lincoln was the most wonderful of men. The seal that President Lincoln always used is in the possession of Mr. Hayes. This beautiful study, with its cheerful fire made me feel like sitting down and enjoying a feast among those books. The exquisite dressing-case, hung with all the little knick-knacks that a woman gathers about her, is of solid mahogany. The upstairs corresponds in beauty with the lower floor. To me it was the finest spot in the Hayes homestead.

The parlor is across the hall from the library. The hardwood floors are a rustic brown. Rich wine-red rugs, with long, soft pile, deaden the sound of walking. On the walls in the parlor are many paintings, conspicuous among the lot being a full-length portrait of Fanny Hayes, the only daughter. Between the parlor and the dining-room is Mrs. Hayes's room. The windows, hung with real lace curtains, open to the south and command a beautiful view of the grove. Some fine oil-paintings adorn the walls. The bedstead is of solid mahogany, with the long, old-fashioned posts. It was the property of Mrs. Hayes's grandmother.

THE CHICKENS AND COWS.

We then went out to see the chickens and the cows, the dogs running ahead and barking, then coming back to us, as if afraid we would not follow. A few beautiful Jersey cows were out in a meadow. In the stable were three calves, which lifted their great, human eyes and whisked their cute little tails and jumped around in their stalls, as if to show us how frisky they were.

"That's a pure Jersey," said the man in charge, pointing out the solitary one. "These here twins are not. They were born since Mrs. Hayes went East. She'll be so delighted and so surprised to see them when she comes home."

The chickens, common breed of a motley kind, number sixty. This does not include the ducks.

"I don't know that the General ever looks at the chickens, but Mrs. Hayes is very fond of them. She doesn't kill any except for sick people. Lay eggs? No. We have so many old hens, and we don't get an egg now. Mrs. Hayes has lots of pigeons," pointing to the dove-cote around which the doves were as thick as bees and as busy. "They all know her. She comes out into the yard and she has a little call at which they all come and sit on her arms and pick her cheeks, and bolder ones sit on her head until she feeds them.

Quote out this way Mr. Hayes has planted some walnut trees in the shape of a church—spire, choir, naves and all. It is perfect in outline. 'In two hundred years from now,' Mr. Hayes said, when the work was completed, 'it will be a church worth owning.'

And Mrs. Hayes! Every one says that she is handsome. She is large and well formed and dresses well, but very quietly. She has black hair, worn smooth over the ears, and large gray eyes which grow black with excitement. She is most lovable and sweet, so all say who know her. She is very fond of music, and still sings. In the Summer she is to be seen every day working in her flower garden or driving. She is very full of fun, and enters into sport with the young folks like a school girl. Her dogs, Dot and Jet, who announced me by their barking, are very dear to her.

MRS. HAYES'S FAMILY.

Mrs. Hayes is the idolized mother of four boys and one daughter. Birchard, the eldest boy, is named in honor of his grand-uncle, Silas Birchard. He married Miss Sherman, of Norwalk, O., two years ago, and resides in Toledo, O. He is a graduate of Harvard and a lawyer, of the firm of Swayne, Swayne & Hayes. He is father of the first and only grandchild, Rutherford Birchard. Webb Hayes, the second son, is in Cleveland, engaged in electrical manufacturing. Rutherford lives at home, and is cashier of the Fremont Savings Bank, of which Gen. Hayes is President. Fanny Hayes is the only daughter, and is said to resemble her father. Scott Russell, the youngest, is very handsome. He is attending Cornell.

Mrs. Hayes entertains a great deal, and is fond of company. Her children make a companion of her, and their choicest jokes are saved for her. Sometimes they are mischievous enough to play their pranks on her.

One time when Mr. and Mrs. Hayes were travelling West Mrs. Hayes endeavored to keep away from the autograph hunters who besieged their train. She kept out of sight until it was time for the train to start, with then she seated herself at the window. There was a crowd outside, and instantly some one handed in an autograph book. Of course she had to write. Then came margins of newspapers, cards and more albums, until she was almost tired out. When the train started Rutherford came in and showed his mother an album that he had been passing in through the window to her. He had her autograph fifty-six times in one album!

VII.

IN RETIREMENT AT MENTOR.

Mrs. Garfield Well Provided For by the Liberality of Her Husband's Friends.

I never experienced such suicidal weather as that which I found at Mentor, O. A Fair was being held in one of the adjacent villages, and I think that it was responsible for the rain—at least it had been raining ever since the Exhibition opened. Mentor is about forty miles from Cleveland. Its former hotel has long since been closed for want of patronage. No through trains stop at Mentor, so I decided to stop in Painesville, the nearest village.

Mentor avenue runs in a direct line from the heart of Painesville through Mentor. It is broad and shady in the summer and, they say, smooth. It had been raining steadily for ten days previous to my visit, and the storms waning strength seemed to revive on my arrival. A man carried an umbrella over me and held it while I climbed the muddy wheel and seated myself in the wagon besides a sixteen-year-old driver. Our horse wore a water-proof.

We had plodded for probably half a mile through mud that almost reached the hubs and through natural lakes of unknown depth which had formed in the middle of the road, when the oilcloth fell off the horse. The first sight of that poor creature made me feel faint. It recalled the many noble steeds bought for a dollar, which I have seen almost propped up in Mexican bull rings to be gored at the pleasure of the festive toro for the amusement of the public. For two hours I endured the shame of making a skeleton draw me over muddy roads. Two hours of misery, and only seven miles! Gusts of wind brought clouds of autumn leaves, red, brown and yellow, all over us, and then they twisted and turned and fluttered to find a nest in close-by meadows or in muddy pools along the road.

A SMALL COUNTRY TOWN.

I hardly knew what that I was in Mentor until I was out of it—a cluster of not more than fifty white houses, with green shutters, modest and plain. Then came one much more pretentious than any of the others. The driver pointed to it with his whip and said that it was the Garfield mansion. I had expected to find a little country home, but this elegant building surprised me. It has been renovated and enlarged until the old home is lost in the handsome residence which has grown from it. A wide lawn, filled with shade trees and shrubbery, surrounds the house. A long portico is at the front, and to the right of it is built a cut-stone wing of artistic design. At the windows hang fine lace curtains. To the rear of the house are large stables and carriage houses. A natural gas well, which supplies the house with fuel and light, is still further back from the road. The estate, some say 100 acres, others say 300, is of the best farming land and is in splendid condition.

"The country home of a millionaire" is what any observer would say who did not know the owner, so perfect and elegant is the tout ensemble. I stopped at the door and was informed by a young boy, who stuck his nose through the crevice of the door when he answered the bell, that Mrs. Garfield was shopping in Cleveland; so there was nothing left for me but to return through the Slough of Despair to Painesville.

While I am forced to wait for Mrs. Garfield we can review her life.

To begin with, Mrs. Garfield is a college-bred woman. To that fact she owes her acquaintance and subsequent marriage to James A. Garfield. Mrs. Garfield's father, Mr. Zeb Rudolph, was a farmer in Garrettsville, O. All his neighbors called him "well to do," and though Lucretia Rudolph was taught the household duties which fall to the lot of a farmer's daughter, at the proper age she entered Hiram College as a pupil. James A. Garfield was a student in the same school, and it was not long before he and Lucretia Rudolph were friends. He was sent to Chester for two years afterwards, and on his return he married Miss Rudolph. Their circumstances did not warrant keeping house, so they boarded, even after some of the children were born. Mr. Garfield was then principal of Hiram College, but afterwards filled the pulpit as a minister of the Campbellites. When the War of the Rebellion opened he entered the army and made a brave record, Mrs. Garfield remaining in Ohio meanwhile, caring for the children, which doubtless at that time and in their pecuniary condition was the more difficult position of the two to fill.

IN VERY COMFORTABLE CIRCUMSTANCES.

When Gen. Garfield went as Congressman to Washington he was accompanied by Mrs. Garfield and the children, four sons and a daughter, the oldest daughter and youngest son having died. Mrs. Garfield lived very quietly in Washington, making no attempt at entertaining and going very little if any into society. She spent her time as a mother should, in looking after her household affairs and the education of her family. Mrs. Garfield is pleasing in appearance. She is slender in figure and dresses elegantly, but in black. Her brown hair is now streaked with gray. As they were anything but rich, Mrs. Garfield's life was not an idle one, but things have changed wonderfully of late. Gen. Garfield's death made her a rich widow. What had been denied to her all her life when he was with her was hers when he was gone. The poor wife found herself, through the sympathy of a generous public, a rich widow. Hundreds of thousands of dollars were subscribed for her and a handsome pension was granted.

Some of the money Mrs. Garfield invested in a handsome home in Euclid avenue, the famous avenue of luxurious homes in Cleveland. It was filled up elaborately and artistically, and here she lived for some time after Gen. Garfield's tragic death. In the mean time the old home in Mentor was rebuilt, and all Gen. Garfield's papers were stored in the new stone wing, which is fire-proof. Mrs. Garfield has now returned to Mentor to live, and the house on Euclid avenue is for sale. Mrs. Garfield has several children. Her son James married this summer. At the same time the only daughter, Miss Mollie Garfield, married J. Stanley Brown, a former private secretary of Gen. Garfield. Both of the newly married

MRS. GARFIELD.

couples went to Europe and at last accounts were still abroad. Mrs. Garfield is considered a distant woman by her neighbors, because she is not the least inclined to be neighborly. This may be the secret of the evident dislike they have for her. She chooses her friends among people in Cleveland. It's like a prophet in his own country.

After waiting some time for Mrs. Garfield I called again to see her. It still rained and I travelled the seven miles after dark, because she was expected home. Her son, a handsome boy of eighteen or twenty, met me and took my card to Mrs. Garfield. He returned very shortly and said:

"Will you tell me what you wish to see my mother for?"

"Certainly, "I replied, "I am writing up the ladies who were once mistresses of the White House, and for that reason I came from New York to Mentor to see Mrs. Garfield."

"Well, it's no use trying to see my mother," he said, turning my card between his two fore-fingers; "she always objects to seeing newspaper people. It is one of her rules to admit none of them."

SHE WILL NOT SEE ANY VISITORS.

"Probably, if you explain the nature of my visit to Mrs. Garfield she will not object," I suggested.

"No, she will not see any one," he replied, firmly.

"It seems too bad," I answered, "for me to write up all the other ladies who have been mistresses of the White House and to omit Mrs. Garfield."

"You might get something from the neighbors," he suggested, "and then you need not omit her entirely."

"I do not get my news and that way," I said. "I go to those interested personally and explain my visit, and if they choose to give me the desired information then they are responsible for its reliability. Outside stories cannot be relied upon."

"That is just it. My mother's friends know when anything appears in print that it is not authentic."

"I don't think that would be pleasant to either your mother or her friends. If there is anything she would wish me to omit I should most certainly respect her wishes if she gave me a meeting."

"No, she would not do it. A woman was writing a book on the ladies of the White House and she wrote to my mother for some information, and my mother would not give it."

"I question her good taste in the matter," I replied, shortly, and took my departure.

Mrs. Garfield was the only woman among all the former ladies of the White House who refused to see me.

VIII.

PRESIDENT ARTHUR'S SISTER.

Mrs. McElroy, the Mistress of the White House During the Former's Term.

A large two-story brick house, with wide windows and long, broad verandas filled with green and red cane chair, down in the heart of a twenty-acre grove of the very handsomest old trees, is the home of Mr. and Mrs. Hayes. It is just within sight of the village of Fremont, O. I do not think it is more than twenty minutes' walk from the very centre of the town. I waited several days for the return of Mrs. Hayes from New York, and then, as I could not wait any longer, I decided to see the much talked-of farm and chickens. I had heard so much about the sweetness of Mrs. Hayes and the genial manner of her husband that it was a disappointment not to meet them.

Mrs. Mary Arthur McElroy, President Arthur's sister, is a lovely woman. I called at her home, No. 170 State street, Albany, and came away completely charmed with her. Their house faces the Capitol and a pretty little park, but it is on a dreadfully perpendicular street. The driver had to go a block above before he could turn and get in to the sidewalk. I could not help admiring the natural toboggan slide. Mrs. McElroy's residence is in a state of renovation. Everything is being pulled to pieces and fixed anew, so I cannot describe her home, only I know that it is to be a gem when finished.

MRS. M'ELROY.

I sent my card I sent in my card and waited near a pile of lumber in the hall until the little card-bearer returned and asked me to follow her. I went with her back along the hall to an open door. A bright fire was burning in an open grate, a centre table was set with some rare china, and a few pieces of silver on the sideboard glinted in the firelight. A low lamp shed a soft, mellow light on the faces of a young man and woman who sat reading on the far side of the table. The other door stood Mrs. McElroy waiting to receive me. I quickly explained to her the object of my visit, and she said:

"If there is anything I can give you I shall be pleased to do so. I never considered myself mistress of the White House. I was merely my brother's guest for several months in the year, but my home was always in Albany."

Just then a handsome man with grayish hair and beard—at least it looked so by the lamp-light—entered, and Mrs. McElroy introduced him as her husband, adding:

"Miss Bly has come up to have me born in some new place." Turning to me, she continued: "I have been born almost everywhere in print—East, West, South and North. Every writer has me born in a different place."

"Where were you born?" I asked. "I'll try to get it correctly."

ONE POINT SETTLED.

"I was born in Greenwich, Washington County, New York, and"—

"Don't you want her age? Ask her her age," interrupted Mr. McElroy mischievously.

"There are two things I never ask in interviewing," I said; "I never ask a woman her age, nor a man how much he is worth."

"I do not object to telling my age," began Mrs. McElroy, but I said:

"I do not wish to know it. I do not consider it news under the circumstances. Tell me something else about yourself."

"There is really nothing to tell," she said, looking at her husband with a smile. "People with the happiest lives have no story to tell. I never said or did anything wonderful. My father was a Baptist clergyman, and I was educated at Mrs. Willard's Seminary, in Troy. I had two brothers and five sisters. I was the youngest."

"Where did you meet Mr. McElroy?"

"I'll tell you, Miss Bly"—Mr. McElroy began, hurriedly.

"Now don't bring up that old thing," Mrs. McElroy pleaded.

"Yes, do, please," I urged, "I know it's a pretty story."

"It was at the fatal picnic," he began. Mrs. McElroy leaned back, with a sigh of resignation, her big, black eyes gleaming with merriment. "It was always called the fatal picnic afterwards," continued Mr. McElroy. "It was at Newtonville, a suburb of Albany, on the 4th of July. I was one of four young men who decided to drive out from Albany to it. The first thing I saw when I reached there was the belle of the picnic. 'Who is that girl with the black eyes?' I asked. 'Mary Arthur,' was the reply. I fell in love with her black eyes at the first glance I caught from them, and the strangest part was that every one of us four young men met four young ladies that day we had never seen before, fell in love with the same young ladies and married them. Strange, wasn't it, four matches in one day among people who had never met before?"

HER IMPRESSIONS OF WASHINGTON.

"That's why it was called the fatal picnic," said Mrs. McElroy, with a laugh.

"How were you dressed that day?" I asked.

"All I saw was her lovely black eyes," said Miss Mr. McElroy.

"I remember well how I was dressed," said Mrs. McElroy. "I wore a plain white muslin and a wide Leghorn hat."

"Did you like Washington, Mrs. McElroy?"

"I loved it very much. I was there only four months in the year because I had other things to do which brought me home. I think mistress of the White House is the most charming position in the world. It is not a difficult one if a woman does not lose her head. Everybody is so kind and considerate. I made many friends there who will be life-long friends. I was only my brother's guest; I could not take the place as mistress of the White House, and so, not being the President's wife, I could accept invitations, which was a great pleasure and allowed me to become more intimate with the people. Although I was not mistress there I did a great deal towards widening the hospitality of the White House. I received every day from 11 to 1. One feature of my stay was the afternoon teas which I introduced. They came after the receptions, and two or three hundred people would attend at a time."

"Were you not frightened or nervous when you first went there?"

NEVER WORE LOW-NECKED DRESSES.

"Never once. I had only one thought and that was to do the best I could and make everyone welcome. I was in mourning, so I confined myself to grays, violet, black and white. One strange fact is that I never wore a low-necked dress. I have no objections to others wearing them, but I do not care for them myself. I think they are becoming to the very fewest possible number. The too fleshy look just as badly in them as the too thin. A gentleman once said to me that I could never be presented to the Queen if I would not wear low dresses, and I told him I did not think that would be any great loss. I never wear jewelry either, excepting a few rings," holding up her pretty little hands, "and my ears have never been pierced."

"I suppose you go to church and belong to missionary societies," I said.

"Yes, I go to the Episcopal Church. I went to St. John's in Washington because I was very fond of Dr. Leonard. I have been asked to join missionary societies, but I never did, for I always had other things to occupy my time."

"You are your own housekeeper?"

"Oh, yes, I keep house because I find it won't keep itself, but I certainly do not go around with a bunch of keys tied to my waist, or in a basket, although they credited me with such things in the White House. Why, I never was even in the White House kitchen," and she laughed. "Everything goes so perfectly there that the mistress has no household affairs to look after. I am fond of society, fond of travel and fond of leisure. I certainly find more pleasures in other things than pining after roasts and stewing-pans."

The McElroy house is in the finest part of Albany. The view from the front is beautiful. They lived on Clinton avenue for twenty-seven years. Mr. McElroy had bought the house and furnished it, and after a quiet wedding in Newtonville he brought his black-eyed bride to the Clinton avenue house, and there she lived until the first of May, when they bought and moved into their present home. Mrs. McElroy has four children. Her eldest daughter is the wife of Mr. Charles Harvey Jackson, a New York lawyer. William and Charles Edward, her two boys, are at home. Her youngest daughter, Jessie, is attending school at Farmington with Mrs. McElroy's niece and ward, Ellen Herndon Arthur. Mr. John S. McElroy, Mrs. McElroy's husband, is a wealthy real estate dealer.

PRESIDENT ARTHUR'S DAUGHTER.

"Ellen Herndon Arthur," Mrs. McElroy said, "President Arthur's only daughter, is my ward. She lives with me during her vacations. The newspapers always spoke of her as Nellie Arthur, but she was never called so. We used to call her Nell, but I never heard her called Nellie. President Arthur's son Alan is in Europe."

I think Mrs. McElroy is a beautiful woman, and I am sorry that the only photograph I could get of her is such a poor likeness. She is five feet five inches in height and of beautiful form. Her hands and feet are small. Her hair, tinged with gray, is parted in the middle, falling in the little soft waves over the head—not banged—and coiled high at the back. She has a lovely nose and mouth. Her face is very Youthful, and when excited a pretty girlish pink creeps into her cheeks. Her eyes are exquisite. They are large, expressive, and a deep, soft black.

"George Bancroft was our very great friend while we were in Washington," said Mrs. McElroy. "Chief-Justice Waite and Mrs. Waite were my intimate friends, and also Randolph Tucker. He has been to visit me since

I left Washington. I received every consideration in Washington. When I left Mrs. Pendleton gave a farewell reception in my honor. I will never forget Gen. Sheridan that day. It was the 3d of March, and Gen. Sheridan was kept busy until the last moment of the hour of the reception. We just greeted a Confederate Major-General who had come in a full uniform of the gayest description, badges, buttons and all that. Directly back of him came Gen. Sheridan in a common tweed suit. The contrast was remarkable. The General excused himself, but said he wanted so much to attend my farewell reception and he was so busy that he had that had he waited to dress he would not have got there, so he came in his tweed suit and we were just as well pleased."

HER DAILY LIFE.

"What do you do generally?"

"We drive every day, and I love to ride. This Summer we took our horses and drove to Massachusetts and all through that State. We take long drives every Summer, and it is a delightful way to spend the warm weather. I read a great deal of good, bad, and indifferent literature, only I very seldom read the newspapers. We generally know of murders and whose husband has run away with another's wife, without them. I am fond of Dickens, Thackeray, Longfellow, Lowell and George Eliot. I read for recreation, but I do not read trash. I go a good deal to the theatre and opera, and I belong to a theatrical club, and I used to take part in little plays, but lately I have been living very quietly."

"What do you think of women's rights and the suffrage question?"

"I think the suffrage question is too broad already and needs drawing in. I don't think it would better women any, so I have no patience with it. You will have to draw on your imagination in describing my home," she laughed as I started to go. "We are living now in one room after another, just as they drive us out. The dining-room is now our only place of abode, but it will be fixed up after a while, not grandly in anyway. We are having everything made for comfort."

NELLIE BLY

Nellie Bly on the Wing

Sunday, November 4, 1888

Some Things She Saw, Heard And Experienced While Traveling

Saidée Polk Fall's Happy Life at the Famous Polk Homestead—A Bit of Amélie Rives's Early History—Poet Riley's Wisdom—Experience with a Southern Quarantine Officer—An Indignant Traveler.

Miss Saidée Polk Fall is the belle of Nashville, Tenn. Her mother was adopted and educated by Mrs. James Knox Polk, whose niece she is. After the death of President Polk Mrs. Fall, then a little black-eyed girl, was the only companion the sorrowing widow had to share her lonely home. Mrs. Fall married, but still made her home with Mrs. Polk. Her only child, Saidée, is the joy and pride of the household, and Mrs. Polk loves to hear her girlish chatter about the house and takes delight in having her young visitors made welcome.

Saidée Fall, who was named in honor of her grandaunt, Sarah Polk, completed her education at Mrs. Reed's school in New York. Afterwards her mother sent her for a short trip through Europe, and she returned to take her place in society as the belle of Nashville. The fame of her illustrious grandaunt has made all social circles cordially open their doors to her. Before the marriage of Grover Cleveland she and her mother were the guests of Miss Cleveland at the White House.

Miss Fall is above the medium height, and dresses in perfect taste. Her waist would break a New York girl's heart, it is so wide. Of course, it is very noticeable in these days of carving waists, and would cause many heads to turn for a second look, but after a first glance of surprise one rather admires it. Miss Fall's face is not quite oval, and nature, aided by a Southern climate, has tinted it most beautifully. The nose is delicate and straight, and the soft red lips curve with a sweet pride as if the owner

MISS SAIDEE POLK FALL.

knew her worth. The eyes are black and deep, and in repose gaze with a dreamy look as if they could tales unfold. The arched eyebrows match the eyes in color, but are unusually heavy. Over the fair, smooth brow and curling round the pink-tipped ears falls her soft, reddish-golden hair. Add to this a graceful ease of manner and dresses that any stylish New York girl would be proud of, and you have Miss Saidée Polk Fall.

Miss Fall's apartments are in the second story of the Polk mansion. She has her own parlor filled with all the little dainties that young girls love. She has her dog-cart and horse, which she drives every day, and a little black-and-tan that likes to lie on the fur rug in the parlor. Miss Fall is quite a musician and plays the piano, guitar and banjo with skill. Besides this she has a clear soprano voice. This is her third year in society. Miss Saidée is a very happy girl. She is the idolized child of her parents, the pride of her grandaunt and the belle of Nashville.

What girl would ask more?

AMÉLIE RIVES'S ROMANCE.

In my travels through Virginia I met a gentleman who has been the life-long friend of Amélie Rives-Chandler. He told me a bit of her life, which is very interesting. Mr. Rives is a civil engineer for the Panama Canal, and Amélie is the pride of the family. They all bowed to her superior genius and she "ruled the roost" at home. In some of her travels Amélie Rives saw John McCullough and became possessed of a passionate admiration for him. She managed to be in several towns where he played and at last was rewarded by making his acquaintance. It is said that a closer acquaintance fanned her admiration into a warmer regard, and that at last John McCullough went to her Virginia homestead to spend his vacation.

"If you have read the book which made her known to the public," said my fellow-traveller, "you can judge what a happy time they had. He undoubtedly admired her and she more than admired him. While he was there she painted a life-size oil portrait of him, which is very artistic. Just after this he became insane, and the shock to Amélie's peculiar temperament was very severe. She became more eccentric than ever, and after his death she decorated the bedstead in which he had slept with a full assortment of angels. They said then that she cherished everything that he had used, even a half-smoked cigar, and locked herself for hours in the room with his portrait. Then she wrote a little play entitled 'Mad as a March Hare,' and played the leading role in it herself. She acted in Richmond, and donated the proceeds to a charity fund.

"She is so peculiar," he continued, "that she never leaves many friends behind her. She trusts to her beauty and genius to save her from any consequence of her rudeness. She makes a rule never to go anywhere until everybody else has arrived. Then she makes such dramatic entrances that I have seen a perfect silence fall on three hundred people as they turned to watch her. In the South she is considered very beautiful. The only objection anyone finds is that she is too 'dumpy.' She is extremely fair, even to pallor, and her hair is of a pale gold hue. Her lips are very full and so blood-red that envious ones have accused her of painting them. Her eyes are peculiar. They are blue, but the iris is so large that it almost covers the pupil, leaving but a tiny blue ring to be seen. We Southerners are very proud of her."

POET RILEY'S KEY TO SUCCESS.

"Do you want to succeed in life?" asked James Whitcomb Riley, the Hoosier poet, whose book of poems has just been most flatteringly received by the English public and press.

"I do," I replied, with an earnestness that might have been felt a block.

"Then dress well," he said. "The secret to success is a good personal appearance. Why, if I struck a town with only 50 cents in my pocket the first thing I'd do would be to go a barber shop. A barber shop is the intelligence office and newspaper of every town. So you see my first move would be to go there. I'd have a shave and give the barber my 50 cents, and when he offered me back the change I'd tell him with a knightly wave of my hand, "It's all right." He would tell everybody else, and it would help me to get an opening somewhere. But about dress. Now, wouldn't you rather give a nickel to a beggar who was brushed and had a clean face than to one who was not? Any one would. When one goes to a hotel doesn't the clerk take an inventory of his guest before he gives a room and doesn't the room always match the appearance? If I want to sell some verses the editor glances at me. If my clothes are shabby he thinks, 'Oh, he's in hard luck and will be satisfied with any price.' If my appearance is that of prosperity he'll be afraid to offer me a small price, or if not afraid at least ashamed. A woman should be even more particular. Her gowns give her her place more than a man's coat. Men always look at the women's dress and in almost every instance judge accordingly. To be successful one must look successful. Good clothing makes everything easier. Take my advice if you wish to succeed—never look shabby."

WANTED—A WIFE.

Who wants a husband?

I have just received a letter from a man in Nova Scotia who is anxious to test matrimony. Somehow I like the ring of sincerity in his letter so well that I wish my acquaintance among women was larger, that I might speak a good word for him. If any girl feels a responsive thrill while reading this and thinks she answers the requirements, I shall be pleased to hear from her and to do what I can in helping two people towards the one glorious end—matrimony. This is the letter:

> MISS BLY: I am much interested in the stories you have given the public, which I have seen referred to in our provincial papers. I write to ask the favor of being referred to some worthy young woman whom I might find eligible and available for a life partner.
>
> I am a farmer in a small way, living in a thinly settled neighborhood on the shores of Annapolis Basin. I am now building a house on my own farm and in selecting a mistress for it nothing would suit me better than to bring some good girl, who might make an efficient helpmeet, from the struggle with poverty and temptation of city life to the homely plenty of country life. Doubtless you could point out to me some such person as I desire, possessing good character, good health, industry, truthfulness, natural refinement of feeling, good judgment and a fair share of those graces of heart, mind and person that constitute the glory and value of the sex.
>
> She should not be above the average height, of the vital or sanguine or vital-motive temperament, and not very much past twenty years of age. Something under twenty would be just as well. If you could place me in communication with a person of this description, who seemed to you likely to possess the ordinary good qualities I have mentioned, you would confer a grateful favor on myself, and possibly on another.
>
> I am a bachelor, aged thirty-five years, 5 feet 8 inches in height, weight 142 pounds; am light complexioned; light-brown hair, somewhat bald at the crown: am not bad looking, have good health and constitution, have a good character, have always been a total abstainer from intoxicants, tobacco, &c.; have no bad habits, strongly inclined to be domestic. I belong to a respectable family and live on the southern shores of Annapolis Basin, a most beautiful spot. Its picturesque scenery and fine climate are making it a favorite summer resort for American tourists. Our Summers are cool, Autumn very fine, Winters moderate. Very little cold weather, but more prolonged than in New York, and backward Springs.
>
> What I ask is that you would kindly give me the address of some worthy young woman who is likely to be unengaged and who appears to you to possess the qualifications I have enumerated. I care not how poor, what her circumstances, percentage or race is—if white—provided she is good and healthy, and calculated for a suitable helpmeet for a poor man.

Or you might merely hand this letter to such a one, who could consider it as addressed to herself and write a reply. A correspondence could thus be opened, photographs exchanged, and New York is not so far from here but that a meeting might be arranged before long. Then, if we were mutually satisfied I could secure the companionship I so much need, and in return supply a poor girl with a good home.

If she could not afford to carry on such a correspondence I would supply her with the means. Pardon my trespassing on your valuable time, but I doubt not that you feel sufficient interest in the poor in whose behalf your pen has often been employed to be willing thus to help one poor girl to find a better home, and also ready to aid a lonely man to find a congenial companion.

Should any one desire references to indorse my good character and standing I can easily supply them from clergymen and other prominent citizens here, but I know no one in New York. I am, very truly yours, —.

PASSING THE QUARANTINE.

"It's too mean for anything!" I heard a girl half sob, and I looked to see what was wrong. She was one of a party of six—two men and four girls—who had started from Nashville at the same time with myself for Chattanooga, Tenn. The party had been very lively, and this dark-eyed Southern girl who was now on the verge of tears had been the jolliest of the crowd. A soldierly looking man in a close-fitting dark blue suit, with cap to match, stood looking first at her and then at a small book he held in a vexed but determined manner.

"I don't see why anything won't do as well," she said as her cheeks grew redder. The young men did their best to hide their amusement, but the soldierly looking man was unrelenting.

"I will go to the office and sign to-morrow," she pleaded; but the man shook his head. "Well, I don't see how it makes any difference whether I put sixteen or thirty-six," she said at last. The officer turned the book upside down and read something from it to the crowd; the young men burst into hearty laughter, and the poor girl, as she wrote something in the book, her eyes filling with tears, said:

"Chattanooga is a mean old town and I will never come here again—so, now."

I watched him have a turn with each of the other girls, which always ended in the girl's defeat, and I was burning with curiosity to know what caused so many tears among the girls and so much laughter among the men. I had not long to wait, for finishing with the party of six the man came to me.

"I am the Quarantine Inspector," he said, slightly touching his cap. "Where did you come from?"

"Nashville," I replied.

"Then fill out this blank, please," he said, handing me the book and a pencil. I did so, and then begged a sample sheet, which is reproduced as I filled one out:

> What is your name? Nellie Bly.
> Age?..
> In what State, county and town do you reside?............................
> In what place or places have you resided in the past fifteen days?
> New York City, Herkimer, Albany, N.Y. Painesville, Fremont, O. Nashville, Tenn.
> To what point are you going? Washington, D.C.
> Has your baggage been disinfected? No.
> Will you stop in Chattanooga? No.
> I solemnly swear that the answers to the above questions are true and correct, so help me God.

"What made the girls so vexed?" I asked the officer, referring to the party he had just left.

"Kicked on telling their age," he said with a grin, as he wrote on the back of the page a description of my color of hair, eyes, dress, hat, cloak, &c. "That one word 'age' causes me more trouble than a hungry mosquito on a hot night. The women try every persuasion to escape, but I just turn up the page and read this"

QUARANTINE OFFICER'S BLANK.
Issued by authority of
CHATTANOOGA BOARD OF HEATH.
Quarantine Ordinance of the City of Chattanooga, Tennessee.

> Any person refusing to answer these questions, or making untrue answers, or refusing to subscribe the oath attached, is guilty of a misdemeanor and may be fined not less than $5 nor more than $100, and forbidden to enter the city, or remain therein, and may also be imprisoned for not longer than thirty days.

"I struck a woman with nice glasses and curls the other day," he continued, "and she was a heap worse to whip than a Yankee soldier. I suspected that she was a back number, and she refused to state her age. I just threatened to have her imprisoned and then she wrote it, but she raved at me until I left the car, and they say that she cried all the way to Chattanooga about the 'outrage perpetrated on a respectable Southern woman.'"

NELLIE BLY

Exposed by Nellie Bly

Sunday, November 11, 1888

A Swindling Magnetic "Doctor" Caught at His Tricks

Prof. Ernest De Blanc, of Brooklyn, Proves to be a Notorious Criminal

---

He Has Advertised to Give a Big Free Exhibition To-Night, but "The World's" Active Reporter Discovered Him Just in Time—His Ingeniously Secreted Electric Wires by Which He Demonstrates His "Personal Magnetism"—A Long Criminal Career in Half a Dozen Big Cities—Convicted of Forgery at New Orleans—His Brilliant Advertising Schemes.

In a New York newspaper of last Thursday I read the following advertisement under the head of "Amusements:"

BROOKLYN ATHENAEUM
cor. Atlantic ave. and Clinton st., Brooklyn.
On Sunday Evening, Nov. 11
Admission Free.

Orchestra in attendance. Doors open at 7.30 P.M.
Commence at 8
THE PUBLIC IN GENERAL IS CORDIALLY INVITED. The AFFLICTED and CHRONIC CRIPPLES are especially invited.
No objectionable persons or children admitted to this REFINED lecture and exhibition.

BROOKLYN ATHENÆUM,
cor. Atlantic ave. and Clinton st., Brooklyn.
ON SUNDAY EVENING, NOV. 11.
Admission Free.

Orchestra in attendance. Doors open at 7.30 P. M. Commence at 8.

THE PUBLIC IN GENERAL is CORDIALLY INVITED. The AFFLICTED and CHRONIC CRIPPLES are especially invited.

No objectionable persons or children admitted to this REFINED lecture and exhibition.

PROF. ERNEST DE BLANC,
the Famous Chevalier Electrician of Paris,
will exhibit HIS SKILL and TREAT THE AFFLICTED FREE on the stage
IN VIEW OF THE AUDIENCE.

Specialist: Chronic Diseases, Deformity, Paralysis, Rheumatism, Consumption, Dyspepsia, Fits, Catarrh, Neuralgia, Nervous Diseases, Blindness, Deafness, Diseases of Indiscretion, and FEMALE DISEASES TREATED SUCCESSFULLY.

STRICTLY CONFIDENTIAL, GUARANTEED IN ALL CASES.

PATIENTS DESIRING TO BE TREATED BY MEDICINE OR SURGERY ARE NOT ACCEPTED FOR TREATMENT.

NO CORRESPONDENCE ANSWERED UNLESS POST STAMP INCLOSED.

Prof. Ernest de Blanc, in order to establish his fame among the WEALTHY CLASS, as well as Working Class Patients, would TREAT FREE a WEALTHY LADY AFFLICTED WITH ANY OF THE ABOVE DISEASES. On application state nature of the case, it MARRIED, SPINSTER, WIDOW and AGE.

CIRCULARS MAILED FREE to any part of the United States.

OFFICE CONSULTATION FREE.

Daily from 8.30 A. M. to 3 P. M. and 6 to 8.30 P. M. Sunday, 9 A. M. to 3 P. M.

Prof. Ernest de Blanc is now permanently located at No. 84 Ashland place, near Fulton st., Brooklyn, N. Y.

PROF. ERNEST DE BLANC

The Famous Chevalier Electrician of Paris.

Will exhibit HIS SKILL and TREAT THE AFFLICTED FREE on the stage.

IN VIEW OF THE AUDIENCE.

Specialist: Chronic Diseases, Deformity, Paralysis, Rheumatism, Consumption, Dyspepsis, Fits, Catarrh, Neuralgia, Nervous Diseases, Blindness, Deafness, Diseases of Indiscretion, and FEMALE DISEASES

TREATED SUCCESSFULLY.

STRICTLY CONFIDENTIAL GUARANTEED IN ALL CASES.

PATIENTS DESIRING TO BE TREATED BY MEDICINE OR SURGERY ARE NOT ACCEPTED FOR TREATMENT.

NO CORRESPONDENCE ANSWERED UNLESS POST STAMP INCLOSED.

Prof. Ernest de Blanc, in order to establish his fame among the WEALTHY CLASS, as well as Working Class Patients, would TREAT FREE a WEALTHY LADY AFFLICTED WITH ANY OF THE ABOVE DISEASES. On application state nature of the case, if MARRIED, SPINSTER, WIDOW and AGE.

CIRCULARS MAILED FREE to any part of the United States.

OFFICE CONSULTATION FREE.

Daily from 8.30 A.M. to 3 P.M. and 6 to 8.30 P.M. Sunday, 9 A.M. to 3 P.M.

Prof. Ernest de Blanc is now permanently located at No. 84 Ashland place, near Fulton st., Brooklyn, N.Y.

I made up my mind to call on this remarkable person, as the advertisement seemed to bear on its face the evidence of fraud. Friday was a bad day for thin boots and Friday night was worse. I had had a long and tiresome day, but I could not rest until I investigated the schemes of the magnetic doctor.

What will you charge to take me to No. 84 Ashland place?" I asked a cabby, who was leaning against his coupé as if asleep.

"Two dollars," he said, straightening up.

THE "DOCTOR" AT HOME.

We arrived at Ashland place in a little more than ten minutes. The street, like the night, was dark and dreary. From what I could distinguish I decided that it was a residence street and a respectable neighborhood.

After much hunting about in the darkness I found the right number and, pulling the bell, asked the man who opened the door if I was right.

"Zees is 84," replied the man, stepping inside the door as the driver returned to me.

THE DOCTOR.

"Good evening, good evening," said the man, as he held the door open for me to enter; "I was just about to close my house."

"Are you Doctor Ernest De Blanc?" I asked, entering the parlor.

"Yes, lady," he replied, with a pleasing accent. A woman, of medium height, with dark eyes and hair, flitted noiselessly out of sight.

"I saw your advertisement in the papers," I said, "and as I am tired taking medicine I concluded to come and try your treatments; you advertise 'no medicine given.'"

"That is right," he said, with a most agreeable smile. "I give no medicine. I cure entirely wizout zat."

"How do you treat patients?" I asked.

"Wiz personal magnetism, wiz animal electricity," he said, spreading out his hands, palms upward, and slightly elevating his shoulders. "Ze electricity all comes from me—from my body. I transmit it to ze patient. I give him treatments. I always cure him."

"Have you been here long?" I asked innocently.

"No. You see my house is yet not in good order," he said, with a sweep of his hands. "I have just moved in. What is wrong with you?"

"I am suffering from sick headaches," I utter plaintively.

"Ah! are they frequent?"

"Yes, every week at the very least, and I am very stupid while they last."

"How long do they last?"

"Usually twenty-four hours at a time."

"Will you come here until I examine you?"

He stepped beneath the chandelier and I went to him. With both hands he pulled the lid of my eye down easily and examined it with a look which rivalled an owl's—in solemnity at least.

"Ah!" he said, with a great deal of force, "ah! I must test your blood. It is greatly impoverished. Remove your rubbers, please, and your gloves."

While I obeyed orders he went out into the hall, and during his absence I will describe his rooms. The parlor, which I entered first from the hallway, is neatly but not luxuriously furnished. Everything is new. Long crimson portières of flannel hide the back parlor from view. This was the room in which the examination took place, and bears the evidence of just coming out of a furniture store. It contains, besides several chairs, a desk and some sketches on the walls. The floor is carpeted, and lace curtains hang at the windows. In one corner, between the window and the mantel, is a red Brussels bed-lounge. In front of it lies a red Brussels rug, bound in gray. This rug is the only article in the two rooms that shows any evidence of wear, and from its appearance I should judge that it had been in the family for a long time.

THE DIAGNOSIS.

Prof. De Blanc placed me on this rug and he stood before me. He touched my wrists and my cheek very daintily with the tips of his fingers.

"You will have to take off your shoes," he said at last. "Your blood is so thin that I can not get a response."

I sat down and unbuttoned my boot while he went out into the hall again and returned. I stuck my boot under a chair and went—two inches higher on one side than the other, thanks to Louis Quinze heels—hobbling across the room to my former position on the rug. The Professor returned and took my arm caressingly in his two hands. My arm tingled at every touch. He touched my face, my eyelids, and his fingers seemed almost to stick to my flesh, so strong was the sensation which communicated itself from him to me.

"It's neuralgia," he exclaimed triumphantly as he led me back to a chair. "A very bad case of neuralgia, and needs immediate treatment."

"Are your treatments similar to this?" I asked.

"Yes, only more exhaustive; each treatment requires about fifteen minutes. You felt me?"

"Yes, very strongly," I replied, still pretending innocence. "What was it?"

"That is my power—my personal electricity."

"Does that electricity all come from you?" I asked.

"Oh, yes it does, it all comes from me—from my body," he said, earnestly. "My cures are marvellous. I cure cripples who never walked; I make the blind see, I heal every known thing, and all by my personal magnetism. On Sunday night I will give a big exhibition at the Athenæum, the aristocratic hall. There I will in public perform my miracles. I will make the paralyzed walk, the deaf hear, the dumb speak. There will be hundreds of reporters—who have never seen me but heard of me—there to write it up, and if you look in THE WORLD on Monday morning you will see a long account of my exhibition."

I just thought if he looked in THE WORLD Sunday morning that he would see a long account of himself, but I held my peace.

"I have two assistants, surgeons from London," he said; "and I have calls from thousands of people."

"Where are you from?" I asked.

"I am from Paris," he said, looking at me sharply and taking up the more decided accent which unconsciously he drops at times.

"You speak very good English for that," I said slowly.

"Oh, I just come from Australia here," he said, with a startled look. "I want to locate here."

"How much will you charge to cure me?" I asked at length.

"Ah, lady," with a sweet smile and outward movement of the hands. "I will be honest wiz you. It ez a little case. I will then only charge you twenty-five dollar in advance for five treatments. After ze first one you have no more a headache."

"How lovely it would be to be rid of these horrid aches," I uttered, with a deep sigh.

"Do ze head aches ever; did you ever have fits?" he asked.

"No, but you can't know how many times I have felt that I would have them," I replied, choking a laugh.

"Ah, ze headaches should make you fear an inflammation of ze brain. It ez threatened," he said. He was working for the $25 in advance, and I knew it.

"What security have I that you will cure me if I give you the money?" I asked.

"I give you a written paper that I will cure you."

"But if you don't?" I urged.

"But I say I will. And when I am so sure of my own power you should not be afraid to trust it," he said very sweetly, but I was not convinced.

THE SWINDLER'S CAREER.

Prof. Ernest De Blanc, as he calls himself, is about five feet four and a half inches in height. He is of rather heavy build—that is, he is not thin. His black eyes are mounted with rather heavy eyebrows. His hair, black in color, grows very thick on the head and is slightly parted in the centre, and his nose is flat. His hands are large and he wore a standing collar, a white waistcoat and black coat and trousers. He talks with a French accent, which is not so marked when he forgets himself.

Ernest De Blanc has not half as much personal electricity as my cat, "Tippecanoe," has on a cold night. I knew his little scheme the moment he took me into his little parlor. It's the most simple thing imaginable. There is an electric battery concealed in the back hall, and a nickel-plated spring at the door by which he turns the electricity off and on. In the much worn rug which lies by the bed lounge are some connecting wires, very badly concealed, I must say. The rug is bound with rubber to make it non-conductive, to prevent the electricity from being transmitted to anything else. The rug is divided directly in the centre with a broad band of rubber. Very well, so far. Electricity is positive and negative. The Professor stands the patient on the side of the rug charged with the negative electricity. He goes into the hall, sees that his battery is all right, stops at the door, and in the face of his patient turns the nickel-plated knob, then plants himself directly on the side of the rug charged with the positive current. The patient feels the tingle of a slight shock, which he has the impudence and boldness to claim comes from his own body. It was such a glaring fraud that it made me disgusted. When people will deceive, why don't they do something well, so that it gives one some work to solve the trick?

This is not Prof. Ernest De Blanc's first effort in this line. A little of the history of his eventful career in America may prove interesting. The first account I could find of him was when he practiced his arts in Portland, Ore., under the name of Dr. Geismardo. While there he assaulted one of his woman patients and was imprisoned. Next I find he appeared in San José, Cal., where he suddenly left town with the money advanced for treatments which people never received.

HIS ESCAPE AT TOLEDO.

He was next heard of in Toledo, O., where he billed the town announcing his lecture and entertainment, but for some reason never appeared. He next worked Detroit, Mich., but his success was of short duration, as shown by the following clipping from the Detroit *Free Press*:

> It will probably be remembered that a man calling himself "Dr. A. E. Geismardo, the world-renowned electricity and magnetic healer," some time since advertised in this city that he would, with a talented company, present a play, written by himself, depicting his experience as a condemned felon and convict in the Oregon Penitentiary. He filled a brilliant engagement of one consecutive night at the Detroit Opera-House and then departed for fields and pastures new. On the 1st of this month he was lucky enough to marry at Chicago Mrs. Eva La Gay, a wealthy widow with one child. He immediately went on the road with his alleged drama and was forced to disband his company a day or two ago at Aurora, Ill. There are any number of suits against him, and he has disappeared, leaving no trace behind.

HE TURNS UP AT BUFFALO.

No longer ago than July 7 he made his appearance in Buffalo under the name of Prof. Albert Le Grand. His record there is briefly told in the following telegram clipped from the Chicago *Herald*. The substance of it appeared in the New York newspapers at the same time:

> BUFFALO, July 7.—Dr. Edward Storck, Chairman of the Erie County Medical Censors, to-day gave "Prof." Albert LeGrand notice to leave town or be arrested for practicing without a diploma. LeGrand gave free lectures in Music Hall and claimed to cure the lame, halt and blind in Biblical fashion. Dr. Storck said: "Prof. Le Grand has decided to leave the city within twenty-four hours. He admitted to me that he had no diploma, and that he was no physician, but a healer. When I asked him if he did not take fees he said that he did. Then, after a good deal of bluster, he gave in. I have learned some of his history. He was a Dr. Geismardo in Portland, Ore., and claimed to be a member of the Society of Sciences of Paris. He also exhibited a decoration, which he claimed to be a cross of the Legion of Honor. He left that city under a cloud, as he was arrested for criminally assaulting a woman patient. He then turned up in Denver, St. Louis, Kansas City, Baltimore and Boston. He was also arrested in Milwaukee. The society could prosecute him here if it wished to, but if he leaves the city that will be enough. Le Grand speaks French fluently and owned up to me that his magnetic touch was caused by an electric belt concealed in the palm of his hand. He had three or four dummies travelling with him who came upon the platform and were cured by him.

In a surprisingly short time afterwards Dr. Geismardo, alias Dr. Albert Le Grand, turned up in New Orleans and advertised himself extensively in the local papers. This was on July 20. He found little mercy there, and after he had spent some $300 in advertising, renting the St. Charles Theatre and paying for rooms and board in advance for himself and his wife, he had to flee the town to escape imprisonment for swindling a New Orleans man some fourteen years before.

SWINDLE IN NEW ORLEANS.

Mr. Chas. D. Lafferranderie, a reputable business man, of New Orleans, says that in January, 1874, there arrived in New Orleans, from Antwerp, a person calling himself Aaron Geismar. Through a common friend Mr. Lafferanderie became acquainted with Geismar. Geismar pretended to be the only child of very wealthy parents, his father being engaged in the ship-chandlery business at Antwerp. He had had a disagreement with his father, so he said, and for that reason had left home, but was given a large allowance by his indulgent parents. Geismar's card contained a full-rigged ship and was printed in both French and English. The latter was:

> Aaron Geismar, To office Knai du Rhin 46 warehouse and store. Digal de Terre, street 31 next to water police, Antwerp. Dealer in old rags, chokens, and old hemp, rop, manlila rop, canvas and old sails, etc., of all kinds paper stock. They heyst price will be payt for it.

So winning and persuasive did Geismar prove himself that when he proposed a partnership in the ship-chandler's business in that city between himself and Mr. Lafferranderie it was gladly accepted. It was agreed, by reason of Geismar's long apprenticeship in his father's shop, that he should come to New York to make the necessary purchases. As a proof of good faith, Lafferranderie was to advance Geismar $100 before his departure, and on receipt of the invoices and the policy of insurance upon the merchandise, forwarded by a reliable New York firm, Geismar would receive a draft of $400.

The result of that transaction I find in the New Orleans *Times-Democrat*:

> In the course of time a receipted bill was received by Lafferanderie, made out to Geismar & Lafferanderie, New Orleans, from Messrs. Baldwin, Hought & Co., No. 66 Sixth avenue, New York, for $1,154.75. The bill was dated New York, Feb. 9, 1874, and stated on its face, "less received for cash on account, $754.75," leaving a balance due of $400.
>
> This was followed by a policy of insurance of the Atlantic and Mutual Insurance Company, No. 55,153, made to Geismar & Lafferanderie, and was stated to cover a shipment of horseshoe nails and other goods shipped upon the steamer Western Metropolis. The policy was signed by J.H. Chapman, Secretary, and W.U.U. Moore, President.
>
> Upon the back was indorsed as follows:
>
> Insurance for $1,150 at 1½.........$14.37
> Policy.........1.25
> $15.62
>
> Record 58, folio 17.
>
> It was signed Feb. 9, 1874. On receipt of these documents Mr. Lafferanderie sent $400 by wire Feb. 14, the receipt for which was shown to the reporter, and bore the signature of J.T. Alleyn, cashier, for manager.
>
> Mr. Lafferranderie then bided the arrival of the goods, which he has been doing ever since.
>
> They never came to hand, and subsequent investigations revealed the fact that the letters purporting to have come from the New York firms were forgeries, as were also the invoices and the policy of insurance. They had all emanated from the brain of Aron Geismar, who had violated the trust and confidence placed within his hands by a too-confiding fellow-countryman.

FOLLOWING UP THE SCOUNDREL.

Mr. Lafferranderie saw a picture of the "Professor" in the Toledo *Bee*, and recognized it as the face of the man who had swindled him. The picture in the newspaper was compared with the photograph in his possession, and though it had been taken years before, they were identical. Mr. Lafferanderie had made an effort to trace the swindling Geismar, and while doing so he learned that he was practicing medicine out West. This was conclusive.

Yet, in order to make no mistake Mr. Lafferanderie called on Prof. Albert Le Grand, pretending he wished to be doctored. The recognition was mutual. Prof. Albert Le Grand, alias Dr. Geismardo and Aron Geismar were one and the same. Mr. Lafferranderie went to make out an affidavit, but before his return Prof. Albert Le Grand had fled the town. He did not even wait to take his electric battery along, but his wife, who professed ignorance as to his place of abode, took it in charge. Thus there was no exhibition at the St. Charles Theatre and numbers of poor people escaped being swindled.

Aron Geismar, alias Dr. Geismardo, alias Prof. Albert Le Grand, alias Prof. Ernest De Blank, is not an over clever swindler. Notice these peculiar wordings in his advertisement for Brooklyn and that for New Orleans.

HIS ADVERTISING SCHEMES.

First: "Admission Free!" appears conspicuously in both.

Second: "No objectionable person, boys or children admitted to this refined lecture and exhibition." Brooklyn advertisement.

"No objectionable person, nor boys nor children admitted to this refined exhibition." New Orleans advertisement.

Third: "Prof. Ernest De Blanc, the famous chevalier electrician of Paris." Brooklyn advertisement.

"Prof. Albert Le Grand, the famous world-renowned Healer and Electrician of Paris, France." New Orleans advertisement.

The following are samples of his advertisements:

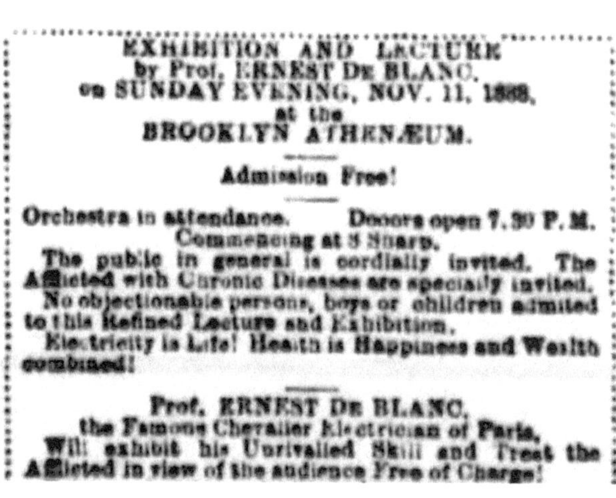

EXHIBITION AND LECTURE
by Prof. ERNEST DE BLANC,
on SUNDAY EVENING, NOV. 11, 1888,
at the
BROOKLYN ATHENÆUM.

Admission Free!

Orchestra in attendance. Doors open 7.30 P. M.
Commencing at 8 Sharp.

The public in general is cordially invited. The Afflicted with Chronic Diseases are specially invited.

No objectionable persons, boys or children admited to this Refined Lecture and Exhibition.

Electricity is Life! Health is Happiness and Wealth combined!

Prof. ERNEST DE BLANC,
the Famous Chevalier Electrician of Paris,
Will exhibit his Unrivalled Skill and Treat the Afflicted in view of the audience Free of Charge!

Patients desiring to be treated by medicine or surgery not accepted.

Diseases treated without medicine and without surgery.

Prof. ERNEST DE BLANC
is now permanently located at No. 87 Ashland place, (formerly Raymond street), near Fulton street, Brooklyn, N. Y.

At New Orleans this was his method of advertising, and is just about the same thing he had adopted for Brooklyn:

ST. CHARLES THEATRE, NEW ORLEANS.
ON SUNDAY, JULY 22, 1888.
ADMISSION FREE.
Come One! Come All! Free!
Commencing 8 P. M. sharp. Doors open 7.30 P. M.
Only one performance in this city. No objectionable persons, nor boys or children admitted to this Refined Exhibition. Full Orchestra in attendance.

PROF. ALBERT LE GRAND,
THE FAMOUS WORLD-RENOWNED HEALER AND ELECTRICIAN OF PARIS, FRANCE.

CONSULTATION FREE!
Diseases Cured Without Medicine and Without Any Surgery.
SPECIAL TERMS FOR THE WORKING-CLASS PATIENTS.

THE POOL OF SILOAM.

THE LAME WALK, THE BLIND SEE AND THE DEAF HEAR AT TREMONT TEMPLE.

Prof. Albert Le Grand is now located for sixty days at No. 14 University Place, formerly Dryades street, New Orleans.

I think I have given enough to show that Prof. De Blanc is a swindler, and of the meanest kind, inasmuch as his victims are among the sick and ignorant. If this exposure saves one such person from expending his hard earned money on Geismar's quackery I shall feel that my work has not been in vain.

NELLIE BLY

Editor's Note: Should Women Propose?

Alice Mona Caird, an English feminist writer engaged with Suffragist movement, wrote a number of novels with subjects such as marital rape, the harmful effects of expecting women to be self-sacrificing, and the idea of career potentially being more rewarding for a woman than marriage.

In August of 1888, she penned an essay entitled "Marriage" for the Westminster Review. *In this essay Caird writes about woman being "punished for all sins and errors with a ferocity and a persistence specially reserved for a sex which is called weak ... Truly the fate of woman, in its injustice, its debasement and humiliating pain, is a tragedy such as Shakespeare never wrote nor Aeschylus dreamt of."*

Though very few people read the Westminster Review, *the much more popular* Daily Telegraph *used Caird's provocative essay as the launching point to debate the question "Is Marriage A Failure?" Printing selected excerpts of Caird's essay, with lengthy, un-edited rebuttal by anti-Suffrage activist Lynn Linton, the* Telegraph *opened up the question to the public, thus instigating the Great Marriage Debate of 1888.*

The Telegraph *received over 27,000 replies, everything from philosophical to complaints of a husband who kept putting his feet upon the mantel-place. They said that "four fifths of it was chaff, but the remainder sincerely written." The question became one of two great obsessions in the Fall of 1888 (the other, in an example of grim irony, being the Whitechapel murders). The responses varied according to sympathy. Several women weighed in with serious and sober consideration, while male wags and opponents of Women's Rights mocked the very posing of the question.*

The question soon went international. In Scotland, the debate evidently inspired Robert Lewis Stevenson's novel The Enchantress. *In Ireland, the* Belfast News-Letter *gave an award for the best epigrammatic answers to the question. Here are two winning entries:*

> *"What! marriage a failure?—ridiculous stuff!"*
> *Said a maid of eighteen as she read the D.T.;*
> *"The writer is surely some chap in a huff*
> *Who has just been dismissed by a charmer like me."*
>
> *O! ladies, ladies, wherefore this outcry?*
> *Shed no more ink, but wipe thy pensive eye.*
> *Know that we males are only one in ten;*
> *Marriage has not failed you-it is men.*

In America, the question was grist for columnists and letter writers from Chicago to Topeka, from Buffalo to St. Paul. In September Bly's own newspaper, the New York World, *asked this question of its readers with tongue firmly in cheek: "Is Bachelorhood A Success?" And it ran a cartoon where Belle asks her pal Dolly if marriage is a failure, and Dolly replies, "No, not while juries continue to give substantial verdicts in breach-of-promise suits."*

Bly was doubtless encouraged by her editors to leap into the fray. However, she might have felt she had covered this topic in her early piece for the Pittsburg Dispatch entitled "Mad Marriages." Not being married herself, she decided to pose a different, if related, query: "Should Women Propose?"

Belle (who is engaged to Mr. Porkprince)—Dolly, is marriage a failure?
Dolly—No, not while juries continue to give substantial verdicts in breach-of-promise suits.

The question was in the air because of the date. 1888 was a Leap Year, and therefore jocularly known as the traditional opportunity for women to propose marriage to men.

This stems from a tradition called Bachelor's Day, sometimes known as Ladies' Privilege. According to this, on Leap Day (February 29) women are allowed to propose to men. Apparently it is based upon a legend of Saint Bridget going to Saint Patrick to complain that men were too slow to propose, and begging for one day in the calendar year when a woman might propose to a man. Supposedly, Saint Patrick countered, suggesting one day every seven years, but Saint Bridget argued him down to one day every four years.

As silly as this legend is, it once had legal basis in Scotland. In 1288, the Queen passed a law that women were allowed to propose to men during Leap Year: "It is stated and ordained that during the reign of her most blessed Majesty, for every year known as Leap Year, every maiden lady of both high and low estate shall have liberty to bespeak the man she likes. But if he refuses to take her to be his lawful wife, he shall be fined in the sum of one pound or less, as his estate may be."

A similar law was passed in France a few years later, and in Italy in the fifteenth century. According to the Every Woman's Encyclopedia from 1912, "in one year alone in Genoa no fewer than 363 prosecutions were instituted against ungallant gallants who had declined the proposals of certain fair damsels."

Almost always this tradition is invoked for humor. A March 21, 1916 edition of The Evening Dispatch of Wilmington, NC, reports that Henry VIII's court jester, Will Sommers, once amused the king by having all the maids in the palace propose to the jester on Leap Day, totally ignoring the king (though I can find no source for the newspaper's fanciful account). In the twentieth century this day became known as Sadie Hawkin's Day, based on the Al Capp comic strip "Li'l Abner" (hence modern Sadie Hawkin's dances). Leap Year being the time for women to propose was referenced in 1944 in an Abbott and Costello radio sketch starring Judy Canova, and all the way up to a 1960 calendar depicting a terrified man fleeing a grasping bride. Always, women proposing was the basis for comedy.

Bly, however, is clearly in earnest in asking the question. She presents her case in the first article, then follows it up with both letters from and interviews with all kinds of people, from playwrights to politicians, including a lengthy and serious response from Belva Lockwood.

Her question was picked up by papers across the country, making perhaps her biggest national splash of 1888. As you shall see, in the course of three weeks Bly herself journeys from encouraged to not a little dismayed by the resulting answers—especially when one enterprising young woman takes Bly's advice and proposes!

Should Women Propose?

Sunday, November 11, 1888

Nellie Bly Advances Arguments In The Affirmative

She Thinks It Is Not Fair for Women to Have to Sit Around and Wait for a Proposal—Mr. Depew Agrees, with His Characteristic Courtesy—Mrs. Frank Leslie Scouts the Idea as Preposterous.

Should women propose?

Leap year is rapidly nearing its end. The unlucky girl who does not win her other soul—her mate—before midnight of Dec. 31 will have to wait three weary years for the right to propose. Is it just? In this day of almost equal rights, when women fill the same positions—yes, and ably too—which were considered man's and man's alone, is it just that women shall not have the right to propose?

Is it just that an able (woman) lawyer shall be allowed to plead for everything except the hand of the man she loves? Is it just that a skillful (woman) surgeon shall dress all wounds except those to her own feelings? Or set all fractures save those of her own heart? Is it just that an eloquent (woman) minister shall teach the way to paradise to others and yet not make a way for herself to woman's heaven? Shall a (woman) dentist fill your teeth and not ask to fill some good man's home and life? Shall a (woman) artist have no right to paint her portrait on some man's heart? Shall a (woman) sculptor not model a Cupid to do her bidding? Shall (women) writers only woo imaginary people in their studies—propose only in stories?

In the days of barbarism, when men stood off and made their selections and afterwards consummated the bargain with the father; or even in the days of our gentle great and great-great grandmothers, whose golden chains and rings were fit emblems of their slavery—when women were animated dolls, having no will but their lord's, having no thoughts of their own—when they were dressed, curled, driven, then it would have been sheer folly to ask such a question.

Women are not confined to their homes now, lamentable or otherwise as different persons may deem the fact. They are in the world—are of it. They write, think, drive and work like men. Should they not, then, have an equal right to propose marriage?

THE PRESIDENT OF THE HOUSEHOLD.

What gives a man the sole right to ask the one he loves to wed him? Does merely being a man make him the more fitted to ask such a question? When one sifts the subject one finds that the greater responsibilities of a home rest on the woman. Should not this fact alone grant her the right to do what she can to secure the man of her choice to share her domestic throne? She is the hub of the wheel in every home. She has charge of the cook, she economizes, she bears the children, watches over their thousand wants, not little ones either; she makes her boys a credit to her family and honorable citizens, or otherwise; the future of her daughters is in her hands; her husband's happiness, his buttons and his comfort generally are under her control. She is the president of the household, her husband the secretary of the treasury. With all this in mind, who shall say that women should not have the right to propose?

Everything in life, and some say afterwards, hinges on love. "Love is life's end; an end, but never ending." It's the mainspring to everything, from a tragedy to a bonnet, and it often even flavors our soup. Shall a woman love and die of love and dare not breath it, or shall she woo? Many women have died old maids because some man courted too long, kept others away and did not propose marriage himself. Such cases are frequent and the girl is always the one who suffers therefrom. If every woman were as straightforward as Juliet, and when men began to pay her idle compliments brought them up to a standstill with a "If thou lovest, pronounce it faithfully," and if he thinks her "too quickly won" she'll "frown and be perverse, else not for the world," people would be better and happier. The rules which govern women in love teach them deceit and to deceive. They debase all that is lovely in woman's character for that very reason. The social rules which govern love teach a girl to hide every sincere feeling and to pretend what she does not feel, yet those who would be first to cry "Shame!" at a woman for deceit would be the first to cry "Bold!" if she gave evidence of her true feelings.

There would be fewer unhappy marriages, fewer divorces and fewer melancholy women if women had the right to propose. I remember when I attended Sunday-school that I was taught "Ask and it shall be given unto you," but I don't know that it was meant for women. I decided to ask the opinion of several people on the subject and then leave the question open to the readers of THE WORLD.

WHAT CHAUNCEY DEPEW THINKS.

First I went to see Mr. Chauncey M. Depew at the Grand Central Depot. I sent my card in and in a few moments was requested to "step this way." I did so and found myself in a room furnished comfortably, but in business-like fashion. Not quite in the centre of the room, but standing distinct and alone, was a desk. In a chair before it, swung half facing the door, sat Chauncey M. Depew, whose handsome, genial face is as familiar to the reading public as that of any President of the United States. Of all the men in public life this noted after-dinner speaker is recognized as the most courteous to newspaper people. I don't think Mr. Depew could be rude or unkind if he wished to.

"And is this Nellie Bly?" he asked, arising from his chair and taking both my hands in a cordial grasp.

I admitted that I was responsible for that person, and continued:

"I have just come to get your opinion on a certain subject which doubtless you will think very silly. It is this"—I took a long breath—"should women propose?"

Mr. Depew gazed at me a moment with a look of surprise in which I detected a faint trace of alarm, then he burst into a hearty laugh. He bent over, lacing his hands on his knees, and laughed until his gold eye-glasses tumbled off. A man sitting on the other side of the room with a large book on his knee joined in, and somehow I began to feel awkward.

"I am not going to propose," I made haste to add, "but really, now, when we have women who do everything as ably as men, don't you think that they should have the right to propose?"

"I do indeed," he replied earnestly, straightening up. "But there are prejudices against it which will not likely be overcome."

"You do not entertain any?"

"No, no; certainly not"—still smiling.

"Then you believe in women proposing?"

"I do." His eyes twinkled, but his tone was serious. "Proposing cost me ten years of my life. I would have lived just ten years longer if I had not proposed. It took me a year to get my courage up to the point. I most certainly believe in women taking that privilege from the men."

"I suppose you feel happy over the election?" I said, forgetting for an instant the main subject of the interview.

"Oh, yes, yes," he replied, pleasantly. "Why don't you telegraph Gen. Harrison and ask him if women should propose?"

"He would be too busy just now answering congratulations to find time to answer my question," I said. "Now, if women would propose," going back to the old subject, "do you think the men would be so ungenerous as to laugh at them or to refuse them?"

MR. DEPEW ILLUSTRATES WITH A STORY.

"Oh, no; they would never do that." His eyes gleamed roguishly. "That reminds me of a friend of mine—I never tell stories, but I'll tell this one. He was lecturing in some small town out West. In the midst of his talk, a number of young girls in the back part of the house began to giggle and laugh; so one of the men, who was conducting the meeting, arose and requested them to please keep better order in the back part of the room. A young man who was sitting by the girls got up and said, 'Please excuse the girls, they couldn't help laughing, 'cause a hornet has just stung me.' Now if the hornet had stung the girls the men would not have laughed, but would have applied the remedies usual in such cases."

Somehow, when I went out, and especially as I had never been stung by a hornet, I wondered what the remedies were for such wounds.

Mrs. Frank Leslie was resting her elbow on a desk, which is thoroughly businesslike in every respect, when I entered her private office. I said:

"Mrs. Leslie, we are going to discuss a question in THE WORLD, and I would like to have your opinion on the subject."

"Yes; I was just reading a lot of clippings containing my opinions on various subjects, and here is one," lifting up one from the desk, "which describes what my mouth is like."

"This question is quite important in this day of almost equal rights," I continued. "Should women propose?"

"Oh!" she exclaimed, and then she laughed. "What an idea! Brigham Young once said that he wished all women had the right to propose."

"And what do you think?"

"Well, I don't think so," she replied, slowly. "The more womanly a woman is, the sweeter she is. Let the men keep that right. It is much easier to use the right of refusal or acceptance than that of proposing."

"Don't you think a woman has as much right as a man to woo?" I urged.

MRS. LESLIE DISCRIMINATES.

"Yes," with a smile, "and she can do it with her eyes and with the thousand little ways she knows so well how to employ, but let her lips be silent."

"But don't you think if women could propose they would more often get those they love?"

"Doubtless, but they must not do it, for it means death," she said earnestly.

"How so?"

"Why, if a man should refuse a woman she would never be satisfied until she killed him. I know I would not," with a tap of her tiny foot.

"Would he dare—would he have the courage to refuse her?" I asked.

"I don't think he would," she smiled. "Then think how wretched a woman would be. She would always fear that he wanted to refuse but did not dare."

We both laughed at this view of the question, and then I said again:

"So you do not believe in a woman having that right?"

"No; let her be as womanly as she can," she said, firmly. "If I had my life to live over, and I know if you had the choosing of yours, we would both prefer a quiet home, obscurity, no knowledge of the world, and no rights except those of a mother and a wife."

I had nothing more to say.

MAYOR-ELECT GRANT FRIGHTENED.

Mr. Hugh J. Grant, the new Mayor, is a tall, handsome man, blessed with all the qualities which endear men to women, yet he is a bachelor. I believe it is only because he is too bashful to propose even if he were in love. I met him in his office two days after his election.

"Before you go," I began, "I want to ask you—Do you think that women should propose?" He almost fell back against the bookcase and his face flushed so red that I was frightened at my own boldness.

"I have often wondered why some one did not propose to me," he said, still flushing deeply.

"Oh, you are not married," I exclaimed. I never knew it until then.

"No," he said, making his way to the door, and I was just as frightened over it as he was.

I went to the stage door of Palmer's Theatre and gave my card to a man who was sitting in a little dimly lighted box to take to Mr. W. H. Gillette. I thought I would like to have the opinion of America's most successful playwright on the subject.

"Miss Bly," I heard called. I looked, and I saw Mr. Gillette leaning on the partition at the head of the uncarpeted stairs. "Will you come up here, or shall I go down?"

"Oh, I will go up," I replied.

"I just wrote you a note," he said, pointing the way to his room, "telling you that I had a long wait later in the evening when you might come, but that I was never interviewed. I always interview. But sit down. You take the chair. I'll sit on this trunk."

"I have come just to ask you one little question," I said, shortly. "Should women propose?"

"It depends on what they propose," he said, crossing one leg over the other and smiling as if he had me cornered.

"Marriage, of course. Should a woman have the right to propose marriage?"

"Yes," with a drawl, "I think she should do all the proposing."

"Really?"

"Yes, really."

MEN ARE NEVER MEAN.

"Do you think the men would be mean enough to say to her afterwards, 'Well, you married me, I didn't marry you,' and all that sort of thing."

"No, no man would ever be so mean," he said, with a laugh.

"Well I am glad you think so and I'm glad you say women should propose."

"Do you want my candid opinion?" he said. "Do you want me to tell you what I really believe?"

"I do, indeed."

"Well, I'll tell you my candid opinion if you will promise to ask me no more questions." I promised.

"You know the story of the one-armed man who worked around a railroad station. Everybody annoyed him by asking him how he lost his arm, so one day he said to a questioner, 'I'll tell you how I lost my arm if you promise to ask me no more questions.' The man promised. 'It was bit off,' he said."

"Then what is your candid opinion?" I asked, answering his smile.

"There should be no such thing—there should be no proposing."

Hum! I bit my lips. He had my promise and I was helpless.

So it rests. Shall women propose, or shall they always tune their harps and sing:

> "Never wedding, ever wooing,
> Still a love-lorn heart pursuing.
> Read you not the wrong you're doing
> In my cheek's pale hue?
> All my life with sorrow strewing;
> Wed, or cease to woo."

NELLIE BLY

Should Women Propose?

Sunday, November 18, 1888

Many Notable People Send Answers To Nellie Bly's Question

Miss Kate Field Says She is a Social Mugwump—Belva Lockwood Writes A Characteristic Letter, and Bill Nye Says He Is Already Provided For—Jenny June Wants No Such Innovation—Marshall Wilder Sees a Chance for Himself.

"Should women propose?"

I was hoisted on a very slow elevator one day last week to Miss Kate Field's eyrie in the Victoria Hotel. I unbuttoned my coat and launched that all-absorbing question at her. Her bright eyes danced and seemed to say she was glad to have a chance to vent her opinion on me. She glanced about at the dainty womanish trifles with which she has brightened up her apartment and then settled herself in an attitude of luxurious laziness in a reclining chair, her soft, red gown falling in graceful folds about her.

"What is the matter with New York?" she asked slowly. "Matrimony seems to provide the atmosphere. Is that the reason we have had such exceptionally warm weather recently? No sooner had I arrived from the glorious climate of California than a noble and manly reporter looked me calmly but firmly in the eye and asked me if marriage were a failure. What did I know about it? I'd had no personal experience. 'The very reason your opinion is valuable,' argued the logical reporter. 'It is because you don't know, that you are unprejudiced.' I confessed I did not see the force of this remark, but as our most enlightened and supposititiously beneficent jury system is founded on the same reasoning I yielded to this tempter and told what I didn't know anything about, save as 'a looker-on in Vienna,' and now you, a woman of THE WORLD, as calmly and firmly ask me if I think women ought to propose for this same stake of marriage, which so many are pronouncing a failure."

Miss Field tapped the arm of her chair with her right hand—a pretty little hand, on which sparkled some costly gems. Somehow I began to feel that she did not favor the proposition. I was ready to argue the question. "I can't say that there is any record of happy marriages," I remarked, "resulting from women proposing. Juliet's marriage was a failure—I always maintained that she began the proposal. Foolish Desdemona hinted so broadly—as Othello was mean enough to tell the Duke, and before all the people—that he had to propose. He boasted:

"She thanked me,
And bade me, if I had a friend that loved her,
I should but teach him how to tell my story,
And that would woo her. Upon this hint I spake."

"Yet the happiest marriage I ever knew of resulted from the woman proposing, and I think the world would be better if they did it more did more of it."

"If marriage is a failure, because men propose, it might be a good idea to give the woman a chance and see whether the returns are more favorable" replied Miss Field, with a smile. "We're to have a change of National Administration, and a general revolution, social as well as political, might purify the air. I was highly amused at the answers given by those to whom you put this awful conundrum in last Sunday's WORLD. One woman thought her sex should wait to be asked. All the men, save one, thought it would be time and money in their pockets if the present fashion were reversed. The soul male exception thought that there should be no proposals whatever! Does he want to get to heaven before his time? You know that in heaven there is neither marrying nor giving in marriage. Evidently Mr. Gillette does not wish to be 'Held by the Enemy.' This is very ungrateful in him, considering what the 'Enemy' has done for his fame and fortune."

A SOCIAL MUGWUMP.

"So you don't believe in women proposing?"

"You know in a republic we are supposed to except the will of the majority," Miss Field said. "As the majority of those interviewed declare that women are to propose, perhaps I should agree with them, but I don't. I am a Social Mugwump and think people should do as they please, providing they harm no one else in the doing. It's absurd to suppose that women have not proposed from time immemorial. Of course we except our first parents, for Adam and Eve could not help themselves. It was 'Hobson's choice.' A woman proposes when she indicates in every tone, and look, and gesture that she prefers one man to all others. A man does the same thing. As there are songs without words, so there are proposals without words, and it is this kind of proposal that women have been making from the beginning of creation."

"Don't you think there are times when a woman is justified in proposing?" I asked mildly.

"I can conceive of situations in which it would he not only proper but perhaps necessary for the woman to speak first, where she has the power, or the wealth, or both, and he has too much pride of sex to tell the story of his heart," she said thoughtfully. "It is natural that a man should wish to give and not receive—though heaven knows you would not think so from the way heiresses are pursued—but I am talking of men who are worthy of the name."

"Don't you think women would fear a possible refusal too much to propose?"

"Be assured that a woman who proposed would know her lover's secret before disclosing her own," she said, with a smile. "Words are the final expression of love, and men and women are tolerably certain of each other before the era of proposals. Unless attraction is mutual there should be no proposal, and when it is both know it. There is nothing to be ashamed of in an honest affection."

"Do you think having this privilege would detract from her womanliness?" I ventured.

"I believe that the dangerous women are not those exceptions who from impulse or conviction have spoken first. But whether men or women propose is a purely individual matter and in no way concerning the public and none of my business."

HOW IT WOULD SUIT ACTORS.

Dion Boucicault writes me this outspoken letter:

> I am for sweeping away every vestige of slavery, let it present itself in what form it may. I hate a privileged class, I detest prejudices however respectable, and respectability itself ceases to be respectable when it protects a corporation of prejudices. My social experiences have been nearly exclusively confined to the stage, where, I feel glad to say, women have the best of it; where they are independent, and where, in the strict attendance to every duty, professional and social, I have noticed and recorded their steadily maintained superiority to the men

employed beside them.

Now, why an honest woman may not freely and honorably acknowledge her preference in selecting a partner for life, I cannot say. Why relegate her to a condition of organized hypocrisy, to exercise which her whole education is directed? She is taught to conceal all her nature, to lie to herself, and to regard perfection in her sex to be the art of concealment.

It is astonishing to me that there is any goodness or truth left in them. Yours faithfully,

DION BOUCICAULT

Mr. Boucicault's opinion, gained by a varied experience in the world, is about the same as expressed by me in last Sunday's WORLD. The rules which govern women of the present day rob them of the loveliest thing in women's character—her truth. Why we ourselves should scorn women for showing that regard for some one and wilfully teach them that the only right way is to practice deceit and cunning is more than I can imagine. It is proper and good form to express everything but that which they honestly feel.

THE PRESIDENT OF SOROSIS SAYS YES.

Mrs. M. Louise Thomas, President of Sorosis, is a representative woman. Her heart is large and charitable and knows no malice. Her life is spent in doing deeds of charity and kindness, and she judges the wrong-doer and those who fall with leniency and gentleness. Every act of hers is motherly, sweet and gentle. See what she says:

You ask me, "Should women propose?" Well, I know of no reason why they should not if they wish to do so, excepting only the unwritten law of usage, which, in this country and at this period of its history, is just no law at all. I do not believe it is to be so uncommon for the proposal of marriage to come from the woman as many may suppose. I have known of many, and I have never known of one wherein the marriage following was not a happy one, from the gentle Puritan maiden, Priscilla, who said to her proxy wooer, "And why not speak for thyself, John Alden?" down to the bride of last year.

An honorable man can confer no higher honor upon a woman than to ask her to become his wife, and I cannot think the distinction would be any less if it should come from the other side if true affection binds them together. The man or the woman who would brag and boast of such experience, with power of refusal, either before marriage or after, is not to be counted in the realm of the true-hearted. Mistakes in mating, together with sharp words and cruel taunts, are too common within the marriage tie for any one to claim that they could be made any worse or harder to bear if to either man or woman should be given

> the sole right of proposal. I believe in the happy marriage without regard to which proposes.
>
> M. LOUISE THOMAS.

This is encouraging. Mrs. Thomas has known of many marriages resulting from the woman proposing, and she has never known of one wherein the marriage following has not been a happy one. If woman had the right of proposal she would not be so apt to accept the first proposal—whether she loved or not—for fear she would never receive another. If I were a man I would have very harrowing doubts about a woman's love if I were the first to propose to her.

BILL NYE HAS NO OBJECTION.

Bill Nye write me the following letter on the subject:

> I do not see why woman should not propose if she so elect, and then suffer the bitter, bitter consequences. Many men who now live on unloved and in a hand-to-mouth manner might be oh, so happy! if the onus of popping did not weigh them down like a large three-cornered incubus.
>
> I am acquainted with several husbands who have been thus acquired and I am happy to say they are turning out well. Several of them who were not self-supporting to start with have married well, having been wooed and won by girls of means. Yours truly,
>
> BILL NYE.
>
> P. S.—I am provided for myself.
>
> P. S. Again.—Mr. James Whitcomb Riley, who, as I write, is brushing his hair with a dummy brush which I carry with me, says he trusts that the day will speedily come when women will propose, and he hopes he will be away up towards the general-delivery window when the office opens. Some good woman could make Mr. Riley very, very happy. Any letter sent to him in my care will be cheerfully read and forwarded it to him.
>
> B.N.

If Mr. Nye's letter does not encourage some girl who thinks the "bitter, bitter consequence, is not any bitterer because of her doing the proposing to utilize her very short time to receive an engagement ring for a Christmas present, I can't see what will. Mr. Nye's marriage certificate seems to hover around his first "P. S." like bumble-bees around clover, but there is a chance for some good woman with Mr. Riley. For those who have not seen him I can vouch for him. He is a handsome and genial gentleman.

BELVA LOCKWOOD'S STRONG VIEWS.

Mrs. Belva A. Lockwood, the Presidential candidate of the Equal Rights party, who has done so much in educating the world into seeing that women are capable creatures, and who reflects so much credit on the sex by the manner in which her last campaign was conducted, writes me as follows:

> Why not? In the ages past men have married their preferences; women, their opportunities. The man may choose, the woman refuse, but she refuses at her peril, as her decision may condemn her to a life of celibacy, especially in our thickly populated New England or Middle States, where the women outnumber the men. The man she accepts may be in no wise the man of her choice; but it may be a marriage of complaisance, of convenience or of necessity under our present system, while the woman looks calmly on to see another fill the place that she has coveted, without any intimation in the male breast of her desire, when a little more frankness on the part of the woman might have added to the happiness of both. A woman would be slow to make application for divorce from the man who had married her on her own calm deliberation and request; while the positive privilege of making another selection should he refuse—and the man should have the same right of refusal as the woman—would give her confidence to approach the man whom she deemed best suited to her condition and happiness. Matches would be more carefully made when considered from both standpoints, and the glamour and indefiniteness that usually hedged around a proposal would be wiped away in the cool consideration of a mutual business contract.
>
> And why should the woman not have a voice and a choice in the man who is to be her life partner—the father of her children, and who is most likely to give the tone and color to all her after life? The majority of women never rise above the character given to them by the man whom they chance to wed, for chance in the past has usually had more to do with marriage than reason. The Catholics make marriage a canon of the Church and indissoluble, but it is considered in most of the States as a civil contract. It should undoubtedly be a civil contract with the utmost mutuality, with both of the contracting parties at liberty to propose and to reject proposals without offense and without any violation of any of the ordinary rules of propriety. This contract should also be construed to contain equal property rights for the man and the woman, and an equal control over the children of the marriage. Why should the woman have more diffidence in selecting the man who is to wed her than in the selection of the house she is to live in and its intricate furnishings when the former has infinitely so much more to do with her happiness and prosperity?
>
> To propose has always been considered the prerogative of queens,

but in this respect every American woman should consider herself a queen. It was not until Queen Victoria had signified to Prince Albert that a proposal from him would be favorably received that he ventured to make advances to that honored lady. Queen Elizabeth, years before, had claimed the right of proposal as England's sovereign Queen. The incident recited in Scripture between Ruth and Boaz, after the day of gleaning in the field, was virtually a proposal by Ruth.

After the formulating of the Gregorian Calendar in 1582, giving to every fourth-year 366 days, it was accounted proper for women to propose every fourth or leap year, but so much facetiousness and ridicule has attached to it, that the customer has been more honored in the breach than in its observance. At this time, when we concede to women equal educational facilities; have arrived at a proximate equality in property rights; have given to her to a limited extent of the ballot and the privilege of holding office; when the trades and the professions are so far thrown open to her that she may compete with man in money-making and money-getting, I can see no good reason why she may not under suitable circumstances propose; but the proposal on her part would always carry with it the tacit agreement to perform her part in the domestic economy of the household. The right of proposal vouchsafed to women would undoubtedly have a moral tendency.

BELVA A. LOCKWOOD.
WASHINGTON, DC, NOV. 13.

Mrs. Lockwood, who is a lawyer, is able to present the case clearly. She certainly advances some new ideas. What slaves are women if they may select their homes but not their husbands! The divorce question which is discussed so much, Mrs. Lockwood thinks would make less trouble if women proposed.

Mr. Lawrence Barrett, in a graceful little letter, confesses himself a poor judge. He writes:

I am a poor judge of the subject contained in your question. I think, perhaps, the matter is quite as well as it is. If women do not propose, they at all events certainly dispose, for good or ill. Yours faithfully,

LAWRENCE BARRETT.

JENNIE JUNE SAYS NO.

Mrs. Jennie June Croly, who was the first woman to make a success in newspaper work, writes the following thoughtful letter:

I certainly do not think it necessary for women to do any proposing. I think they are altogether too ready to except proposals made to them. If I could exert any influence it would be to induce them to refuse all proposals for twelve months at least; and thereafter, until they brought

> men to their knees—where it would be good for them to once in a while find themselves. George Eliot says: "The homage of a man is delightful until he asks for love, by which a woman renders homage." For women to sue and allow men to be wholly the recipients of this homage would be to deprive the woman of her birthright and reduce her still more to the subjection which her organization and motherhood lay upon her. There are plenty of ways in which a modest girl can show her preference without departing from the reserve and dignity which belong to and are the best defenses of her womanhood; and if a man does not avail himself of these indications he will not be likely to be reached by appeal or demands.
>
> As a rule men are precipitate when they are in earnest—they are mortally afraid of losing what they want—and do not allow any question which affects their own inclinations to remain long in suspense. Women would find them more ardent lovers if they held them in suspension for awhile; then, by at once reversing the situation and by eager acceptance, become themselves the worshipers.
>
> JENNIE JUNE.

Here is another chance for some girl. Humor seems to pine for a congenial mate:

> Yes, I believe in allowing women the right to propose marriage, for, between you and me, I fear that will be the only chance I will ever have to marry, and I am in a dreadful hurry to begin. Merrily yours,
>
> MARSHALL P. WILDER.

There are many interesting letters left over until next Sunday's WORLD. In the mean time the question is open to all—men, women, married and single—Should women propose?

NELLIE BLY

Should Women Propose?

Sunday, November 25, 1888

One Girl Has Taken Nellie Bly's Advice And Is Now Married

Gen. Butler Writes to Say That the Question No Longer Interests Him—E.H. Sothern Claims Exclusive Rights for Men—Dr. Talmage Says Women Have Always Exercised the Privilege.

Should women propose?

I am not a fairy godmother. If I were I would waive my wand and, with my blessing, say to all:

"Let common sense guide you. Do what your heart urges. If you think that you are going to lose a prize speak. Don't let false rules—nor any rules, for that matter—keep you from seizing happiness while it is within your reach."

But just imagine what a calamity it would be if people spoke their minds. Then novelists could not drag us through 450 pages of agonizing misery in order to make a man on the four hundred and fifty-first page tell a girl in two lines what he could have told her in the first chapter, "And live happily ever afterwards."

I am going to withdraw. I would rather be responsible for harmony in an opera chorus than responsible for a marriage. It's dreadful. Why, I would never say "yes" myself, because I haven't courage enough to be responsible even for my own marriage. And yet I have this to bear:

> I have always admired Nellie Bly ever since she told her first wonderful experience in The World, and now I love her.

> Miss Bly, I owe my happiness to you. I have loved a young man for a long time, and often have I been unhappy because he did not speak what I wanted to hear. He was too modest—being poorer than myself—to propose.
>
> I asked him if he had read your "Should women propose?" He said he had, and we began to discuss it. I cannot recall exactly how it occurred, but before many minutes I was in his arms, and we were betrothed and happy.
>
> I write you this to let you know that you are responsible for our great happiness. Nellie Bly shall always be a household word with us.

This wouldn't be so hard to bear if it were the end of it. But I shall be haunted with the thought that probably they were too hasty. Responsible or not, if the question, "Should women propose?" were to be decided by a majority women would undoubtedly be given the right to propose. Among the many letters which have come in I find the majority of the women are in favor of their rights being asserted, and the majority of men are urging that the privilege be given them. It is impossible in this edition to attempt to publish all the letters, but the subject has awakened interest among the married and single; even the cartoonist is touching it up with his expressive pencil.

Everybody throughout the land knows of general Benjamin F. Butler. Personally Gen. Butler is charming, his matter is dignified and courteous. He sent me the following letter:

> LAW OFFICES OF BENJ. F. BUTLER.
> Washburn & Webster, No. 6 Ashburton Place,
> Boston, Nov. 19, 1888.
>
> Dear Miss: You must excuse me from answering your question, "Should women propose marriage?" for I am past having any interest in it. Yours truly,
>
> BENJ. F. BUTLER.

"What do ministers think of women proposing?" a woman asked me last week. "They are supposed to be our guides and teachers. I should be guided by their opinions."

"You don't mean to say if ministers said it were right for you to propose you would do so, regardless of your own opinion?" I asked.

"Now, my dear," she laughed, "I did not propose. My husband did, and I am much too old to take personal interest in such things; but I do believe girls would not commit many improprieties or do much wrong if they were guided by their ministers. When the matter does not affect themselves they can generally give the best advice. It's a case of 'don't do as they do, but do as they say.'"

We can at least know what one eminent divine thinks of the subject:

> Should women propose? Why, you are centuries too late in asking that question. Women always have proposed and always will propose. Words are very weak things compared with womanly affability and loveliness. The most splendid being on earth is a good woman, and when, with all her attractiveness, she makes up her mind that it would be well for her to be the wife of some good man and that it would be equally well for him she captures him as easily as a regiment captures one corporal. It does not make any difference whether her tongue proposes or not, her eyes propose, her smile proposes, her mode of entering a room proposes.
>
> Until a man gets from a woman a proposition of that style he had better not make a proposition of his own unless he wants to be made to feel ridiculous the rest of his lifetime. Yours, &c.,
>
> T. DE WITT TALMAGE.

A young woman in the following letter thinks with Rev. Dr. Talmage in his opinion that "women always did and always will propose:"

> In answer to the invitation extended it to the public to express its opinion as to whether women should propose, I beg to answer in the negative. It is my opinion that if the first woman had not been so ready to propose the rest of her sex need not be troubled with this question to-day. We are told that we would be still dwelling within the walls of Paradise to-day if our first parents had not eaten of the forbidden fruit. Eve proposed to Adam that they eat of it. They did, and we see the consequences.
>
> If Madame Eve had not been so willful we would not have to worry about proposing, for "matches are made in heaven;" so our matches would be made in Paradise.
>
> A good woman is like a flower blooming upon the dreary way of life; let her then be womanly; if there is anything we dislike it is a womanly man or a man-like woman, and surely to propose is not womanly. Why should they propose? Surely if the man loves her he will take that duty upon himself. He is timid, you say. Well, to that I reply, "Faint heart never won fair lady," and if he has not enough courage to ask a woman who, he has reason to believe, loves him, well, then, he is not worth having. And she? Women have a thousand little arts by which to tell in eloquent silence of their love. The eyes are the windows of the soul, and if you see a woman follow you with her eyes full of tender light or gives a quick laughing but loving glance into yours; if she says she has missed you, if she tells you she has dreams of you, if she likes to talk with you more than any one else, or looks pleased when you sit with her, be sure she loves you. Tennyson has written how the Lord of Burleigh proposed:

In her ear he whispered gayly,
"If my heart by signs can tell,
Maiden, I have watched thee daily,
And I think thou lovest me well."

Yes, by signs we can tell; that is, if she is like the Lord's lady-love, a good, artless girl, not a fashionable flirt.

A good, pure girl may give these signs without over-stepping the bounds of modesty; and a good, pure girl would rather die in silence than express her love in so many words. Miss Cory tells us:

'Tis hardly worth the proving,
We often give our hearts away,
And are not loved for loving.

I would as soon go into a man's house and propose to be his cook or scrub-girl as to ask to be his wife. I hope we will always be able to be independent enough to hold our own and support ourselves without asking any man to do it; that is well enough for the English, who are under the impression that it is degrading for women to work outside their homes, and therefore the women are on the watch for husbands, but for our liberty-loving Americans no, a thousand times no.

It is only those women who have no independent spirit in them and want a prop in life to support them, who like the idea; and a nice prop he'll be, a fine man to look up to, if he has not the courage to propose! Only a narrow-minded woman would think of such a thing, for if she loves him that love will be sufficient for her till he thinks fit to declare his love. What if he never does? Well, he does not love you, and it is better for you to love in silence. Hear what our own American poet says:

Talk not of wasted affection;
Affection never was wasted if it enrich not the heart of another.
Its waters returning back to their springs,
Like the rain, shall fill them full of refreshment;
That which the fountain sends fourth
Returns again to the fountain.

CATHARINE C.
WASHINGTON D.C., NOV. 21.

Everyone who has seen "Lord Chumley" and heard him tell the girl he loves that he "C-can't smoke, c-can't drink, c-can't sleep, c-can't eat, c-can't stay, c-c-can't go," because she is unkind and will not return his love, will thoroughly believe him when he says that he would surely accept the first pretty girl, probably the second and possibly the third. This is what he writes:

In reply to your question, "Should women propose marriage?" I say certainly not. I quite agree with Mrs. Leslie's opinions, as expressed in your first article on the question. A woman can we do quite well enough with her eyes. If she were permitted to "pop of the question" we should have no means of escape at all. I am quite sure, for my part, I should accept the first pretty girl who proposed, probably the second, and possibly the third. I should wind up my life in Sing Sing.

How could one help it?

Whoever arranged that men alone should propose marriage, made a most wise law. A man has time now, after some eyes have vanquished him, to go home and put a wet towel on his head and reflect—but who could reflect if a pretty girl said: "I love you; will you marry me marry me?" I believe the wisdom of ages tells us that reflection is a great thing in these matters, not that I reflect much myself. Yours very truly,

BOSTON, NOV. 14, 1888. E. H. SOUTHERN.

A young doctor, who does not want his name published lest all the girls be angry with him, sends me the following:

It is apparent that one cannot be really "in the swim" unless he (or she) expresses an opinion on the question propounded by you. "Should women propose?" I have a very decided opinion about the subject under discussion. So I am going to free my mind!

I consider that your fair sex has been guilty of a mean, selfish, stingy, cheese-paring policy throughout all these ages in throwing the onerous burden of proposing matrimony on us men, and right here I want to thank you, Miss Bly, for taking up the cudgels in our behalf. Just think of us in the Summer time! I need not say to a young lady of your attractions and experience that the Summer is our "busy season." It is undoubtedly in the Spring that the "young man's fancy lightly turns to love," but just the same he don't propose till the frost gets well out of the ground, and the scent of new-mown hay is wafted with the musical mosquito upon the balmy Summer air. Now this is what I am getting at: If you ladies will only help us out during the heated Summer term, say July, August and September, we promise not to complain about the Winter, but will take up our burdens on the 1st of October and plod our weary way as men have had to do since Time was an infant. What my bruised and battered heart needs is balm. I want to wander with some fair girl down into the damp, dewy mead beside the stilly brook, under the silvery moon, and tell her I can never care for her "in that way," but will always be a brother to her. If I could only do that nine times I am sure the look of sadness which now clouds my countenance would leave it, and the old happy smile return. Gratefully and sneeringly yours,

M. D.

P. S.—If this whole scheme falls through I have an idea for a universal drop-a-nickel-in-a-slot proposer, and I think there is money in it.

And now what more can be said? It is as in matters of religion, life and death, marriage and divorce, Republican and Democrat, Mugwump and Equal Rights, Prohibitionist and Free License, fried or boiled—everyone has his own opinion and all the talking and writing in the universe will not change it one iota. Only be brave enough to claim happiness at every turn regardless of obstacles. Laugh in the face of frowning misery until he smiles upon you.

NELLIE BLY

Visiting the Dispensaries

Sunday, December 2, 1888

Nellie Bly Narrowly Escapes Having Her Tonsils Amputated

Treated as a Charity Patient in the Throat, Skin and Ear Infirmaries

---

She Joins the Throng of Poor Invalids and Finds Out How Free Medical Aid is Dispensed—One Brusque Old Doctor Probes Her Throat and Nose and Wants to Perform an Operation—A Young Physician Tells Her Never to Wash Her Face with Soap—The Druggists' Big Profits—What She Saw and Heard.

I started out the other day to investigate some of the New York dispensaries and see for myself how the poor girls fare who are really sick and have to seek charity. Naturally I concluded before I started that only the very poor were the recipients of free medical aid, so I spent some time over my make-up. When it was completed I flattered myself that I looked as poor as any of them.

My first visit was to the Metropolitan Throat Hospital, 351 West Thirty-fourth street. As I read the words, "Open the door," on a big silver plate, and was obeying the order, I heard the most heartrending cries from an inside room. I stood holding the door for a moment and heard again those dreadful cries of pain:

"Oh! ow! Doctor! ow!"

My bangs curled at these sounds, yet I stretched my ear-drums lest I should miss one.

"I won't hurt you. I won't hurt you, my good woman. Keep perfectly still one moment," came the answer in a sharp, metallic voice. Then in lecture style, slow, with many impressive pauses, it continued: "This, causes the tonsils, to turn, outward, and, so allows, a—a better view, of the—of the throat."

"O-w!!" a prolonged cry.

"Don't move; I am doing that on purpose." Then resuming the discourse: "You see, in this way"—

"Ow! My! Doctor!"

"Keep still. I am only spraying your throat." A strong "whistling" sound like a stage storm, then the lecture goes on. "The object, is, to make them, wear away, gradually, not to, make them burst, as was, formerly the practice. By this method, they come away, in white, or opaque chunks. It is as well"—

By this time I had come to the conclusion that some poor girl had called to have her throat attended to and had been taken into the operating room as an illustration for a lecture. Closing the door, I entered and quietly sat down beside a woman who occupied one end of a long bench in the hall. She was better clad than I, which made me feel quakish on my ability to "make up" appropriately, A woman with a very small waist and extra large shoulders came out of the first room and looked me over.

"Do you wish to see the doctor?" she asked.

"Yes," I replied, curtly.

"Throat?"

"Yes."

"Come in here," she said, leading the way into the room she had just left. It was a small, uncarpeted hall room, with long benches on one end. The front end, cut off with an iron fence, held a desk and a small apothecary shop. Over the mantel was a black tablet inscribed in commemoration of John D. Jones, esquire's gift of the building in 1886. Below it sat a small box, whose plain face bore the words: "Charity Fund for the Hospital."

"What is your name?" asked the girl behind the railing.

THE PRELIMINARY EXAMINATION.

"Norah Simpson," I replied modestly, as she dipped her pen in the ink preparatory to recording my answers.

"Where were you born?"

"Rhinebeck."

"New York State?"

"Yes."

"Where do you live?"

"No. 110 West Twenty-fifth street."

"Married or single?"
"Single."
"Present occupation?"
"Making scarfs."
"Ever been here before?"
"No."

All these questions were printed in a small book in which she wrote my answers. Then marking my copy "9,585," she gave it to me with this card, one side of which was printed in German:

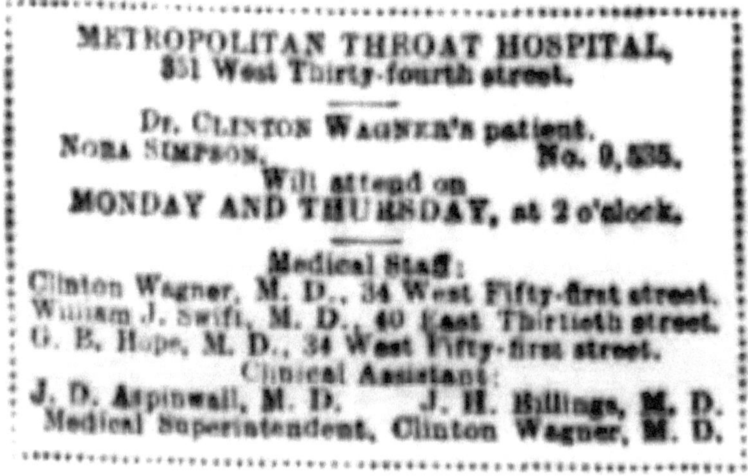
METROPOLITAN THROAT HOSPITAL,
351 West Thirty-fourth street.

DR. CLINTON WAGNER'S patient.
NORA SIMPSON, No. 9,585.
Will attend on
MONDAY AND THURSDAY, at 2 o'clock.

Medical Staff:
Clinton Wagner, M. D., 34 West Fifty-first street.
William J. Swift, M. D., 40 East Thirtieth street.
G. B. Hope, M. D., 34 West Fifty-first street.
Clinical Assistants:
J. D. Aspinwall, M. D. J. H. Billings, M. D.
Medical Superintendent, Clinton Wagner, M. D.

"Sit out in the hall, and when the doctor is ready for you I will tell you," she said.

"They have had her in there for an hour," whispered the woman beside me on the bench. "They're experimenting on her so as to teach a young doctor. I wish the old doctor won't go away afore my turn. I hate young doctors to learn on me."

I echoed her sentiments.

"What is wrong with the woman?" I asked, her "ouches!" occasionally punctuating our conversation.

"She thinks she has cancer," she whispered. "It's all down here," indicating the middle of the collarbone, "and it's hard to get at. She suffers awful with it. Hear how bad they have made her voice. It wasn't so husky at first."

"How are the doctors, kind?" I asked.

"Oh, yes, they're kind enough. Then it doesn't cost anything unless you let 'em know your man gets good wages; then they'd want ter visit your house an' be paid."

More patients were coming. First came a young man, who I should judge from his clothing was in comfortable circumstances. Then a young woman came whose gown was so neat that I thought she had mistaken the place; but no, she sat down on the bench opposite. Two more young men, likewise well clad, joined the group. I was the poorest dressed in the hall.

A bell tapped twice and the young woman came from the room to say that the doctor wished to see the new patient first. It was I.

A HORRIBLE SITUATION.

Stepping suddenly into the room from the dark hall made the brilliancy of the gas and reflectors dazzle me. Only for an instant, though; then I saw a doctor sitting at one side of the table motion to me. I sat down facing him and glanced about. The walls were covered with pictures of the throat in all conditions. The table was strewn with all sorts of gleaming instruments. Large reflectors made an unusual brilliancy. On the opposite side of the table, trying to make a young man open his mouth wider than nature had most liberally made it, was another doctor. Standing near by, intently watching every move, was a bald-headed pupil. Both of the doctors had glass reflectors bound over their right eyes. It looked so much like an engine headlight in a snow-storm that when it was turned on me I had a lively impulse to laugh.

"What is wrong?" he asked, curtly, taking my book and glancing through it.

"My throat," I replied, with ebbing spirits.

"Let me see," he said, taking a small instrument out of a finger bowl. "Open your mouth wide."

I opened it. I did not want to, but I knew I was in for it. He caught my chin firmly and ran the instrument down my throat. Just then the horrible thought came that with the same thing he had looked into the other woman's throat. And she had cancer! Ugh!

"What's wrong? What's wrong?" he asked sharply as I involuntarily jerked away and held my breath to prevent my disgust from materializing.

"I'm sick, that's all," I replied faintly.

"Well, if you're going to pull away in that manner I can't do anything for you. Open again. Now say ah—ah."

"Ug—ug," I grunted, he meanwhile holding my tongue down.

"Ee—ee," he commanded.

"Ech—e–! I 'em th'iek," I pleaded.

"Very well. I want you to be," unfeelingly. "If you get sick it won't hurt you. I am making you that way on purpose."

The thing goes away down my throat again. My stomach rocks most frightfully. I know it is useless to beg off. I have half an inclination to laugh and half to box the doctor's ears.

"That tonsil needs a piece cut off," he said, dropping the probing instrument and taking up another whose bright gleam gave me a chill.

I'll do a great deal, I think pathologically, to get a story, but I won't give up half a tonsil. But how to get away? I can't run for the door, and if I object to giving up all claim to a useless tonsil, he will discover that I am not a bona fide patient.

I look at him in fear and alarm. He takes up a piece of linen. He throws his head-light into my eyes, I am blinded! With a quick movement he catches my tongue and wraps the linen tightly around it. I am by force speechless! Mercy, mercy, will he cut a tonsil out and not allow me a word of explanation?

Many warnings, which my acquaintances have hurled at me, time after time, about some day getting caught in my own trap flash like a spectre before me. It's an agonizing thing to be able to think and not to speak in moments like these. Upon disagreeable realizations one always thinks of unpleasant things, instead of comedies, the latest jokes and the last minstrel show. I couldn't keep my mind off the doctor and the silver knife, try as I would.

He turns, still holding my tongue—more than I can do myself. I see again; he reaches for the dreaded instrument. I wildly catch his hands with both mine and pull my tongue free.

"I won't be cut," I cried. "I am too nervous, don't you know. I—I will come again when—when my nerves are better."

"That's all foolishness," he answered, shortly. "You must not give way to your nerves."

"But, somehow, I do lately," I pleaded, eagerly. "I am run down. My nerves are very bad to-day. I will come again."

"That's very foolish" (rubbing the knife). "They are no worse to-day than they will be any day."

"Oh, but I sat out there and heard that woman yell, and that has shattered me," I explained.

"I did not hurt that woman. Let me make one more examination." He took a piece of cotton, and wrapping it around a probe, dipped the end into a bottle of dark fluid. He held my head back and ran this up my nose until I could almost feel it touch my brain. It left a burning sensation in my nose and throat, and as he removed it I half choked.

"Spit it out, spit it out," he said. Too late!

"It's gone down," I gasped meekly.

"I can't do anything for you if you are going to act this way." Then writing something in the book, he told me to leave it where I got it, and so I left.

TRYING THE HOSPITAL.

My mood was anything but cheerful the next day when I started out on my second visit. I had started it and I would persevere. I decided this time to complain of my ear. I had no idea as to the manner of treating such cases, but I felt confident that they could not attempt to amputate an ear. Anything but cutting for me. This visit was to the West Side German Dispensary, 411 West Thirty-eighth street. It occupies the parlor floor in a small brick building with a high stoop. No one ever heeds the bell, so tiring out at last I open the door and walk into the uncarpeted hall, back to a half open glass door. In this room, waiting on the bare benches, are some half dozen men and women. One corner held a little drug store, and near it a conspicuous sign gave forth this warning:

"None but the poor treated here."

A man in a wet, worn suit sat shivering on a bench. I sat down between him and a woman who had herself and her baby wrapped in one shawl.

"Is the doctor engaged, do you know?" I asked the woman. She had one knee crossed over the other. When I addressed her she set the under foot into a soothing movement, for the benefit of her babe.

"Yah, him mit a sick voman."

"Has he been in there long?"

"Yah, mit some time already."

"Is your baby sick?"

"Yah, him vas sick mit him's ears."

"Oh, how sad!" I reply sympathetically. Then, with a harrowing remembrance of my throat experience, I ask cautiously, "How does the doctor treat your baby?"

"Dreat him? Vas es dot—doctor him? Yah, yah! Him dakes mine Yocob and runs him drough mit his nose to his ear. Mine Yocob schreams so loud as never vas, und den all der dimes mine doctor he runs it mit mine Yocob's ear again some more. Mine gracious! I shust tink der nefer vas notings so bad."

"Do you mean that he probes through the nose to the ear?" I asked in horrified accents.

"Yah, yah! dot es it."

No. I did not stay to be probed. I got up and quietly made my way to the door. My breath came with more regularity when I was outside and my heart resumed a more dignified pace.

Over a half million people every year receive free treatment in the New York dispensaries and hospitals. It may be well to state here that dispensaries are maintained by charity. Many bequests are made by private people, and some of the dispensaries have been richly endowed. They are intended only for the use of the worthy poor, but many times are they imposed upon by people well able to pay. For this very reason some of the medical journals have protested against there being so many dispensaries. They claim that treating people who are able to pay robs young physicians. Then again, wrong can be done by a physician opening a dispensary and working it for an advertisement, at the same time charging a small fee "because he does not want to be blamed for taking patients away from his opponents." A ten-cent fee will make a dispensary pay very well. I don't think there is any law to prevent a doctor from opening a dispensary if he chooses, and the chances for abusing it are great.

I have understood that probably one or two dispensaries pay their physicians. The majority do not. Young physicians, while waiting their practice to grow to a supporting point, are glad of the chance to gain experience. Dispensaries are especially beneficial to young physicians who wish to make a specialty of any disease, so while benefiting the poor gratuitously they do the same for young physicians.

The Northwestern Dispensary, corner of Thirty-sixth street and Ninth avenue, was the next one I visited. Although the rain was coming down in torrents I found people going there as they go to church—in squads. I followed in their wake, up bare stairs, through empty, deserted looking halls, to a dark inside room. The only windows in it were shut off by the drug department.

IN THE CROWD OF CHARITY PATIENTS.

This dark room was filled with benches. Each bench held from two to half a dozen specimens of humanity with all sorts of aches and ills. I quietly slipped into the last bench so as to command a view of the room. A pale, sad-faced woman, with silver-gray hair sat beside me. On her knee she held a baby whose misproportioned head, half covered with a gray wool hood, reminded me of photographs I have seen of an 8½ head on a six months' old baby. The case of "big head" did not seem to interfere with the child. He beat a tattoo with his woollen heels on his mother's knee, meanwhile tugging away, with dirty fists and mouth, at something tied up in a linen cloth which had once been white.

On towards the front were women in shabby gowns, many nursing babies, others holding little tots by their sides. There were some few young girls who made an attempt at display in their apparel. Tottering, white-haired men, strong young workmen with bandaged arms or heads, sad little boys with large bottles were waiting. Everything was as quiet and orderly as in a church. Sometimes one woman would gossip in low tones with another. Then a mother would whisper, "Sh, sh," to her fretful babe. Then a new patient would quickly enter and take a place among us. A continual stream kept going with bottles and boxes in their hands to the drug window. An iron rail prevented crowding. They would hand in their prescriptions and bottle or box, as the case called for, and when it was returned moved more quietly out.

At last a man came into the room in a quiet, jerky way and took a stand near a hall door.

"Those to see the doctors come this way," he called, and an assistant helped get me in line.

"What is wrong with you?" he asked the first.

"An aching in my joints," replied the old man in a quavering voice.

"That room," pointing somewhere out in the hall. Then to the next, "What is wrong with you?" and so on down the line until it came my turn.

"What is wrong with you?" he inquired.

"My skin is rough," I replied.

"Breaking out?"

"Yes, a little," I answered, stretching the truth a trifle to fit the occasion.

"Room two. Next—What is wrong with you?"

I went into the room indicated. Two old men were waiting there. One sat in a corner in a drooping, despondent way; the other, in the opposite corner, leaned back with a rakish air as if the world pleased him well. He was old, but roguish. I was conscious that he was trying to catch my eye. At last when he did so, he gave a little smile. I was surprised at his audacity and looked again, thinking my sight deceived me. No, he smiled again, and I kept my eyes fixed on the blank wall thereafter.

A good deal after the right hour a young doctor came bustling in.

"First," he called, entering a small room at the end. One of the old men went in.

"Have you been here before?"

"Yes, sir," I heard the old man reply.

"Where's your card?"

"Sir?"

"Where is your card? You must bring your card if you want to be treated."

"I forgot it, sir. I will bring it the next time, sir. My leg, sir, is much worse."

"Have you received regular treatment?"

"No, sir; I 'ave n't been 'ere more'n a month."

"You will never get well if you do not come regularly. Get this prescription filled and apply the salve every night. Good day. Next."

NEVER WASH YOUR FACE WITH SOAP.

The third time he said "Next," I went in. I found the room as bare as the others. Two chairs, one table and a wooden box filled with sawdust, for the use of weed inebriates.

"Have you ever been here before?" the doctor asked, and when I answered in the negative he asked my name, address and occupation, all of which he wrote in a large book on the table before him.

"What ails you?"

"My face gets rough when I wash," I replied.

"Do you use soap?"

"Yes."

"Well, no young lady can have a good complexion and use soap. It ruins the skin."

"But how else will I keep clean?" I asked.

"Bathe your face in hot water and rub with a coarse towel. I keep clean and I have not used soap for eight years. Take this prescription," handing me one, "have it filled—you must bring your own box for it, you know—and every night, before retiring, bathe your face in hot water—as hot as you can stand, then rub this salve well into your skin. In a short time you will have a nice complexion. Come back next week, I may have to put you under other treatment. Always bring this card with you."

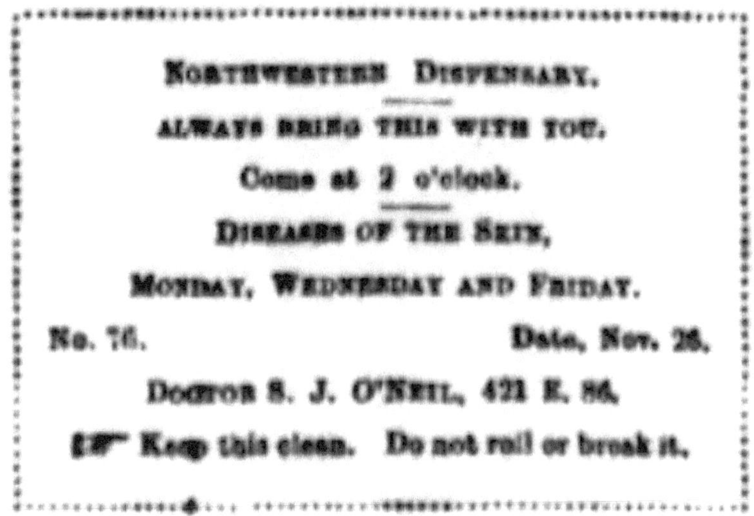

NORTHWESTERN DISPENSARY.

ALWAYS BRING THIS WITH YOU.

Come at 2 o'clock.

DISEASES OF THE SKIN,

MONDAY, WEDNESDAY AND FRIDAY.

No. 76. Date, Nov. 26.

DOCTOR S. J. O'NEIL, 421 E. 86.

☞ Keep this clean. Do not roll or break it.

I went to the drug department and handing the man the prescription asked what it would cost.

"Ten cents," he replied. "Where's your box?"

"I have none to-day. I'll bring it back to-morrow. Do you ever charge any more for other prescriptions?"

"Certainly not. All prescriptions are 10 cents each."

HOW THE DRUGGISTS GET RICH.

Hoping to gain some estimate of what druggists' profits are, I decided to have the prescription filled at an independent drug store. Dispensaries fill all prescriptions for 10 cents and yet they are said to clear all expenses by their drug department alone, and make a profit. What becomes of this profit? Whether it returns to the original charity fund I could not learn. This is the prescription I was given:

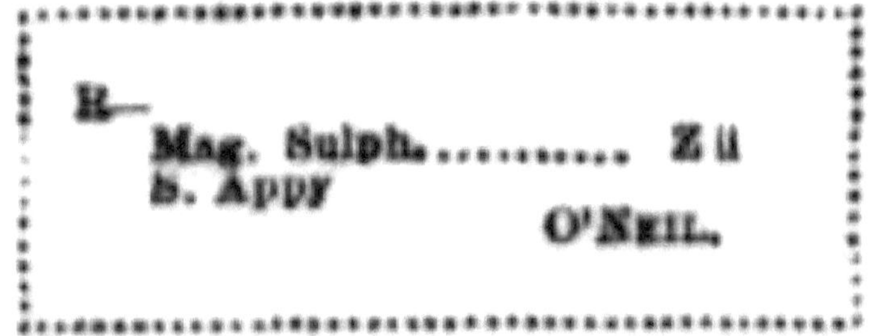

R—
Mag. Sulph. .... Z ii
S. Appy
O'Neil.

A druggist near the union of Broadway and Sixth avenue filled it.

"How much, please?" I asked as he handed me the small box.

"Fifty cents," he said, and I paid it. This makes the druggists' profit over and above the dispensary profit 40 cents, less the price of a small glass jar not costing more than two or three cents.

I did not wait to be treated at the Demilt Dispensary, corner Second avenue and Twenty-third street. It is one of the oldest in the city and is kept in splendid running order. In disguise I visited several more, among them Bellevue Hospital Dispensary, but found nothing of especial note differing from that which I have already described. In all I found the poor kindly treated, although in many instances the doctor's manners were quite brusque.

I have come to four conclusions:

First—That New York is the most charitable city in the world.

Second—That charity is daily outraged in numerous cases.

Third—That the poor have a much better chance to improve their conditions than those in moderate circumstances.

Fourth—That too much and ill-directed charity breeds pauperism.

NELLIE BLY

A Day in a Diet Kitchen

Sunday, December 23, 1888

The Sad Procession of Invalids Begging For the Simplest Food.

Nellie Bly Visits the Wretched Homes of Some of the Sufferers.

A Charity that Dispenses Nourishment to the Afflicted Poor with Liberal Hand and Irrespective of Race, Religion or Character—The Matron Tells of Her Long Experience—Mrs. Nugent's Wretched Garret in Mulberry Street—A Hopeless Invalid, Blind and Penniless—The Quarrel Over Mrs. Healy's Bank Account—Mrs. Siffert's Misery and Suffering.

It was so near Christmas time—so near the one day in the year when almost the whole world rejoices and is happy, that my thoughts turned to those sad homes where misery, poverty and sickness give little chance for joy. I made up my mind to search out some of these afflicted households, and I turned for a few days from the gay stores and happy shoppers to the narrow streets were poverty and want was sadly apparent at every step.

But it is no simple matter to find the really worthy poor. I have had some experience among the very poor and I know whereof I speak. It occurred to me that I could find no better starting-point than the New York Diet Kitchen, at 137 Centre street, and I went there. I sat down beside the heater in the small, but very clean, oil-cloth floored room, and waited until the matron had given out an allowance to a patient. A little counter, covered with white oil-cloth, separated her from those who entered. A small desk in the rear of the room and several chairs completed the furnishings.

"If you do not object," I said to the matron as she turned to me, "I would like to sit here for awhile and watch the people who come in for food. I would like to write something about the Diet Kitchens for THE WORLD."

"I will assist you all I can," she replied with a pleasant smile. "For I think the Diet Kitchen Association is the greatest charity in existence. We only help the sick, so we are not likely to do a wrong by keeping up indolent, unworthy persons."

"Do you ever have any frauds?" I asked.

"No," she said, again smiling, as she sat down. "That is one of the good results of keeping one matron for a long time. I have been here eight years, and I do believe I know everybody in our neighborhood, so I could not be deceived by unworthy ones. But then we do not forsake the sinner when he becomes ill. We help the sick without a question as to creed, race, color or character. Our patients, or customers, are treated at the dispensaries, and any dispensary doctor, knowing that a patient is in need of food or nourishment, can send them to us with one of these blanks filled out:

CENTENNIAL DIET KITCHEN,
No. 137 CENTRE STREET.
NEW YORK DISPENSARY DISTRICT.

New York, ——, 188 .
Per—— No. —— St.
Age—years—month of —— parentage.
Please issue to bearer——
——
——, Physician.

Kitchen open from 10 A. M. to 3 P. M.
Take CLEAN VESSEL with you to the Kitchen.

"You see on the last line they write what to give the patient and how long to continue the supply. We give them milk mostly. The doctors do not favor beef tea any more. They claim that there is more nourishment in milk. Two quarts of milk is an allowance. We also give boiled rice, mutton broth and such things. I use from fifty to one hundred quarts of milk every day."

"How are the Diet Kitchens kept up?"

"By charity. We receive donations of every kind, and we are very glad to get them, especially old clothing and rags."

THE THRONG OF CHARITY PATIENTS.

The door opened, and with a wave of cold air in came a thinly-clad woman, whose hair was the only warm thing about her.

"Good morning, Mary," the matron said, rising from her chair. "How is your baby to-day?"

"He's no better," Mary replied, taking a tin pail from beneath her shawl and setting it on the counter. "Can ye give me a double allowance this mornin'? I can't leave 'im very well every mornin' to come for the milk."

"Have you enough medicine for him?" the matron asked, as she lifted the measure filled with creamy milk.

"I have about two teaspoonfuls left yet from that you bought 'im," Mary said, while trying to get the tin lid to fit the pail.

"I will give you some money to buy more to-morrow," said the matron, and the woman left with her filled pail under her shawl, hardly thanking the matron for her kindness.

A little old woman, her shoulders all humped over from age and hard work, with a red nubia over her whitened head and a large gray shawl pinned about her, came in as Mary went out.

"Good mornin', Mrs. O'Donnell," she said to the matron, in a voice which sounded like a bagpipe on the next block.

"Good morning, Ann," Mrs. O'Donnell responded cheerily. "How are you to-day?"

"Oh, God knows I'm no better, Mrs. O'Donnell," she cried in a chant, without inflection of any sort. She had only one eye, and that she now turned upon me, letting a large splint basket which she carried slide to the floor.

"Is your daughter well, Ann?" asked the matron.

"Yes, please God, 'un still workin'," replied Ann, sitting down by the heater and rubbing her hands.

Mrs. O'Donnell asked me if I would not like to see her kitchen, and then telling Ann to "keep shop" until she returned we went down a flight of stairs to the basement. The kitchen was very bright and very clean.

"Do you do all the cooking?" I asked.

"Yes;" she replied, glancing with pride at the row of shining pans. "I come here at 7 o'clock and cook everything ready for the patients, who are served from 10 to 3. Occasionally I get a woman to help me clean up. The position is not an easy one. It shatters the nerves to be face to face with misery for five and six hours all day. After my hours are over here I visit all new patients in order to see that all is right and what they may possibly need. Still I love the work, and think this is the greatest charity association in existence."

We went upstairs again, and a woman very fat and rather untidy, to say the least, was waiting for her allowance, which was promptly given to her.

LIFE-LONG DEVOTION.

"This is one of the noblest women I ever saw," said the matron, nudging me hurriedly as the door was pushed open by a tall, plainly clad woman. Turning to her the matron said:

"Good morning, Miss Maxwell. How is your brother this morning?"

"He is no better, thank you, Mrs. O'Donnell. I think his end is near," and she tried to smile though the lips quivered and the tears were near the eyes. She was unlike any of the others. Her pale, sad face had an expression of resignation. Her poor little bonnet and gown and shawl were plain, but spotlessly clean.

"What is wrong with your brother?" I asked her.

"It was rheumatism at first, but it is a complication of diseases now. The only work I can do is the fine finishing to vests. I cannot leave my brother alone so I take my work home."

"She only gets three cents a vest for finishing work," said Mrs. O'Donnell indignantly.

"Yes," Miss Maxwell said, with one of her slow, sad smiles, "I worked yesterday, last night and to-day, and up to this time have just finished 21 cents worth. I cannot leave my brother and I cannot get anything else to take home. He was at the hospital once, but they would not keep him because he is incurable. I went to work when I was ten years old to support my mother, who was helpless and bed-ridden from rheumatism," Miss Maxwell said in a sad, low voice. "She was my charge for the twelve years which she spent in her bed. Her death did not free me, for a short time before my brother has been taken to the hospital with the same disease. My mother was hardly buried when he was discharged incurable. There was no one but myself to care for him, so I took him, and it is now seven years since he left his bed, and in all that time he has been my charge. His disease at last affected his mind and has run into consumption. When he dies I will be too old to marry and too old to go into a factory to work." And the tears would come to her eyes though she bravely tried to smile.

A little woman whose face had wasted away until she was nothing but great black eyes and a hollow cough came in gasping for breath. She sat down, unable to speak.

HOW SHE KEEPS THE FIRE BURNING.

"I've had no fire for several days," chanted Ann by the heater. Somehow she reminded me of the raven above the chamber door. "My daughter works in a store, and it takes her wages—$3 a week—to dress her. If she don't dress well she'll lose her place. If it hadn't been for Mrs. O'Donnell I could never have lived this long. I pray God's blessing on her every day and night."

"Have you got any coal yet?" the matron asked.

"I hadn't money enough to buy a pail of coal. It costs 15 cents; but I bought a pail of cinders from the Italians for five cents."

"Where do Italians get the cinders?" I asked.

"They gather them out of ash-barrels and then sell them at five cents a pail."

"Did you get any stockings for me yet?" piped up the woman with the great eyes to Mrs. O'Donnell.

"Not yet. None have come in. How are you feeling?"

"Very much worse, and I have no under-clothing and the cold makes me worse," and she broke down coughing again.

I stayed at the Diet Kitchen until I was heart-sick with the world's misery, and then, following Mrs. O'Donnell suggestion, I made a list of several patients and set out to visit them.

First I want to see a blind woman, Mrs. Ellen Nugent, at 76 Mulberry street. It was a high tenement, with narrow, dark, uncarpeted stairs that wound round and round to the top. On each floor were four doors to as many rooms for as many families. I knocked on one door after another, and dark Italian faces glanced out at me, and in reply to my questions said that they did not understand English. At last one woman made me understand that there were no English people in the house except one family on the top floor. When I reached that place, wading through all the débris in the hallways, I wondered how I would ever get out. I knocked and the door was slightly opened. I asked if Mrs. Nugent lived there, and the woman said she did, but did not offer to let me in until I said that I was from Mrs. O'Donnell. That opened the door for me and I went inside. It was a little room, with a small, fireless stove, a few broken chairs, a table and an open cupboard that had a hungry look. A few colored prints of a religious character were hung on the dirty walls, and the ceiling was low enough for me to touch without getting on my tip-toes. A large woman was attempting to set a few dishes in order in the cupboard.

THE EXTREMIST POVERTY.

I stepped softly into the small room. I cannot describe it. The ceiling almost touched the head of the bed and the plastered walls had never known a finishing touch or paper. Bundles of rags and worn bed-clothing lay in the only corner. The only light came through one pane of glass about six by nine. On the bed, amid feather bolsters and some dirty sheets, lay a little old woman with a baby-white face and snow-white hair. She raised herself on her elbow and turned her sightless eyes toward me.

"Mrs. O'Donnell sent me to see you," I said by way of explanation as I pressed the wrinkled old hand held out to me.

"Heaven bless her; she is so good and kind," she answered, in a strong, clear voice.

"How did you lose your eyesight?" I asked.

"It came very strange like, about fifteen years ago, when my husband owned a little store. One day I started out to cross the street—my eyesight was as clear as anything that morning—and a green color came before me, so I turned back and went into the store. Then everything was black. My husband took me to a doctor and he examined my eyes, but he said nothing could ever be done for them. I would be blind all my life. Then three years after that my husband died, and all my acquaintances forgot me and I was alone—alone in the world and blind. I hadn't one friend, one relative, nor one acquaintance to go to. I moved into this house, and for eleven years I have never been out of this room. I am away in the eighties, and for seven years my back has kept me in this bed."

"How do you get enough to live on and pay your rent?"

"Sure, and she has no appetite. For four years she has lived on the milk which Mrs. O'Donnell gives her. She hasn't tasted anything else," said the woman outside.

"That is Mrs. Bagner," explained Mrs. Nugent. "She is not a relative of mine, but she has been kind to me. She had rooms in this house, but work was so scarce, and her husband is too sick to work, and she has her grandchild to keep, so she moved in here and takes care of me. We pay $7 a month for these two rooms. The Blind Society gives me $40 a year and Mrs. Bagner makes up the rest for the rent."

"Do you ever have any one to read to you or to visit you?" I asked the old blind woman.

PRAYING FOR DEATH.

"No one but Mrs. O'Donnell. I am always lying here alone, and Mrs. Bagner has to go out to work all day. We have had no fire for several days now, because Mrs. Bagner had no work. Ah! the ways of God are so strange. For fifteen years I have prayed night and day to die. So many strong people, and happy ones, and young ones have been compelled to go in that time, and here I lie begging to be taken away."

"She spends the whole night praying to die," Mrs. Bagner called in.

I bought them some coal, and left.

My next visit was to No. 86 Mulberry street. I went through a narrow, cobbled court and up darker and dirtier stairs than I had yet seen. I went to the top of the house, asking at every door for Mrs. Healy. All the occupants were Italians and could give me no information. When I turned to go down the stairs some boys above amused themselves by throwing pebbles and cinders after me, but I kept close to the wall and hurried on. I stopped in a small candy store underneath the tenement and asked the proprietor for Mrs. Healy.

"Go to the rear house an' you'll find one room with a lot of widows in it, an' I s'pose she's among 'em."

A STRANGE EXPERIENCE.

When I explained further what I wanted I was told that Mrs. Healy had a small bank account, and her two daughters were tearing one another's eyes out to see who would get the money when their mother died. Through the court and filthy back yard I went, and felt my way up the dark stairs and brought forth several Italian families. At last I found Mrs. Healy's.

A small Irish woman opened the door, and when I asked where Mrs. Healy was she pointed to the side room. I walked to the door and looked in, and as I had had no luncheon and it was past 1 o'clock I felt my spirits weaken. Two beds had been set up in the room, which left a space about two feet square near the door. The only light came through this door, and by its dim rays I saw two of the filthiest beds I ever gazed upon. A gaunt, ghastly form was propped up on one. As I stepped into the little square the form raised itself to a sitting position and stretching out long, bare, bony arms and claw-like hands to me. The woman made some of the most agonizing sounds that I ever heard. I looked at her, and as my eyes became accustomed to the dim light I saw splotches of blood on the death-like face, the wide, staring eyes, the straggling gray hair.

"What is the matter with your mother's face?" I asked.

"You see she is alone all day, except when I can come to her, and I have a house of me own to look after. Me sister is a widow an' she works out by the day, so me mother is locked up here alone. Somehow one day she fell out of bed an' the people next door heard her moaning, an' when they came in she was lying with her feet in bed an' her head on the floor, an' her face was all scratched full of blood as you see it."

"As you have a home, why don't you take your mother there and care for her?" She entered into a long explanation about her refusing to keep her husband's mother, and now he would not keep hers.

"I wish God would take her, bless his holy name," she whined. "She is a burden to me an' to herself an' I wish God would call her, bless his holy name."

"What does she have to eat?" I asked, shortly.

"Only the milk from the kitchen, and sometimes I bring her a bit of tea meself."

"Why don't you use the money she has in the bank?"

She looked at me in a startled way and then dropping her eyes whined:

"She hasn't much, God knows, blessed be his holy name, an' she's a saving that to bury her when God calls her to him."

A SAD PICTURE OF SUFFERING.

I visited several other old women and divided my little with them. I was called names by young women who were parading the streets; I was hooted at for "a lady" by rude children, and a "Gospel slinger" by others. Altogether my life was made miserable while I investigated Hester and Mulberry and Mott streets. My last visit was a very sad one. It was to Mrs. Siffert, at 137 Mott street.

It was the old, old story. She has two little rooms, for which the rent is paid by kind neighbors. In the front room are two little children—Willie, six years old, and Frances, four—and in the back room, with the seal of death on her quiet face, lies the widowed mother, with her white lips stained with the blood which surges up every few moments from her wasted lungs. The two innocent children talked and laughed together while the mother wiped the blood from her lips and talked to me.

"Four years ago," she said, "my husband died and I went to washing to keep the children. Frances was born five months after her father died. I was always well and strong until one day I turned from the washtub to have a hemorrhage. That was seven months ago, and ever since I have been in this bed. I know it is consumption, although the doctor does not say so. Since yesterday I have been coughing blood. The neighbors are very kind and see that things are cared for. The kitchen furnishes me with milk every day, and we live on that; but I have such an appetite," and the strangely bright eyes glance up to me with a smile. "Isn't it strange? I am hungry all the time and the milk does not satisfy me. I feel I could eat anything.

"The children will have no Christmas," she continued, glancing out at her little ones. "They do not understand. You wonder why I do not send them to a home? Think how many years they will have to be without a mother and what a little time I have to be with them. I cannot let them go until it is all over with me. If it had only been God's will to give me strength how happy I would have been to work for them! If it only been his will"—

The poor, wan face turned on the pillow, and several tears trickled slowly down. The children still whispered together in the corner. "Our birdie is dead," I heard Willie say, and I glanced at the empty cage in the window. Pressing the thin, feverish hand I went quietly out.

Nellie Bly

ABOUT NELLIE BLY

Nellie Bly was born Elizabeth "Pink" Cochran. Her father, a man of considerable wealth, served for many years as judge of Armstrong County, Pennsylvania. He lived on a large estate called Cochran's Mills, which took its name from him.

Being in reduced circumstances after her father's death, her mother remarried, only to divorce Jack Ford a few years later. The family then moved to Pittsburg, where a twenty-year-old Pink read a column in the *Pittsburg Dispatch* entitled "What Girls Are Good For." Enraged at the sexist and classist tone, she wrote a furious letter to the editor. Impressed, the editor engaged her to do special work for the newspaper as a reporter, writing under the name "Nellie Bly." Her first series of stories, "Our Workshop Girls," brought life and sympathy to working women in Pittsburgh.

A year later she went as a correspondent to Mexico, where she remained six months, sending back weekly articles. After her return she longed for broader fields, and so moved to New York. The story of her attempt to make a place for herself, or to find an opening, was a long one of disappointment, until at last she gained the attention of the *New York World*.

Her first achievement for them was the exposure of the Blackwell's Island Insane Asylum, in which she spent ten days, and two days in the Bellevue Insane Asylum. The story created a great sensation, making "Nellie Bly" a household name.

After three years of doing work as a "stunt girl" at the *World*, Bly conceived the idea of making a trip around the world in less time than had been done by Phileas Fogg, the fictitious hero of Jules Verne's famous novel. In fact, she made it in 72 days. On her return in January 1890 she was greeted by ovations all the way from San Francisco to New York.

She then paused her reporting career to write novels, but returned to the *World* three years later. In 1895 she married millionaire industrialist Robert Seaman, and a couple years later retired from journalism to take an interest in his factories.

She returned to journalism almost twenty years later, reporting on World War I from behind the Austrian lines. Upon returning to New York, she spent the last years of her life doing both reporting and charity work, finding homes for orphans. She died of pneumonia in 1922.

Books by Nellie Bly

JOURNALISM

Ten Days in a Mad-House

Six Months In Mexico

Nellie Bly's Book: Around the World in 72 Days

NOVELS

The Mystery of Central Park

Eva the Adventuress

New York By Night

Alta Lynn, M.D.

Wayne's Faithful Sweetheart

Little Luckie

Dolly the Coquette

In Love With a Stranger

The Love of Three Girls

Little Penny, Child of the Streets

Pretty Merribelle

Twins and Rivals

THE MYSTERY OF CENTRAL PARK

A rejected marriage proposal and the corpse of a dead beauty confound Dick Treadwell's hopes for happiness, until his beloved Penelope sets him a task: she will marry him if he solves—*the Mystery of Central Park!*

EVA, THE ADVENTURESS

Nellie Bly's ripped-from-the-headlines novel of a poor girl determined to revenge herself upon the world, only to find that, in the battle between love and revenge, only one can triumph.

NEW YORK BY NIGHT

Setting out to solve the bold diamond robbery, millionaire detective Lionel Dangerfield finds himself in competition with Ruby Sharpe, daring young reporter for the *New York Planet.* Will "The Danger" solve the case before Ruby can steal the story—and his heart?

ALTA LYNN, M.D.

A prank goes awry and Alta Lynn finds herself wed against her will. Leaving love behind, she throws herself into the study of medicine, only to find that love has other plans for her!

WAYNE'S FAITHFUL SWEETHEART

Beautiful Dorette Lover is rescued from poverty when she finds work as an artist's model. That same day she witnesses a seeming murder. To protect the man accused, she agrees to become his bride—only to fall desperately in love with him!

LITTLE LUCKIE

Luckie Thurlow longs to be accepted by society and gain the man she loves. But she harbors a dark secret—she is the daughter of the murderous Gypsy Queen, who plans to use Luckie to gain her own revenge!

IN LOVE WITH A STRANGER

Kit Clarendon is in love! Trouble is, she doesn't know her love's name. But she is determined to track him down and force him to love her! A wild pursuit filled with disguises, desperate deeds, and declarations of love as Kit determines to go through fire and water to win him!

THE LOVE OF THREE GIRLS

An heiress in disguise, a factory girl with dreams of wealth, and a sweet child of charity are forced into rivalry when they all fall in love with the same man! Murder, fever, fallen women, and a desperate villain conspire against—*the love of three girls!*

INTO THE MADHOUSE

Never before collected! "Who is this insane girl?" asked other papers, completely taken in by Nellie Bly's plan to infiltrate Blackwell's Island. The complete reporting surrounding her daring expose, including details not included in her initial accounts and her scathing rebuttal of the doctors' excuses!

NELLIE BLY'S WORLD - Vol. 1

1887-1888

Bly's complete reporting, collected for the very first time! Starting with the stunt that made hers a household name, Nellie Bly spends her first year at the New York World going undercover to expose frauds, sharpsters and boodlers, interviewing Belva Lockwood and Hangman Joe, and tackling Phelps the Lobbyist!

NELLIE BLY'S WORLD - Vol. 2

1889-1890

Bly's complete reporting, collected for the very first time! Nellie buys a baby, has herself followed by a detective and arrested, interviews Helen Keller, champion boxer John Sullivan, and convicted would-be killer Eva Hamilton, all before setting out on her greatest stunt of all, a race around the world!

COMING SOON:

NELLIE BLY'S WORLD, Vol. 3 & 4

NELLIE BLY'S DISPATCHES, Vol. 1 & 2

NELLIE BLY's JOURNALS, Vol. 1 & 2

ALL FROM SORDLET INK

ABOUT DAVID BLIXT

David Blixt is an author and actor living in Chicago. An Artistic Associate of the Michigan Shakespeare Festival, where he serves as the resident Fight Director, he is also co-founder of A Crew Of Patches Theatre Company, a Shakespearean repertory based in Chicago. He has acted and done fight work for the Goodman Theatre, Chicago Shakespeare Theatre, Steppenwolf, the Shakespeare Theatre of Washington DC, and First Folio Shakespeare, among many others.

As a writer, his STAR-CROSS'D series of novels place the characters of Shakespeare's Italian plays in their historical setting, drawing in figures such as Dante, Giotto, and Petrarch to create an epic of warfare, intrigue, and romance. In HER MAJESTY'S WILL, Shakespeare himself becomes a character as Blixt explores Shakespeare's "Lost Years," teaming the young Will with the dark and devious Kit Marlowe to hilarious effect. In the COLOSSUS series, Blixt brings first century Rome and Judea to life as he relates the fall of Jerusalem, the building of the Colosseum, and the coming of Christianity to Rome. And in his bestselling NELLIE BLY series, he explores the amazing life and adventures of America's premier undercover reporter.

David continues to write, act, and travel. He has ridden camels around the pyramids at Giza, been thrown out of the Vatican Museum and been blessed by John-Paul II, scaled the Roman ramp at Masada, crashed a hot-air balloon, leapt from cliffs on small Greek islands, dined with Counts and criminals, climbed to the top of Mount Sinai, and sat in the Prince's chair in Verona's palace. But David is happiest at his desk, weaving tales of brilliant people in dire and dramatic straits. Living with his wife and two children, David describes himself as "actor, author, father, husband - in reverse order."

WWW.DAVIDBLIXT.COM

Books by David Blixt

Nellie Bly
What Girls Are Good For
Charity Girl
Clever Girl

The Star-Cross'd Series
The Master Of Verona
Voice Of The Falconer
Fortune's Fool
The Prince's Doom
Varnish'd Faces: Star-Cross'd Short Stories

Will & Kit
Her Majesty's Will

The Colossus Series
Colossus: Stone & Steel
Colossus: The Four Emperors

Eve of Ides - a play

non-fiction
Shakespeare's Secrets: Romeo & Juliet
Tomorrow, and Tomorrow: Essays on Macbeth
Fighting Words

MORE FROM SORDELET INK

PLAYSCRIPTS

ACTION MOVIE - THE PLAY BY JOE FOUST AND RICHARD RAGSDALE

ALL CHILDISH THINGS BY JOSEPH ZETTELMAIER

CAPTAIN BLOOD ADAPTED BY DAVID RICE

THE COUNT OF MONTE CRISTO ADAPTED BY CHRISTOPHER M. WALSH

DEAD MAN'S SHOES BY JOSEPH ZETTELMAIER

THE DECADE DANCE BY JOSEPH ZETTELMAIER

EBENEZER: A CHRISTMAS PLAY BY JOSEPH ZETTELMAIER

EVE OF IDES BY DAVID BLIXT

THE GRAVEDIGGER: A FRANKENSTEIN PLAY BY JOSEPH ZETTELMAIER

HER MAJESTY'S WILL ADAPTED BY ROBERT KAUZLARIC

IT CAME FROM MARS BY JOSEPH ZETTELMAIER

THE MOONSTONE ADAPTED BY ROBERT KAUZLARIC

NORTHERN AGGRESSION BY JOSEPH ZETTELMAIER

ONCE A PONZI TIME BY JOE FOUST

THE RENAISSANCE MAN BY JOSEPH ZETTELMAIER

THE SCULLERY MAID BY JOSEPH ZETTELMAIER

SEASON ON THE LINE BY SHAWN PFAUTSCH

STAGE FRIGHT: A HORROR ANTHOLOGY BY JOSEPH ZETTELMAIER

A TALE OF TWO CITIES ADAPTED BY CHRISTOPHER M. WALSH

WILLIAMSTON ANTHOLOGY: VOLUME 1

WILLIAMSTON ANTHOLOGY: VOLUME 2

WWW.SORDELETINK.COM

www.ingramcontent.com/pod-product-compliance
Lightning Source LLC
Chambersburg PA
CBHW061220190726
48288CB00001B/259

* 9 7 8 1 9 4 4 5 4 0 8 9 0 *